DATE DUE

Brodart Co. Cat. # 55 137 001 Printed in USA

Controlling Desires

CONTROLLING DESIRES

Sexuality in Ancient Greece and Rome

Kirk Ormand

Praeger Series on the Ancient World
Bella Vivante, Series Editor

Westport, Connecticut
London

Library of Congress Cataloging-in-Publication Data

Ormand, Kirk, 1962–
  Controlling desires : sexuality in ancient Greece and Rome / Kirk
Ormand.
      p. cm. —(Praeger series on the ancient world, ISSN 1932–1406)
  Includes bibliographical references and index.
  ISBN 978–0–275–98880–7 (alk. paper)
  1. Sex customs—Greece—History.   2. Sex customs—Rome—History.
3. Sex in literature. I. Title.
  HQ13.O76 2009
  306.70938—dc22   2008036656

British Library Cataloguing in Publication Data is available.

Library of Congress Catalog Card Number: 2008036656
ISBN: 978–0–275–98880–7
ISSN: 1932–1406

First published in 2009

Praeger Publishers, 88 Post Road West, Westport, CT 06881
An imprint of Greenwood Publishing Group, Inc.
www.praeger.com

Printed in the United States of America

The paper used in this book complies with the
Permanent Paper Standard issued by the National
Information Standards Organization (Z39.48–1984).

10 9 8 7 6 5 4 3 2 1

Copyright Acknowledgments

The author and the publisher gratefully acknowledge permission for use of the following
material:

"Impossible Lesbians in Ovid's Metamorphoses," from *Gendered Dynamics in Latin Love
Poetry*, ed. R. Ancona and E. Greene, 79–112. Reprinted with permission of The Johns
Hopkins University Press, copyright 2005.

This one is for Ella.

Contents

Series Foreword

The lives of ancient peoples may seem far removed, socially, linguistically, and especially technologically, from the concerns of the modern world. Yet the popularity of historical subjects on both the big and little screens—*Troy, Alexander, 300;* HBO's *Rome,* the many History Channel programs—demonstrates the abiding fascination the ancient world continues to exert. Some people are drawn to the dramatic differences between the ancient and modern; others seek to find the origins for contemporary cultural features or the sources to provide meaning to our modern lives. Regardless of approach, the past holds something valuable for all of us. It is literally the root of who we are, physically through our actual ancestors, and culturally in establishing the foundations for our current beliefs and practices in religious, social, domestic and political arenas. The same ancients that we study were themselves drawn to their own pasts, often asking questions similar to the ones we pose today about our past.

The books in Praeger's series on the Ancient World address different topics from various perspectives. The ones on myth, sports, technology, warfare, and women explore these subjects cross-culturally, both within the ancient Mediterranean context—Egypt, Mesopotamia, Greece, Rome, and others—and between the ancient Mediterranean cultures and those of the Americas, Africa and Asia. Others, including the volumes on literature, men, sexuality, and on politics and society, examine their topic more specifically within a Greek or Greek and Roman cultural framework.

All renowned scholars committed to bringing the fruits of their research to wider audiences, each author brings a distinctive new approach to their topic that differentiates them from the many books that exist on the ancient world. A major strength of the first group is their multi-cultural breadth, which is both informative in its comprehensive embrace and provides numerous opportunities for comparative insights. Likewise, the books in the second group explore their topics in dramatically new ways: the inner life of male identity; the contributions of both women and men to the social polity; the ancient constructions of concepts of sexuality and eroticism.

Each volume offers amazing windows into aspects of ancient life. Together, the series provides an invaluable overview of how ancient peoples thought about themselves and the world, how they conducted their lives, and how they expressed their views in creative terms. Enjoy the journey into the past that each one provides.

Bella Vivante
Series Editor, Praeger Series on the Ancient World

Preface

The Western world has long known that the ancient Greeks and Romans thought about sex differently than we do and that they considered men's homoerotic desire for attractive young men as entirely normal. At one time, this fact was passed over in embarrassed silence. For some time now, however, it has been the object of lively and sometimes boisterous conversation, both within academia and in the general public. These conversations have, until quite recently, assumed that the Greeks and Romans categorized individuals according to sexuality in the same way that we do (that is to say, gay, lesbian, or straight). In the past 30 years, however, spurred on by important work in the history of human subjectivity, gender studies, and the growing field of queer theory, scholarship on Greek and Roman sexuality has come to see ancient erotic experience in a different light.

This moment of growth has not been without serious controversy. Pioneering work on the Greeks, especially, became quickly mired in a debate between those who held that sexuality is biological, natural, and transhistorical (the "essentialists") and those who held that it is a product of culture and as such must be understood in the context of a specific society at a specific time (the "constructionists"). At virtually the same time, arguments arose about the relative importance of sexuality and gender as defining terms in the study of human sexual interaction. Some parts of these debates have taken place in public forums, but for the most part, they have existed in scholarly publications, away from the eyes of everyday readers. Only in the last 10 years or so have books appeared that present this material to those readers who are not fully conversant with the history, culture, and literature of ancient Greece and Rome.

In this book, I outline the basic structures of sexual practice and the fundamental categories through which the Greeks and Romans understood the world of sexual behavior. I assume that my reader is not familiar with the bulk of Greek and Roman literature and history. As a result, this book is organized chronologically, with each chapter dealing with a particular kind of evidence. Beginning with the earliest Greek literature and ending in the second century CE in Rome, I go through a series of different texts, showing what each has to tell us about Greek and Roman sex. Though most of my evidence is, in some sense, literary, I have also included chapters dealing with laws and social institutions that limited and defined sexual behavior.

The reader will not find a thorough discussion in this book of the visual, material evidence for Greek and Roman sexuality. Although this material is indeed important, I found it intractable to deal with in a brief and suitably comprehensive manner. I have indicated some studies for further reading that are highly accessible to the nonspecialist.

In making this survey, I have included as much of the original Greek and Latin literature (in translation) as I have been able to squeeze in. I hope that my reader will find the translations here sufficient to support the arguments that I make, but I also hope that he or she will be inspired by this book to seek out translations of whole texts, and thereby to experience these products of ancient Greek and Roman culture in all their complexity and detail. Although this book is long, I must say that I have had to be quite selective. There are many texts, authors, and even entire kinds of work that are not treated here. I decided early on that it would be better to treat a few texts in depth than to cover more works in a more summary fashion.

In writing this book, I have tried to acknowledge my intellectual debts fairly. But I have made no attempt to cite every scholarly work that deals with a given text, or even those that deal with the sexual aspects of every text. This work is a product of my own work and teaching in the area of sexuality for the last 15 years; even if I could remember where I learned everything that I now think about Greek and Roman sexual behavior, any attempt to cite it all would have resulted in a different kind of book for a different kind of audience. The reader is strongly encouraged to seek out the books provided in footnotes and recommended for further reading for more specific and scholarly discussions of the subjects I have included here.

Sex and sexual practice have a way of permeating a wide variety of cultural products and institutions, and the study of sex has taken me on some surprising and intriguing tangents. I hope that my reader will find this book engaging, at times amusing, perhaps at other times irritating, and always thought provoking. Many of the arguments I present are controversial; throughout, I have tried to indicate the bounds and terms of the controversy and to make my own opinions clear. Now, however, it is time for the reader to form his or her own opinions, and that is best accomplished by turning to the evidence at hand. I have presented here a broad range of material; I hope it will bring the reader of this volume to new ways of thinking about sex, sexual behavior, and sexual identity.

Acknowledgments

This book could never have been completed without the encouragement and help of many people. I would like to thank Bella Vivante, who first suggested that I should write a book on this topic for a general audience; David Halperin, Craig Williams, and Edward Harris, for their assistance with particular matters and unflagging encouragement in general; and my fine colleagues Tom Van Nortwick, Drew Wilburn, and Ben Lee, who gave me good advice and were always willing to help with sticky questions. I must also give sincere thanks to my research assistant, Lizzie Ehrenhalt, who helped me track down bibliography and images at the very start of this project. I would never have begun my study of ancient sexuality had I not had the good fortune to study, briefly, with the late Jack Winkler.

Many of the ideas presented here were tested and refined by two classes of students at Oberlin College and a graduate seminar at the American School of Classical Studies in Athens. To the members of those classes, then, my thanks for your questions and challenges. None of the people mentioned previously can be considered responsible for any errors that remain; those are mine alone.

My family, Gayle, Kevin, and Ella Boyer, have given me constant love and support, even when I spent too much time on this book and not enough with them. Ella is too young to read this book, but I hope that she will take some satisfaction from the dedication to her when she is older.

Thanks also go to institutions: Oberlin College has supported this book with a sabbatical leave, as did the American School of Classical Studies in Athens with an Elizabeth A. Whitehead professorship. I also thank the Johns Hopkins University Press for allowing me to republish, in modified form, "Impossible Lesbians in Ovid's Metamorphoses," which appeared first in *Gendered Dynamics in Latin Love Poetry,* edited by R. Ancona and E. Greene, on pages 79–112. That material appears here as chapter 12.

One

Introduction

WHAT'S SO DIFFERENT ABOUT ANCIENT GREEK AND ROMAN SEX?

Sex is difficult to talk about and even more difficult to analyze as a feature of a particular culture. There are several reasons for this, and they all have to do with how sex is perceived and discussed in our own society. First, we tend to think that because sex is a natural part of life, the particular forms of sex that are prevalent in our society are also natural. Though we may not put it in exactly these terms, our assumption is that these value judgments (i.e., that certain kinds of sex are or are not normal) are universal and that they transcend both time and space. Second, we think of sex as particularly private; while we think we know what normal sex is, and what most people do, we generally don't want to talk to our neighbors about what they do. This sense of privacy serves to hide common sexual practices that may not fit the norm at the same time that it fuels anxiety about such practices. Because we think of sex as private, moreover, we sometimes do not see that we deal with sex in a public way all the time: our popular culture, from teen romance movies to supermarket magazines, is littered with artifacts that describe in great detail and variety how we think about sex in our lives.

When we look closely at some of the ancient Greek and Roman conversations about sex, most of these rules also apply. The ancient Greeks and Romans thought of certain kinds of sex as normal or abnormal; certain aspects of sexual life were considered private and therefore not spoken about. When we scrutinize the ways in which they did speak about sex, however, we rapidly discover that the Greeks and Romans speak in ways that are foreign to us. In fact, we may be initially a bit shocked at how publicly they seem to discuss what are, for us, embarrassingly private moments. The reason for this is that their sense of what should be private and what constitutes an acceptable public forum for sexual discussions is not exactly the same as ours. Further confusing the issue is the fact that Greek and Roman conventions about sex itself are not always the same as ours, so that sexual content may appear so different from our own experience that we do not understand it at all.

It is useful to begin by emphasizing that we are not as private about sex as we sometimes think. The modern West also has a long tradition of talking about sex, though we do so in a series of metaphors and images that have become conventional; such metaphors tend to reduce the shock value of these public conversations. The distance of even a few hundred years also serves to reduce the impact of what were, at one time, quite racy discussions. To get a bit of perspective on this problem, consider the last lines of a famous love poem from the English tradition:

The Grave's a fine and private place,
But none I think do there embrace.
Now therefore, while the youthful hew
Sits on thy skin like morning glew,
And while thy willing Soul transpires
At every pore with instant Fires
Now let us sport us while we may;
And now, like am'rous birds of prey,
Rather at once our Time devour,
Than languish in his slow-chapt pow'r.
Let us roll all our Strength, and all,
Our sweetness, up into one Ball:
And tear our Pleasures with rough strife,
Through the Iron gates of Life.
Thus, though we cannot make our Sun
Stand still, yet we will make him run.

I first read these lines, as I suspect many Americans did, in high school. They are from Andrew Marvell's "To His Coy Mistress" and are the closing part of the speaker's argument, in which he tries to persuade his beloved to waste no time in going to bed with him. Though there is no explicit description of sex—quite—the imagery of "tear our Pleasures with rough strife / Through the Iron gates of Life" does not leave much to the imagination. These lines also provide some fairly standard metaphors for the passion of love: the speaker compares his beloved's youth to the freshness of morning, and in the next lines, he imagines that she feels like she is on fire. It all adds up to an argument for haste, a desire on the part of the speaker to enjoy sex while both he and his beloved are young; it is a celebration of the passion of youth in the face of the fact that time will not stop at this fleeting, precious moment. If his beloved waits too long, both speaker and beloved will be dead—and then it is too late: "The Grave's a fine and private place / But none, I think, do there embrace."

Compare that fairly explicit reading experience to the following poem of Strato, a Greek author of erotic poetry writing at the time of the Roman emperor Hadrian:

"Know the right time," said one of the seven sages, Philippus.
For all things are loveliest at their prime.
Even the cucumber is valued, when first seen on the garden's border.
But too ripe, becomes fodder for pigs.[1] (*Greek Anthology* 12.197)

The first thing the modern reader might notice is that this poem does not seem all that sexy. If it were not found in a book of fairly explicit love poetry, he might not even think of it as being about love or sex. It is found in such a collection, however, and that fact begins to open up some familiar patterns of thought. The speaker of the poem indicates urgency, and the reader might recognize something like Marvell's argument in the line "all things are loveliest at their prime." In fact, the poem is in the form of an argument, and much like Marvell's poem, the argument is that the beloved (Philippus) should not wait to have sex. Even the gardening imagery is not entirely foreign to us. Though contemporary poetry does not often compare the beloved to a cucumber, the idea of a lover as a flower (as in Burns's famous "My love is like a red, red rose") is familiar enough.

The temptation, then, is to read the preceding poem and think that it is not so far from the love poetry of the English tradition—it is just another poem urging the beloved to "seize the day." Unfortunately, the Greek poem hides some meanings from modern readers, simply because we are not steeped in the poetic tradition from which it comes. First, the speaker (who is male) is addressing his little poem to a person named Philippus (also male). In our terms, that makes this a homosexual poem, though as we will see, that terminology doesn't quite work for the ancient Greeks. What is more important to understand is that in the Greek system of erotic relationships that is being celebrated here, it was considered quite normal for older men (30 to 50 years old or even older) to try to seduce young men—that is, men between the ages of, say, 13 and 22. More specifically, there is a concrete physical limit at which these young men cease to be attractive, and that limit is the appearance of secondary sexual characteristics, especially hair on the cheeks and buttocks. So, for example, Strato writes in another poem,

Especially among them see how Milesius blooms,
As a rose resplendent with sweet-smelling petals.
But perhaps he does not know that, as a fair flower by the heat,
So young beauty is destroyed by a hair. (*Greek Anthology* 12.195)

These beautiful young men are only attractive as *objects* of affection, so long as they are young. Once they become older, they are supposed to switch roles and become the older men who are attracted to the younger ones. Moreover, this shift of roles is accompanied by a rather strict shift in sexual roles as well: the lover (the older man) is assumed to be the penetrating partner, and the beloved (the younger) to be the penetrated. (I will examine these roles in more nuance and detail later.) Once a man grows hair on certain parts of his body, he is no longer the beautiful darling sought by all the older men, and instead he finds that he must become the pursuer rather than the pursued. Since the age of attractiveness is tightly defined, there must always have been more men pursuing than youths being pursued, and the loss of one's physical attractiveness must have carried with it a certain sense of loss of status. It is a transition that is described in harsh terms in many of the poems of the *Greek Anthology*.

So it turns out that what looked at first like a similarity between our own tradition and the Greek contains something a little different. Strato's poem is not simply saying "Gather ye Rose-buds while ye may" (to quote Herrick's "To the Virgins, to Make Much of Time"), but is rather pointing to a specific moment in Philippus's life that is fast approaching. Soon, he will not be the valued cucumber on the edge of the garden, but, once past his prime, fodder for pigs. The sentiment is similar to that in Marvell's poem, but the specific cultural associations are very different.

All of the preceding may seem a bit shocking. But I have saved the greatest shock of all for last. Strato's poem is, by modern standards, quite obscene. For, as it turns out, it relies on two sexual images that were absolutely standard for the Greeks but are foreign to the later Western tradition. Cucumbers are used regularly as a metaphor for a man's phallus, and pigs are a regular metaphor for female genitalia. Suddenly, the poem takes on a completely different, and surprisingly graphic, meaning. What the speaker is warning is this: "Right now, Philippus, your 'cucumber' is attractive to men like me. But soon, when it grows larger, it will only be useful for having sex with women. And won't that be a shame? You'd better have sex with me—a man—while you still have time."

So now the poem is not only about the sense of urgency that Philippus ought to feel, but it also gives a succinct, elegant snapshot of the different kinds of sex that the Greeks were interested in. It suggests, further, a specific value system that is not quite ours either. At the very least, the poem suggests that Philippus ought to prefer sex with the (male) speaker of the poem to the kind of sex he will have later, with women, when he becomes an adult male.

Some of my readers will be shocked by what I have just explained, some amused. But in any case, the point is this: the ancient Greek and Roman systems of erotics were different from ours (and from each other). When we understand the ways in which they were different, their erotic poetry looks rather different from ours, too. And whatever one thinks of the Greek and Roman systems of erotics and of their love poetry, we can only understand the latter when we look unflinchingly at the former. In the next few chapters, we look at a vast tradition of erotic writings, in contexts ranging from the legal system to comedy to love poetry. In the end, the reader will come to understand a system of erotic life that is, in some ways, not like our own and, in other ways, surprisingly similar, but in any case, coherent, interesting, and a real pleasure to study.

FIRST PRINCIPLES

This is a book about ancient Greek and Roman sexual practices and attitudes. As the brief example given previously demonstrates, those practices and attitudes may be shocking to some of my readers. I should warn you, therefore, that my tolerance for discussion of sex is rather high, and I do not intend to flinch away from a literal description of what the Greeks and Romans said and did. If this material offends you, please look elsewhere.

Those who are interested in what this book offers should know that this study is based on a virtual explosion of scholarly discussion on the topic of Greek and Roman sexuality that began, in a variety of venues, in the 1970s. Much of what I will have to say is still controversial, and I will, at times, refer to scholarly works with which my own views disagree. For the sake of the reader, I have kept footnotes to a minimum, and I refer only to a few of the most recent and relevant discussions of the issue at hand. Scholars interested in a more thorough treatment of the secondary literature should turn to the works suggested for further reading. Readers should be aware, however, that most of the texts I refer to are now easily available in an excellent collection of translations by Thomas Hubbard.[2] Though I have translated most of the sources in this book myself, interested readers may want to turn to Hubbard to read fuller versions of the texts in reliable translations.

Before we begin, it will be useful to be clear about a few definitions. Three interrelated terms are paramount: sex, gender, and sexuality. When I talk about *sex* (as in "the sex of the speaker is female"), I am referring to the biologically determined indicators of human distinction on the basis of sex. Although modern science has blurred the permanence and significance of these indicators considerably in recent decades—a person born a man no longer has to stay man, if he chooses to undergo a sex change operation—in common practice, this is a matter of genitalia. Men have penises, and women have vaginas. Even in the ancient world, these distinctions were not crystal clear: ancient Greece and Rome knew of a type of person known as a *hermaphrodite*, a person with ambiguous sexual organs. On a deeper level of biology, it is a matter of chromosomes: XX or XY.

Gender, on the other hand, is not a stable biological fact, but rather a matter of cultural definition. Gender refers to the cultural interpretation that is ascribed to the biological fact of sex. In other words, certain traits and behaviors are marked as masculine or feminine. The important thing to remember about gender is that the traits that are valued are not necessarily the same across time and culture. Greek men viewed Persian men as suspiciously feminine, in part because (unlike the Greeks) Persian men wore pants. Long hair is still something of a feminine trait in our society, though men can wear their hair long if they are willing to deal with the social pressures that accompany this slight deviation from the norm. Many other signs are less obvious, though no less powerful: studies have shown that in modern-day America, women move their heads when they talk more than men, and they tend to end their sentences with a slight upward pitch, whereas men end theirs with a downward one. Try doing the opposite sometime (i.e., if you are a man, raise your voice at the end of your sentences and bob your head around while you talk), and you will quickly see what I mean.

Sexuality, similarly, is, at the most basic level, the cultural interpretation of a person's sexual identity, determined by whether or not a person arranges her sexual life according to the norms of her society. Again, it is important to note that these social norms are not fixed across time and place. There have been, and are still today, many societies in which it is normal for younger men to engage in sexual activities with fully adult males. Though such men would, in the modern West, be considered gay (or at least bisexual), within the context of their own societies, such a term simply makes no sense. They are not thought of as belonging to any particular sexual orientation or sexuality; they are simply young men.

Sexuality, then, is the most complex of these three terms, in large part because it interacts with both of the other two; that is, the definitions of gender play a large role in determining what is appropriate sexual behavior for an individual. In the modern West, men who prefer to engage in sex with other men, rather than women, are gay. Whether true or not, one prevalent set of assumptions in our society is that gay men are less fully masculine than straight men, and gay women are presumed to be, in some senses, more masculine than straight women. So a violation of sexual norms means, in effect, that an individual runs a risk on two cultural axes at once: a gay person can be marginalized because he or she is gay (i.e., discrimination based on sexuality) or marginalized as inappropriately gendered (i.e., discrimination based on perceived gender slippage).

All of that is something of an oversimplification. In the modern world, one's sexuality is much more than the outside world's perception of one's sexual role. We also think of sexuality in terms of identity: a person is not just homosexual or heterosexual, but is *a* homosexual or *a* heterosexual. The object of one's desire—and whether he is of the same or the opposite sex—becomes a powerful indicator of a kind of person and is taken as a key that unlocks deeply secret aspects of that person's psyche. Being homo- or heterosexual also expands outward to suggest a person's orientation toward the world and toward culture at large; once thought of as an identity, sexuality takes on the power to define a lifestyle, that is, it becomes an attitude toward society that goes well beyond sexual activity.

As we have already seen, the terms most commonly used today when we think about categories of sexuality simply will not work when we discuss ancient Greece and Rome. If we begin with the presumption that the Greeks and Romans divided the sexual world into homo- and heterosexual, then we are left with rather curious inevitable conclusions: that virtually every man in Athens was gay, or at least bisexual, but that at the same time, the Greeks and Romans expressed, in some kinds of texts, extreme forms of homophobia. A simpler and more reasonable assumption is that the Greeks and Romans thought of sexual roles differently than we do—that, in effect, their sexual universe was oriented on a different set of axes than ours is.

Even more fundamentally, it is far from clear that the Greeks and Romans thought of sexual roles as sexualities—that is, as deeply seated internal elements of one's psyche that determine not only sexual roles, but character and lifestyle. For reasons that I will discuss later in this chapter, Michel Foucault has argued that that notion of sexuality only comes into existence in the nineteenth century, as a necessary product of the discursive power of the field of psychology. Foucault's thesis has been challenged, and it is certainly worth looking at closely; but for now, let us assume that it is an open question whether or not the Greeks and Romans had a category of thought that we can legitimately call "sexuality."

DOWN TO BASICS: PSEUDO-LUCIAN'S *EROTES*

All of this is somewhat difficult to discuss in the abstract, so I will turn now to a description and discussion of a specific text. Although most of this book is arranged in chronological order, the first text I discuss, pseudo-Lucian's *Erotes* (or *Loves*) is quite late. Most scholars put it in the years 200–300 CE. (Originally, it was thought to be the work of Lucian, an author of the second century CE. Experts now believe that it is not really his work, but since we do not know, in that case, whose work it is, we are forced to refer to the author as "pseudo-Lucian," that is, someone imitating the style of Lucian.) This text, written in Greek by a Greek living under the later Roman Empire, illustrates with particular clarity how the ancient sexual system was different from ours. Reading it allows us to deduce what the unstated social assumptions were behind a particular piece of literature, and it serves as a useful springboard to examine how the Greeks and Romans thought of sex, and if they thought of sexuality at all.[3]

The form of pseudo-Lucian's *Erotes* is one that most American readers are not familiar with. The text presents itself as a philosophical dialogue on the forms of love; that is, two speakers, Callicratidas (from Athens) and Charicles (from Corinth), hold a formal argument on the question of whether it is better to love boys (i.e., young men before the onset of adulthood) or women. Each of these speakers is interested in only one sex: Callicratidas loves boys, Charicles, women. It is tempting, therefore, to see them as representatives of homosexuality and heterosexuality, but as will become clear, that distinction breaks down on careful examination. This is a lighthearted and not terribly serious text, but one with clear literary pretensions. The author recalls, through several small allusions and references, various works of high Greek culture. The text is most clearly indebted to Plato's *Symposium* (discussed later in this book), in which Socrates recounts the teachings of Diotima on the topic of love in a more serious vein.

Before the formal debate even begins, it is clear that something other than our sexual value system is at play. A character named Lycinus is having a conversation with one Theomnestus, and in the course of their discussion, it comes out that each of them represents a certain sexual type. Theomnestus declares that Lycinus will make an impartial judge of the debate between Callicratidas and Charicles since he is not interested in sex with either boys or women (*Erotes* 4). Theomnestus, we learn in the next paragraph, is interested in sex with both. Lycinus compares Theomnestus's attitude with that of Callicratidas and Charicles, saying, "You who, thanks to your easy-going spirit, go sleepless and earn double wages, 'One as a herdsman of cattle, another as a tender of white flocks.' "[4] (This last sentence is a quotation from *Odyssey* 10.84–85.) What is remarkable about this description, from a modern point of view, is that Theomnestus's bisexuality is not particularly remarkable and certainly has no overtones of immorality. Rather, describing him through a learned literary allusion, Lycinus likens Theomnestus to a man who has two jobs—and jokingly suggests that because he is willing to sleep with either sex, he does not get much sleep.

The two speakers who frame the dialogue proper, then, provide the reader with two fairly normal Greek sexual types. What defines their sexual behavior, however, is not whether they choose to sleep with boys or women, but rather whether they are interested in sex at all. One is, one is not, but the one who does enjoy sex is presumed to enjoy sex with both men and women, and this aspect of his sexual behavior is not seen as problematic. Between the two of them, Lycinus and Theomnestus define the poles of an axis on which every Greek and Roman man had to locate himself.

By contrast, the two men who have the debate about the preferable form of love are described in terms that make it clear that each of them is really quite an odd duck. Callicratidas, the Athenian, is only interested in boys. We might assume that his preference is abnormal, but it is worth noting that Lycinus describes him as "a man of straightforward ways. For he was preeminent among the leading figures in public speaking and in this forensic oratory of ours" (*Erotes* 9). There is evidently no concern about his love for boys as such. What is odd about his preference is that he loves boys exclusively. Later in the dialogue, Callicratidas engages in a misogynistic diatribe that is extreme, even for an ancient Greek.

Even more noticeable, though, is the fact that Charicles' predilection for women, and only women, is also thought of as abnormal. Here is how Lycinus describes his household:

Charicles, however, had in attendance a large band of dancing-girls and singing-girls and all his house was as full of women as if it were the Thesmophoria, with not the slightest trace of male presence except that here and there could be seen an infant boy or a superannuated old cook whose age could give even the jealous no cause for suspicion. (*Erotes* 10)

Charicles, whom we might be tempted to think of as heterosexual, is not just a normal guy. As in the case of Callicratidas, his exclusive preference is worthy of comment and thus marked as a bit bizarre. His house resembles the Thesmophoria, an annual festival of Demeter in which only women participated, itself set off from the normal activities of civic business. We do hear that Charicles allows very young and very old men in his household, and it is worth noting here that this exception to his rule is itself somewhat ambiguous. The men who are excluded from his household are those who are of a sexual age. But are they sexual as *objects* of desire, or as desiring subjects? The Greek translated literally says that he allows those "whose age held no suspicion of rivalry." But rivalry for whom—the women of the household, or for Charicles himself? I believe that Charicles allows no men in his house who might be *his* rival for the affection of his female attendants, but it is impossible to know for sure. The first point we must note about this debate, in any case, is clear: this is not an argument between a normal heterosexual and a less normal homosexual about whose kind of sex is better; rather, it is a disagreement between two men who are both odd in their strongly held preference for one kind of perfectly acceptable sex over the other. The grounds of the debate are simply not those that would occur in our day.

In the course of the debate itself, the speakers confirm the idea that this is an argument about two kinds of fully comparable and interchangeable sexual activity. Each of them discusses the characteristics and advantages of their preferred kind of love. Charicles begins with a set of arguments that are familiar: he suggests that in early days, before the corrupting influence of civilization, men had sex with women, as nature intended. It was only with the arrival of a more decadent time that men began having sex with boys, and "they were ashamed neither at what they did nor at what they had done to them, and, sowing their seed, to quote the proverb, on barren rocks they bought a little pleasure at the cost of great disgrace" (*Erotes* 20). He goes on to argue that animals do not engage in same-sex activity (*Erotes* 22). Then, anticipating that Callicratidas will rely on the philosophical precedent of Socrates, he argues that when the philosophers claim that their love for boys is really something more virtuous (i.e., love of beauty or virtue), they are giving "honorable names to dishonorable passions" (*Erotes* 24).

All of this sounds rather like a modern denunciation of homosexuality, which is often decried as "unnatural" (though in fact, same-sex sexual activity is not uncommon among cats, dogs, and other animals). We should note, however, that Charicles never suggests that feeling this sort of desire is unnatural or unlikely; rather, his argument thus far is simply that although we all feel such desires, we would do better not to act on them because they do not lead to the survival of the species. The more serious problem with such love affairs, he argues, is that they do not last very long because the beloved boy will inevitably grow up and cease to be an object of desire. Women, he says, are desirable "from maidenhood to middle age" (*Erotes* 25). But should a man pursue a man over the age of 20, Charicles argues, then things begin to be repugnant:

For then the limbs, being large and manly, are hard, the chins that once were soft are rough and covered with bristles, and the well-developed thighs are, as it were, sullied with hairs. And as for the parts less visible than these, I leave knowledge of them to you who have tried them! (*Erotes* 26)

In other words, love of women is better than love of boys because it lasts longer—and not because there is anything unusual or shameful (in this part of the argument) about feeling desire for boys.

Charicles continues on similar lines, arguing that there is a structural problem in affairs between men and boys, namely, that the boys derive no pleasure from the sex (*Erotes* 27). Ideally, Charicles argues, sexual preference should be mutual and reciprocal. Here we see clearly one of the assumptions that underlies the Greek sexual system being described; that is, while it is presumed that the active partner in the sexual relationship—the adult man— will derive pleasure with either partner, the boy, who is being penetrated, is presumed not to experience pleasure, but rather to put up with the sexual imposition in return for other kinds of favors. Here, as we will see repeatedly in Greek and Roman texts, that which is shameful and truly deviant is for a man to enjoy being penetrated. Penetrating, whether the object is a boy or a woman, is presumed pleasurable.

Indeed, at the very end of his argument, Charicles indicates that in a fundamental way, the pleasure that the male subject experiences with a boy is interchangeable for that with a woman. His penultimate point is that women can be used like boys—that is, they can be penetrated anally—but that boys cannot be penetrated vaginally. While the overt point of this argument is that women provide "two paths to pleasure," while a boy has only one (*Erotes* 27), the underlying understanding is that anal sex with a woman is more or less the same thing as with a boy.

Charicles does not oppose same-sex amours, then, on the sort of moral grounds that we commonly hear today; rather, for him, there are specific aspects of the adult male–young man relationship that are disadvantageous. It is a relationship that does not result in procreation; it is necessarily of limited duration; and it is one-sided in the bestowal of pleasure. Of these three arguments, only the first one can be applied to the modern idea of homosexuality. Here, then, the Greeks are thinking differently than us.

Callicratidas responds to Charicles' charges of same-sex desire being unnatural first. He concedes that sex with women is necessary as a means of procreation but then argues that, with the advent of civilization, we should not limit ourselves to this required act, but enjoy the results of the greater leisure that comes with an advance in human comfort. This argument reaches a conclusion with a comment about animals, answering Charicles' earlier observation of their heteroerotic practice: "Lions do not have such a love, because they are not philosophers either" (*Erotes* 36). In other words, same-sex sexual activity (between men) is part of the advantage of civilization—along with higher reasoning, better clothes, more elaborate foodstuffs, and all the rest that we enjoy now that life is a little less nasty, brutish, and short.

Callicratidas next tries to justify his idiosyncratic banishing of all women from his life, and he does so by again appealing to a notion of what is natural. Women, he points out, rely on artifice for their beauty, in the form of makeup, clothing, and jewelry. Boys, by contrast, live a life of unfeigned and natural valor:

He rises at dawn from his couch, washes away with pure water such sleep as still remains in his eyes and after securing his shirt and his mantle pins at the shoulder, he leaves his father's hearth with eyes bent down and without facing the gaze of anyone. . . . next come the glistening wrestling schools, where beneath the heat of the midday sun his developing body is covered in dust; then comes the sweat, that pours forth from his toils in the contest, and next a quick bath and a sober meal suited to the activities that soon follow. . . . Who would not fall in love with such a youth? Whose eyesight could be so blind, whose mental processes so stunted? (*Erotes* 44–46)

In this argument, it is the boy's natural beauty, won by hard exercise and dedication to the study of virtue, that trumps the more artificial beauty of the heavily made-up and perfumed woman.

Finally, Callicratidas must respond to the argument that relationships with young men are not mutually pleasurable and are necessarily short-lived. He does so by invoking the image of Socrates, whose love for young men was presented (by Plato) as part of a program of virtuous instruction, from which the young men would benefit as they grew older. Indeed, Callicratidas says,

> For, when the honorable love inbred in us from childhood matures to the manly age that is now capable of reason, the object of our long-standing affection gives love in return and it is difficult to detect which is the lover of which, since the image of the lover's tenderness has been reflected from the loved one as though from a mirror.[5] (*Erotes* 48)

Given this model for the love of young men, however, Callicratidas also acknowledges that it comes with a set of limits. He suggests that since such long-standing friendship is the goal of these relations, the lovers in such an amour must keep their affections carefully under control: "Do not for the sake of a brief pleasure squander lasting affection, nor till you've reached manhood show counterfeit feelings of affection, but worship heavenly Love and keep your emotions constant from boyhood to old age" (*Erotes* 49). This last set of comments is indicative of one of the core values of ancient Greek sexual practice. Far more than one's choice of erotic object, the ancient Greeks were concerned with the demonstration of temperance, or self-control.

The two speakers have made their case; at the close of the dialogue, Lycinus gives his judgment. He tries, briefly, to steer a middle course: he declares that all men should marry, but that only philosophers should be allowed to love boys for "perfect virtue grows least of all among women" (*Erotes* 51); that is, he accepts the philosophers' argument that their love of boys is a necessity since boys better embody virtue than women do. Though this has sometimes been taken as a victory for Callicratidas—and indeed Charicles seems to take it that way—the final section of the dialogue undercuts it significantly. For Theomnestus, our lover of both women and boys, has the last word, and he decrees that it would be unfair to require him to love boys but never enjoy them sexually (*Erotes* 53). Nor, he says, did Alcibiades arise from lying with Socrates "unassailed" (*Erotes* 54). At the close of the dialogue, then, Theomnestus insists on the physical aspect of men's love of boys and begins an argument to defend that aspect, suggesting that Achilles and Patroklos—the great heroic pair of the *Iliad*—were lovers as well as friends (*Erotes* 54).

I have described this dialogue at some length, and given the reader numerous quotations from it, to give the reader a taste of what the ancient Greeks worried about when they worried about sex. Let me now summarize a few of the main assumptions that underlie this entertaining dialogue. First, we note that although both of the speakers hold exclusive erotic tastes—one loves only boys, the other only women—neither they nor Lycinus assume that either of these positions is the social norm; rather, the dialogue could only take place as it does in a society that assumes that most men are interested in both boys and women. The question, then, is not why some percentage of the population is homosexual, but rather, of the commonly available and desirable options, which should men prefer? For the most part, moreover, the arguments for that preference are not cast in terms of one kind of love being inherently wrong; rather, each presents certain advantages and disadvantages.

Second, although the dialogue is set as a debate between two men whom we might call "gay" (Callicratidas) and "straight" (Charicles), it is clear that neither of them represents a common type of sexual being; rather, both of them are depicted as unusual, if not unique, in the exclusivity of their tastes, and moreover, there is no Greek word or term that can be used to describe either of them because of those tastes. In fact, it is a mistake to think of them as having distinct sexual *identities* in the modern sense of the word. Callicratidas loves boys, but he is not labeled a "boy-lover." He is not invested with particular physical, social, or emotional characteristics as a result of his preference. Rather, we should think of both speakers as expressing a *preference of personal taste,* no more and no less.

Some scholars have, nonetheless, pointed to Charicles' arguments, in which he suggests that the love of boys is unnatural, as evidence that the ancient Greeks did express homophobia. But again, Charicles' views are presented as unusual, and extreme. By the same token, Callicratidas expresses severe misogyny in his description of the made-up and luxuriant women whom he prefers to avoid. Although both their arguments rely on common philosophical and poetic ideas, there is nothing in the text that suggests that either of them is presenting the mainstream view when attacking the other.

Finally, we must discuss one of the great blank spots in the text, a part of this discussion that the dialogue simply refuses to deal with, that is, what about women and their desires? Charicles discusses them briefly, in suggesting that women can feel pleasure in sex in a way that boys do not (or should not). But the text as a whole is simply unconcerned with what women think, feel, prefer, or desire. The erotic *subject* of the text is the adult male, and it is with his desires, pleasures, and preferences that the speakers are concerned. There is, however, one exception to this rule, and it is a telling one.

At the end of his argument, Charicles, the great lover of women, makes a bold and unusual move. If men are to love boys, he suggests, then we might as well take the further, and evidently completely outrageous step, of allowing women to love women:

Let them have intercourse with each other just as men do. Let them strap to themselves cunningly contrived instruments of lechery, those mysterious monstrosities devoid of seed, and let woman lie with woman as does a man. . . . And how much better that a woman should invade the provinces of male wantonness than that the nobility of the male sex should become effeminate and play the part of a woman. (*Erotes* 28)

Here, I suggest, the speaker is still not really concerned with the desires of women; rather, women are being set up as a bogey-man (so to speak) to terrify the reader away from the notion of male-male love. In particular, Charicles seems hysterically concerned about the women's potential use of dildos ("those mysterious monstrosities devoid of seed"), further proof of the unnatural aspect of such love. But even more important, the passage is particularly alarmed at the idea of gender slippage. What is really upsetting about what we would call lesbianism is that one of the women will play the part of a man—that is, be the active partner in sex ("invade the provinces of male wantonness"). Bad though this is, it is not as frightening to Charicles as the possibility that a man, in male-male sex, should "play the part of a woman."

This last section, then, confirms what many scholars of ancient sexuality have been arguing for the last 30 years, namely, that the ancient Greeks are not concerned with homosexuality per se. What they are concerned with is a notion of masculinity that requires a man to be the active, penetrating partner in sex. To be a man (not a boy) who desires to be penetrated is, then, the deviant position. For women, the opposite is true. Women are assumed to be passive by nature, and the deviant woman is not deviant because she desires women, but because she desires to take on the active, penetrating role in sex. Thus for the Greeks, sexuality is closely bound to their understanding of gender roles.

MICHEL FOUCAULT AND *THE HISTORY OF SEXUALITY*

My reading of pseudo-Lucian's *Erotes* would not have been possible without the pioneering work of Michel Foucault. A distinguished philosopher and social critic, Foucault set out in the 1970s to write a history of sexuality. The first volume, which appeared in 1976, is a dense, theoretically sophisticated analysis of sexuality in its modern sense. While scholars are still arguing about the implications of much of this work, I will attempt a brief description of some of its main points. In 1984, the second volume (subtitled *The Use of Pleasure*) was published in French, and a translation into English followed swiftly. In this volume, Foucault began his analysis of the Greeks' discussions of sex, pleasure, and sexuality. Volume 3, *The Care of the Self,* was published two years later and treats several works of Greek and Roman authors living under the Roman Empire.

To say that this history was controversial within the field of classics is a vast understatement. Scholars attacked Foucault on several fronts at once. Feminist scholars argued that Foucault, while profiting from their critiques of classical literature, had failed to cite much of their work.[6] Others pointed out that Foucault's understanding of the classical world was deficient in several areas and that, in particular, he failed to distinguish between the different attitudes of Greece and Rome toward various sexual practices.[7]

Most important of all, however, some scholars took issue with Foucault's assertion that homosexuality, and indeed the entire discursive field currently thought of as sexuality per se, did not exist in ancient Greece and Rome— that it was, in fact, only possible to speak of sexuality with the advent of psychoanalysis in the nineteenth century. Today, this debate rages on, and many scholars (including Thomas Hubbard, whose sourcebook I referred to earlier) continue to argue for the existence of homosexuality as a sexual identity in the ancient world, with an accompanying homophobia. While I have read much of this controversy and considered it carefully, I should warn the reader that I am not an impartial judge in this matter. I have come to the conclusion that, in the main, Foucault was right: sexuality is a concept that is culturally specific, and we do not find homosexuality or homophobia in ancient Greece or Rome. Readers interested in the debate are encouraged to read Foucault and his detractors.

How can I argue that homosexuality did not exist, especially after having discussed the *Erotes* of pseudo-Lucian? First, it is important to distinguish between the raw fact of same-sex desire (which certainly did exist in ancient Greece and Rome, as it does today) and the idea that such desire is abnormal and that it constitutes one as a kind of person. Indeed, in the first place, the Greeks and Romans simply did not seem to be concerned about one's choice of love-object as a way of distinguishing sexual behavior. As Foucault wrote in volume 2,

As a matter of fact, the notion of homosexuality is plainly inadequate as a means of referring to an experience, forms of valuation, and a system of categorization so different from ours. The Greeks did not see love for one's own sex and love for the other sex as opposites, as two exclusive choices, two radically different types of behavior. The dividing lines did not follow that kind of boundary. What distinguished a moderate, self-possessed man from one given to pleasures was, from the viewpoint of ethics, much more important than what differentiated, among themselves, the categories of pleasures that invited the greatest devotion. To have loose morals was to be incapable of resisting either women or boys, without it being any more serious than that.[8]

In other words, it simply does not make sense to talk about Greek and Roman homosexuality when four conditions are true: (1) virtually every man is assumed to be interested in sex with boys; (2) this desire for boys is not assumed, normally, to exclude an equally strong desire for women; (3) with rare exceptions (if any), the desire is depicted as that of an adult man for a so-called boy below the age of 20 or so, rather than a reciprocal desire between equals; and (4) neither the Greeks nor the Romans have a word, or seem to have a category, for individuals who prefer sex with one gender rather than the other.

If the Greeks thought of sex in terms so different from our own, how did we get to where we are today? This is the subject, more or less, of volume 1 of Foucault's *The History of Sexuality*. The argument in this first volume is complex, closely argued, and contested. I can do no more here than provide a bare outline of some of the most salient points.

First, Foucault moves the idea of sexuality into the realm of history by arguing that the idea of sexuality itself—that is, the idea that each of us has a sexuality, a deeply held, private, and secret psychic reality that governs our sexual behaviors and inclinations—is not constant across time and space; rather, it came about because of a particular set of historical conditions. Seen through this lens, it is not the Greeks who are odd, but us; and in fact, it does appear that the notion that one can divide the world up into homosexual, heterosexual, and bisexual is a particularly modern one.

Foucault points out that despite a tendency to believe that we are secretive about sex, in fact, the culture of the modern West is characterized by a drive to "confess" about sex. We talk to psychotherapists, to religious leaders, to parents, and to teachers; we take quizzes in supermarket magazines; daytime talk shows prominently feature abnormal sexual relationships and are watched by millions of people. Foucault then argues that this confessional mode, which has its roots in the early Christian church, makes certain assumptions about sex that have carried through to modern times, namely, that one's sexual behavior and desire contain an essential truth about a person, but that this truth is by nature hidden and must be elicited through the intervention of a trained professional. Confession of this sexual truth will, ideally, bring about good effects, whether a cure of deviancy or an assurance of salvation.

The other key aspect of the mode of confession, however, is that it always enacts a relationship of power between the confessor and the one extracting the confession. In its most extreme form, as under the Inquisition, this relationship can take on the brutality of physical torture. In less extreme forms, say, a young woman confessing her emotional desires to a guidance counselor, it is still true that the counselor is responsible for extracting the true confession, interpreting it correctly, and then helping the confessor to derive benefit from the act of talking about her desire.

Perhaps the boldest and most important theoretical move in Foucault's *History* follows: he argues that the modern practice of psychoanalysis, especially as described and practiced by Freud, follows this same model of confession, "constituted in scientific terms"[9]; that is, a patient goes to a psychoanalyst and confesses his sexual secrets to this trained professional. As before, there is a clear relationship of power: the psychoanalyst has the power, not only to interpret these confessions, but to extract the truth of them in the first place. In fact, the act of confession in classic psychoanalysis is much more than a mode of diagnosis. Once the sexual secret has been confessed and correctly interpreted, the act of bringing the secret truth of the subconscious mind to the level of consciousness is also how the patient is cured. Thus psychoanalysis has become the modern, scientific mode of confession.

It is within this context, of course, that the notion of homosexuality first came into being. Freud and his followers were concerned with what Foucault calls "a psychiatrization of perverse pleasure"; that is, the question for a psychoanalyst was not, is this sexual act or desire sinful? but rather, is this sexual act or desire healthy and normal? Unhealthy sexual desires, those that do not fit the norm were (and some still are) put into a scientific catalogue of types, and homosexuality became thought of a sickness to be cured. More important, someone who exhibited this sickness became a type of person, similar to a schizophrenic or neurotic.[10] From this scientific recasting of the mode of confession, then, came the modern notion of a homosexual, and indeed of sexuality itself, both normal and abnormal.

Ancient Greece, as Foucault argues, does not exhibit this kind of discussion of sexual practice and desire; rather, the ancient Greeks thought of sexual desire as an appetite, best managed when it was kept under close control. But unlike the modern notion of perversity, to have this or that sexual desire did not, in most cases, mark one as a particular kind of person. When a person was marked by his sexual activity, it was not the case that the desire itself was thought of as inherently wrong (let alone sinful), but rather that some men were not in sufficient control of the desires to which all men were subject.

That does not mean, however, that the Greeks and Romans lived in a world free from moral valuation about sex—far from it. It is simply the case that their rules are not ours. In the first place, it is clear that numerous texts— legal oratory and Aristophanic comedy, most markedly—do attach negative values to certain kinds of sexual behavior. Adult men were not supposed to desire to be penetrated. To be penetrated was to accept a submissive stance in regard to the partner who was doing the penetrating—to give up, in other words, control of one's own body. That was never good, and it carried with it a much broader set of social and political connotations. As we observed when discussing pseudo-Lucian, the assumed *subject* of the sexual desire in that dialogue was an adult male—and neither speaker ever broached the idea that being penetrated might be preferable to penetrating; rather, their dialogue is about the advantages of the two acceptable kinds of sex for penetrating men such as themselves.

If normal men were assumed to be active, and desiring of both women and boys, then the boys who were their objects of desire were placed in an ambivalent position. Citizen boys in Greece were depicted as highly desirable objects. But at a certain age, such boys were expected to make a transition to full adulthood and cease being penetrated. Considerable anxiety shows itself, not only about the future active citizenship of these boys, but about their integrity while still boys. The better the family, the more closely guarded the boy would have been, and it appears that actual *penetration* of a citizen boy was regarded as damaging to him. A man might, then, be criticized for damaging a boy in this way—or even brought to trial for *hybris,* a violation of the person, and a very serious charge. This criticism should not be confused with homophobia, however; such a man could have homoerotic sex freely with a prostitute without fear of reprisal.

Even the active adult man in an erotic relationship was not entirely free from constraint. One of the most important advances of Foucault's work (and of classicists John Winkler and David Halperin) was the understanding that the Greeks thought of desire in much the same way that they thought of other appetites: for food, for sleep, and so on. While in some ways, this way of thinking makes sex less fraught with danger, in others, it exactly locates the danger that desire possesses. For, as Foucault showed through an analysis of various philosophical and medical texts, adult citizen men aspired to a state of *enkrateia,* or "self-control." Their control over their own bodies was thought of in ways analogous to their control over their households and wives, and to give in too readily to a desire—for food, for sleep, or for a boy or woman—indicated a lack of self-control that made a man suspect in other arenas, especially the political. Thus, as we will see, one of the most devastating things a man could do was prostitute himself. Doing so was a complete giving-over of self-control, and in fifth-century Athens, such a man could be stripped of his rights as a citizen.

When dealing with the sexual desires and acts of women, we must admit that we are at a severe disadvantage. Like every aspect of women's lives in ancient Greece and Rome, when it comes to sex, we have (almost) no first-person accounts. The vast majority of Greek and Roman literature was written by men, about men, and for men. When they do consider women, these male authors are frankly less concerned with the women as thinking and feeling subjects than as potential threats to the male subject. As such, though we can deduce what the Greek men thought was normal behavior—that is, behavior that fit into the male notion of femininity—we have to exercise considerable ingenuity to glimpse what the women themselves might have thought, felt, or done.

From this masculine perspective, women were thought of as naturally lacking the kind of self-control that defines masculinity. As such, their sexual desires were often characterized as insatiable. For a woman to achieve the ideal of modest temperance—for which the most common word is *sophrosyne*—was to be chaste. Again, the discourse on love produced by pseudo-Lucian simply is not concerned with women's desires; there is no dialogue concerning whether it is better to have sex with a man or a boy (or with a man or a woman) from the point of view of a desiring woman. That is not the ethical or erotic position that the Greek texts concern themselves with. There is, however, a position of deviance for a woman, and we have seen it already: for women to be *active* in sex, that is, to penetrate, was deviant, as a denial of their natural gender role.

None of this, of course, is to say that the Greeks did not distinguish between sex with women and sex with boys. If that were the case, pseudo-Lucian's text could never have been produced. There are different rules governing these two kinds of desire, they have different characteristics, and it is even possible to find characters in the ancient world who express a strong preference for one over the other. But again, this preference is best thought of in terms of an appetite, not as a deep psychological trait that characterizes a certain type of person. It is a recognized difference, in other words, but not a meaningful one in terms of ethics, or values, or, in modern terms, sexuality.

SUMMARY: WAYS OF THINKING ABOUT SEXUALITY

There are different ways of thinking about sexuality that will be helpful to keep in mind in the following chapters. Various works present people who have certain kinds of sexual preferences, who are characterized in certain ways by their sexual behavior, and who are occasionally described as having identities that are defined by their sexual practices. In looking at these people, it will be helpful to break what we usually call "sexuality" down into four related, but not identical, subcategories.[11]

First, does the person described have a sexual *orientation*? That is, does he express a strong or exclusive preference for erotic partners of a particular gender? Second, does the person have a sexual *identity*? Does her sexual desire mark her as a kind of person, and more important, does she think of herself as inhabiting that identity because of her particular kind of desire? Third, does the person have a sexual *morphology:* can he be spotted on the street as a particular kind of sexual being because of certain tell-tale signs in his physical being, including hairstyle, dress, mode of walking and talking, and the like? And finally, does the person analyzed demonstrate a particular *gender role*? Is she considered feminine or masculine because of the kind of sex that she prefers, and is the person's sexual behavior defined by whether she is active (penetrating, masculine) or passive (penetrated, feminine)?

When we think about the modern category of homosexuality, the answer to the first three of the preceding questions is probably a qualified yes. Sexual orientation is, for the modern West, the most basic aspect of homosexuality: gay men and women are defined as those who prefer sex with members of their own sex. We generally also think of this as an identity, an entire mode of life, and deeply held aspect of one's personal being. The third category is a bit trickier. Although it is commonly assumed that homosexuality results in demonstrable physical traits and personal characteristics, one of the things that homophobic people find most threatening about gay men and women is their apparent ability to blend into society and to appear straight. The final category, gender role, is one that does not apply directly to homosexuality; that is, a gay man can penetrate or be penetrated, can be effeminate or masculine in affect, and this has no effect on whether or not he is gay. For modern lesbians, the notion of penetrating or penetrated may well not apply at all.

In general, in the ancient world, the last category is the one that turns out to be most crucial: sexual actors are defined according to their gender role and according to whether they are penetrating or penetrated. On the other hand, the question of sexual orientation rarely, if ever, comes up. Most men were assumed to be interested in erotic objects of either gender. Most women were not thought about as sexual subjects at all. The other two categories, those of sexual identity and sexual morphology, are more slippery and will bear careful investigation in each of the texts that we encounter.

ANCIENT TERMS FOR SEXUAL BEHAVIOR

In reading almost any translation of a classical work that deals with sex, the reader will sooner or later stumble across examples that seem to directly contradict what I have just said. Translations of Aristophanes' plays or Catullus's poetry, for example, are full of jokes and insults against apparent homosexuality because their translators choose to render critical statements about certain kinds of people into modern slang terms such as *faggot*, or *bugger*, or *lesbian*. These passages sound like modern homophobia and make it sound as if the ancient Greeks and Romans thought of sex in the same ways that we do.

Unfortunately, what the reader must realize is that the translators of those texts are translating Greek and Roman sexual terms into terms from our own culture, and that in the process, a certain amount of distortion takes place. The fact of the matter is that the vast majority of these insults and jokes are directed against men who wish to be penetrated in sex (or women who are active in sex, "playing the part of the man"). Very rarely, a man will be criticized for penetrating a boy, and if he is, it is generally not in terms that suggest that such action is in itself wrong—rather, he is criticized for damaging a wellborn citizen boy, or for failing to keep his desires in proper check, or (as in pseudo-Lucian) for engaging in nonprocreative sex. None of these insults, then, are attacks on homosexuality itself.

Following are a few of the words that are commonly translated into a modern sexual idiom:

erastes/eromenos: In the system of pederasty described previously, in which an older man had an affair with a younger one, the older partner is referred to as an *erastes*, or "lover." The younger, passive partner is referred to by a word that is itself passive in form and can be translated as "beloved." There is considerable controversy over how passive any given *eromenos* was, but the ideal was that he was younger, penetrated, and did not so much enjoy sex as endure it for the sake of the social relationship that his *erastes* offered him.

kinaidos: A *kinaidos* was a gender-deviant man. He embodied several feminine characteristics, including a decadent style of dress and speech, a tendency to give himself over to physical luxury, and often (though not always) a willingness to be penetrated in sex. This term was taken up by the Romans (spelled *cinaedus*) and will be discussed at greater length in the second half of this study.

euryproktos: Literally, "wide ass," this is a term of reproach common in the plays of Aristophanes. As the literal meaning of the word suggests, a man who was *euryprokotos* was given to being penetrated, often with a sense of having done so indiscriminately.

katapugon: This is another Aristophanic insult. *Katapugon* is of less clear origin and meaning than *euryproktos*. Often, it seems to mean simply "lecherous," that is, given to indulging sexual desire. It may originally have had a meaning that referred to being penetrated but seems to have lost this sense by the classical period (fifth century BCE).

tribas: In pre-Roman Greek literature, there is almost no discussion of women who prefer sex with other women; when Plato discusses such people (in the *Symposium*, discussed later), he uses an unusually rare word—*hetairistriai*—to name them. In Rome, however, we have a more common term. A *tribas* is a woman who played the active role in sex, usually with another woman. (In some Roman texts, *tribades* are said to penetrate boys.) Originally, the word appears to derive from a verb that has to do with rubbing or grinding. This word is often misleadingly translated as "lesbian."

The tendency of modern translators to render all these modern terms in terms that invoke modern sexual categories is a clear impediment to understanding what goes on in the ancient texts. As a general rule of thumb, however, it is not a bad idea to mentally replace words that refer to our modern sexual system with words that describe the ancient one. When you run across the word *fag* in a comedy by Aristophanes, for example, simply think "passive" or, if you like, *kinaidos*. You will not often be wrong.

Two

Homer, Hesiod, and Greek Lyric Poetry

This book will traverse nearly a thousand years of literature, law, history, and art. During such a long period of time (covering two major cultures), the reader must expect that attitudes and ideas about sex will change considerably. Unfortunately, my investigations are hampered by some of the same difficulties that also affect investigations into modern sexual practice. Although the Greeks and Romans were in some ways much less concerned about obscenity than the modern West, at other times, they seem hesitant to talk about specific sexual acts. Just as when dealing with current events, then, the researcher must sometimes read between the lines.

Further affecting this inquiry, moreover, is the fact that there is not a full record of sources for every time period under investigation. Often we have, essentially, only one. Thus, for the archaic period in Greece (dating from roughly 800–500 BCE), the primary sources consist of a body of heroic, didactic, and erotic poetry. The latter century of this period also produced some painted vases having to do with same-sex and opposite-sex love, which scholars can use to supplement their interpretation of texts. History, in the modern sense of the word, had not been invented yet. By the classical period (500–340 BCE), a new set of sources emerged: the comedies of Aristophanes, the philosophy of Plato, and a set of legal speeches that sometimes dealt with sexual matters.

Because the kinds of sources that remain are different for different periods, it is difficult to know if what appears to be a historical difference—for example, a increase in concern with heteroerotic romantic love—is due to an actual change in attitude or simply to the kind of source that is present at that time. It is almost impossible to talk about sexuality in archaic Greek law, for example, because we do not have any archaic Greek legal speeches (though we do have the texts of some laws that are said to come from the archaic period).

In this chapter, I discuss the evidence for sexual attitudes and practice in the archaic period. As will become evident, all of my sources are poetic. Even within this limitation, the kind of poetry matters: in the love poetry of

Anacreon, sex is a primary concern. A different kind of evidence is presented by the heroic epic of Homer. These variations do not necessarily indicate a historical change in sexual practice; they are probably the result of the separate requirements of different kinds of poetry. As a result we must take care when using poetry as an indication of sexual practice in the real world. Nonetheless, this is the evidence that exists, and my strategy is to make the most of it.

What is particularly striking about the poetry from this period is that even when the works in question describe sexual desire in explicit terms, none of the poets discussed in this chapter seem to be concerned with the question of sexual orientation. Nearly all the erotic poetry from the archaic period presumes a masculine subject of desire, who may be interested in sex with either boys or women. Sappho is a notable exception because her poetry often takes the narrative voice of a desiring woman, but even in her case, the question of which gender constitutes an appropriate object seems of greater concern to us than to her. In other words, archaic Greece does not give evidence of *sexuality* in the modern sense of the word. It does, however, provide striking examples of anxiety about the proper behavior of lovers and beloveds, within the roles of penetrating and penetrated, discussed in chapter 1.

For the most part, this chapter is arranged chronologically. Homer and Hesiod are the earliest of the poets that I discuss, and Anacreon and Theognis, who follow, are roughly contemporary. Sappho is somewhat earlier than Anacreon and Theognis, (though later than Homer and Hesiod) but I have reserved her for the end of the chapter because it will be easier to understand her poetry once we have considered the approaches and attitudes of the predominantly male lyric poets with whom she shares both genre and time period.

SEX IN THE HOMERIC EPICS

The texts of Homer's *Iliad* and *Odyssey* are little short of miraculous. Though they appear in the eighth or seventh centuries BCE, they contain mythic material from a period some 500 years earlier. In the modern era, Millman Perry showed definitively that these were the products of oral poetry; that is, they were composed and transmitted in spoken form only for some hundreds of years before attaining their current, written form. In a real sense, then, these epics have no single author, and even the name "Homer" cannot be identified with a particular individual who lived at a particular time and wrote these works; rather, "Homer" is the name traditionally assigned to the poems as they were transmitted in canonical form to the Greeks of archaic and classical periods. Almost every aspect of this transmission is the subject of lively scholarly debate. It is also important for our purposes, however, because of the difficulty that it presents in discussing so-called Homeric society.

In brief, there is no easy way to determine how historical the epics are. If, as some scholars think, they preserve accurate depictions of social institutions (marriage, law, inheritance), there is little agreement as to what era those social institutions come from. Are they from the time of the poem's setting, in the 1200s BCE? Or from the time of the poet, in the 750s BCE? Or somewhere in between? For my part, I have become convinced that the poems primarily reflect the society and conventions of Homer's own day, which is to say, the eighth century BCE. It is almost certain, however, that no actual person ever lived under a society exactly as Homer describes it.[1] His is a poetic and heroic world, often depicting an upper-class ideal. We must assume that many aspects of real life are simply not depicted in Homer, any more than we would take a modern romantic comedy as presenting documentary truth.

That said, the only sexual activity referred to in the *Iliad* and *Odyssey* is clearly heteroerotic. There are no explicit descriptions of sex, though some characters do go to bed together, and we do hear occasionally that they enjoyed each other's company in this way. But more important, the conflict that causes the Trojan War is that between the Greek king Menelaus and the Trojan king Paris. Paris has stolen away Menelaos's wife, Helen, who is the most beautiful woman in the world. As a result, Menelaos, his brother Agamemnon, and the other kings of Greece unite in an expedition to bring her back. Subplots have the same structure: Agamemnon and Achilles fight over who should possess Briseis, a young woman captured from the Trojans.

Helen is a particularly problematic character in this story, and one whose alliances and affections are not always easy to discern. Her beauty is her defining characteristic, and it holds a terrible force for those who see it. Neither the poet nor the characters in the *Iliad* ever describe Helen physically, beyond a few stock adjectives (she is blonde and lovely-armed). Instead, we see the reaction of people who look on her. In book 3, for example, Helen appears on the walls of Troy. This is in the 10th year of the war, and Troy has suffered greatly because of her presence there. Here is how the old men of Troy see her:

And these, as they saw Helen along the tower approaching
murmuring softly to each other uttered their winged words:
"Surely there is no blame on Trojans and strong-greaved Achaians
if for a long time they suffer hardship for a woman like this one.
Her face is frighteningly like that of the immortal goddesses.
Still, though she be such, let her go away in the ships, lest
she be left behind, a grief to us and her children."[2] (*Iliad* 3.154–60)

Helen's appearance is frightening in the sense that it drives men to do crazy things, even when they know that they would be better off not to. She compels the Trojans, quite literally, to "suffer hardship" on behalf of her beauty.

This beauty is Helen, and it gives her a form of power that is unmatched by other women in literature, even extremely beautiful ones. In a later poem known as the *Catalogue of Women,* ascribed to Hesiod (but probably dating to 100 or more years later than Homer), the poet tells us the story of the princes of Greece wooing Helen before she was wed. Throughout the *Catalogue of Women,* there are stories of men marrying women, and the formulaic phrase describing their aspirations is "and he made her his blooming bride." In the story of the suitors of Helen, however, the relative power of groom and bride is reversed. Over and over again, we read a new formula: "for greatly he wished in his spirit to be the husband of lovely-haired Argive Helen." A man can make another woman his wife, but Helen's beauty is such that whoever marries her will become her husband. (This story, in fact, is the only place in the *Catalogue of Women* where the word *husband* appears.)

The most sexually explicit scene in the *Iliad,* and the only sex scene between mortals, occurs between Paris and Helen. In book 3, Paris engages in single combat with Menelaos, and he does not fare well. As he is on the verge of losing, Paris is whisked out of battle by Aphrodite, the goddess of lust and attraction. She takes him to Helen's bedroom, pretties him up, and more or less forces Helen to sleep with him. Paris, here, is clearly beautiful himself. But it is also worth noting that his preference for love over the manly arts of war makes him a bit of a fop. Helen initially tries to dismiss him:

"So you came back from the fighting. Oh, how I wish you had died there
beaten down by the stronger man, who was once my husband.
There was a time before now you boasted that you were better
than warlike Menelaos, in spear and hand and your own strength.
Go forth now and challenge warlike Menelaos
once again to fight you in combat. But no: I advise you
rather to let it be, and fight no longer with fair-haired
Menelaos, strength against strength in single combat
recklessly. You might very well go down before his spear." (*Iliad* 3.427–36)

Helen seems torn, here, between her disgust for Paris, who has proven himself less than a man, and her attraction to him. She does not, after all, want him to be so brave that he dies. Similarly, when Hektor, Paris's brother and the leader of the Trojans, arrives in book 6, he can hardly believe that Paris is lying around with his wife, rather than fighting the enemy:

But Hektor saw him, and in words of shame he rebuked him:
Strange man! It is not fair to keep in your heart this coldness.
The people are dying around the city and around the steep wall
as they fight hard; and it is for you that this war with its clamour
has flared up about our city. You yourself would fight with another
whom you saw anywhere hanging back from the hateful encounter.
Up then, to keep our town from burning at once in the hot fire. (*Iliad* 6.325–31)

Manliness, here as often in the idealizing pages of Greek literature, requires bravery in the forefront of battle, not dillydallying with beautiful women.

Even if Paris is a little bit less than a man, however, he does engage in sex with Helen, and there are no clear suggestions of men desiring other men in this epic. Can we say, then, that the *Iliad* shows us a clear heterosexual ethic? Not quite yet. In the first place, it is worth noting that here, as in much of later Greek literature, the poet presents a hero who is particularly attractive to women, but who is not, on that account, considered particularly manly. In fact, Paris's attractiveness to Helen, and his tendency to be with her, rather than out on the field of battle, suggests that he is somewhat effeminate. Rather than being a sign of masculinity, then, spending too much time with women could have been a sign of gender inversion, of being womanish.

Even more important, however, there is one other deeply emotional and affective relationship in the epic, and that is the heroic friendship between Achilles and his companion and double Patroklos. When Achilles, angry at Agamemnon, refuses to fight for the Greeks, it is Patroklos who keeps in touch with the troops and reports back. When the Greeks are in dire straits, Patroklos urges Achilles to loan him his armor so that he can scare the Trojans and win some breathing space for the Greek troops. And finally, when Hektor kills Patroklos, Achilles lets go of his grudge against Agamemnon and rejoins the fray to recover Patroklos's body. It is his relationship to Patroklos, finally, that acts as a kind of social glue, bringing Achilles back into the group of heroes who are his peers.

Though the two heroes are never shown in any kind of physical intimacy—and at night, we are told, they lie in separate beds, each with a woman by his side—they are emotionally bound to one another. When Patroklos requests to borrow Achilles' armor, Achilles expresses a wish that only he and Patroklos might survive the war together (*Iliad* 16.97–99). After Patroklos has died, Achilles' mother (the minor goddess Thetis) comes to him and tries to ease his grief and convince him not to reenter the battle. She tells him that if he does enter battle again, he will win great fame, but is fated to die soon. A distraught Achilles responds,

My mother, all these things the Olympian has brought to accomplishment.
But what pleasure is this to me, since my dear companion has perished,
Patroklos, whom I loved beyond all other companions,
as well as my own life. I have lost him, and Hektor, who killed him,
has stripped away that gigantic armour. . . .
As it is, there must be on your heart a numberless sorrow
for your son's death, since you can never again receive him
won home again to his country; since the spirit within does not drive me
to go on living and be among men, except on condition
that Hektor first be beaten down under my spear, lose his life,
and pay the price for stripping Patroklos, the son of Menoitios. (*Iliad* 18.79–93)

In rejecting Thetis's advice, Achilles fully realizes that he is giving himself over to death; he really does love Patroklos more than himself.

Achilles, however, still has something to learn about desire and its unfulfilled nature. After Patroklos has died and Achilles has killed Hektor in an act of brutal violence, he finds that revenge is ultimately unsatisfying, that it cannot replace his lost friend:

. . . only Achilles
wept still as he remembered his beloved companion, nor did sleep
which subdues all come over him, but he tossed from one side to the other
in longing for Patroklos, for his manhood and his great strength
and all the actions he had seen to the end with him, and the hardships
he had suffered; the wars of men; hard crossing of the big waters.
Remembering all these things he let fall the swelling tears, lying
sometimes along his side, sometimes on his back, and now again
prone on his face. (*Iliad* 24.3–11)

It is not too much to say that Achilles here is acting much the way that we expect unrequited lovers to behave in films and stories today. He constantly thinks of his lost friend, wishes that Patroklos were still alive, and is himself unable to eat or sleep in his longing. Achilles' friendship for Patroklos is, in these terms, the strongest emotional bond in the entire epic.

Does that, however, make Achilles and Patroklos lovers? This is a question that has been raised, and contemplated, from the classical period in Greece down to the present day. Though the argument has been made that they are, I must say that there is no evidence in the text for a physical relationship between the two heroes; rather, their friendship falls into that somewhat anomalous category of male-male relationships that persists in the West today, particularly in conditions of intense competition such as war.

What is particularly interesting about the story of Patroklos and Achilles, though, is that in the fifth century in Athens, it appears that the natural assumption was that the two heroes were lovers. In a legal speech that we will look at in more detail later, the speaker (a professional orator named Aeschines) argues that Homer hides their love for one another, "thinking that the greatness of their affection would be apparent to those of the listeners who were educated" (Aeschines *Against Timarchos* 142). Aeschylus, the great Athenian playwright, wrote a tragedy in which the two were portrayed as lovers. But as Plato points out in the *Symposium* (180a4–7), Aeschylus seems to have gotten their sexual roles wrong. Aeschylus portrayed Achilles as the lover, that is, the *erastes*. But as Homer makes clear, Patroklos is the older of the two and so, under the pederastic system of the fifth century in Athens, should have been the lover and Achilles the *eromenos,* or beloved.

All of this demonstrates a simple fact, which is that each society tends to read the *Iliad* with its own cultural assumptions in mind. For most modern scholars, the two heroes are not, and cannot, be lovers. The idea of presenting a gay Achilles is, to say the least, a bit subversive. But to the Greeks of the fifth century, it is clear that they must have been lovers, even if they did not seem to fit into the pederastic model that was their cultural norm. Ultimately, the question of whether or not these two fictional characters were lovers is both unanswerable and, perhaps, irrelevant. What matters most is the way in which this fundamental text elicits the unspoken assumptions of its readers.

HESIOD AND THE FIRST WOMAN

Like Homer, Hesiod is less a person whom we can identify than a name attributed to a set of poetry from the early archaic period. Unlike the heroic epics that Homer is known for, however, Hesiod is best known for a poem describing the origins of the Greek gods, called the *Theogony,* and a didactic poem about farming and justice, called the *Works and Days.* Perhaps the most famous passage in Hesiod's work is the story about the creation of the first woman on Earth; this story appears in both the *Theogony* and the *Works and Days,* though in slightly different form in each.

Myths of origin are always revealing of the ways in which people think when the myth is created (or retold), and the story of the first woman is no exception. As a paradigm for how the Greeks thought about women, then, the story of Pandora is particularly valuable. In the *Theogony*, in particular, this first woman (who is not named in this version) is given to humankind as a punishment. It seems that the god Prometheus, who generally rivals Zeus in mythical texts, has tricked the chief Olympian god twice, both times in ways that benefit humankind. Zeus's revenge is to create a woman, who is described explicitly as a "snare" herself; so Zeus is paying back humans in kind.

How is this first woman a snare? The outstanding thing about her is that she looks exceedingly beautiful—we should think of Helen here—but that she hides a dangerous and destructive nature. Following is the description of her creation in the *Theogony:*

. . . for the famous Hephaistos made out of clay,
as Zeus decreed, an image of an untouched virgin.
And the goddess gray-eyed Athena girdled and dressed her
in a silver-white gown and over her head drew a veil,
one that was woven with wonderful skill, a marvel to look at;
and over this a garland of spring flowers, bright in their freshness. . . .
Then the gods and mortal men were struck with amazement
when they beheld this sheer inescapable snare for men.
From her descend the race of women, the feminine sex;
from her come the baneful race and types of women.
Women, a great plague, make their abodes with mortal men,
being ill-suited to Poverty's curse but suited to Plenty.[3] (*Theogony* 571–93)

This, then, is a story about the creation of gender. Before this first woman, evidently, all humans were male. (How they reproduced is not a question that the text asks, or answers.) From now on, however, reproduction will be sexual. Significantly, that mode of reproduction is always marked by deception: men are taken in by the woman's beauty, a beauty that hides her true nature. Two anxieties are at play here. First, we see the concern that men will not be able to control their own desires when faced with feminine beauty. Second, and equally important, is a fear that women are by nature greedy, that they consume, but do not produce, and this uncontrolled appetite is the thing that fundamentally defines them.

This uncontrollable appetite that characterizes femininity is more marked in the version of the story in the *Works and Days*. There, the woman is similarly created as beautiful on the outside, but her destructive interior is made even more explicit. At the end of her creation, the poet tells us, "And Hermes, the Slayer of Argos, enclosed in her breast / lies and wheedling words and the treacherous ways of a thief" (*Works and Days* 77–78). And in this story, her action suits her character. Pandora has exactly one action in the narrative: she opens the lid on a jar, letting all of the evils out into the world, and closes the lid in time to save only one quality, that of hope. This myth is more familiar to most readers in later versions, in which Pandora lifts the lid on a box, and this act is an explicit violation of an injunction from her husband. In this early Greek version, however, the emphasis is not on her act as a transgression against an order, but rather on the fact that she is a *consumer*. The lid that she lifts is on a *pithos* jar, the type of jar that archaic Greeks used to store up food, oil, and wine to feed on during the lean months before harvest. Here, Pandora's opening of the jar is an act of consumption and one that threatens the male householder.

It may seem that this has little to do with sex or sexuality, but I suggest that there is a careful correspondence created here. Just as Pandora presents a threat because she consumes food—that is, she does not control her appetite—the story contains a subtle message about women being unable to control their *sexual* appetites. As we have already seen, Pandora is slinky and seductive, posing a threat to men, who should know better than to be taken in by her looks. Later on in the *Works and Days,* the poet speaks directly to the reader and warns him not to be fooled by a beautiful and sexy woman:

Let not a woman with buttocks attractively covered deceive you,
charmingly pleading and coaxing while she seeks out your *barn.*
He who trusts in women is putting his trust in deceivers. (*Works and Days* 373–75)

The anonymous woman's appetites are thus brought into close congruence. She cannot control her appetite for sex, but what that appetite hides is another, more dangerous appetite for food; it is up to the man to resist both (female) appetites and keep them both under control. Again, later in the poem, the poet talks about a woman's appetite for sex and the damage that it can do to a man:

For a man gets to possess nothing better at all than a wife,
if she is good, nothing more horrible if she is bad,
if she's a gluttonous woman who roasts her husband without fire,
withering him, though he's a strong man, prematurely to old age. (*Works and Days* 702–5)

Here again, the woman's sexual appetite is likened to an appetite for food, and the danger is that she will consume her husband's vital energy before its time.

Hesiod's poem, then, provides us with important evidence about the way the Greeks thought about the division of humanity into two genders. More important, it shows us how the gender of femininity is mapped directly onto a kind of sexuality: women are defined by their inability to control appetites. They pose a risk to men specifically because men must resist their charms, thereby controlling both their own appetites and those of their wives.

THE CHARMS OF GREEK LOVE POETRY

From the seventh century onward, Greeks from different cities wrote some of the most striking love poetry in the Western tradition. Most of this poetry falls into the ancient genres of lyric and elegiac poetry, by which the

Greeks and Romans meant that these poems were written in specific meters. Lyric poetry was so named because it was accompanied by music played on the lyre. Elegiac poetry is written in a variant of the meter used for epic poetry. More important for modern readers, however, is the fact that lyric and elegiac poems are generally short, tend to treat intensely personal subjects, and evoke a strong emotional response. Though the traditions of lyric and elegiac poetry continue in the fifth century and beyond, the poetry of the sixth century carries an extraordinary vibrancy; it is little wonder that these early poets became canonical.

In this section, we will look at four archaic poets. They all come from different parts of Greece, write in slightly different dialects, and have different approaches to writing the subject of love. With all such poetry, however, certain formal aspects create a particular relationship with the reader. Unlike epic poetry, in which an omniscient narrator speaks directly to us, much erotic poetry is written from the point of view of a smitten lover, a man (or woman, in the case of Sappho) who declares himself powerless in the face of his erotic desire. What is more, many of these poems are addressed to the beloved himself or herself. This creates the illusion that we are eavesdropping on a personal correspondence, as if we were reading a private love letter. The reader is not explicitly a part of the poem, but of course, we are always there. These are, in fact, not love letters, but poems meant to be read by us. We are positioned, then, as voyeurs into this erotic world, and part of the pleasure of reading these poems comes from the sensation of illicit access to secret pleasures.

As with epic poetry, however, it is important to remember that this portrayal of private pleasure is, nonetheless, a fiction. Too often, the love poems of Sappho or Anacreon have been read as unmediated outpourings of emotion, a kind of verse biography of their love lives. On the contrary, the function of these poems is to invest us, the readers, with an erotic experience through reading. Though these poems can and do tell us about the assumptions and expectations of the ancient Greeks, they cannot be taken as biographical fact.

Theognis

Boy, don't wrong me—I still want to
please you—listen graciously to this:
You won't outstrip me, cheat me with your tricks.
Right now you've won and have the upper hand,
But I'll take you from behind, as they say, while you run away.
The virgin daughter of Iasius,
Though ripe, rejected wedlock with a man
and fled; girding herself, she acted pointlessly,
abandoning her father's house, blonde Atalanta.
She went off to the soaring mountain peaks,
Fleeing the lure of wedlock, golden Aphrodite's
gift. But she learned the point she'd so rejected.[4] (Theognis 1283–94)

Theognis is a poet traditionally said to be from the city of Megara; like many early Greek poets, it is unclear whether his work was actually written by one man or is the product of a group of people writing in a particular style (referred to by modern scholars as the Theognid school). This also means that we cannot be sure of the date of any particular poem, though Theognis is said to have lived in the sixth century.

The content of the poems in the corpus of Theognis, however, forms a consistent thematic and poetic whole. The poems are addressed to a boy, Cyrnus, and form a kind of educational program. Many of the verses are not erotic at all, but concern various political and social concerns in the city of Megara, written from the point of view of an aristocrat. In some of the poems, however, it is clear that Cyrnus is Theognis's beloved (*eromenos*), and Theognis's attempts to educate him are inextricably woven into their erotic relationship. As such, Theognis's poetry provides us with one of our clearest examples of an aristocratic pederastic relationship.

In such a relationship, an older man befriends a younger and educates him in the ways of the world—erotic, political, and social. The poems of Theognis show a good deal of anxiety on two levels. On the first level, the poems are addressed to Cyrnus to convince him to remain with Theognis, his lover. The poet warns against trading his affections for those of a baser man. On the second level, however, these poems are concerned with maintaining the integrity of Theognis's and Cyrnus's social circle. Theognis does not want his beloved to fall in with the wrong crowd. The erotic, then, becomes a metaphor for the social: to spurn Theognis's affections (for someone else's) is also to betray the social circle to which Cyrnus belongs. And that, in addition to causing personal pain to the poet, is bad politics.

The definition of a social circle is most clear in brief poems that make reference to "our friends" (*philoi* in Greek), like the following:

Boy, your slutting around has wrecked my affection
you've become a disgrace to our friends.
You refreshed me for a short time. But I've slipped out of the squall
and found a port as night came on. (Theognis 1271–74)

Again, we should note that there does not seem to be any criticism here of the pederastic relationship; there is nothing wrong with the boy sleeping with men. What is unacceptable to the poet is that the boy has been indiscriminate in his affections and has slept with men who are, apparently, not in their circle of *philoi*. At the same time, the relationship with the boy, now past, or at least in abeyance, was like a "squall" for the poet, a metaphor for the intensity of the erotic relationship. Most likely, the relationship was stormy specifically because of the boy's indiscriminate "slutting around."

Elsewhere, the people outside the circle of friends are seen as even more deliberate enemies:

Don't leave the friend you have to find another,
Yielding to the words of vulgar men.
You know, they'll often lie to me about you,
to you about me. Don't listen to them.

You'll take pleasure in the love that's gone
and that one will elude your mastery. (Theognis 1238a–42)

Here the "vulgar" men are *deiloi,* a word that means something like "cowards" or "base men," so Theognis's advice is about more than just love. He is also concerned to advise the boy about his appropriate social station. The cementing of community works here on two levels at once. First, the poet suggests that those outside their social circle are unworthy and not to be trusted. They are an active threat to the speaker's social group. At the same time, their lies threaten to destroy Theognis's erotic relationship with the boy, to the boy's disadvantage; in time, the boy will learn that the love he had (with Theognis) was superior, after it is too late.

Similar to these poems, but with a slightly different emphasis, are some pleading verses in which the poet warns the boy of the danger of spurning his lover. He is at the height of his physical attraction now, but soon, he will be too old to be pursued, and then he will know the torments of pursuing a flighty but beautiful boy. This theme will reverberate throughout Greek same-sex love poetry; it is beautifully presented in Theognis 1327–34:

Boy, as long as your cheek is smooth, I'll never
stop praising you, not even if I have to die.
For you to give still is fine, for me there's no shame in asking,
since I'm in love. At your knees . . . I beg,
Respect me, boy, give pleasure if you're ever
to have the gift of Cypris with her wreath of violets,
When it's you who's wanting and approach another. May the goddess
Grant that you get exactly the same response.

The beloved's era of attraction is clearly marked: "as long as your cheek is smooth." The argument that the lover makes, moreover, is one that suggests reciprocity over time. One day, the boy himself will be a lover, and the poem ends with a wish that the boy receive exactly the answer then that he gives now.

We should also note, however, that the relationship thus defined is rigorously unsymmetrical. The speaker wants the boy to "give pleasure," but there is no suggestion that the pleasure would flow in the other direction. Moreover, the boy's motivations for giving this pleasure are perhaps not those we would expect: "respect me," is the poet's request. Theognis is quite cagey about how exactly the boy should show this respect. These poems are fairly decorous in their portrayal of love. In another epigram, the speaker hints at physical limits:

Boy, my passion's master, listen. I'll tell no tale
that's unpersuasive or unpleasant to your heart.
Just try to grasp my words with your mind. There is no need
for you to do what's not to your liking. (Theognis 1235–38)

Here the speaker positions himself as a teacher, his beloved as a recalcitrant student. He promises that his teachings will not be unpleasant. In the last line, though, the emphasis shifts to what the beloved boy will *do* (Greek *erdein*). Just as the speaker's story will not be unpleasant, he assures the boy, neither will he cross the line of acceptable sexual behavior. But the speaker does not tell us what that line is.

There are hints in this poetry about such a love relationship creating a sense of shame, usually in the form of the speaker saying that there is no shame in what he does. In 1327–34 (given previously), the poet assures the boy that it is "fine" for him to give, and that "for me there's no shame in asking / since I'm in love." This implies that such a relationship could be shameful, outside the confines of the pederastic relationship. If the poet were a different kind of man, if he did not really love the boy, their relationship would, perhaps, be a more sordid one. But again, the speaker does not suggest that same-sex relations are shameful, but rather indiscriminate ones.

The lover in this kind of relationship is open to criticism himself, however, in that his lust for the boy implies a lack of self-control. Consider the following:

Alas! I love a smooth-skinned boy, who to all friends
displays me against my will.
But I'll put up with it and not hide. Much is compelled, even unwilling
for I was not shown tamed by an unappealing boy. (Theognis 1341–44)

The poem (as modern editors have it) goes on to point out that even Zeus fell in love with Ganymede, so why should the speaker not give in to a similar desire? Here again, we see the same circle of friends that the poet has urged solidarity with in other poems, but in this case, the circle turns inward for a bit of good-natured ribbing. The boy possesses a certain kind of power here, embodied in his beauty. Because he is so good-looking ("smooth-skinned" is an erotically charged description), he is able to lead the speaker around by the nose. He boasts a bit, showing off how he has tamed this older, sober, respectable teacher. And though the teacher does, clearly, feel some embarrassment, he puts a brave face on it: at least he was tamed by a beautiful boy. So much, though embarrassing, is not shameful; it is rather that sense of embarrassment that a modern college youth might experience at the hands of his friends when in the early stages of romance.

With Theognis's poems, then, there are always onlookers, always a circle of friends watching, teasing, approving, and participating. The poetry itself becomes a way of solidifying this social group: if the boy misbehaves (especially by consorting with men outside the circle), the poems act as a way to shame him into better behavior. If that fails, he can be excluded. The speaker himself alternately tries to win his love, and consoles himself when that love is gone, but whatever he does, he does in the watchful eye of his *philoi*. The education of Cyrus, then, is not only represented in these poems, but rather, it is enacted by them. The poetry creates a community of readers whose behavior is consistent with the values that the poems espouse.

Anacreon

Once again Eros has struck me, like a bronze smith,
with a large axe, and washed me in a wintry mountain stream.[5] (Anacreon 413)

Anacreon is said to have been born on the island of Teos, in the first quarter of the sixth century BCE. He lived and worked as a court poet, for both Polycrates of Samos and Hipparchos of Athens. His lyric poetry is written in the persona of a single speaker and was regarded in antiquity as among the finest of its kind.

Unlike Theognis, the poetry of Anacreon is not exclusively directed to a single boy, and it does not purport to have an educational function. Anacreon writes poems to both boys and young women, and his love poetry is characterized by strong (and sometimes graphic) metaphors like the one in the preceding brief fragment. Some of Anacreon's poems can be put in a particular context, that of the all-male symposium (on which, see the following discussion). Others are not so easily placed. Since most of Anacreon's poetry comes to us in fragments, bits of poetry quoted by later authors, it is often impossible to be sure of the exact context of the few lines we have. Nonetheless, Anacreon's imagery, particularly that describing the speaker's helplessness in the face of love, provides us with insight into archaic Greek attitudes toward Eros, that most fickle of deities.

Anacreon is particularly known for his poems composed for the symposium. In archaic and later Greece, upper-class men regularly got together at drinking parties known as symposia. The men drank wine, engaged in witty

Greek wall painting from the tomb of the diver Paestum, early fifth century BCE. Two couples recline on dinner couches. Each couple consists of an older bearded man and a young man with light hair on his cheeks. The older man in the center appears more interested in the other couple than in his own partner. Museo Archeologico Nazionale, Paestum, Italy. Photo taken by the author.

Greek wall painting from the tomb of the diver Paestum, early fifth century BCE. Two couples recline on dinner couches. The boy to the far right plays the *aulos*; his partner throws his head back in a stylized indication of ecstasy. Museo Archeologico Nazionale, Paestum, Italy. Photo taken by the author.

and sophisticated conversation, listened to poetry and song, and were entertained by flute girls. (Respectable women were not invited as members of the party.) To judge from numerous vases depicting these symposia, such parties were often suffused with eroticism. Older men gaze longingly at smooth-cheeked "boys," who either return the gaze or look absently elsewhere. Within the sexual system of ancient Greece, then, these parties were a place for the upper classes to meet eligible young men.

Several of the poems of Anacreon make reference to these symposia and indeed declare proper behavior there, such as 96D:

I do not love the one who, drinking too much wine,
speaks of strife and tearful war,
But rather he who, mixing together the shining gifts of the Muses and Aphrodite,
remembers seductive pleasantries.

The word I have translated as "seductive" in the last line is *eratos*, a word derived from Eros, the god of erotic desire. These lines, then, are about the kind of poetry that should be recited at a symposium: not, like Homer's verses, the heavy epic poems about war and strife, but rather poems that are in themselves pleasant and charming—poems about love. The person who does this successfully becomes the person whom Anacreon himself loves.

It is in this context that most scholars place a number of other poems, ranging from the simple to the more complex. In fragment 359, we see a charming depiction of the poet's obsession with a boy named Kleobolos:

I lust after Kleobolos,
I am crazy for Kleobolos,
I gaze at Kleobolos.

The last line is something of an anticlimax, perhaps intentionally so. After declaring the strength of his feelings, the speaker, in the end, can do no more than look on and admire his beloved. He is stuck there, gazing, but not acting despite his manic lust. His own powerlessness is enacted in the contrast between the strength of his feelings and his lack of any action beyond looking.

A more complex poem is addressed to an unnamed boy and enshrines an image that will be picked up by Plato in his dialogue the *Phaedrus:*

Boy, you who glance like a girl,
I look at you, but you do not notice,
not realizing that you hold the reins
of my soul. (Anacreon 360)

The lines are carefully crafted, and work in several registers at once. The boy is said to glance "girlishly" (*parthenion*), a word that carries connotations of innocence, a lack of guile. But then it is confusing to find that, though the speaker is looking at the boy, the boy does not notice, or perhaps appears not to. If he is not noticing, at whom is he glancing modestly? Is the boy innocent, or merely coy? In any case, what the boy does not notice, or appears not to, is that he has enthralled the speaker of the poem. The image of "holding the reins" is one of control, mastery of a horse. As with much erotic poetry, this self-abasement is both a real expression of the loss of control one feels in the face of erotic desire and mildly ironic. It is the boy who is presented as young, innocent, and unknowing; yet he is in control of the wise, worldly, and speaking poet. Even this image of erotic submission, moreover, is less straightforward than it might appear. Though the phrase "you hold the reins of my soul" certainly sounds decorous, it is also a bit naughty. Riding a horse is a common metaphor for having sex in archaic and later Greek poetry. The poem, then, creates a tension between the graphic image that it calls up, that of the boy "riding" the speaker, and the sublime expression of the poet's devotion to the boy. This tension is quintessential of Anacreon's poetry, and it is what makes him such a brilliant erotic poet. Eros always exists in a state of tension.

In the corpus of Anacreon's work, we also find poems addressed to young women. We do not know if these are any more or less biographical than those addressed to boys, but in any case, Anacreon exhibits no conflict about writing poems in the voice of characters who desire girls as well as boys. Again, some of the fragments are so short as to defy interpretation, such as the line quoted by Athenaeus (a rhetorician from the second to third centuries CE, writing in Egypt), as an example of the power of thirst: "For you are a friendly girl towards strangers; since I am thirsty, allow me to drink" (Anacreon 389). One can easily imagine a context for this line that has nothing to do with the erotic, or one can read it as a somewhat crude come-on. Without more from the fragment, we will never know the meaning with any certainty.

One of Anacreon's most famous poems, however, allows for no such ambiguity of intent, though its meaning has been much debated. Again, we do not know the context of the poem; it appears to be a love poem in which a (male) speaker tries to seduce a young woman:

Thracian filly, why do you look askance at me,
and flee heartless—do you think that I know nothing clever?
Know this, I would put the bit in your mouth beautifully,
and holding the reins I would turn you around the end post of the track;
But now you feed in the meadows, and you play, frisking lightly,
for you have no one skilled in horse riding to mount you. (Anacreon 417)

As a heteroerotic attempt at seduction, these lines are not terribly subtle. An aspect that is clearer in the Greek than in translation, however, is the suggestion that the girl move from a position of innocence to one of experience. At the moment, she is simply out frisking freely in a meadow, a paradigm for innocence about to be lost. The meadow is itself uncultivated, and her activity there is enjoyable, but without purpose. The speaker offers to bring her into a world of culture, here represented by horse racing, where she will enjoy the experience of being ridden. The entire poem operates on this idea of transition to the world of experience, and nearly every line works as a double entendre in which sex equals knowledge, and knowledge equals a submission to the speaker.

At the very least, then, we can say that Anacreon writes poems to both boys and girls, though again, we should remember that in none of these poems is the speaker to be identified with the poet. One point, however, is quite interesting about the poems addressed to boys and the poem addressed to the Thracian girl. When Anacreon addresses a boy, or when he speaks of Eros, he tends to declare his utter helplessness in the face of his desire. We saw this in the poem about the boy who "held the reins" to the speaker's soul most clearly. Here, however, when the speaker wishes to seduce a young woman, he positions himself as the rider—he is the one in control, the one who holds knowledge that the beloved needs. In general, this relationship holds true for most male Greek lyric poets: helplessness before a boy, mastery before a young woman. The same is not quite true, as we will see, when we deal with the only female poet of whom we have significant fragments left: Sappho.[6]

We have one poem in which Anacreon is harshly critical of another man, and we might be tempted to see here a notion of sexual orientation, or perhaps sexual identity:

Before, he used to wear a ragged hat, a tightly tied hood,
and wooden dice in his ears, and a smooth skin
of an ox around his ribs,
the filthy wrapping of a poor shield, and he held company
with bread sellers and willing whores, the rogue Artemon,
finding a counterfeit life.
Many times he placed his neck in stocks, many times on the wheel,
many times he was flogged on the back with a leather whip, and his hair
and beard were plucked out.

But now he rides a woman's carriage wearing gold earrings,
the son of Cyce, and he carries an ivory parasol
just like a woman. (Anacreon 388)

The speaker would have us believe that this fellow Artemon is worthless, and at the end of the poem, he attacks him, in particular, for his womanish ways. Artemon's behavior is suspect but in manner consistent with the sexual system that I discussed earlier; that is, Artemon is not attacked for loving boys. In fact, the "willing prostitutes" of the second stanza could have been of either gender. He is attacked, rather, for violations of his gender role, both before and after his acquisition of wealth. Moreover, the attack on him is double. It is not merely that Artemon is an effeminate, but rather that his newfound ostentation is ridiculous to those who know his character from before. Whereas before he was a cheap effeminate, now he is a rich one; the reader recognizes with the poet that nothing fundamental about his character has changed. Artemon, then, can be said to have a sexual morphology, a deviant gender role, and perhaps even a sexual identity. But unlike a modern homosexual man, he has no clear sexual orientation, and it is his gender role that is most strikingly criticized.

Anacreon, in brief, provides a lens through which we can see how Greek aristocrats thought about erotics. The poems present the somewhat fanciful and overblown declarations of helpless love for boys that characterized the erotic interaction of the symposium; the speaker's masterful, if amusing, attempt at seducing a young woman; and finally, the reassertion of proper masculinity and social class in the attack on a lowborn effeminate like Artemon. Anacreon is a proper aristocrat. For all that, his love poetry is clever, highly charged, and brilliantly constructed.

The Problem of Sappho

A single sweet apple blushes on the topmost branch
way up on the tip-top, but the apple gatherers do not notice it;
Or rather, they notice, but they are not able to reach.[7] (Sappho 105a)

No archaic poet is more important for our understanding of ancient sexuality than Sappho, and no Greek poet has been so variously understood, or misunderstood. Though very little is certain about her life, Sappho is reported to have been born in the last quarter of the seventh century. Of the nine books of poetry she is supposed to have written, we have a few hundred lines, and only one complete poem.[8]

Although Sappho wrote in various meters and genres, she is best known for her love poetry, in which the speaker expresses erotic desire for a number of named women. Sappho lived on the island of Lesbos, and it is from this island that we derive the modern word *lesbian*. As soon as one makes this observation, however, we are forced to point out that the ancient world did not make the same associations with Lesbos as we do. In fact, ancient Greek has a verb, *lesbiazo*, but in most instances, the specific meaning of that word is "to perform fellatio." With one notable exception (discussed later), the women of Lesbos are not known for their single-sex attraction, but rather for a general enthusiasm for sex.

In fact, no contemporary of Sappho's ever mentions her (poetic) desire for other women. It simply does not seem to be worthy of comment. Although we know of some comedies from the fourth century BCE that may have poked fun at Sappho's sexual behavior, these works have been almost entirely lost. Not until the Roman period is Sappho's homoerotic desire clearly made a problem, and then her behavior is likened to that of the *tribas,* or masculine woman. Sappho was seen by Greeks of the sixth and fifth centuries as remarkable, to be sure, but more as a female poet than as a homoerotic one. Within this context, the ancient readers regarded her as unusually skillful and her poetry as unmatched in beauty. Plato referred to her as "the tenth muse."

Needless to say, the history of the reading of Sappho is complex and fascinating; I cannot do justice to it here.[9] Every generation has invented its own Sappho and read her poetry in the light of that invention. In modern times, her so-called lesbianism (in the modern sense) has created a significant problem for classical scholars, and until quite recently a variety of strategies were used by scholars to rescue Sappho from the socially problematic category of lesbian. Some scholars fixated on later biographies of the poet, which suggested that Sappho fell in love with a man name Phaon and give birth to a daughter, though virtually none of the so-called facts in these biographies can be confirmed. Her sexuality thus assured, it was argued that her poems were addressed to women because she was taking on the persona of a male love poet.

Other strategies have been less ingenious, but equally debilitating. For Denys Page, who produced the standard philological edition of Sappho's work, the operative strategy was to divorce Sappho's work from her person. Though her poetry shows us her inclinations, he says, there is no evidence that she ever acted on them.[10] While in general, Page's principle is a sound one—it is, indeed, dangerous to assume that a poem's speaker is to be identified with its author—in this case, the argument feels like special pleading. We have very few female poets; Sappho is clearly the most important, and as it happens, she writes about desire for women, in a way that is distinct from the way men write about desire for women. It seems uncharitable at best, and homophobic at worst, to deny that Sappho ever enjoyed any erotic experience.

More devastating and more long lasting than either of these strategies, however, was the invention of the image of Sappho as a schoolmistress.[11] In this reading, the origin of which can be found at the end of the nineteenth century, Sappho's inclination for sex with girls was explained away as a kind of initiation rite. Young aristocratic girls, it is supposed, were sent to Sappho, poet and etiquette expert, for finishing school before they entered the adult (and heterosexual) world of marriage. In this way, Sappho's love affairs were also likened to the male institution of pederasty, which, as we have seen, could have an educational function. Needless to say, there is no evidence for such a school, and reading the poems in such a context is distorting at best.

And yet, it is not easy to say how one *should* read Sappho. Her poetry is beautiful, deeply affecting, much imitated, and largely anomalous. The ancients seem not to have noticed the anomalies that so distract us; this, again, may simply be evidence that their sexual expectations were wildly different than ours. It is also possible, however, that the ancient Greeks are silent about Sappho's love for women because they *did* find it a problem and that the near-universal silence about it is the result of an unspoken conspiracy.[12] The simple fact is that Sappho is one of the very few sources from the ancient world that gives us an idea of how a woman might have thought of herself as a sexual subject. She does so, however, within the same kind of literary constraints that operate in the poetry of Anacreon or Theognis. We will do best, then, by trying to read her poetry in the context of other erotic poetry from the same period, and not by trying to make her fit with our ideas about either modern or ancient sexuality.

When we read Sappho in the context of other lyric poets, several striking features of her poetry emerge. Though it has sometimes been overemphasized, her work presents a greater degree of mutual pleasure and affection between the lovers than the work of male poets. Sappho also demonstrates an exquisite ability to render personal helplessness in the face of passion. Though the same could be said of Anacreon, the difference in Sappho is that her helplessness does not depend on the willful power brokering of her beloved; she simply *is* helpless when faced with a woman she desires, even if that woman is completely unaware of the watching poet. And finally, Sappho's poems represent, more than any other poet from the ancient world, the poignancy of desiring someone who is absent; Sappho's narrator concerns herself repeatedly with the idea of past pleasures, future pleasures, and lost companions. We almost never hear of pleasure in the present.

Sappho's poems often show a complicated narrative situation. Perhaps her most famous expression of erotic experience comes in the following lines (the fragment, we should note, is not complete):

That man looks like a god to me,
whoever sits across from you,
and listens close to your sweet talk
and desirable laughter, which sets aflutter
my heart in my breast.
For as I look at you quickly, so I can no longer speak
But my tongue breaks, silently, and thin
fire steals straight under my skin
and there is no sight in my eyes, and my ears hum,
a cold sweat holds me down, a trembling seizes
all of me, and I am paler than grass,
and I seem—to myself—little short of dying.
But all must be endured, since even a poor . . . (Sappho 31)

The description here of the speaker's incapacity is a remarkable poetic achievement, not least because of the way in which the poet takes us through such a variety of sensations: blindness, humming in the ears, simultaneously being on fire and cold with sweat. Eros, here, is a force that so overwhelms the process of sensation that it leaves the speaker unable to make sense. This, of course, is the most blatant of poetic conceits since this expression of complete helplessness exists not only articulated, but in a complex and regular metrical scheme. There are two Sapphos here: one who appears to speak not to us, but to her beloved, about her inability to speak; and another who presents to us with clinical and metrical precision the symptoms of that desire.

Perhaps even more remarkable, and more problematic, however, is the narrative situation that is set up in the beginning lines of the poem. With the first line, it looks initially as if the narrator is going to write a poem to, or at least about, a man. This man is given conventional, but high, praise: he looks like a god. But in the next line, it turns out that the speaker has no interest in this man—if there even is a man—but rather in the "you" whom the poem addresses, the you who sits across from that man whispering sweet nothings to him. The idea of a male lover has been called up only to be made dazzlingly irrelevant, an outsider to the love relationship that the rest of the poem will explore.

In the history of this poem, a vast amount of ink has been spilled trying to pin down a historical moment that the narrative could be describing; critics have, in fact, been obsessed with the identity of the man. But as John Winkler pointed out some years ago, the man in the poem is not a particular person.[13] The pronoun that introduces him in the second line, which I have translated "whoever," is used to indicate a general situation. Whoever happens to sit across from the "you" of the poem is the one who looks like a god—not, however, by any virtue of his own. He is generic male. He looks like a god because he entertains "you." In this regard, the poem is also a brilliant bit of erotic rhetoric. What appears to be a praise of "your" boyfriend turns out to be lavish praise of "your" erotic appeal. What could be more seductive than that?

On another level, however, the crucial aspect of this poem is the uncrossed distance between the speaker of the poem and her erotic object. As far as we can tell, the "you" of the poem is completely unaware of the speaker. If the man to whom she is supposed to speak and sweetly laugh is generic, then she, likewise, is not actually in the situation described; rather, she exists only in the speaker's imagination; she is only a way to express the effects of Eros on the speaker. Unlike the boys of Anacreon's poems, however, she is not deliberately tormenting the speaker of the poem; there is no intentional exercise of erotic power. Rather, the poem is an expression of a purely one-sided desire; what the response of the "you" in the poem will be remains outside the experience of reading the poem.

Some other fragments of Sappho are in a less complete state but suggest actual erotic experience, though not in the present. Among the most beautiful is fragment 94 (I have marked gaps in the text with ellipses):

and frankly I wish I were dead.
She left me as she wept
much and she said this to me.
"Alas how terribly we have suffered,
Sappho, indeed unwilling I am leaving you."

And I answered her,
"Farewell, go and remember
me, for you know how we cared for you.
But if not, I wish to remind you
. . . and we endured lovely things
For with many wreaths of violets
and roses and crocus
. . . you placed by me,
and many garlands woven
of flowers you placed
around a soft neck
and with much oil of
myrrh . . .
you anointed and for a queen
and on a soft bed
the gentle . . .
you would satisfy desire for . . .
and again someone . . . not any
shrine nor . . .
where we stayed away
nor grove . . . dance
. . . rattling

As the reader can readily see, the fragment is in such poor condition that it is difficult to know what is going on. The images, however, are more sensual in their way than anything we have seen from the male poets. Sappho pays attention to the softness and suppleness of the young women's bodies. The poem describes a scene that affects sight, touch, smell, and even hearing. Scented oil, wreaths of flowers, and soft necks—as here—are all fairly common in her poetry.

More important than all of this, however, is the narrative situation that appears in the first few lines. Though even this is not entirely clear, it appears that a young woman is speaking to Sappho just before leaving her company. She does not want to leave and claims to have "suffered" much. Sappho responds by reminding her how much she, Sappho, has cared for her in the past, in the process using a compound of the same verb that I have translated as "suffered," literally, "and we suffered lovely things." Sappho then enumerates these past pleasures as a way of bringing them physically into the present. The girl who goes away will carry with her these past delights into her new situation, whatever that is. The poem, then, highlights the tension between present sadness at parting and past delight in company and brings the two forcibly together.

A similar technique is used in another, similar fragment, number 96:

. . . Sardis . . .
many times holding her thoughts here,
as . . . we . . .
you like a well-known
goddess, and she especially enjoyed your song.

But now she is outstanding among Lydian
women as when, after the sun sets,
the rosy-fingered moon
outshines all the stars; and the light
spreads over the salt sea
and over the many-flowered fields;
And the dew is poured out beautifully, and the roses
bloom and the delicate chervil
and the flowering melitote.
But wandering much, she remembers gentle
Atthis with desire,
and consumes her delicate heart over your fate.

Again, we must extrapolate a dramatic situation between the speakers. It appears that the speaker of the poem is consoling Atthis over the loss of a mutual friend, who has gone to Lydia. This consolation again makes use of memory as a way to survive the tragedies of passion. First, the speaker reminds Atthis of how their friend used to enjoy Atthis's company, and especially her poetry. We are then taken on an imaginative flight in which the missing girl's life is described, using familiar images from epic and erotic poetry. Then memory is called up again, but this time in the other direction: the speaker suggests that the missing girl is herself remembering Atthis and longing for her. Thus the speaker becomes a bridge between the two other women, each of whom experiences (again) her love for the other through memory.

Significantly, when the speaker describes the missing girl, the images that she uses are deliberately feminine. Particularly striking is the image of the "rosy-fingered moon." The adjective *rosy-fingered* is familiar from Homeric epic, where it is inevitably used to describe the sun at dawn. The sun, however, is resolutely masculine. Here, the girl is compared not to the harsh light of day, but to the moon—significantly, a feminine noun and perceived as a female entity—in her brilliance. The purposes of the adjective *rosy-fingered* can only be to call up, and then deny, the idea of masculine epic poetry. This is a female poem, about female desire and experience.

Both of the poems described previously suggest a community of women who have shared erotic experiences with one another; it is perhaps on the strength of these two fragments, primarily, that the idea of Sappho's school for girls was devised. But we need not postulate Sappho's finishing school to imagine a circle of women who shared love and poetry together. More important, I think, are the tone and feel of these poems. They are poems of consolation, and they suggest both mutual pleasure and mutual care. We do not see here the kind of male-female power dynamic of Anacreon's "Thracian filly" poem, or even of the bartering for sexual favors that underlies so many of the poems addressed to boys. At the risk of a dangerous essentialism of gender, Sappho's poems appear to represent a different, feminine, mode of erotics.

Before we are lulled into a sense of joy about this supposedly feminine, cooperative erotic experience, however, it would be wise to consider the only complete poem that we have from Sappho, fragment 1. In it, what looks initially like a reciprocal relationship of desire turns out to be rather closer to the masculine model:

Lovely-robed Aphrodite,
crafty-weaving child of Zeus, I beg you,
do not tame my spirit with pains
or anguish, queen,
but come here, if ever before
you heard my voice from a distance
and listened, and leaving the house
of your father, you came
having yoked your golden chariot.
And the beautiful swift sparrows led you,
over the dark earth, swiftly whirling their wings
through the middle atmosphere,
and straightaway you arrived. But you, blessed one,
with a smile on your immortal face
asked what again I suffered and why again
I was calling,
and what exactly I want to happen
with my crazy heart. "Whom again do I persuade
to lead you into her friendship? Who, Sappho,
is doing you wrong?
For if indeed she flees, swiftly she will pursue;
if she does not receive gifts, still she will give them;
and if she does not love, swiftly she will love
even if she does not wish to."
Come to me again now, and free me from harsh
sorrow, and whatever my heart desires to happen,
make it happen. And you yourself
be my ally.

Once again, we see a complicated narrative situation. The poem begins with Sappho calling on Aphrodite for help. She then reminds Aphrodite of a previous time when Aphrodite had answered such a prayer, and quotes, in direct speech, the goddess's words from that time. Aphrodite, we must notice, is a bit sharp with Sappho, calling to attention the repeated nature of her prayers, and asking, in brief, "What is it *this* time?" The poem ends with Sappho repeating her request, asking that Aphrodite be her battle ally (Greek *summachos*) again in yet another erotic conquest.

In Sappho's quotation of the goddess's past visit, Aphrodite reportedly made a series of promises to Sappho, and these promises have been read as evidence of reciprocal desire: if she flees, she will pursue; if she rejects gifts, she will give them; and so on. It seems here as if the rigorous one-sided nature of desire in the male poets is not so for women. Sappho's beloved can, in this reading, turn the tables and pursue. In such an interpretation of the poem, women's desire is less hierarchical than men's, their roles more fluid. Admittedly, this reversal of roles will require some compulsion on the part of Aphrodite, but it is nonetheless possible.

An interpretation of the poem by Anne Carson, however, suggests that this is a mistaken reading altogether.[14] Carson argues that this reversal of roles is not going to happen *now;* it is not that this unnamed woman whom Sappho pursues will turn about and pursue Sappho. Indeed, the poem does not indicate that the object of her affections will be Sappho; it does not say who it will be at all. Rather, this poem is parallel to those works by male poets who tell boys that they had better hurry up and enjoy the lover's offer now, before they find that they are too old to be erotic objects and find themselves in the harsh position of offering gifts to other beautiful boys (see Theognis 1327–34, given previously). In Carson's reading, Aphrodite's promise is simply that of age. She tells Sappho, simply, that if some beautiful young thing is fleeing her now, the time will come when that beloved object will have to pursue, and then she, too, will understand the pain that comes with asking and not receiving.

This second interpretation has on its side considerable philological support and has the further advantage of placing Sappho's poem in the context of contemporary love poetry. Though I am sorry to lose the idea of a mutually desiring lesbian couple, poetically enacted by Sappho, I find Carson's reading compelling. In this poem, at least, the experience of Eros is still one-sided, defined by power and all too short.

I conclude this chapter, then, by asking the crucial question, is Sappho a lesbian, in the modern sense of the word? The answer can only be ambivalent, and that ambivalence marks the divide between our modern erotics and that of the archaic Greeks. If by *lesbian* we mean simply that Sappho is a woman who loves women, and that her expression of desire for those women provides evidence of a less hierarchical, more mutual form of desire than that expressed by male poets, the answer is yes. But we still have very little evidence that Sappho's desire for women was thought of as a *different kind* of desire than that of men for women, or women for men, or men for young men. And there is no solid evidence that Sappho or other women from Lesbos were thought of as belonging to a particular sexual *type.* Sappho may have a sexual orientation, but to the ancients, her poetry does not seem to have suggested a sexual identity or a sexual morphology.

There is one exception to this rule, and it is especially troubling because it is, like so much of our evidence, completely unique. Anacreon has one other poem that suggests that women from Lesbos were, in our sense, lesbian. He writes,

Again golden-haired Eros strikes me
with a purple ball, and calls me to play
with the girl with the fancy sandals.
But she, since she is from well-built
Lesbos, finds fault with my hair
(since it is white) and gapes
at another (girl).[15] (Anacreon 358)

What exactly do those words mean, "since she is from well-built Lesbos?" And how, exactly, does the speaker's white hair come into it, to say nothing of the fancy sandals? The poem seems littered with irrelevant references and is almost as likely to refer to a preference, among Lesbian women, for young partners as for female ones. Nonetheless, we must admit that here, if only here, we have a contemporary reference to a Lesbian woman's preference for women, and perhaps a criticism of that preference. This is hardly a sexuality in the modern sense of the word, but it does suggest the idea of a sexual orientation coupled with a sexual identity. This poem, then, lends support to the idea that the Greeks might, despite their near-universal silence on the subject, have been made anxious by women who had no erotic use for white-haired old men.

Three

Sexual Roles and Sexual Rules in Classical Athens

We have more information about the fifth and fourth centuries in Athens than about any other time or place in the Greek world. In large part, this is due to a wealth of different kinds of sources: we have literature in the form of Greek tragedy and comedy, both of which interact with cultural and social institutions in unique ways; we have access to numerous legal speeches, from which scholars are able to reconstruct a picture of the entire legal system; we have philosophical treatises by Plato, Xenophon, and Aristotle; we have narrative political and military history. Beyond these purely textual sources, there are numerous inscriptions (writings on stone) that provide hard data to support historical narrative and a vast repertoire of Athenian pottery depicting a wide variety of mythological and real-life events.

There were, of course, other city-states operating in Greece in the classical period. But Athens came to be recognized as the center of cultural and artistic achievement, and so, some thousands of years later, it is a daunting challenge to try to isolate the specific cultural institutions of other city-states such as Sparta and Thebes. Often, when we do have information about other city-states, it comes from Athenian authors and is therefore subject to a certain amount of Athenocentric distortion. For the classical period, then, this book will focus on Athens, with its relative abundance of information.

ATHENIAN SOCIETY IN THE CLASSICAL PERIOD

The fifth century in Athens saw remarkable political changes. In 507, a politician named Kleisthenes enacted a series of reforms that created the Athenian democracy. With these reforms, the aristocratic families that had been ruling Athens lost formal power, and a great deal of authority was given to citizens in general, who were organized into 10 *phylai* (tribes). Membership in the *phylai* was determined by *demos,* a smaller social and political institution that was defined, at least in part, by area of residence. Of particular importance was Kleisthenes' reorganization of the *boulê,* the administrative body of the government, into a group of 500 people, consisting of 50 from each *phylai,* chosen by lot. Kleisthenes' reforms, then, ushered in an era of radical democracy. As with all such political reforms, however, it is important to realize that the aristocracy did not go away. The rich and powerful families in Athens continued to hold important offices, propose laws to the assembly, and exercise political influence in myriad ways.

Many of these aristocrats were not particularly fond of the democracy, and social tensions between the elite and the less wealthy remained. This is particularly important in the study of sexuality because some sources that purport to represent middle-class views (such as comedy) often make jokes about the aristocracy, and these jokes are frequently of a sexual nature. In examining these texts, then, one needs to consider carefully whether what is being targeted is sexual practice, or social status, or some combination of both.

We also need to bear in mind the overwhelming social effects of the Persian wars. In the year 490 BCE, under Darius, and again in 480 BCE, under Xerxes, the vast eastern empire of Persia attacked Greece. An alliance of Greek states, with Athens at the head of the navy and Sparta at the head of the land army, successfully held off the invasion and sent the Persians packing. This victory proved a crucial moment for Greek self-definition; Athenian historians, in particular, attributed their victory to the moral character of their mode of life and of their form of government. In brief, the Persians, who were led by a monarch, were characterized by the Athenians as everything that the Athenians (ideally) were not: self-indulgent, seduced by luxury, ruled by a monarch, and above all, effeminate.[1]

Just as Athens thought it completely unacceptable to be ruled by a monarch, so individual Athenians prized their *enkrateia,* or "self-rule." A real man controlled his desires, his person, his wife, and his household. The Persians, ruled politically by a king, were judged unable to rule themselves as persons. They were therefore depicted as given to indulgence and luxury, soft, decadent, and effeminate. How could they be otherwise, when every Persian man owed obedience to the Persian king? For Athens, self-control operated on every level.

This ideology comes through most clearly in the histories of Herodotus, who wrote of the Persian wars from an Athenian perspective. (Though Herodotus was not born in Athens, it appears that he lived for a time in the Athenian colony of Thurii in Italy.) Before the battle of Thermopylae, at which 300 Spartan soldiers would stand to the death against a vastly superior Persian army, Herodotus reports a conversation between Xerxes and an advisor, Demaratus. Demaratus tries to convince Xerxes that the Greeks, though inferior in numbers, will fight to the death:

There has never been a time when poverty was not a factor in the rearing of the Greeks, but their courage has been acquired as a result of intelligence and the force of law. Greece has relied on this courage to keep poverty and despotism at bay. . . . As for the size of the army, there's no point in your asking how, in terms of numbers, they can do this. If there are in fact only a few thousand men to march out against you . . . then a thousand men will fight you.[2] (Herodotus 7.102)

Xerxes, of course, does not believe his advisor. He argues that if the Greeks had a single leader whom they feared, they might be willing to fight against superior numbers, "urged on by the whip"; but given that each of them is free, he believes they will not do so. Demaratus tries one more time:

The point is that although they're free, they're not entirely free: their master is the law, and they're far more afraid of this than your men are of you. At any rate, they do whatever the law commands, and its command never changes: it is that they should not turn tail in battle no matter how many men are ranged against them, but should maintain their positions and either win or die. (Herodotus 7.104)

Demaratus is here speaking specifically about the Spartans, who indeed had a policy of never retreating in battle, and whom Xerxes' forces would face at Thermopylae. The debate about motivation in battle, however, clearly applies to all of Greece. Xerxes assumes that fear of a monarch is the only thing that will motivate a man to fight against superior numbers. Not so, says Demaratus: the Greeks' bravery is greater because they obey the law, which they themselves have made. This, rather than fear of a despot, allows them the bravery necessary to stand against overwhelming numbers. This freedom—which is to say, self-rule—is what makes the Greeks superior men.

The Athenian aristocracy had a tendency to sympathize at times, however, with Persia and their form of rule. More important for this study, they were also seen as potentially embodying the faults of the effeminate East. If an Athenian wanted to insult an aristocrat, a common mode was to suggest that he was soft, given to overindulgence in food, sleep, and/or sex. All such characteristics were understood to be antithetical to the democracy itself and so were all the more easily ascribed to the less-than-fully-democratic upper classes. In other words, the Athenians drew parallels between their personal and political lives.

At the same time, we must recognize that the institution of democracy had wide-ranging and complex effects for women. As the fifth century progressed, Athenian society became increasingly closed; Athens was always miserly with the granting of citizenship rights to non-Athenians, and in 451–450, the great statesman Pericles passed legislation stating that citizens could only be born to two citizens. Previous to this, presumably, a citizen man could marry a respectable woman from another city-state, and their offspring could be Athenians. After this, however, only citizen women could produce more Athenian citizens.

Under such laws, sexual control over women appears to have been extensive. In legal terms, women were always under the protection and control of a male guardian, or *kurios*. Before marriage, the woman's father was her *kurios;* after marriage, her husband was. In theory, citizen women's lives were rigorously private. Wives were expected to stay indoors and not to wander about outside without an escort; they could not participate in the assembly or bring lawsuits on their own behalf; and they appear to have been limited in the kinds of economic transactions they could make. This thumbnail sketch is, of course, much too simple even as a description of a civic ideal, and women clearly exercised informal power and influence in many ways.[3]

One unfortunate effect of this ideal of women as private creatures, however, is that it is unusually difficult to find evidence for women's attitudes, experiences, and private practices. We do, of course, have dramas—comedies and tragedies—that make a pretense of representing women. But the reader must remember that these dramas are written by men, for a notional audience of men.[4] Even the women on stage were played by men; comedy often makes fun of this tradition of cross-dressing and in this way provides some interesting information about the perils of masculinity. But as evidence for women's lives, these plays can only be used with great caution and must be read against their own assumptions.

HOPLITES AND *KINAIDOI*

The ideal man in Athens was a citizen-soldier known as a hoplite.[5] These hoplites, at least in the ideal, exhibited the kind of strong moral character that one would expect from their disciplined moral training and personal bodily strength. As a person, he was a strong, well-disciplined man whose emotions and desires were under his own control. As a political being, he contributed his person to the Athenian hoplite army, ensuring that Athens would remain a free state, under the rule of the people. The essential quality of the hoplite was manliness, *andreia,* a word that initially had a specifically martial context. *Andreia* was the ability and willingness to stand one's ground in battle.[6]

At the other end of the axis of masculinity was a type of person known as a *kinaidos.* The word itself is of obscure origin; it may be related to the verb *kineo,* "to move," which in some contexts can have the sexual meaning of "to screw." The word often indicates an adult male who desires to be penetrated anally. The term, however, has a wider range of meaning than the purely sexual and is better understood as a full gender-deviant, that is, a man who is inappropriately feminine in every aspect of behavior.

The distinction between hoplites and *kinaidoi* is brought to the fore by Aeschines in a brief passage, in which he attacks his rival orator, Demosthenes:

But I am amazed if you dare slander Philon, and that, too, in the presence of the most respected men of Athens who, having come here to render their verdict for the best interest of the state, are thinking more about our lives than our words. Which do you think they would pray for: ten thousand hoplites like Philon, fit of body and temperate of soul, or thirty thousand *kinaidoi* like you? (Aeschines *On the Embassy,* 150–51)

Everything in the preceding passage is about respectability and self-control. The hoplites are *diakeimenoi,* "fit" or "settled" with respect to their bodies. The word I have translated "temperate" is *sôphrôn,* which has as its basic meaning "self-controlled." It is closely related to the term *sôphrosyne,* which appears as a particular virtue of men and women in a variety of Athenian texts. For men, *sôphrosyne* embodies the idea of restraint of all sorts of appetites; for women, the word is usually synonymous with sexual chastity. The audience, Aeschines points out, consists of respectable men who are worried about the reality of the political situation, not about the persuasive words that the orators produce. They are good, strong Athenian men. The speaker further suggests through contrast that Demosthenes should be ashamed to attack such a man as Philon because he himself is not such a man. A little later in the speech, once Aeschines has turned to Demosthenes' attacks on him, he suggests that he, at least, demonstrates the kind of self-control that Demosthenes apparently does not: "By what pleasure have I been mastered? Or what unseemly act have I ever done for money?" (Aeschines *On the Embassy*, 152).

All this, however, does not tell us exactly what a *kinaidos* is. On this point, Aeschines is fairly circumspect. The following passage from Aeschines' first speech shows that it has to do with more than just sex (I discuss this speech in greater detail later):

> . . . and common report called him "Batalos" with justification, because of his unmanliness and his *kinaidia*. For if, Demosthenes, someone should strip off those exquisite, pretty mantles of yours, and the soft, pretty shorts that you wear while you are writing speeches against your friends, and should pass them around among the jurors, I think, unless they were informed beforehand, they would be at a loss to say whether they were holding the clothing of a man or of a woman. (Aeschines *Against Timarchos* 131)

The bit about the nickname "Batalos" is confusing, and I will discuss it shortly. The most obvious thing about this passage, however, is the way that Aeschines ridicules Demosthenes for his clothing: his shirts and mantles are inappropriately soft for a man. There is, moreover, a salacious suggestion in Aeschines' hypothetical situation. "If someone were to strip off those clothes of yours," he says. Who would do this? If anyone were to strip off Demosthenes' clothes in real life, Demosthenes could justifiably bring a charge against him for *hybris,* unless it were done with Demosthenes' consent. But Aeschines can suggest it safely enough, and by doing so, he calls to mind an image of Demosthenes in a socially, if not sexually, submissive position, being undressed.

All of this is brought up as a justification for the name "Batalos," which Aeschines says was given to Demosthenes because of his lack of manliness (*anandreia*) and kinaidos-like nature (*kinaideia*). Now, the origin of this nickname is obscure. If you look up the word in a standard ancient Greek dictionary, you will find that when spelled *battalos,* the word means something like "stutterer," and we are told that as a child, Demosthenes did have a stutter. But spelled as Aeschines does (with only one *t*), the word is used in only one other place in classical literature: in a fragment of a comedy by Eupolis. There, the word appears to mean "buttocks." It looks very much like what Aeschines has done is mispronounce Demosthenes' nickname to give it a sexually suggestive meaning; this, combined with his accusation of unmanliness and *kinaidia,* impugns Demosthenes' masculinity.

In none of this is any specific sexual act described, or even mentioned, though the meaning of "Batalos" is suggestive. The point, however, is not a particular sexual behavior, but rather a complete failure to live up to the requirements of masculinity. The softness and prettiness of Demosthenes' clothes suggest a corresponding softness and prettiness of person, an implication that he is simply not man enough. This passage, then, helps us to understand the full import of the contrast between hoplites and *kinaidoi* in Aeschines *On the Embassy* 150–51. A hoplite is a manly man; a *kinaidos* is soft and womanish, in every respect.

THE PERILS OF BEAUTIFUL BOYS

As Michel Foucault pointed out in volume 2 of *The History of Sexuality,* a great deal of anxiety revolved around boys in Athens as erotic objects, the kind of anxiety that later European and American societies have expended on young, unmarried women. In part, this anxiety appears to have to do with the fact that these young men, especially the sons of the aristocratic elite, would someday need to grow into manly, active hoplites.

The concern to protect boys from the perils of penetration can be seen, in part, in a variety of laws that are clearly designed to protect them from the sexual advances of suitors. Aeschines tells us in his prosecution of Timarchos, for example, that schools and gymnasia were not to be open before dawn or after sunset to keep boys out of these public spaces after dark (Aeschines *Against Timarchos* 10). He goes on to state that penetration of a man, woman, or boy constitutes an act of *hybris,* a very serious criminal charge. To commit *hybris* against another is to violate his physical person against his (or her) will, and the term is often used to indicate forcible rape of a boy or of a woman. The penalty for *hybris,* if convicted, was a loss of citizenship rights (Aeschines *Against Timarchos* 15–17).

Obviously, however, not all sexual acts with boys resulted in charges of *hybris;* if they had, then no Athenian man would have taken the risk of being a lover, an *erastes.* Indeed, later in the same speech, Aeschines admits that he has been the *erastes* of several beautiful boys. At issue, in part, is the behavior and decorum of the lover. A charge of *hybris,* in fact, requires that the person committing the *hybris* do so against the will of the person against whom it was committed, either through physical strength or some other form of compulsion.[7] At issue, then, is whether or not the boy has willingly acceded to the advances of his lover. If he has, then he enters a somewhat difficult moral realm since giving in too easily or too often could result in the suggestion that he has made himself a prostitute. If he has not, a charge of *hybris* can be leveled against his sexual aggressor.[8] In other words, the law against *hybris* only comes into play if a lover's advances are improper, or not approved of by the boy (or perhaps his parents). But even giving in to a proper lover, if it involved penetration, might be accompanied by a sense of shame for the boy.

The erotic vases give us another look at this anxiety. Of the many hundreds of vases that show men and boys in erotic situations, it is extremely rare to see scenes of actual penetration.[9] We do see intercrural sex, in which the lover's penis goes between the beloved's thighs. And there are numerous pots depicting quite explicit sex with female prostitutes. We cannot, therefore, assume that this gap in the visual record is due to general squeamishness about showing sexually graphic scenes. It seems most likely that this penetration is not shown because such practice is forbidden, not out of homophobia, but out of concern for young men's reputations and futures as male citizens. Again, we should not assume on the basis of a few pots that only intercrural sex took place between *erastes* and *eromenos*. No doubt, many boys did go "all the way." But what one does in bed and what one admits to in public might be different things, and the hesitancy on the part of pots to show full anal penetration is probably an indicator of what was fully socially acceptable.[10]

A more general concern, however, is more akin to that articulated in the poetry of Theognis; that is, a praiseworthy boy must demonstrate sufficient discrimination in choosing friends and lovers. This concern is two pronged: the proper boy must avoid accepting too many lovers and must avoid accepting even one lover of the wrong sort. A text that provides a good look at the difficult tightrope of desire that a beautiful, high-class boy must walk is the *Erotikos* (or *Erotic Essay*) ascribed to Demosthenes.

Orgy scene. Men and youths make free use of (female) prostitutes. The hairstyle on the woman in the center may indicate that she is of servile status. Reunion des Musees Nationaux, Louvre, Paris, France/Art Resource.

(Many scholars believe that the essay was not written by Demosthenes, but it does appear to have been written in Demosthenes' time, i.e., the mid-fourth century BCE.) This brief piece contains the speaker's polished praise of an exemplary boy, followed by an exhortation to the same boy to study philosophy as a means of self-improvement.

Early on in the piece, the speaker enumerates those qualities that a perfect boy must have:

I think that everyone would agree with me that it is especially pressing for people of your age to possess beauty in your appearance, self-restraint *[sôphrosyne]* in your soul, and bravery *[andreia]* with regard to both, and to achieve charm in speaking. (*Erotic Essay* 8)

Already we see the importance of two qualities that will be crucial for such a boy when he becomes a citizen, namely, self-discipline and bravery. Charming speech might be useful if he becomes an orator, though the word here for "charm" (*charis*) also has connotations of erotic desire. And beauty of person is, of course, only important so long as the boy is an object of desire, rather than its subject.

The speaker, we should note, is quite taken with this boy's physical appearance, though he avoids naming particular parts with a quaint rhetorical flourish:

I will begin by praising first, that quality of yours which is first apparent to all who see you, your beauty, and your coloring, through which your limbs and your whole body shine. When I look to see what appropriate comparison to this I might bring forward, I see none; but it occurs to me to request of those who read this speech that they see you and gaze at you, so that I will receive their pardon for not being able to find anything similar. (*Erotic Essay* 10)

A little later on, the speaker praises the boy's character as well, and in particular, his *andreia* ("bravery" or "manliness"). He lavishes compliments on the boy's athletic competition, especially his choice of events:

Knowing, therefore, that even slaves and resident aliens take part in the other events, but that it is only allowed to citizens to take part in the "dismounting" *[apobainein]*, and that the best men strive after it, you have set out to take part in this sport. (*Erotic Essay* 23)

The boy's choice is particularly appropriate because in it, he has reaffirmed the class structure to which he belongs. By competing in an event peopled only by citizens, and especially by the "best men," he demonstrates the kind of discriminating character that, as an aristocrat, he must have.

Now, a boy of such beauty, with character to match, must necessarily have had a number of competing suitors. One temptation for such a boy, apparently, was simply to turn down all suitors to protect his reputation. But this is not, in the speaker's view, the most admirable course. The truly remarkable thing about the boy to whom the speaker addresses his essay is that he manages to grant favors discreetly and with proper judgment, erring neither to the left nor to the right:

Concerning your lovers *[erastai]*, if I must speak of these, you seem to me to inter-act with them beautifully and with restraint *[sôphronôs]*, so that, even though most of them are not able to behave with restraint with the one whom they have chosen, you have been able to please them all a great deal. And this is the clearest indication of your excellence; for not one of them comes away from you without having got-ten a share of what is just and good; but of those things that lead to shame, no one arrives even at the hope of achieving them. Your self-restraint *[sôphrosyne]* provides such great accommodation to those reaching out for the best things, and makes such cowards of those who wish to act brazenly. (*Erotic Essay* 20)

Again, a veil of discretion falls over the speaker's description, so that we do not know exactly what actions this boy so adroitly discourages. The boy's bril-liance, however, also lies in the direction of encouraging the right kind of lover. He gladly gives those favors "which are just and good," and somewhat para-doxically, his own self-control (*sôphrosyne*) is figured as an impetus for those who intend their affections in the right way. The entire passage is saturated in language of appropriateness, discrimination, and self-control. In this regard, the speaker of the essay constructs the boy's erotic experience as a kind of practice for his adult life. In accepting only the right kinds of propositions, and gently discouraging those that lack self-control, the boy is developing the kind of discrimination of thought that he will need as a full-fledged citizen.

Of course, this praise also has an ulterior motive. The *Erotic Essay* is addressed to the boy himself and is itself a form of seduction. By prais-ing the boy for recognizing the right kind of proposition, and by suggest-ing that the right kind of proposition can be accepted without shame of any kind, the speaker positions himself as the right kind of suitor. He, no doubt, hopes that the boy, pleased by this rhetorical offering, will choose to please him "exceedingly." The entire text can be read as an adept game of erotic cat and mouse, and it demonstrates the careful line of behavior that a beautiful boy had to adopt—between refusing every suitor and accepting the wrong one—if he wanted to maintain his reputation.

OBSCENITY

In the age of the Internet, the question of what constitutes obscenity has become a constantly evolving legal and social problem. What is acceptable in one country (or part of a country) is not in another, but the Internet knows no such geographic boundaries. Material that is appropriate for fully de-veloped adults is not for children; a huge industry has sprung up designed specifically to protect children from what is considered harmful exposure to such material. We live in a time in which these boundaries of acceptable, appropriate, harmful, and enjoyable are constantly being pushed, pulled, re-examined, and variously enforced.

To the person who first comes to study Greek art and society, it may ap-pear that the Greeks had no sense of the obscene at all. Consider, for ex-ample, the festival of the Greater Dionysia in Athens, at which tragedy and comedy were performed. On the first day of the festival, before the plays began, a procession led the cult image of the god from the outskirts of the city to the theater in Athens, reenacting the arrival of the god Dionysus from Eleutherae. In this procession, according to our sources, were citizens and resident aliens (called *metics*) of both sexes. Girls of high birth carried baskets of offerings to the god; young men carried large erect phalluses, symbols of the god's gift of fertility. It is difficult to imagine such an explicitly sexual demonstration at a modern Western civic or religious festival (though similar processions still take place at Easter time in small villages in Greece).

Once the dramas began, things became, by our standards, even more outrageous. The tragedies were staid enough, but by convention, each playwright produced, after his three tragedies, a so-called satyr play. These satyr plays were so named because their choruses consisted of satyrs, mythical creatures associated with Dionysus who were men from the waist up, goats from the waist down, and who generally sported outlandish erections. Images from vases often depict these satyrs pursuing female followers of Dionysus (*maenads*) with obvious sexual intent.

All that is before the comedies. In the comedies (discussed at more length later), the male characters' costumes included large, strap-on erect phalluses. The more manly the character, or, as dictated by some plots, the greater his sexual need, the larger and more outlandish was his equipment. Women's bodies, too, were burlesqued. The men who played female parts in these plays donned exaggerated body padding that represented breasts and female buttocks. As we will see, the plays themselves are chock-full of sexual jokes, ranging from innuendo to flat-out sexual derision. These plays took place, it is important to note, at a large public festival, open to, and attended by, large segments of the general population of Athens.

Then there are the pots. The study of erotic situations on Greek pots is somewhat technical and beyond the scope of this work. Here let me simply mention that the pots made for symposia are often decorated with graphic sexual details. Men fondle boys' genitals, men engage in sex (oral, anal, and vaginal) with naked women (presumably prostitutes), and on it goes. In his outstanding study of Greek art, Robin Osborne discusses a late-sixth-century drinking cup, the interior of which shows a suggestive symposium scene. The foot of the cup, which the drinker would have held to drink, is in the form of a male penis and two testicles.[11] There is simply no way to drink from this cup without being confronted with sex.

All of this sounds surprisingly open to us, but we must realize that the Athenians did have an acute sense of obscenity. Like other aspects of ancient culture, it was simply not the same as ours. The incredible, graphic scenes on many Athenian pots need to be put in context: they are virtually always on pots used at symposia, that is, used by men in the company of other men. Pots on which citizen women's sexual activity is referred to—for example, the water vases on which wedding scenes are frequently depicted—can be suffused with eroticism. But the women are always shown fully clothed, and the bride's erotic availability is signaled by decorous and formulaic gestures, such as lifting up the shoulder of her outer garment. Vases for household use, or women's use, do not show explicit sex scenes.

Similarly, though Aristophanes could have characters in his plays refer to each other as "wide-assed," we must remember that the context of those statements allows a certain freedom, just as comedians in modern America are allowed certain liberties of political and sexual license that would not be allowed, say, on the editorial board of a newspaper. When we look at the evidence from legal speeches, the speaker is often frustratingly circumspect. Consider, for example, the following passage from Aeschines' *Against Timarchos* 74–75:

You see these men who sit in the brothels, the ones who on their own admission practice this activity. Yet these men, when they are required to engage in the act, still throw a cloak over their shame and lock the doors. Now if someone were to ask you, the men passing by in the street: "what is this person doing at this moment?" you would immediately give the name of the act, without seeing who had gone in; no, once you know the chosen profession of the individual you also recognize the act. So you should investigate Timarchos in the same way and not ask whether anyone saw him but if this man has engaged in the practice.

At this particular moment in the speech, the prosecutor (Aeschines) is trying to convince the jury that Timarchos has prostituted himself. The difficulty, however, is that he does not have a witness willing to come forward as having hired Timarchos. Nonetheless, he argues, if everyone *knows* that Timarchos is that sort of person, there cannot be much question about whether or not he has engaged in the activity.

Notice, however, how many careful phrases there are in the paragraph whose only purpose is to avoid saying, "Timarchos sold himself to be penetrated." Even when the speaker is speaking about a hypothetical prostitute engaged in a hypothetical act, he does not name the act. In fact, he calls up a scene in which the observer might be asked what is going on, but even when playing this drama about naming the act, he talks around the issue: "you would immediately give the name of the act." If this strikes us as uncommonly delicate, we should take it as another sign of the cultural divide between us and Athens. Aeschines can say that Timarchos has sold himself (and he does). He cannot, apparently, say what service he sold himself for, at least not in this context.

Obscenity, then, is relative and context-specific. It is worth reminding ourselves that many of the images we see every day at the supermarket—for example, of citizen women in skimpy bikinis on the covers of magazines marketed primarily to women—would have been shocking to a fifth-century Greek audience. We are less concerned with maintaining the privacy of women's lives than the Athenians were, even while we are a bit more restrained in the decoration of our drinking cups.

PEDERASTY

We have already seen the institution of pederasty at work in the lyric poetry of the archaic period and in the attempted seduction of Demosthenes' *Erotic Essay*. All of our evidence indicates that this practice continued in fifth-century Athens and was adopted wholeheartedly by the elite classes as a mode of introducing boys into the social order of men. Older men pursued beautiful boys, and in exchange for sexual favors, provided them with gifts, advice, protection, and education.

We should not assume, however, that this model, so familiar to us from the dialogues of Plato, is the only acceptable form of same-sex desire in ancient Greece. Readers will sometimes find it argued that pederasty was practiced only by the aristocratic elite and that Athenian men in the street found it repugnant and made fun of it. Indeed, Athenian men in the street do make fun of the aristocratic elite, and not least for their sometimes excessive attachment to boys, or their soft and luxurious mode of living. But vast evidence exists suggesting that *most* Athenian men, whether or not they could afford the lifestyle of the aristocracy, found boys to be attractive sexual objects.

In the passage from Aeschines quoted previously, the speaker speaks quite casually about a male prostitute and his potential client. Even if the passage is only hypothetical, the fact that Aeschines could call up this presumed situation and expect it to be recognizable to his listeners indicates how common it must have been. Note, moreover, that although Aeschines speaks of "throw[ing] a cloak over his shame," no particular shame appears to cling to the client of the prostitute for visiting him and engaging in the unnamed act that is so broadly hinted at. In brief, the scene must have been neither shocking nor morally reprehensible, and the desire of the client must have been considered fairly normal.[12]

Why, then, do we find attacks against the aristocratic elite for their sexual practices? I see two common kinds of attacks. First, aristocratic boys growing up would have been under a social microscope. As the future orators and politicians of Athens, their every move would have been intensely scrutinized. At the same time, because of their high social standing and prominent place in the city's public life, to say nothing of the gymnasia, they would have been particularly desirable erotic objects. What this means is that as adults, the aristocratic leaders of the city could be tweaked for having had multiple affairs as youths. In Aristophanes, then, we see Alcibiades, a brilliant general and former student of Socrates, described as *euryproktos*, or "wide-assed" (Aristophanes *Acharnians* 716). These kinds of attacks are a way to undercut the superior social status enjoyed by the Athenian upper class.

Another fairly common attack suggests that the elite adult males tend to give themselves over to pleasure, especially the pleasure of boys, but that such men justify their actions by arguing that these seductions are motivated by the noble purpose of education. We have seen this already in the pseudo-Lucianic *Erotes,* in which the judge of the debate decides that only philosophers should pursue boy-love. He is immediately countered, however, by Theomnestus, who says that it is unfair to suggest that men can pursue boys, but not enjoy them sexually, and who denies that Socrates refrained from physical contact with Alcibiades. The gist of these jokes, again, is not that desire for boys is wrong, or even strange; rather, the point is that the elite are dressing up their common, understandable sexual activity as something more noble than it is. The modern equivalent is perhaps the jibe against an upper-class heterosexual man who subscribes to *Playboy* and claims that he reads it for the articles. The elite, these middle-class speakers suggest, are just like everybody else: they too enjoy their sex with boys and need not put on such philosophical airs.

PROSTITUTION

I cannot provide a full discussion of prostitution in ancient Athens, fascinating though that topic is.[13] It is worthwhile, however, to note that the city of Athens subsidized state-run brothels and that the establishment of this institution was ascribed to the sixth-century BCE lawgiver Solon. Both male and female prostitutes worked in these establishments, which provides further evidence for the assertion that men thought of boys as normal erotic objects. Sex at these brothels was quite cheap and available to any Athenian man. So far as we can tell, no great shame was attached to visiting a prostitute for recreational sex.

Though it has sometimes been asserted that most prostitutes in Athens were foreigners, the evidence for this assumption is fairly thin. It was not illegal for Athenian citizens to act as prostitutes, though doing so meant that they could no longer exercise full citizenship rights, including introducing legislation in the assembly and bringing an accusation for a criminal charge. Noncitizens, then, would have had less to lose by becoming prostitutes than citizens; but as Edward Cohen has pointed out, the only solid evidence we have consists of legal cases against citizens who allegedly prostituted themselves and then tried to exercise their citizenship rights.

The logic behind the loss of citizenship rights is also revealing. As Halperin has argued, the idea that a man would sell his body for someone else to use in sex is a fundamental denial of control over one's sexual self. If he is willing to sell himself in this way, then can the state trust him not to do other shameful things for money? Might he sell his interest in the state to an enemy or intruder? Again, the parallel between the man's control over his own body and the state's ability to self-rule is paramount. A person who would sell one cannot be trusted with the other.

The ready availability of sex for hire also must have had an effect on Athenian citizen women. Indeed, in Euripides *Medea* 244–47, the title character complains bitterly about the asymmetry of availability for men and women:

A man, whenever he is tired of those at home
can go outside and end his distress,
turning to some friend or one of his age mates.
But for us it is necessary to look at only one soul.

The speaker does not suggest prostitutes, but does seem to resent the idea that men have a world of companionship available to them, whereas women are cut off, dependent on their husbands for company. Indeed, like most other aspects of citizen women's lives, their sexual lives are largely a mystery to us because the ideal is that they had no public sexual life.

What of women who were prostitutes? Like men, women could not be prostitutes and exercise full citizenship rights at the same time. It is clear that citizen women were prostitutes, however, and there was nothing illegal about that, strictly speaking. Men, moreover, could not be prosecuted of violating the law against adultery if they had sex with a woman who worked in a known brothel.[14] As in the modern world, there were different levels of status for prostitutes, from common brothel workers and streetwalkers to the "companions" (*hetairai*) who were especially associated with symposia. The most successful of these *hetairai* entered into long-term relationships with aristocratic men and wielded considerable economic power. For a fascinating look at the life of an (alleged) *hetaira,* and the ways in which she parlayed her sexual relationships into economic, social, and political status, readers are encouraged to read pseudo-Demosthenes *Against Neaira.*

CONCLUSIONS

While no form of consensual sex was illegal in Athens, there were significant and sometimes confusing restrictions on whom a citizen could have sex with. The law against *hybris* protected both citizens and noncitizens, even slaves, from unwanted sexual advances. If a person was willing to be penetrated, however, whether male or female, citizen or noncitizen, no shame fell on the active male citizen who chose to have sex with him or her. Within this understanding was a second set of unwritten rules, by which adult citizen males were supposed to exercise *enkrateia,* "self-rule," and *sôphrosyne,* "moderation." Failure to exercise such self-control could open an adult man up to the charge of having been a prostitute, and this carried with it an implicit lost of citizenship rights. The citizen's control over his own person was considered analogous to the Athenian state's control over itself and its own institutions, and a good citizen was one who was unwilling to sell either himself or his state for any price.

Beautiful boys, as Foucault recognized, were in a particularly fraught situation. They needed to demonstrate a level of self-control to protect their own reputations. At the same time, however, the most highly praised of such boys (such as the object of Demosthenes' *Erotic Essay*) were those who did not reject all comers out of hand. A proper beautiful boy, behaving with the right decorum, became all the more beautiful and desirable to his potential lovers. The trick was to grant sexual favors, but not too easily, too often, or with the wrong people. As often with social institutions, the lines that defined these borders must have been a bit blurry at times, and staying within them must have required considerable skill and discretion.

Four

Sexuality in Greek Comedy

There is nothing quite like Greek comedy in modern Western culture. Our best evidence for the genre comes from Aristophanes, a writer of the late fifth century who continued on into the 380s BCE, and from whom we have a total of 11 complete plays. We know a few things about some of his competitors, and we have some fragments of their plays (usually only a line or two), but for the most part, when we speak of comedy, we mean Aristophanes.

The plays themselves took place in the same context as Greek tragedies, probably on the fourth day of the Athenian tragic festival, which was a festival honoring the god Dionysus. Dionysus was a potentially dangerous, boundary-crossing deity whose realms of influence included wine, drama, male and female sexual fertility, ecstatic dance, and song. In myth, women who worshipped him became *maenads*; they left the safety of their homes for the mountain wilds, where they were said to drink wine, take part in typically masculine activities such as hunting, and engage in uninhibited sexual behavior. In some ways, the comedies preserve certain Dionysiac elements more completely than do the tragedies: the actors in the comedies who played male parts wore, as part of their costumes, large erect phalluses, recalling the procession of young men carrying phalluses that preceded the festival. Nearly every play, no matter how much things get out of hand in the course of the drama, ends with a metaphoric celebration of fertility, as the hero—usually a solid middle-class Athenian—walks offstage with at least one sexy slave girl on his arm. And the comedies themselves are built on a convention of temporary violation of boundaries of all sorts.

The comedies share some features with modern satiric comedy: jokes refer to contemporary political events, and the playwright often names specific politicians or public figures as the butt of those jokes. A few public figures, like the demagogue Kleon, the tragic poet Euripides, the philosopher Socrates, or the well-known effeminate Kleisthenes,[1] are parodied as characters within the plays. At times, the mockery of these public figures had serious consequences. Kleon evidently brought a lawsuit against Aristophanes for slander after a particularly unsympathetic portrayal in a play, now lost, called the *Babylonians*. It appears that Kleon lost his lawsuit, and he continued to show up as an object of ridicule. More chilling is the fact that in his version of Socrates' *Apology*, Plato blames "the comedians" for stirring up public resentment against his teacher. Socrates had been the object of a scathing satiric portrayal in Aristophanes' *Clouds*, originally produced in 423; he was convicted in 399 BCE of corrupting the youth and sentenced to death.

The most astonishing thing about the plays for the modern audience, though, is the open and frank obscenity. Characters refer to sex as well as other bodily functions (defecation, urination) with an ease that would be considered pornographic if written by a modern playwright. Insults are often of a sexual nature, and some of the most common refer to men as being sexually passive, such as *euryproktos* (wide-ass) or *katapugon* (anally penetrated). Such profanities do not always have their literal force; just as, today, we can call a person a "bastard" without actually meaning that he was born out of wedlock, a man could be called *katapugon* in Aristophanes with no more specific meaning than that of many modern profanities. At times, however, these words do seem to maintain their literal meaning.[2]

Jeffrey Henderson suggests that the Greeks simply had a different notion of obscenity than we do; that is, although the obscenities in his plays maintain a certain shock value because they bring private matters abruptly into the public eye, Henderson argues that the Greeks did not think of sexual or bodily functions as fundamentally dirty in the way that later Western cultures do. Be that as it may, Aristophanes' plays, because of their concern with sexual humor, the relations between the sexes, and the examination of sexual norms, are among our best evidence for Athenian attitudes toward sex and sex roles.

ARISTOPHANES AND THE WIDE-ASSED ATHENIANS

Consider the following passage from Aristophanes' *Clouds*, in which the playwright turned his comic eye on the philosopher Socrates and his followers. In the course of the play, the objects of attack are the Sophists, a group of private teachers in Athens whose influence had grown during the 420s. (Socrates was not a Sophist but was sometimes misunderstood to be one— but that is another matter.) The Sophists were among the West's first moral relativists: they taught, or so they boasted, that winning arguments had less to do with being right than with presenting your argument in a pleasing and persuasive way.

As part of his attack on this position, Aristophanes creates two characters whose names literally translate to "Weaker Argument" and "Stronger Argument." The two hold a debate over which should be allowed to educate the youth of Athens, represented here by a young man named Pheidippides. In so doing, Aristophanes makes concrete a theoretical position that was particularly well known from the Sophists; that is, the Sophists claimed that they could teach an orator to speak such that the weaker argument—that is, the position that held less intrinsic merit—would defeat the stronger. So from the beginning, this scene has a certain surreal quality to it. The characters are less people than representatives of an idea.

Stronger Argument goes first—always a bad idea since the second speaker generally has an advantage in Aristophanic debates—and advocates an old-fashioned strict moral upbringing. His speech is all nostalgia, not unlike the kinds of speeches that every older generation makes, even today, about the decadence and lack of discipline of the younger generation. In particular, Stronger Argument claims that his educational method was responsible for the men who defeated the Persians at the battle of Marathon in 490 BCE. In the course of praising the youth of his day, however, it has been noted that Stronger Argument seems to be concerned with these young boys as sexual objects:

The boys in the gymnasium used to cross their legs when sitting down
so they would not expose to those outside anything cruel;
When they got back up, they would smooth the sand and take care
not to leave behind the image of their manhood for their lovers.
No boy would ever oil himself below the navel:
So that dew and down bloom on their genitals, as on peaches. (*Clouds* 973–78)

This is only one tricky moment in the scene, and it raises questions about how we should think about Stronger Argument. If we read the scene with a modern sexual sensibility in mind, then the humor is quite broad. Here is this strict moralist, hearkening back to the days of Marathon, and he turns out to be gay.

The problem with reading the scene this way, however, is that there is no indication that there is anything abnormal in Stronger Argument's desires and inclinations, nor any suggestion that it is morally problematic for him to display this interest in young men's genitals. At the same time, the scene is gently funny. What is mocked here, however, is not the *fact* that Stronger Argument is interested in boys, but rather the manner of his desire. He seems on the verge of losing his self-control. Indeed, if the impression of a boy's genitalia in the sand is enough to send him over the edge, he is pretty far from attaining the Athenian ideal of self-mastery. He may have a sexual preference for boys, but he is not depicted as having a sexual orientation, or even a particular sexual identity. Nothing about the scene suggests that it is odd for him to feel these desires; and in fact, we know from Aristophanes and other authors that the gymnasia were common cruising grounds, where older men would go to scope out, and perhaps engage, attractive young men.

So far, however, we have not come to the real point of the contest between the two speakers. After Stronger Argument is done, Weaker Argument engages his rival in a brief dialogue. Through a series of deliberately facile arguments, he confounds a number of Stronger Argument's positions. His final bit of sophistry, however, comes when Weaker Argument suggests that there is no harm in a boy growing up to be *euryproktos,* "wide-assed." This term, as discussed earlier, is used commonly in Aristophanes as a general term of abuse. When it has a specific sexual connotation, it refers to someone who (willingly) submits to anal penetration. Following is the scene, at some length:

WA   What harm is there in turning out to be wide-assed?
SA   What? What greater harm could be endured than being wide-assed, ever?
WA   And what would you say if I refute your argument on this point?
SA   I'd be quiet. What else could I do?
WA   All right, then, here's a question. From what kind of person do we get lawyers?
SA   From the wide-asses.
WA   Quite right. And from what kind come tragic poets?
SA   Wide-asses.
WA   Well said. And from what kind come politicians?
SA   Wide-asses.
WA   Now you see, your argument was nonsense. What about the audience? Of which sort do you see the most?
SA   I see them all right.
WA   And what do you see?
SA   Most of them, by gods, are wide-assed. (*Pointing into audience.*) I know that one is, anyway, and that one there, and that one with the long hair.
WA   So, what do you say?
SA   I'm beaten. Here, you passives, by the gods, take my cloak so I can desert to your side. (*Clouds* 1085–1104)

The greatest single shock of the preceding scene is the suggestion by Stronger Argument that, in effect, the entire Athenian audience consists of men who have been penetrated in anal sex. Certainly the lawyers and tragedians have. To add to the humor, the actor also breaks the dramatic illusion, not only referring to the spectators, but pointing to specific members of the audience as he casts his aspersions. We can imagine the actor having a bit of fun as he scans the audience for appropriate targets; perhaps, in the performance, he would have pointed at leading politicians like Kleon or Alcibiades.

But what do we do with the idea that all of Athens is wide-assed? It is one thing for satirical comedy to make fun of public figures, as *Saturday Night Live* or *The Daily Show* does regularly. It is quite another to suggest that every member of the Athenian audience is sexually passive. I see in this brief passage a clear expression of embarrassment with the double-bind that the Athenian sexual system put on every citizen man; that is, as I discussed earlier, Athenians assumed that every adult male would want to seduce attractive young men. And the young men were supposed to welcome these advances, in a limited and careful way. What this means is that every adult male in the audience, even those who are now properly masculine (and active in sex) *may* have been a passive partner in his youth. As passivity was forbidden to respectable adults, this past, which they all shared, was nonetheless a source of mild embarrassment and subject to the kind of tweaking we see in the scene described previously.

WOMEN CONFOUND THE STAGE

Three of Aristophanes' remaining plays involve women as main characters and explicitly address women's view of the state and its operation. The most famous of these in recent times is the *Lysistrata,* in which the women of Athens refuse to have sex with their husbands until the men find a way to end the ongoing Peloponnesian War. Less well known is the *Thesmophoriazousae* (literally, "The Women Attending the Festival of Demeter and Kore"), in which the women at the festival attack Euripides for his portrayal of women. In the least popular of the three, the *Ecclesiazousae* (Assemblywomen), the women actually take control of the Athenian assembly and pass a new set of laws, establishing a radical socialist state in which even sex must be evenly shared.

All of this provides opportunities for some good fun, and there are a number of scenes in which the "women" on stage talk directly or indirectly about sex. In saying this, however, we must remember that all the parts on the stage would have been played by men, and that those playing women were wearing exaggerated body padding to represent breasts and large buttocks. Nor can we assume that Aristophanes' female roles represent real women's views; in fact, as we will see shortly, the poet regularly hijacks women's traditional social roles to provide an outsider's perspective from which to criticize the men who are misleading the Athenian state. Nonetheless, the plays are interesting evidence for what *men* thought women were like, even if we must make some allowance for comic exaggeration.

With all that said, what are Aristophanes' women's views of sex? They like it. In fact, they are generally represented as sexually voracious, nearly unable to control their desire. In the *Lysistrata,* it appears at times as if this expectation is reversed. In fact, the plot turns on the unusual idea that the women will be able to do without sex longer than their husbands will. (In the imaginary world of the play, the husbands apparently do not have access to prostitutes or mistresses; similarly, all the women on stage are already married.) Despite this reversal of the normal expectation, here Aristophanes gets considerable comic mileage out of the idea that the women cannot live without sex. When Lysistrata proposes the sex strike, for example, the idea is presented with comic buildup and a response:

LYSISTRATA	Would you, then, if I found a way want to end the war with me?
MYRRHINE	I sure would! Even if I had to throw down my cloak today and begin . . . drinking.
KALONIKE	And I would split myself like a flounder[3] and give half of myself.
LAMPITO	And I would climb to the top of Mt. Tagyetos in order to see Peace again.
LYSISTRATA	Then I'll tell you. For I should not keep it secret. Women, if we are going to force our husbands to make peace, we must abstain . . .
KALONIKE	From what? Tell us.
LYSYSTRATA	But will you do it?
KALONIKE	We will do it, even if we must die.
LYSISTRATA	We must abstain, then, from . . . cock. (*As other women begin to leave.*) No, wait, why are you leaving? Where are you going? You there, why are you pouting and shaking your head? Why are you turning pale? Why this crying? Will you do it, or not? Or what will you do?
MYRRHINE	I will not do it. Let the war go on.
KALONIKE	By Zeus, I won't do it either; let the war go on. (*Lysistrata* 111–30)

We cannot look too closely at the logic of this scene. The reason that the women give for wanting peace is that their husbands are never home; it is not clear, then, what sex they would be giving up in their attempt to force an end to the war. The joke works, however, because the audience is willing to accept the idea that this group of wives, however earnestly they desire an end to the war, are unwilling to give up sex with their husbands.

Eventually, of course, Lysistrata convinces the women that the sex strike is worth enduring, but the joke is not over yet. Later in the play, there is an entire scene that consists of women trying to sneak out of their encampment to visit their husbands; again, the image of sex-crazed women is one that the comic audience is willing to entertain. The one notable exception in this play, and indeed in all of Aristophanes, is Lysistrata herself. She is the heroic figure in the drama, and she embodies the kind of self-restraint that even the men do not. It is worth noting, however, that at the end of the play, Lysistrata disappears from the stage. An Athenian and a Spartan negotiate peace by discussing which parts of a girl, named "Peace," each of them will claim as his own; the men then disappear for a round of drinking, rapidly return, and end the play with celebratory hymns. The world is once again constructed as safe for men's drinking, song, and sexual activity.

In a similar way, the *Thesmophoriazousae* claims to show us the world of an all-women's festival, but the women in that festival seem to be the product of male sexual paranoia. Euripides has heard that the women at the festival intend to pass judgment on him for his negative portrayal of women in his tragedies. He convinces his kinsman (named in most productions, simply, "Kinsman") to dress in women's clothes and infiltrate the all-female *Thesmophoria*. Once there, he is to spy on the women and represent Euripides' interests.

The women do indeed attack Euripides, but their argument is somewhat surprising. Rather than arguing that Euripides has unfairly depicted them as shallow, hypersexed beings, the women claim that by (truthfully) depicting them in this way, Euripides has made their *husbands* jealous and suspicious. The end result is that it is nearly impossible for these women to entertain lovers. In one of the crudest scenes in the play, the Kinsman, dressed as an old woman, "defends" Euripides by listing some of the things that the women do that Euripides has *not* put into his plays:

Or here's a really terrible thing:
When I had been married for three days,
my husband was sleeping next to me. I had a lover,
who deflowered me when I was seven.[4]
He came and scratched at my door, ready for some action.
Right away I knew it was him. Then I went down stealthily.
But my husband asked, "Where are you going? Where?"
"I have a stomachache, husband, and cramps.
I'm going to the outhouse." "Go now," he said.
And then he began mixing up some stomach remedies.

But I poured water on the hinges [to keep them from squeaking]
and went out to my lover. Then I was getting screwed
next to the pillar of Apollo [by the door], holding on to a laurel bush.
Euripides never talked about this, you see." (*Thesmophoriazousae* 477–90)

The Kinsman's complaints here are an exaggeration of the kinds of things that the (dramatically portrayed) real women had been saying just a few lines earlier. Their complaint was that Euripides focused only on the negative, never the positive; as one woman puts it, his plays are about Phaedra (a woman who conceived an overwhelming desire for her stepson in Euripides' *Hippolytus*) rather than about Penelope (Odysseus's wife, famous for her fidelity to him). The Kinsman's defense is both more prosaic and considerably more crude. Nonetheless, the women do not object to the substance of what he says. None of them says "no woman ever did that"; rather, they become upset only because he is taking Euripides' side.

When a character representing the well-known effeminate man Kleisthenes arrives with the news that a man has infiltrated this women's festival, the women rapidly seize on the Kinsman and discover his true sex. He is revealed as a proponent of Euripides, which becomes justification for his earlier misogynistic confession. But again, the supposed women on stage do not object to the substance of that confession, but rather to the Kinsman's apparent betrayal of the women's shared and, they hope, secret activity. The layers of costume here are dizzying: the Kinsman is distinct from the women in the play in that he is a man dressed as a man disguised as a woman, whereas the rest of the women are men simply dressed as women. If these "women" object to Euripides's portrayal of women, however, they are participating nonetheless in Aristophanes' portrayal of women as even worse.

Again, however, we must remember that this is a depiction not of real women, but of men's fears about women. Male anxieties are projected onto these characters, and what the men of Athens are worried about, it appears, is that their wives will have affairs right under their noses. A corollary of this fear is that the women in these plays are always shown as being particularly interested in drink; whenever they have an opportunity to drink wine, they do. A female character in the *Thesmophoriazousae* has even dressed up a wineskin in little Persian booties and is pretending that it is her daughter. Drinking, in the Athenian male imagination, leads to sex, and both need to be rigorously controlled by watchful husbands.

At the same time, Aristophanes demonstrates a clear knowledge of the double standard at work, in which each man wants his own wife to be faithful but the wives of others to be available for affairs. In most of the plays of Aristophanes, there is a passage known as the *parabasis* (literally, the "stepping aside"), in which the chorus speaks, outside of the drama, directly to the audience. Often the narrator of the *parabasis* speaks in the voice of the poet. In the *parabasis* of the *Thesmophoriazousae,* the chorus chides the men in the audience for claiming that women are an evil (*to kakon*) and yet being so attracted to this evil that they marry it and then guard it jealously. If women were really an evil, the chorus says, the men should be happy to see them leave the house, instead of keeping them sequestered in it (*Thesmophoriazousae* 785–813). Even if the *parabasis* exposes men's foolishness, however, it must be admitted that the play does little to tell us what *women* really thought or felt. It is a conscious exposure of the inconsistency of men, much of which is then embodied in the rest of the drama. The real views of real women are simply not here.

Indeed, nowhere in all of Aristophanes do we hear anything about women's desire for, or sexual activity with, other women. This silence might not seem so significant if it were not for the unbridled relish with which Aristophanes talks of men's sexual activity, with boys, with other men, and with women. The poet thinks nothing of tossing off a one-liner in which one man suggests that he would be more than happy to screw another. Nor can we easily write this silence off to a lack of opportunity; in the three plays mentioned previously, we have scenes in which the chorus and all the speaking parts are women. In the *Thesmophoriazousae,* the women are representing, however unrealistically, an all-women's festival, the rites of which were kept jealously secret from men. Athenian men were more than willing to assume that women, when left alone, were absolutely prey to their desires. Why, then, is it never suggested that these women might enjoy one another's company sexually?

The closest that we come is in a passage from the *Lysistrata,* in which the women of different city-states (Lysistrata and Kalonike of Athens, Lampito of Sparta) admire one another's bodies. The Athenians comment on Lampito's musculature, a reference to the fact that Spartan girls were out-of-doors and got more physical exercise than Athenians did. And Kalonike comments on an unnamed Boiotian girl's "cultivated and well-plucked plains," which appears to be a reference to her depilated genitalia. But the women never suggest that they would like to have sex with one another or make mention of such activity taking place in the world off the stage. Other sources are equally reticent to discuss female-female sexual contact (or, in the case of pottery, to depict it). This overwhelming lack of evidence is so striking in contrast to the easy mention of male-male sexual activity that Kenneth Dover has suggested that it amounts to a conspiracy of silence on the part of the Athenians.[5]

NORMAL MEN

The protagonist of most Aristophanic comedy is recognizable as a solid upper-middle-class Athenian citizen. He is usually not an aristocrat, but neither is he entirely without means. If there is one thing that we can say about his sexual life, it is that he is randy. He is interested in sex, often with women, but not infrequently with boys or effeminate men. Though this protagonist may be married, this fact never impinges on his desire or ability to enjoy sex with others. Ideally, he is in control of his sexual urges, but sometimes, for the sake of the comedy, he is shown to be in the thrall of an overwhelming desire. At the end of many of the plays, the male protagonist exits with a slave girl on either arm, going offstage to enjoy unfettered (and unrepresented) sex.

Often, Aristophanes presents this protagonist in direct contrast to a man who is not sexually normal—an effeminate man, or a passive. But even the normal men in Aristophanes' plays can be the subject of extended comic routines. In the *Lysistrata*, we meet the husband of Myrrhine, a man named "Kinesias." Kinesias is a one-scene character, inessential to the plot. Even his name is a joke; it is derived from the verb *kineo*, a word that means "to move" and is used at times as a euphemism for the active role in sex. A reasonable translation of his name, then, would be "Screwer."[6]

In Kinesias's one scene (lines 845 and following), he has been reduced to a distressed state by the sex strike. He arrives at the Acropolis and begs his wife to have mercy on him and allow him to have sex with her. We should remember at this point that the standard costume for men in Greek comedy included a strap-on erect phallus and that this could be used to comic effect. I imagine that Kinesias's phallus was even larger and more erect than usual to visually represent his distress. Myrrhine, though she is also interested in sex, demonstrates admirable self-control in their shared scene. She teases her husband mercilessly, promising him sex, but never delivering; she keeps putting him off by declaring that they need various accoutrements: a mattress, pillows, perfume, and so on. As he grows increasingly desperate, Myrrhine gets Kinesias to promise that he will argue for peace in the assembly; having accomplished her goal, Myrrhine leaves Kinesias, unsatisfied and still in a state of painful erection.

Of course, Kinesias's scene only works as long as we forget, for the moment, that there are other alternatives open to him. (Given the bawdy humor of much of Aristophanes, one is tempted to wonder why he does not simply masturbate.) Apparently, there are no prostitutes available. Moreover, he cannot be interested in having sex with boys or young men; only his wife is an acceptable outlet for his sexual desires. This was, in fact, more like the situation of most young Greek wives, who could only have sex with their husbands. But in real life (and in other places in Aristophanes' plays), boys and prostitutes are viable options for the male characters.

It is true that Aristophanes makes considerable fun of men who have been, or are willing to be, penetrated. Some modern readers are astonished, however, at the casual ease with which normal males suggest having sex with other men. The crucial point is that it is never shameful to desire to penetrate another man; some gentle needling of one's inability to manage this desire is possible, but it is quite clear that neither Aristophanes nor his audience thought that there was anything odd, unusual, or shameful about the desire itself. Consider two examples from the *Thesmophoriazousae*.

In the first, Euripides and his Kinsman have arrived at the house of Agathon, a real person from fifth-century Athens. Agathon was an aristocrat and a tragic poet, and he is depicted as such in Aristophanes as well. He is portrayed as silly, and he composes a bit of tragedy while on stage, which is clearly meant as a parody of his high-flown, bombastic style. More important, though, he is dressed bizarrely, in half-male, half-female clothes. The

Kinsman, faced with this oddly effeminate character, is critical of Agathon but also finds him attractive. He questions Agathon about his clothing; Agathon responds that he dresses in an effeminate manner when he is composing poems about women—a sort of early precursor to method acting:

AGATHON Old man, old man, I heard this ill-willed reproach, but it didn't hurt me any. I wear clothes that are appropriate to the idea. A male poet must have the proper manner with respect to what the drama requires. For instance if he is composing a feminine drama, it is necessary for his body to take part in the manner of women.

KINSMAN So, do you ride bareback when you are writing a Phaedra?[7]

AGATHON *ignoring the last comment.* And if someone is writing a manly play, he has what he needs in his body from the start. But what he has not acquired, imitation helps him hunt down.

KINSMAN Whenever you write a satyr play, give me a call so that I can help you out from behind, with my hard-on. (*Thesmophoriazousae* 146–57)

Satyr plays were semicomic plays in which the chorus was represented as a group of satyrs, half-human, half-goat creatures who are often represented with enormous erections. Here the Kinsman's offer picks up on Agathon's language of imitation. The Kinsman, probably with aspersions cast on Agathon's manliness, offers to imitate a satyr for him, and in so doing, to penetrate him "from behind" to help Agathon write his next satyr play. The comment, like the one before, is a throwaway. But the very ease with which he throws it out is indicative; the Kinsman feels no sense of embarrassment about offering to penetrate Agathon.

If the Kinsman is a bit of a boor in the preceding scene, he is paid back later in the play. Toward the end of the drama, the Kinsman has been captured by the women, tied to a plank, and is under the watchful guard of a Scythian archer. As an attempt to escape, the Kinsman and Euripides begin playing parts from a play by Euripides (now lost) on the theme of Perseus and Andromeda. Euripides plays the bold hero Perseus, slayer of the Gorgon. The Kinsman, already dressed as a young woman in saffron robes, plays the part of Andromeda, chained to a rock as a sacrifice to a horrific sea monster. Although the characters' decision to reenact this play as a means of escape does not make much realistic sense, it makes a kind of metatheatrical sense. If the Kinsman and Euripides can convince their on-stage audience—the Scythian—that they are who they say they are, then "Perseus" can effect "Andromeda's" escape.

The guard, however, is having none of it. He is simply baffled when Euripides, in the guise of Perseus, claims to be madly in love with what is clearly an unattractive old man. Here is the critical scene:

EURIPIDES (AS PERSEUS) Oh, maiden, I pity you, seeing you hanging here.

SCYTHIAN That's not a maiden, but a deviant old man and a thief and a rascal.

EURIPIDES You're babbling, Scythian. She is Andromeda, daughter of Kepheos.

SCYTHIAN Look at her cunt. (*Ironically.*) Doesn't it look small?[8]

EURIPIDES	Come, give me your hand, so that I may touch it, girl. Come, Scythian. Emotions touch all men. And lust for this girl has seized even me.
SCYTHIAN	I don't envy you. But if his ass were turned around in this direction, I would not prevent you from leading him away and buggering him.
EURIPIDES	Why will you not allow me to set her free, Scythian, and fall into a marriage bed [with her]?
SCYTHIAN	If you want to screw the old man, drill a hole in the plank and bugger him from behind. (*Thesmophoriazousae* 1110–24)

This is as rude and crude as Aristophanes ever gets, and a good deal of the humor comes in this scene at the Scythian's expense as well as that of Euripides and the Kinsman. He is too dense to understand that they are putting on a play for him, so he keeps reacting to the literal situation, rather than to the dramatic one. Even so, Euripides' declaration of love for the Kinsman strikes him as odd, but not immoral. The Kinsman is, as he points out, old and no longer attractive. But the only thing preventing Euripides from enjoying sexual activity with the Kinsman, at least as the Scythian sees it, is that he is bound with his back to the board. That problem could be solved by turning him around or, even more crudely, simply drilling a hole in the plank.

Again, there is humor here in the contrasts: the old man is compared to a young and traditionally beautiful young maiden. A hero's desire to rescue this maiden is understood, instead, as a man's simple, if unusual, lust for an impersonal and demeaning sexual penetration. But if there is something disturbing about the Scythian's understanding of Euripides' desires, it is not that he sees those desires as unusual in the gender of his object; rather, it is the age and ugliness of Euripides' love object that strikes him as bizarre. Euripides might be said to have a sexual identity, of sorts, but there is no indication here of a sexual orientation or an inappropriate gender role (on his part). The Kinsman, on the other hand, is subject to a certain amount of humiliation because he has taken on a feminine role, and the natural assumption of the Scythian is that he is therefore in a position to be sexually penetrated.

PATHICS AND EFFEMINATES

As the preceding discussion makes clear, one common way to reproach men in Athenian comedy was to suggest that they were effeminate, especially if this characterization involved being penetrated anally. In the *Thesmophoriazousae*, both Agathon at the beginning of the play and Kleisthenes in the middle of it are mistaken for women, on first sight. As Agathon comes out of his house, the Kinsman says, "But, am I blind? For I don't see a man there at all; rather I see Kyrene" (*Thesmophoriazousae* 97–98). Kyrene is evidently the name of a well-known (female) prostitute. Similarly, as Kleisthenes is making his entrance, one of the women at the festival identifies him: "Indeed, here comes some woman, and she's hurrying. Before she gets here, be quiet, so that we can learn properly what she will say" (*Thesmophoriazousae* 571–73). In both instances, the joke that this man could be mistaken for a woman is meant to be funny.

Although both men lack a certain manliness, however, it is worth noting that there are subtle differences in their characterization. Agathon, as we have seen, defends his wearing of women's clothing as necessary to his art. Nonetheless, his indeterminate gender characteristics also appear to be linked to sexual passivity. In one of the funniest sequences in the play, Euripides tries to identify Agathon to the Kinsman before either sees him:

EURIPIDES	There is a certain Agathon—
KINSMAN	Do you mean the dark, muscular one?
EURIPIDES	No, another one. Have you never seen him?
KINSMAN	Not the one with the shaggy beard?
EURIPIDES	You haven't ever seen him.
KINSMAN	No, by Zeus, I haven't, at least not that I know of.
EURIPIDES	Yet you've screwed him; but perhaps you didn't know that. (*Thesmophoriazousae* 30–35)

The point is not just that Agathon has, apparently, been screwed by the Kinsman (and perhaps many others). The previous lines, in which the Kinsman asks about Agathon, contain the standard markers of masculinity. When the Kinsman asks, "You mean the dark one? The one with the heavy beard?" the audience is already laughing, because these are precisely the characteristics that the well-known public figure Agathon does not possess. His smooth cheeks, lack of musculature, and pale complexion all mark him as effeminate, and this is part and parcel with his sexual passivity.

Kleisthenes, on the other hand, is perhaps even more effeminate than Agathon. After all, he is mistaken for a woman, despite the fact that he is not dressed as one. More important, however, there is no indication in *this* play that he is sexually passive. In fact, if anything, he describes himself as too closely attached to women:

Women, friends, you who innately share my manners,
it is clear from my [smooth] cheeks that I am your friend.
I am crazy about women, and I act as your proxy always.
And now I've heard about an important bit of business affecting you,
gossiped about in the marketplace a little bit ago. (*Thesmophoriazousae* 574–78)

Here, what marks Kleisthenes as dangerously feminine is the fact that he spends so much time with women. He is, in essence, their ambassador in the world of men. His sex allows him to listen to what is being said in the agora (marketplace), but his alliances are with the women who are elsewhere. We might even say that here he is gender-deviant, more feminine than masculine, *because of* his affections for women.

All of this points to the conclusion that Aristophanes and his audience are more concerned with violations of the boundaries of *gender* than they are with transgressions of *sexuality*; that is, what is of primary significance is that Kleisthenes is effeminate. The possibility that he may also be pathic—an idea that is raised in one line of the *Lysistrata,* but never brought up in the *Thesmophoriazousae*—is a subsidiary concern to the larger anxiety about the blurring of gender roles.

This understanding of Athenian society is confirmed by the experience of the Kinsman in the *Thesmophoriazousae.* In the scene discussed earlier, in which he has been captured by the women and is going to be bound to a plank, the Kinsman has only one request to make of the Athenian official who has arrested him. Because he has been trying to infiltrate the women's festival, he is dressed as a woman. He asks, in particular, that he be allowed to shed this clothing:

KINSMAN   Officer, by your right hand, which you love to hold out so that someone
           can give you a bribe, please do me one small favor as I am about to die.
 OFFICER   What favor?
KINSMAN   Order that the guard undress me, leaving me nude, and bind me to this
           plank, so that I, an old man will not provide laughter in my saffron robes
           and headdress, as I feed the crows. (*Thesmophoriazousae* 936–42)

We might think that being exposed nude would be less comfortable than being exposed in women's clothes. And in fact, the Kinsman's speech recalls a passage in Homer's *Iliad,* in which the old father of Priam expresses his fear of the fact that when he dies, his nude body, and especially his genitals, will be exposed to dogs (*Iliad* 22.65–76). But however shameful this eventuality may be, nudity is still an acceptable costume of masculinity. It is worth remembering that Olympic athletes competed in the nude and that Greek heroes are often depicted in art either nude or with cloak hanging open and genitals exposed. Faced with a choice between exposing his nude body to the birds or being dressed in a saffron cloak like a marriageable young girl, the Kinsman has no hesitation about which he should prefer. Femininity, even in the form of a dress that everyone in the theater saw him put on as a disguise, is the ultimate disgrace. The point about Kleisthenes, then, is not that he is seen as sexually passive, although that is a possibility. Rather, the fact that he can be mistaken for a woman is an indication that he is not sufficiently masculine, and this is the primary mode of criticism against him.

At the end of the play, order is restored by restoring proper gender distinctions. The Scythian guard, having been bamboozled by Euripides and the women (with whom Euripides has reached an accord) goes offstage with a young prostitute. The Kinsman escapes and is sent home to his wife and children. This restoration of the correct order of things is, more than anything, a return to carefully defined limits for men and women and the idea, however illusory, that the lines between masculine and feminine are never crossed. Euripides promises not to portray women badly in the future, and as a result normal Athenians—here represented by the Kinsmen—are rendered safe in their role as active, securely masculine men.

CLASS-BASED SEXUAL CRITICISM?

It has sometimes been asserted that only the upper classes in Aristophanes' plays are proponents of pederasty and that the lower- and middle-class characters in his plays ridicule the aristocratic elite for their practice of same-sex desire.[9] While it is true that politicians, orators, tragedians, and Sophists all come in for such criticism, some important distinctions should be made. First, the vast majority of such criticism is directed at the passive partner in any sexual situation. Violation of the proper gender role always leaves a character open to an attack of softness, lack of self-control, and passivity. If the lower classes in Athens regarded same-sex eroticism itself as wrong, it is curious that in comedy, they reserve their insults for only one of the partners in the vast majority of cases.

Even more important, however, is the fact that the passages from the *Thesmophoriazousae* discussed previously demonstrate that lower-class characters do not see anything inherently wrong with the desire to penetrate other men. The Kinsman, though related to Euripides, is not marked in the play in any way as aristocratic. His language, in contrast to most of the other characters on stage, is fairly crude. He uses far more obscenities than anyone else in the play. Yet he is perfectly happy to suggest that he would enjoy penetrating Agathon. Even more telling is the Scythian bowman. He is not even an Athenian citizen and can in no way be assimilated to the aristocratic elite. Yet his response to Euripides' professed desire for the Kinsman (dressed as Andromeda) is to suggest that Euripides is a bit odd to be attracted to an old man. He finds nothing questionable about the nature of Euripides' desire for a man in general.

What is subject to attack on the part of the upper classes is the suggestion that they may be a little soft and therefore objects of desire for other men beyond the age when this would have been appropriate. Agathon certainly falls into this category, as do the "wide-assed" Athenians who are recognized by Stronger Argument in the *Clouds*. But again, this is not an indictment of their homosexuality, but of their femininity and associated passivity.

Finally, the plays do sometimes criticize the upper classes for trying to dress up their sexual escapades as somehow more noble than those of the lower classes. A telling passage from Aristophanes' *Wealth* gives the sharpest example of this. Two characters, Chremylus and his slave Karion, are discussing the behavior of prostitutes, and they make a pointed comparison to aristocratic boys. Chremylus, I should point out, is described early in the play as poor; his wife's name is even *Penia*, which literally means "poverty":

CHREMYLOS	They say that Corinthian prostitutes, when a poor man makes a try for them, they pay him no notice. But when a rich man tries, they turn their ass towards him right away.
KARION	And they say that boys do this very same thing, not out of desire, but for the sake of money.

CHREMYLOS   Surely not the noble boys, but the sluts; for the noble boys do not ask for money.
KARION   What do they ask for, then?
CHREMYLOS   One asks for a noble horse, another for hunting dogs.
KARION   Perhaps because they are ashamed to ask for money they cover up their wickedness with another word. (*Wealth* 149–59)

Again, the point of this passage is not that only the upper classes indulge in pederastic relationships; rather, as Karion makes clear, both upper-class boys and boys who are professional prostitutes are doing the same thing. The only difference is in the manner of their payment. Both boys are engaging in behavior that is moderately shameful since they are allowing themselves to be penetrated; but while the boy who is a "slut" (*pornos*) affects no airs about the commercial nature of the transactions, the wellborn boys are pretending that their behavior is somehow different.

The upper classes, then, can be the target of sexual barbs in Aristophanes. But they are not singled out as participating in a kind of sex that normal Athenians eschew; rather, they are criticized for pretending that their affairs are for the purpose of education, or are somehow different from common prostitution because they are paid in horses, rather than money. The elites are not marked by their sexual practice, but by their elitism.

CONCLUSIONS

Aristophanes presents us with a dazzling array of sexual types: normal men (who are often randy), women whose sexual desires are only exceptionally held in check, effeminate men, and men who are willing to be penetrated in sex. Any of these types can be the target of a sexual joke, even the normal men. But we see no evidence in Aristophanes of a particularly marked sexual orientation on the part of any of these characters. Some, like Agathon, might be considered to have a sexual morphology since his alleged passivity is accompanied by a particularly odd form of dress and manner of speech. But even Agathon is held up not so much as a type as a distinct aberration: his sexual and social oddity is a product of being a tragic playwright more than anything else.

Far and above, however, the most common sexual joke in Aristophanes is to suggest gender inversion on the part of a man, that is, to suggest that he is effeminate and willing to be penetrated. These jokes are leveled, usually, at two kinds of characters: men who are notorious in Athenian society for their effeminate mode of speech and dress, like Kleisthenes, and members of the aristocratic elite. This latter group is not singled out, however, as having a monopoly on homoerotic sex or even passivity; rather, the joke that men who were rich and powerful today were penetrated boy toys in their past is a common and effective way of deflating their elitist status. Aristophanes' aristocrats are not gay, nor even necessarily pathic. But their softness, their love of luxury, and their undemocratic attitudes make them prime targets for accusations of being overly effeminate.

Five

Legal and Illegal Sex in Ancient Greece

ATHENIAN LAW AND THE COURTS

The Athenian legal system was significantly different from our own. To begin, juries were much larger: for private suits, a minimum of 201 jurors sat in attendance; for public suits, a minimum of 501 jurors attended, with more important cases having as many as 1,501 jurors. These jurors were selected by lot, initially unpaid, and had to be full citizens over the age of 30. (At some point in the fifth century, the state began paying jurors a nominal daily wage.) A majority vote was required to convict, and a person who brought a public suit and failed to get at least one-fifth of the vote was subject to a substantial fine.

Perhaps most important of all, though, was the fact that there were no public prosecutors, even for crimes that were considered harmful to the general public; rather, any Athenian citizen man who had not lost his citizenship rights (*timia*) could bring either a public or a private suit. Trials took only one day, and both prosecutor and defendant had only a few hours to present their cases. The men involved in the case could write their own speeches or could hire a professional orator, such as Lysias or Demosthenes, to write a speech for them. Jurors did not formally deliberate before voting and were not prevented from indicating their approval or disapproval during the course of testimony.

Courtroom trials, then, were something of a public spectacle. We must imagine professional orators playing quite skillfully to the crowd, perhaps to loud cheers and jeers, and indeed, the texts of the speeches that we have are often highly entertaining. It is also important to realize, however, that although the courts were overseen by an administrator, there was no judge running a trial, and there were no rules of evidence like those that govern modern court cases. A prosecutor could bring in whatever evidence he thought would be effective in persuading the jury and could, moreover, engage in some rhetorical exaggeration when describing Athenian laws.

This last element is particularly important for modern scholars because we do not have a systematic record of Greek law in the way that we do for

Roman law. Modern scholars have painstakingly reconstructed the content of Greek law by carefully reading legal speeches and culling the laws that are referred to in the context of those speeches. Even here, there is considerable uncertainty; it is generally agreed, for example, that orators tended to ascribe laws to Solon, an important lawgiver from the sixth century BCE, even if the laws were passed after his time. It is not always easy, then, to know exactly when a certain law went into effect, or even what its specific provisions were.

Finally, it is important to realize that certain kinds of cases were particularly the domain of an aristocratic elite, whose lives were under constant public scrutiny. One law in particular is important for the study of ancient sexuality, and that is the law brought forward in an "indictment of prostitution" (*graphe hetairesis*). This law did not make being a prostitute illegal, but rather stated that men who engaged in prostitution lost key citizenship rights, among them the right to speak in the assembly, to propose legislation, or to bring criminal charges against other citizens. In a speech by Demosthenes against a man named Androtion, the speaker argues that Solon intended this law to have a relatively limited effect:

For he saw this, that although many of you are able to speak [in the assembly] but do not, so that he thought this was not at all heavy; and he could have instituted many harsher measures, if he wanted to punish these offenders [i.e., prostitutes]. But he was not concerned with this, but he forbid these things for your sake and for the sake of the state. (Demosthenes *Against Androtion* 30–31)

Whether that was, in fact, Solon's intent or not is somewhat beside the point. But Demosthenes' speech makes it clear that a certain class of men—the rich and powerful who were accustomed to speak in the assembly—had to deport themselves with more care than ordinary Athenians. If a man had no intention of being involved in the high-stakes games of the assembly and the courts, then he need not fear careful scrutiny of his sexual life. Men like Demosthenes, Aeschines, and Lysias, however, were under something of a social microscope and had to be prepared for public attack in the form of legal suits.

A FIGHT OVER A BEAUTIFUL BOY: LYSIAS *AGAINST SIMON*

Early in the fourth century BCE, a man named Simon brought a charge of attempted murder against a man (his name is not known) who hired the celebrated orator Lysias to defend him. Lysias's defense speech is packed with surprising and salacious details. It appears that Simon and the defendant were both infatuated with a young man, probably a citizen, named Theodotus. In the event, it appears that the defendant was more successful in obtaining Theodotus's affections; in his account, however, this did not deter Simon, who on at least two occasions resorted to violence in an attempt to

win Theodotus back. Here is the description of one such event, as described
by the defendant:

We were both enamored, members of the Council, with Theodotus, a boy from Plataea. I thought to make him my friend by means of treating him well, while he [Simon]
thought to force him to do what he wished by treating him outrageously and contrary
to the law . . .

Having learned that the boy was at my house, he [Simon] came to my house at
night, drunk. Breaking down the doors, he went into the women's quarters, in which
were my sister and nieces, who lived in such an orderly way that they were ashamed
to be seen even by their family members . . .

He called me out of doors, and the moment I came out, he tried to hit me. When I
defended myself against him, he stood away from me and began throwing stones at
me. He missed me, but Aristokritos, who came with him to my house, he struck with
a stone and bruised his forehead. (Lysias *Against Simon* 5–8)

This story contains a number of fascinating elements. In reading it, we
must remember that the speaker is hardly an unbiased reporter; rather, he
has been charged with a serious crime, and it is in his best interest to make
Simon look as bad as possible. Nonetheless, by looking at the ways in which
he constructs his arguments, we can gain a good understanding of what the
Athenian jury would have considered normal behavior and what would have
constituted a serious breach of laws and social conventions.

First, there appears to be no particular disgrace associated with the fact
that both of these adult men have fallen in love with a boy. (The Greek word
used for the boy, *meirakion,* is regularly used to denote objects of erotic attention; we might translate it as "boy toy.") Though the speaker does admit
in a later part of the speech that he was not keen to advertise his affair with
the boy, this reticence does not appear to stem from the fact that it is a *boy* he
is interested in. And Simon, whom the speaker is keen to depict as entirely
brazen, clearly has no compunctions about causing a public brawl to take
the boy back—physically, if necessary.

Simon's behavior is marked as outrageous on several counts. The first is
the way in which he courts the boy. While the speaker claims that he tried
to win the boy over with acts of friendship, Simon is accused of "outrage"
(*hybris*) against the boy. This is a significant legal term: to commit *hybris*
against another is to violate his physical person, against his will. In sexual
contexts, *hybris* generally means something like our modern term *rape*. So
while the speaker is trying to seduce the boy according to the acceptable
rules of gentlemanly behavior, Simon (he claims), by trying to force the boy
to do what he wants, is guilty of a serious crime.

Next, the fact that Simon breaks into the speaker's house, and the fact that
he goes into the women's quarters is particularly shocking. In the Athenian
ideal, the women of respectable families were protected from the public by
their houses and family members. They did not go out in public without a
guardian, and their quarters in the household were protected and free from
male intrusion. In this speech, the speaker claims a particularly stringent
adherence to this rule: his female relatives are embarrassed to be seen even

by (male) family members. Simon's intrusion into their private space, then, is paramount to a sexual violation.

Finally, there is the attack on the speaker's person. Simon's attempt to strike him would again be subject to a charge of *hybris,* as a violation of the speaker's body. The fact that he then stepped back and began throwing stones indicates, perhaps, a bit of cowardice on Simon's part. A real man might have continued to fight hand-to-hand. Here, however, the story begins to lose a bit of credibility. How it was that Simon hit his own comrade, Aristokritos, rather than the speaker, and in the forehead, no less, is a matter that the speech leaves unexplained.

The speech also leaves somewhat open the question of the status of the boy, Theodotus. The fact that he is specified as from the deme of Plataea suggests strongly that he was an Athenian citizen. It also appears that he may have been a prostitute, though this is somewhat less clear. In a later passage in the speech (*Against Simon* 22), the speaker says that Simon had, at one point, paid Theodotus 300 drachmas (a considerable sum of money), "having made an agreement with him." The terms of this agreement are, of course, not spelled out. But if such an agreement had been willingly entered into by the boy, then he could be accused of having been a prostitute and therefore stripped of certain citizenship rights. The speaker, however, will later claim that no such agreement was ever arranged:

For, Council members, all this has been made up and devised by him; he says that he gave the money, so that he would not seem to behave badly, if he dared to commit *hybris* against the boy with no such agreement having been struck. (*Against Simon* 26)

Though we will never know for sure if Theodotus was a highly paid call boy, this passage gives us one of the clearest explanations of the law against *hybris* as it relates to sexual matters. Simon, it appears, has done things to Theodotus which, in some circumstances, would constitute *hybris.* The only way that they would not constitute *hybris,* the speaker intimates, is if Theodotus agreed to them, that is, if he had prostituted himself. In that case, he could not bring a charge of *hybris* because he would have already, and willingly, given up the protection against *hybris* that was afforded to every citizen. *Hybris* is only *hybris* if it is done against the recipient's will.

Was there any shame associated with frequenting a boy prostitute? The speaker takes pains to indicate that Simon is a thoroughly reckless person, so in any case, he would not feel such shame. The speaker, however, admits to some embarrassment over his own love affair with Theodotus. In this admission, he again seeks to draw a distinction between himself and Simon:

I am especially irritated, Council, because I will be forced to speak to you about these matters. I was ashamed of the idea that many people would know about them, and so, although wronged, I held off [i.e., from taking legal action]. . . . I am worthy, Council, if I have done wrong, to meet with no sympathy. But if I show that I am not guilty of the things about which Simon has taken an oath, even if it appears to you that my attitude toward this boy was a bit senseless for a man of my age, I ask that you not think me the worse for that. For you know that all men experience desire, but that he is best and most temperate who is able to bear misfortunes in the most orderly way. (*Against Simon* 3–4)

What exactly is the speaker ashamed of? Not, evidently, the fact that he has fallen in love with a boy, rather than a woman. In section 5 (quoted previously), the speaker makes no bones about this attraction; rather, it appears that he feels a bit foolish. He recognizes that for a respectable man of his stature to fall head-over-heels in love with a youth is not entirely appropriate. Similar to a modern unmarried man who has an affair with a woman half his age, his behavior is personally questionable, but not inherently immoral. He would rather not talk about it in public. A mild social reprimand is at stake here, not denunciation for unacceptable behavior or, still worse, any sort of legal action.

The form of this social reprimand is made clearer in a later section of the speech:

I thought, Council, that I was suffering badly; but I was ashamed, as I told you before, of this misfortune, and I held off. I preferred not to receive justice for these wrongs rather than to seem foolish to the citizens, since I knew that these deeds would be considered appropriate for this man's [Simon's] disgraceful nature, but that many would laugh at me for suffering such things. Many people are accustomed to be jealous, if anyone desires to be useful to the city. (*Against Simon* 9)

Again, the real problem is that the speaker is not only a responsible adult, but someone who takes an active role in the governance of Athens. This puts him, necessarily, in the public eye. Were he merely a private citizen, or, like Simon, a known reprobate, there would be no need for him to be concerned. But as a public figure, he is subject to the kind of reprimands that are reserved for those politicians who do not exhibit sufficient self-control and respectable behavior. Indeed, in the last clause, the speaker suggests that he does not even deserve such reprimand and that, on the contrary, the criticism he will receive will come from those people who feel envy toward the city's benefactors.

From this discussion, several points can be established. First, it appears that there were male prostitutes in Athens, even if Theodotus may not have been one. To be a prostitute was not illegal, though as we will see, it did involve the voluntary renunciation of certain rights as a citizen. Moreover, the competition for particularly beautiful boy prostitutes could evidently be intense. And though a gentleman might be a bit embarrassed to admit that he was infatuated with such a prostitute, it was not a crime to have sex with one. It could be a matter of considerable public embarrassment to have to admit to being infatuated—particularly for an older man, and one involved in public life—but even this was not, in itself, legally or socially out-of-bounds.

LEGAL RESTRICTIONS: AESCHINES
AGAINST TIMARCHOS

A different set of circumstances surrounds the most famous legal speech from Athens regarding a same-sex liaison. In the mid-fourth century, a well-known orator named Aeschines brought a suit against Timarchos. The charge was a *graphe hetairesis*, that is, an "accusation of being a prostitute." This might lead us to think that prostitution was illegal in Athens, as it is in most of the United States; but in fact, this is not the case. Prostitution was not only legal, as various passages from this speech demonstrate, but it was state-sanctioned. There was even a regularly collected prostitution tax. What, then, is the point of a *graphe hetairesis*? A citizen who was convicted of having been a prostitute suffered the punishment of *atimia*, literally, "loss of honor." In practical terms, this meant that he could no longer engage in the activities that were, in theory, the privilege of all adult male citizens: he could not propose laws in the assembly, he could not serve as an embassy for the state, and perhaps most important, he could not bring charges against another citizen in a court of law.[1]

Aeschines was engaged at this time in a series of legal disputes with another great Athenian orator, Demosthenes. Timarchos sided with Demosthenes in this conflict, and it appears that when Aeschines brought his suit against Timarchos, it was a politically calculated move. Timarchos was planning to bring a suit against Aeschines for corruption while in political office. By successfully arguing that Timarchos had engaged in prostitution, then, Aeschines effectively made it illegal for Timarchos to bring this charge against him and thereby headed off an embarrassing and potentially damaging trial. This linking of sex and politics, hardly foreign in modern political campaigns, was far from coincidental.

Among other things, Aeschines' speech against Timarchos provides us with considerable information about the presence of prostitution in Athens and social attitudes toward it. We learn, for example, that Athens had a specific tax levied on prostitutes (*Against Timarchos* 119). We also learn that it was possible for prostitutes to have written contracts that could, evidently, be called on as evidence in a court of law (*Against Timarchos* 160). Perhaps most important of all, however, is the simple fact that men were prostitutes (serving male clients) and that the presence of brothels in public was well known. At one point, to make the argument that everyone understood what sort of thing Timarchos had been up to, Aeschines describes a hypothetical street scene:

Consider the situation from examples. Of course, the examples must be very similar to the behavior of Timarchos. You see these men sitting on their doorsteps, the ones who openly practice the profession. These, however, whenever they engage in this . . . necessity, nevertheless because of shame they throw a cover over themselves, and they shut the doors. If, of course, some one should ask you, as you go along the street, what at that moment the man is doing, immediately you would say the name of the deed, even without seeing it, nor knowing who it was that went in; but knowing the chosen profession of the man, you also know his deed. (*Against Timarchos* 74)

Aeschines is careful in this speech not to name sexual acts explicitly; earlier on, he begged the court's indulgence for doing so, lest he be thought as coarse in his speech, as he says Timarchos has been in action (*Against*

Timarchos 37–38). Nonetheless, he is quite circumspect in his language, here as elsewhere.

Even so, the point that Aeschines makes is that everyone knows what goes on in these kinds of houses. Furthermore, although the man who engages in prostitution is assumed to be at least somewhat ashamed of his deeds, there is no suggestion here that the client would feel a similar shame. Elsewhere, Aeschines argues that free men must be careful not to corrupt citizen youths, but here it is only the one who has sold his body to another for sexual use who must cover his actions.

One of the central problems that Aeschines faces in this speech, however, is that however disreputable Timarchos may have been, he was not clearly and legally identified as a prostitute; that is, there are no signed contracts to bring into court, nor has he ever paid a prostitution tax. Aeschines must therefore argue away the necessity for such supporting documents and rely instead on the power of rumor and public reputation to make his case. In essence, much of Aeschines' argument consists of statements to the effect that the audience all knows what kind of person Timarchos is; and if he is that kind of person, then they must regard him as having prostituted himself. Public opinion functions as a kind of evidence in making this argument. A bit later in the speech, Aeschines cites common report almost as if it were a material witness:

Call to mind, men of the jury, what rumor you have heard about Timarchos. Is it not the case that when his name is spoken you ask the question, "Which Timarchos? The slut?" (*Against Timarchos* 130)

Simply put, if everyone thinks he is a prostitute, he must be one.

Why does Timarchos have the reputation of being a prostitute? It is possible, of course, that his sexual behavior has taken place in public and is well known. But more important, the kind of person who is a prostitute is presumed to exhibit other types of unacceptable behavior. This common assumption allows Aeschines to make a further argument (based entirely on rumor and public perception) about Timarchos's status:

What would you say, Timarchos, concerning another person on trial for this same charge? Rather, what must one say, whenever a young boy toy leaves his father's house and spends the night in other people's houses, a man distinguished from others by his looks, and dines on costly dinners for free, and keeps the very most expensive flute girls and courtesans, and gambles, risks nothing himself, but another man puts down stakes for him? Do we need a prophet to explain this? Is it not clear enough that a person making such arrangements must, in return, provide some pleasures to those who are paying the money up front? (*Against Timarchos* 75–76)

In essence, the passage just quoted makes one thing quite clear: Aeschines does not have any solid evidence that Timarchos was a prostitute; rather, he must argue from analogy that Timarchos has behaved *like* a prostitute. The modern reader will, I hope, have noticed that the behavior that makes Timarchos susceptible to such an argument includes some information that we might not immediately link to (male) prostitution, especially the idea that the hypothetical person described here "keeps . . . expensive flute-girls and courtesans." Timarchos, here, is accused of sleeping with men for pay to keep up his heteroerotic flute girl habit. We might find this counterintuitive, but for an Athenian, it was not so at all. The idea is that a person like Timarchos lacks all self-control, and his dissipation exhibits itself in multiple outlets: prostituting himself, excessive sexual pleasure with women, gambling with money not his own, and so on.

Clearly part of what makes prostitution so problematic is the fact that the (male) prostitute is willingly taking the part of the penetrated partner in sex, beyond an age when such a role is appropriate. Again, this does not mean that homosexuality, or even passivity, was illegal in Athens; but it was a matter of public disgrace. This aspect comes to light in another anecdote, in which the ostensible point is that Timarchos and his lover Hegesandros had previously tried to defraud the city. Aeschines claims that at the time, a man named Pamphilos spoke against them:

"Athenian men, a man and a woman together are stealing a thousand drachmas from you." When you were astonished and asked how "a man and a woman," and what this meant, he waited a bit and said, "Do you not understand what I mean? The man is that Hegesandros there, who before was Leodamas's woman. But the woman is this Timarchos." (*Against Timarchos* 110–11)

Timarchos's relation to Hegesandros is not gender-appropriate: he is playing the part of a woman. To make it worse, he is passive with a man who himself was passive earlier, pushing him even further down the hierarchy of proper manliness. Later in the speech, Aeschines refers to Timarchos as "this man with a man's body, but who has sinned womanly sins" (*Against Timarchos* 185). None of that is illegal, but it adds to the sense of shame that is heaped on Timarchos for having prostituted himself.

Another paragraph in Aeschines' speech brings up a curious point about Timarchos's relationship with a man named Misgolas. Misgolas, the speaker warns, is one of those people who looks considerably younger than he is. The jury should not, on seeing him, be fooled into thinking that Misgolas and Timarchos are roughly of the same age:

For he [Misgolas] happens to be the same age as I am; we were *ephebes* (young men on the verge of manhood) together, and he is forty-five years old. And I have as many gray hairs as you see, but he does not, because of which I say the following: so that when you see him suddenly, you are not amazed and do not think in the following way: "By Herakles, this guy is not much older than the other one." (*Against Timarchos* 49)

Why this concern? What would it matter if one of Timarchos's lovers were his age-mate? Although the text does not say so explicitly, I believe that the issue is that age-mates, especially when still young and beautiful, like Timarchos evidently is, might have been expected to engage in some sexual activity with each other. Such activity would not have been thought of as a pederastic relationship, but neither would it have been considered prostituting oneself. For Misgolas's relationship with Timarchos to count as evidence that Timarchos

Courtship scene. Young men and boys in various stages of amorous activity. None of the youths pictured here has the beard of a full adult man. Each couple, however, consists of an older, taller youth and a younger boy. Bildarchiv Preussischer Kulturbesitz, Antikensammlung, Staatliche Museen zu Berlin, Berlin, Germany/Art Resource, NY.

is a prostitute, Misgolas has to be significantly older than Timarchos as well as being one of a series of such lovers.[2]

One might still ask why, exactly, being a prostitute should exclude one from legal participation in the life of the city. In this speech, there is a good deal of rhetoric about the moral unfitness to lead the city of those who have led dissolute lives. The speaker identifies four classes of men whom the law prohibits from speaking in the assembly: those who beat their father or mother, or do not support them; those who fail in their military duty; those who have prostituted themselves; or those who have squandered their patrimony. Again, it is reasonable to see a consistent pattern of thought here. Those men who violate these basic duties of a citizen are considered too uncontrolled, too undisciplined to administer the government. As Aeschines argues (about those who squander their inheritance),

For he [the author of the law] thought that a man who managed his own household badly, likewise would mismanage the common affairs of the city; and he did not think that the same person was able to be shameful in his private affairs, but useful in public life. (*Against Timarchos* 30)

Timarchos, it should be noted, is accused of also having spent away his inheritance (*Against Timarchos* 96); he is profligate both with sex and with his private property, if we are to believe the speaker.

All of this points to a mode of thinking by analogy that pervades Athenian politics. If a man cannot control his own desires, then the assumption is that he cannot control his household; if he cannot control his household, he should not be allowed to take part in controlling the state. The sexual quickly becomes political. This mode of thinking is seen most baldly toward the end of the speech, when Aeschines argues again that Timarchos must not be allowed to execute state offices:

And shall we send out as an ambassador of the city this man who has lived shamefully at home, and trust this man with the most important matters? What would he not give away, this man who has sold the right to abuse his body? Whom would he pity, who has not pitied himself? (*Against Timarchos* 188)

If he would sell his body, he would sell the state's interest. Clearly there is no trusting such a man.

PROSTITUTES AND BEAUTIFUL BOYS: AESCHINES
AGAINST TIMARCHOS, AGAIN

As I have argued already, Athenians did not always think it particularly shameful for a citizen boy to give himself to an older man under the right circumstances. When a boy did so, he could expect to receive gifts in return for the sexual favors that he granted. Such was the system of pederasty, idealized by Plato, made fun of by Aristophanes, and generally accepted by the Athenian citizenry. This raises interesting questions about Timarchos's case; if the evidence against him amounts to the fact that he has had lovers, and that the citizenry gossips about him as being a prostitute, what is to distinguish him from the respectable young men of Athens who took lovers in exchange for gifts? At what point does being a popular boy cross the line and become prostitution?

There is no easy answer for this, although Aeschines works hard to establish a clear demarcation. At one point, he gives a three-point definition of a prostitute: "For a person who does this recklessly, and with many men, and for pay—this one seems to me to be liable to this exact charge" (*Against Timarchos* 52). But as in modern life, this line is never quite as clear as the legal system implies. In fact, Aeschines anticipates his opposition and realizes that Timarchos and Demosthenes will bring up his own love affairs with various boys against him. He attempts, therefore, to respond to this line of attack in advance:

And here, as I have heard, he intends to make a certain attack against me, asking if I am not ashamed—I who have been a nuisance in the gymnasia, and who have been the lover *[erastes]* of many—to bring this practice into reproach and danger. And finally, as some people have warned me, in order to make some of you laugh and engage in gossip, he will exhibit all the love poems I have ever written to anyone. Moreover, he will provide witnesses to all the quarrels and brawls I have been involved in as a result of this practice. (*Against Timarchos* 135)

As a legal point, Aeschines is quite correct here. He has done nothing illegal, and this strategy of Timarchos (if indeed it is his strategy) is one of blurring distinctions. Engaging in pederasty is not the same thing as being a prostitute.

Nonetheless, the fact is that Aeschines must argue against this line of attack at great length. He goes on from this point to quote Homer, Euripides, and a number of other poets who wrote about noble loves between two men (including, e.g., Achilles and Patroklos); he cites the example of Harmodios and Aristogeiton, two lovers who were credited with overthrowing the tyranny of Hipparchos in 514; he even goes so far as to name living Athenian citizen youths who "because of their good looks have had many lovers" (*Against Timarchos* 155) but who, because they behaved appropriately, have not fallen prey to the bad repute that has dogged Timarchos. He then lists several young men who, he says, have ruined their own reputations by their bad behavior (*Against Timarchos* 141–59).

All of this goes, as Aeschines says, to prove that there is a difference between those boys who have sex with men in the right way and those, like Timarchos, who are prostitutes. The fact that he must make this argument at such length, however, is a strong indication that knowing which class a particular boy might belong to at any particular time is not necessarily easily determined. Indeed, the fact that Aeschines has written potentially embarrassing love letters and been involved in "disputes and brawls" over his love affairs with boys demonstrates how pervasive the practice was. What distinguishes this practice from that of Timarchos, moreover, is not any clear legal distinction, but a matter of the intention and the ethical behavior with which the love affair was carried out.

It must have been, then, a difficult thing to be a beautiful boy from a noble family, especially if one had designs on taking an active role in the city once an adult. And indeed, this speech provides us with good evidence that considerable care and legal weight was brought to bear to prevent young men from being corrupted before they were of an age to make responsible judgments themselves. Strict laws protected boys from being hired out by their fathers, brothers, or guardians as prostitutes and, at least as Aeschines summarizes the law, "it does not allow the charge to be against the boy himself, but against the one hiring him out, and the one hiring him, the one because he hired him out, and the other, they say, because he hired" (*Against Timarchos* 13). This may seem odd in a state where prostitution even by citizens was legal, but at stake here is not the morality of a particular sex act, but the future of a freeborn Athenian boy. If, at an older age, he prostitutes himself, there is no charge to be brought; but before that time, his future must be diligently protected by those who hold guardianship over him.

Indeed, the protection of boys from improper sexual advances comes up indirectly in another part of the speech. In the course of establishing Timarchos's shameful past, Aeschines says that at one point, he was supposed to go to the festival of the City Dionysia with Misgolas and another Athenian, named Phaedrus. When he did not show up on time, the two men went looking for him. They found him having lunch with a couple of foreigners, or *xenoi*. Misgolas and Phaedrus, we are told, were angry, and evidently, they did not want to share Timarchos with these foreigners:

They threatened the foreigners and ordered them to follow them immediately to prison [i.e., they put them under arrest], because they [the foreigners] had corrupted a free boy; and the foreigners were afraid, and fled, leaving behind all their belongings. (*Against Timarchos* 43)

Aeschines is not, of course, arguing that these foreign men had corrupted Timarchos; indeed, the point is that he was already thoroughly corrupt by the time he met them. But the fact that Misgolas and Phaedrus could threaten the men with having corrupted Timarchos, and that the men took the charge seriously enough to leave in a hurry, rather than face arrest and trial, indicates that the sexual use of a citizen youth could result in serious legal charges.

This concern certainly underlies the end of the speech. Aeschines suggests that the three kinds of people who will side with Timarchos are those who have wasted their own inheritances, those who have prostituted themselves, and those who would make use of such young men. As for this last group of men, Aeschines suggests that the Athenians should "order them to turn to foreigners and resident aliens, so that they would not be deprived of their sexual preference, nor would you be harmed" (*Against Timarchos* 195). In other words, it is fine with Aeschines if they corrupt the youth—just not the citizen youth.

FEMALE PROSTITUTES: PSEUDO-DEMOSTHENES
AGAINST NEAIRA

It is striking how different the concerns are in another legal speech from the mid-fourth century BCE. The speech *Against Neaira,* which comes to us attributed to Demosthenes—the same Demosthenes mentioned in the preceding sections—but is now generally thought to be by another, unknown contemporary orator. Much of the speech consists of a discussion of the life of Neaira, who seems to have been a highly paid and popular prostitute. Here, however, whether or not Neaira is a prostitute is not in itself the principal legal question; rather, the prosecution (a man named Apollodorus) contends that Neaira is not a citizen but has been living with an Athenian man (Stephanus) as if she were.[3]

As always, it is important to understand the precise legal point. Upperclass Athenian men evidently kept concubines; such behavior only became an issue when the men tried to pass such women off as their wives. Since 451–450 BCE, under a law introduced to the assembly by the general Pericles, only people born of two citizens could be citizens in Athens. The citizenship of one's father could generally be established (or disproven) more easily than the citizenship of one's mother since there were a number of public rituals at which a man's citizenship was affirmed. But women occupied a somewhat les well defined position, and proving that a woman was, or was not, Athenian was not always easy. If a man tried to claim that his non-Athenian concubine was his legal Athenian wife, then what was at stake was her citizenship and the citizenship of any of their offspring.

This is exactly the issue in the case of Neaira. The speech gives us a brief version of her life: she was raised as a slave, eventually (with the help of her lovers) contrived to purchase her own freedom, and moved to Athens. Once there, she continued to live as a courtesan, engaging in highly questionable activities such as dining openly with men. At one point, it appears, Stephanus and a man named Phrynion came to an agreement to share her; Neaira was to live with them on alternate days (*Against Neaira* 46). Though there are a few comments about "this kind of woman" and quite frank discussions of her affairs with various men, the real problem is not her moral character, but the fact that she is not an Athenian, and Stephanus has been pretending that she is. Once more, it does not appear that it was illegal for Athenian women to be prostitutes. But, similar to the situation for men, such women gave up their rights as citizen women to participate in various religious ceremonies (see *Against Neaira* 85–87). Even more important, such women could not be regarded as legally married, in the sense that their relationships were not protected by laws against adultery. Adultery with a married woman was, in Athens, a serious crime. In fact, if an adulterer was caught in the act, the husband had the right, if he acted immediately and without forethought, to kill the adulterer.[4]

Whether the husband killed the adulterer on the spot, or brought him to court, however, the Athenian laws on adultery deal rather differently than do modern laws when it came to the wife. A husband who knew that his wife had committed adultery was required by law to divorce her. Failure to do so amounted to an admission that she was not his wife, but a prostitute, and that the husband was running a brothel. Indeed, there seems to have been some market for prostitutes who could pass as legitimate wives. Apollodorus claims that after Stephanus had set Neaira up in his household,

. . . she continued to practice the same work no less than before, but she charged higher fees from those wishing to consort with her, since she had now a certain respectability and was married to a husband. (*Against Neaira* 41)

It appears that some Athenian men's sexual tastes included an enjoyment of partners who could pretend, at least, to be out-of-bounds.

Such pretence was clearly illegal, however, and the law went to some length to distinguish such women from legitimate wives. In fact, it appears that exactly this situation came up during the life of Neaira. At one point, a man named Epaenetus, allegedly a former client of Neaira, was charged by Stephanus of adultery with Neaira's daughter. Apollodorus suggests that Stephanus brought this charge with a view to extort money from him. Epaenetus brought countercharges against Stephanus and, in his defense, argued that Stephanus's household was not a home, but a brothel:

In addition he brought forward the law that does not allow [a man] to seize a man as an adulterer with such women, that is with women who sit in a brothel or who sell themselves openly. He said that Stephanus' household is just this, a brothel, and that they [i.e., Stephanus and Neaira] prosper especially from this business. (*Against Neaira* 67–68)

The point of Apollodorus's prosecution, then, is that Neaira cannot be a legally married Athenian wife. She is not from Athens (as he establishes early on); she was originally a slave; and she seems to have had sex with quite a few men, even after she set up house with Stephanus. Such a woman clearly cannot be a citizen, and even if she were a citizen, she is not legally married.

The threat that Neaira poses, interestingly, is not primarily one of morality. Though Apollodorus is indignant that Neaira's daughter, Phano, has taken part in religious observations that she should not, he does not speak out against the practice of prostitution itself, as does Aeschines in *Against Timarchos*. Perhaps if Neaira really were an Athenian, and Stephanus really were allowing his legally married wife to behave as a prostitute, the speaker would work up a bit more high rhetoric about the immorality of the situation. But as it is, what is clearly at issue is the threat that Neaira poses to the integrity of Athenian citizenship. This is particularly true because Stephanus has been claiming that Neaira's children are his own.

The legal concern over this behavior comes to its sharpest point in the discussion of Neaira's daughter Phano. Stephanus gave this young woman away in marriage to a man named Phrastor, who, according to Apollodorus, thought that he was marrying a legitimate Athenian citizen woman. He noticed shortly after the marriage, however, that Phano's behavior was not appropriate: "she did not know how to suit herself to Phrastor's ways, but she imitated her mother's manner, and her general intemperance, having been raised, I suppose, in such lack of restraint" (*Against Neaira* 50). Phrastor eventually came to the conclusion that he had been duped, and the language used here is significant:

. . . having learned now clearly that she was not the daughter of Stephanus, but of Neaira, and that he had been tricked in the first place, when she was betrothed, taking her as the daughter of Stephanus and not of Neaira, but his [i.e., Stephanus's] with a citizen woman, from before he lived with her [i.e., Neaira]. (*Against Neaira* 51)

The point is not only that Phano is not Stephanus's child, but that she is *Neaira's*. Children are always identified for legal purposes by their father's name. The fact that Phano here is identified as the daughter of Neaira is an open declaration that we do not know who the father is. We know only that her mother is a woman who has slept with too many men, and Phano can neither be a citizen woman nor produce citizen sons.

Under the circumstances, Phrastor divorced Phano, though she was pregnant with his son. It appears that later he was reconciled with her and attempted to register their son with his relatives (*genos*) as a legitimate member of the family, which would have been a first step in establishing the boy's citizenship. In this action, Phrastor was apparently opposed by members of his *genos*, and the boy was not so registered. We see here, however, the extent of the threat that Neaira poses: not only has she attempted to pass as a citizen, but Stephanus has contrived to marry off her daughter as a citizen, and that daughter has produced a son whose father tried to register *him* as a citizen. The integrity of Athenian citizenship has been threatened across three generations before all is said and done.

In a particularly interesting move, the speechwriter closes by inviting the jury to imagine what will happen when they go home and talk to their (legitimate) wives about the day's business. They will tell their wives that they tried Neaira, and they are encouraged to imagine what their wives will say if their husbands have to admit that they have acquitted her. "Certainly then the most virtuous of your wives will be angry with you, because you judge that this one is entitled equally with them to take part in the affairs of the city and of religious matters" (*Against Neaira* 111). A few sentences later, the speaker declares that if Neaira is allowed off the hook, there will be no distinction between legitimate citizen women and prostitutes. The speaker here imagines that the wives themselves will vigorously defend their status as citizen women, and it is worth considering that though citizen women had no direct part in legal affairs, these women might well have held considerable influence with their husbands.

It is useful, here, to note that a similar rhetorical tactic is used by Aeschines in his prosecution of Timarchos. Near the end of his speech, he suggests that the jury should think about how they will answer their sons when asked how they voted in the case of Timarchos. And again, the speaker suggests that a failure to convict will, in effect, destroy the critical distinctions on which Athenian society is built:

When you agree that you acquitted Timarchos, do you not overturn our common system of education? What use to keep teachers or trainers or educators to watch over our children, when those who have responsibility for keeping the laws are twisted to shameful behavior? (Aeschines *Against Timarchos* 187)

We have, then, two cases in which alleged prostitutes are put on trial. In both cases, there is some legitimate question over whether the defendant is really a prostitute. And in both cases, the jurors are invited to imagine how the relevant members of their family will react if they, in spite of the evidence the speaker has presented, vote to acquit. Timarchos, we are told, poses a threat to citizenship in his very body. Having allowed others to shamefully mistreat his person for pay, he can no longer be trusted not to sell the Athenian state to the highest bidder. He gives us a picture of what can happen when a citizen man is has no control over his appetites, his finances, or finally, his own body.

Neaira, on the other hand, is not a citizen, so she has less to lose and considerably more to gain. She is figured throughout as an outsider, a dangerous woman who, through the exercise of her sexual beauty, threatens to infiltrate the closed system of Athenian citizenship. For all Neaira's documented sexual activity, it is Timarchos who draws the greater condemnation on personal and moral grounds. He is castigated for having done unspeakable things with his body, the speaker even suggesting that he has committed *hybris* against himself (*Against Timarchus* 108, 185). For a woman, especially a noncitizen woman, to engage in such behavior was, evidently, fine with everyone (so long as she did not try to pass as a citizen). But the idea that a man would abdicate his citizen status in this way was shocking and outrageous, and posed a lurking threat to every Athenian boy who would grow up to be a citizen.

Six

Philosophical Sex

In the second half of the fifth century BCE, an uncompromising and critical philosopher named Socrates was active in Athens. Socrates left behind no writings himself, preferring, evidently, to engage in active teaching with students who were present. But two of his students, Plato and Xenophon, wrote dialogues in which a character named "Socrates" is one of the speakers. He is depicted as a challenging, clever, and often annoying man who was surrounded by boys and young men of the aristocratic families of Athens. It should be noted that Socrates himself is portrayed as quite uninterested in the trappings of wealth and willing to discuss philosophical issues with virtually anyone. But it was no doubt the wealthier young men of Athens who had the time and leisure to spend their days listening to him.

An older man, a series of young, beautiful, wealthy boys—it looks very much like a typical pederastic relationship. Several of our extant works—most notably Plato's *Symposium* and Xenophon's *Symposium*—show a Socrates, however, who did not engage in sex with his pupils as a matter of principle. This may be an instance of special pleading, as later critics attested, since Socrates was put on trial, found guilty, and executed by the Athenian state in 399 for "introducing false gods and corrupting the youth." In any case, his reluctance to engage in sexual relations with boys did not stem from a notion that such activities were immoral or unconventional, as we will see.

One member of Socrates' philosophic circle was Plato, who went on to become a preeminent philosophical writer of the early fourth century BCE in Athens. Plato wrote a copious collection of dialogues, philosophical discussions in which two or more characters debate important ideas—the nature of justice, for example, or the relationship of courage to knowledge. In nearly all of Plato's dialogues, a character named "Socrates" leads the discussion (in a few of the latest of Plato's works, he is not present). This Socrates typically asks a series of questions challenging the views of the person with whom he is conversing (whom scholars commonly call the "interlocutor"); through a process of question and answer, Socrates convinces his interlocutor that the topic at hand is not as easily defined as originally thought. Socrates consistently argues in favor of true knowledge as the guiding element of a moral life: the only way to achieve the good, in brief, is to understand what it is and to work deliberately toward it.

This figure of Socrates, I should point out, may be significantly different from the historical Socrates who taught Plato and his fellow students. We should not imagine that Plato was a mere parrot, transcribing the conversations that Socrates had with various illustrious Athenians; rather, he was himself a brilliant thinker who used a fictional character based on his primary teacher to write dramatic dialogues in which he developed his own thoughts.

Plato's writings are important for this study in two ways. First, there are a number of passages in which the subject under discussion is not desire itself, but in which we can glean information about popular attitudes about sex and pleasure. In the *Charmides,* for example, Socrates engages in a conversation with an unnamed interlocutor after a battle at Potidea, in which Socrates had evidently taken part. Socrates asks if there are any distinguished young philosophers in Athens, and in the course of the discussion, in walks Charmides, a youth distinguished for his physical beauty. Socrates comments on the effect of the young man:

Nothing should be measured by me, my friend, for I am a useless measure when it comes to beauty—nearly everyone in that age-group appear beautiful to me. But I must say, at that time he appeared amazing to me both in size and beauty, and all the others seemed to me to be in love with him—they were so struck and thrown into confusion when he came in. And many other lovers followed him in from behind. That my group of men were admiring him was not that amazing; but I noticed also the children—none of them were looking elsewhere, not even the smallest of them, but all were gazing at him as if he were a statue. And Chaerephon called to me, and said, "How does the young man appear to you, Socrates? Does he not have a beautiful face?"

"Beautiful beyond nature," I said.

Then he said, "If he were to decide to strip, he would seem not to have a face; for his body is completely beautiful." (*Charmides* 154b–c)

The passage is important for two reasons. First, it gives us some indication of the power that a boy's beauty in Athens could have. Charmides evidently has the kind of face that stopped traffic. As such, he gets gossiped about by men in all-male company, in a manner comparable to a group of modern straight men discussing a female supermodel or movie star. Second, the passage suggests that not only older men are attracted to this kind of beauty. Though young boys could hardly hope to be *erastai* of the older Charmides, they too are struck by, and attracted to, his remarkable physical beauty. This text provides us with evidence, then, that the Athenians thought of a boy's beauty as attractive to virtually everyone, even if only those older than him would be expected to act on that attraction.

Another such incidental passage provides evidence about Athenians' views on the status of the type of sexual deviant known as a *kinaidos.* In a passage from Plato's *Gorgias,* the two speakers are discussing the nature of happiness. Callicles has argued that for those who are powerful, self-restraint is unnecessary for happiness since they have the ability to satisfy their desires. Socrates begins a series of questions to call into doubt this position:

SOCRATES   First off, tell me: suppose a man has an itch, and he scratches it, and is able to scratch it without restraint, and scratches his whole life; does he live happily?

CALLICLES   How unusual you are, Socrates, and what a simple crowd-pleaser.

SOCRATES   Yes indeed, Callicles—that is how I drove Polos and Gorgias off-course and made them ashamed. But don't you be distracted nor feel shame; for you are courageous. But just answer the question.

CALLICLES   Yes, then, I say that even the one who scratches would live pleasantly.

SOCRATES   And if pleasantly, also happily?

CALLICLES   Certainly.

SOCRATES   What if he scratches only his head? Or shall I ask you anything more? Consider, Callicles what you would answer if someone asks you all the things that logically follow these. For the logical end of this sort of question, the life of *kinaidoi,* is this not terrible and shameful and wretched? Or do you dare to say that these people are happy, if they have what they want without restraint?

CALLICLES   Are you not ashamed to lead the argument to this point, Socrates? (*Gorgias* 494c–e)

This text is a rare and important moment in which the figure of the *kinaidos* is acknowledged, and it provides several pieces of useful information. First, there is the somewhat muted reference to the well-known habit of *kinaidoi* by which they can be identified: scratching their heads with one finger. More important, perhaps, is the analogy that Socrates' line of argument implies. To be a *kinaidos* is to satisfy a certain kind of desire, to scratch a particular itch, as it were. Almost as soon as this desire is conjured up, however, it is disavowed, both by Socrates and by Callicles. Indeed, Callicles suggests that it is shameful for Socrates even to bring it up. This, then, provides an exact and careful image of the way the Athenians thought about *kinaidoi,* with a mixture of prurient interest in this perverse form of pleasure and immediate rejection of such pleasure as shameful, terrible, and wretched. From this point, it is easy enough for Socrates to convince Callicles that not all pleasure is good and that satisfying every desire is not the key to happiness. He has found the crucial counterexample, a pleasure that Callicles must acknowledge but cannot claim as acceptable for those who have the power to fulfill it.

In addition to these sorts of incidental passages, however, Plato was also the most sophisticated theorist of desire in Greek history. Several of his dialogues, generally thought to come from the middle of his long and productive career, deal specifically with the nature of *eros,* or erotic desire. In this chapter, I will discuss one of the most important, Plato's *Symposium.* In this work, Socrates attends a symposium, or drinking party, at the home of the well-known tragic poet Agathon. In attendance are several notables, including Phaedrus (who is the interlocutor in another of Plato's dialogues on the nature of *eros,* the *Phaedrus*), a physician named Pausanias, and the comic poet Aristophanes. Each of the people at the symposium gives a speech on the nature of love.

SEXUALITY IN THE *SYMPOSIUM*

By far one of the most amusing, interesting, and problematic speeches in the *Symposium* is that of the comic poet Aristophanes. This speech has been one of the central texts in modern discussions of sexuality in the ancient world, and in particular, it appears to support the idea that the ancient Greeks did think of people in categories similar to ours;[1] that is, the speech explains why some men are primarily attracted to other males, why some women and men are attracted to each other, and even why some women prefer to have sex with other women. This certainly looks like our categories of homosexual men, lesbians, and straight men and women; and even if the configuration of these categories is not exactly the same as ours, the speech suggests that the Greek conception of sexual types is not so different, as I have suggested elsewhere in this book.

Aristophanes was, of course, a well-known comic poet in Athens, so it should not surprise us to find that his speech has funny moments. And indeed, he begins with a proposition that is fairly comical. Originally, Aristophanes says, there were not two sexes, but three, because each individual consisted of two of today's people. Some were made of two male parts and were masculine; others were made of two female parts and were feminine; and some were made of one male and one female, and were so androgynous (a word that literally means "male-female"). Each of these double people had four arms and four legs, and when they wanted to move quickly, Aristophanes says, they stuck out all their limbs and rolled along at high speed—one of the first amusing moments in the story that suggests that we should not take it entirely at face value.

Unfortunately, these hyperhumans eventually made the sort of mistake that tends to fell tragic heroes: they challenged the gods. In fact, these humans tried to ascend Olympus. Zeus, realizing that they were too powerful, decided that to render the threat less dangerous, he should slice them in half, "as people do when they slice eggs in preparation for pickling them" (*Symposium* 190d). This splitting of individuals led to some unfortunate consequences: the new half-people (whole people of today) spent their lives looking for the other half, and once one found her other half, the two halves would simply embrace until they died of hunger and exhaustion. So then Zeus made a few more changes, the most important of which was that he moved the humans' genitals around to the other side—that is, the new fronts of these creatures—and invented the process of sexual reproduction (previously, Aristophanes says, we had reproduced "in the ground, like grasshoppers" [*Symposium* 191c]).

Once we have reached this point, the logic of the myth seems inescapable. Men who came from male-male pairs would be attracted to men; women from female-female pairs would desire women; and individuals from mixed-sex pairs would be what we think of as straight. And indeed, that is what the myth says, in so many words. It is worth pointing out that this story is unique in Greek literature and that its many comic elements suggest the sort of thing that a poet like Aristophanes might come up with. We should not assume, then, that anyone in Athens actually believed this story to be literally true. All the same, it does seem to be a "just so story" to explain the presence of what look like modern sexual categories.

A closer reading of some key passages, however, reveals that the logic of the myth does not quite correspond to the sexual system that Aristophanes is used to or is thinking with. The first clue comes immediately after Zeus has switched human genitals around so that they can reproduce sexually. Aristophanes explains what Zeus had in mind thus:

He did it for this reason: so that if a man should happen on a woman and embrace, they would reproduce and beget descendents, and if a male happened on a male, they would be fully satisfied with their intercourse and then stop, return to their work, and take care of the rest of their lives. (*Symposium* 191c)

Note the distinction of the two kinds of sex: one is for procreation, the other pleasure. The assumption is that the male-male sex will not result in a lasting relationship, just a momentary pleasure before the two males return to their lives. More important than that, Aristophanes is careful to use age-neutral language when he discusses the two males; that is, in discussing the opposite-sex couple, he refers to them as a "man" and a "woman" (the words here can also mean "husband" and "wife"). But when discussing the same-sex couple, he refers only to their gender: when a "male" meets a "male" (the Greek word is *arrên*). The reason for this is clear enough: the logic of the myth would suggest that the two halves that are searching for one another would be of the same age. But as we know, that would not be a normal sexual coupling for the Greeks. So rather than saying "if a man happened on another man," which would be a bit shocking to Aristophanes' audience, Aristophanes uses the generic term *male,* allowing the audience to imagine a pederastic couple.

We should also note that in the preceding passage, no mention is made of two women who come together for sexual satisfaction. Where the two kinds of couples discussed each had a recognized place in Athenian society, Athenians were much more hesitant to imagine two women together. Even though the myth dictates that such couples must have existed, Zeus apparently gives no thought to them, and the purpose of their sexual attraction remains, for now, a mystery.

The paragraphs that follow make it even clearer that when Aristophanes is discussing male-male relations, he has a pederastic model in mind. As Aristophanes says, the entire human race is always looking for his or her "other half," and he runs through the three possibilities that this entails. The categories of individuals that result, however, contain a few surprises. I have translated the key passage as literally as possible. In the discussion that follows, I elaborate on a few key words:

The men who are divided from the shared-sex originals, the one that was called "androgynous," these are woman-lovers, and many adulterers are born from this race. And the women [from this origin] are man-lovers, and adulteresses come from this race. But the women who are divided from the female originals are not at all interested in men, but are rather turned toward women, and prostitutes who serve women *[hetairistriai]* come from this race. And the ones cut from the male origin, these pursue males, and so long as they are boys, since they are cut from a male, they love men and they enjoy lying with them and being embraced by them. And these are the best boys and boy toys, since they are the most manly in nature. Some people say that they are shameful, but these people lie. For it is not from shamelessness that they do this, but because of courage and manliness and masculinity that they enjoy what is similar to themselves. The proof of this is significant. For when they are adults and enter into public life, only this sort are men. But when they have become men, they are boy-lovers, and are not interested by nature in marriage or child producing, but are forced into these things by convention. (*Symposium* 191d–192b)

It is true that this passage provides something that we have little seen elsewhere; that is, it suggests that because of some circumstances of a person's birth, he will have a particular, and apparently exclusive, sexual orientation.

When we try to identify these sexual orientations, however, things quickly become complicated. Consider, first, those men and women whom we would identify as straight. The words that I have translated here as "woman-lovers" and "man-lovers" mean just that in a literal sense. But they are relatively rare words, and when used elsewhere in Greek literature, they indicate an excessive obsession with the opposite sex. For this reason, *man-lovers* is sometimes translated "nymphomaniacs," and *woman-lovers* has the sense of "womanizers."[2] In addition, we note that this particular origin is responsible not only for a person being attracted to the other sex, but for a tendency to do so as an adulterer or adulteress. Again, the sense here is of someone who is not in control of his sexual desires, so that he gratifies them in ways that are not socially acceptable. Not only is this not the same as our notion of straight, but the people here described are clearly not normal.

What about the category that was passed over in the previous passage, women who are attracted to women? Again, this is a topic that is almost never talked about in our literary sources. What we find here is unique and therefore difficult to assess. As in the previous example, Aristophanes first tells us about their orientation—they are interested in women, not men—and then he gives us a specific example: *hetairistriai* are found in this group. Unfortunately, the word *hetairistriai* is of uncertain meaning and appears in Greek literature here for the first time. (Lucian uses it some centuries later, in his *Dialogue of the Courtesans*.) At its root is the word *heataira,* a word used in Plato's time to indicate a prostitute. By comparing the word to other words formed with a similar morphology, Dover comes to the conclusion that it might mean what I have translated it as in the passage: a (female) prostitute who specializes in servicing women.[3] If that interpretation is correct, this, too, seems like a bit more than a simple sexual orientation.

When we get to the male-male pair, however, the careful structure that the myth has set up simply begins to break down. As we noted before, the logic of the myth would seem to dictate that men who are attracted to other males would be attracted to men who are their equals. But Aristophanes does not even begin to discuss these male-male relationships in those terms; rather, from the outset, he assumes a pederastic structure, involving an older man and a younger one. And since both partners play different roles in such a relationship, the playwright is at some pains to explain how it is that a common origin results in these different roles.

First Aristophanes justifies the boy's willingness to give himself to a lover, and he argues that such an action is taken because of qualities in the boy that are entirely appropriate to his gender: courage, manliness, and masculinity. Modern readers may find some of the other statements in this passage even more surprising, especially the notion that these kinds of people are those who play a significant role in public life and who are the only "men" when they grow up. We may want to recall here that the real Aristophanes frequently took a swipe at leading Athenian politicians by reminding the audience that they had been popular boy toys when younger. In any case, this formulation again marks a sharp break with our own notion of sexual orientation. Few, if any, modern cultural products suggest that young men who have affairs with older partners are especially manly and particularly well suited for public service.

Finally, Aristophanes discusses what happens to these male-oriented men when they grow older. They are still attracted to males, it turns out, but now as the active partner or *erastes*. He does not suggest that they will be attracted to men of their own age, which would have been considered deviant. Again, their orientation is excessive: not only do they prefer boys, but they actively avoid marriage and the production of children. This is distinctly odd behavior for an adult male Athenian citizen. Indeed, in the paragraph that follows, Aristophanes describes these people in a way that suggests that they are outside the norm:

These are the ones who spend their entire lives with one another, and they could not say what they wish for themselves from each other. No one would think that what each wishes is only sexual intercourse, or that on account of this each of them takes such pleasure in being with the other with such zeal. But it is clear that the soul of each wishes something else, which it is not able to express, but it prophecies what it wants, and speaks in riddles. (*Symposium* 192c–d)

These are not just everyday Athenian lovers and their boy toys, but rather exceptional lovers, whose relationships expand beyond the physical and extends throughout their lives. These unusual couples do begin to look like gay men, in that they have a lifelong sexual orientation, except that it is not clear that they remain sexually active in the later phase of the relationship. More important, for the course of Plato's argument, Aristophanes here introduces the notion that such lovers are grasping intellectually for something beyond their physical desire, for a metaphysical satisfaction of which their erotic impulse is only the initial phase. This idea will be more fully developed in Socrates' speech, discussed later.

In brief, then, none of the so-called orientations described previously are exactly like ours, and more important, none of them would be considered normal by Plato's Athenian audience. Each of them is a type of excess, and the story turns out to be not about how to produce gay or straight men and women, but how certain kinds of odd and excessive preferences came to be. When describing those preferences, Aristophanes still assumes a pederastic model for the male-male couple. The category of homosexual male, in which two men of the same age would be attracted to each other, and either at any given time could be thought of as lover or beloved, simply seems not to be thinkable; rather, when he speaks of male-male desire, it can only be expressed as a boy's willingness to give in to an older lover, and an older lover's fondness for boys.

PLATONIC DESIRE AND THE *SYMPOSIUM*

When we use the phrase *platonic relationship*, we mean a close, potentially romantic relationship, usually between a man and a woman, that does *not* involve sex. In fact, the phrase is used specifically to exclude the idea of sex in the relationship. We can go still further. When we describe such a friendship using those words, we do so because we have a need to define the relationship in a particular way. It is not sexual, but it is unusually close—close enough that some people might think that it is sexual, but, in thinking so, would be wrong. The idea, then, is that the relationship embodies *something,* some idea of close friendship that is *in place of* sex.

What is that something, that thing that defines this relationship as different from other kinds of casual friendships? In part, it is an idea that the two friends share personal or intellectual interests, that they find their friendship to be emotionally and intellectually stimulating and satisfying. Those outside the relationship (and looking in) may sometimes have the sense that the two friends have channeled their sexual attraction for one another into these other areas of mutual interest. It is this idea of having channeled romantic energy into some other, less sexually fraught area that one can most easily trace to the philosophical writings of Plato.

This understanding of platonic relationships stems from a line of thought developed most fully in the *Symposium.* There Socrates recounts a speech that he once heard from an enigmatic figure, a female teacher named "Diotima."[4] The doctrine of Diotima, briefly, is that the love of a beautiful boy should lead the lover to love not just one boy, but to love the beauty itself that is inherent in this one boy; and that from there, the lover should be drawn to the pursuit of beauty, which is to say, the pursuit of the Good, which is naturally most easily achieved through philosophical inquiry. I will discuss this passage at more length later; for now, it is simply important to note that this philosophical doctrine underlies our notion of a platonic relationship: a relationship without sex, in which erotic desires are sublimated to the pursuit of philosophic virtue.

How does Plato come to this somewhat curious idea, that erotic desire is most perfectly realized in the practice of philosophy (rather than, say, sex)?

The argument in the *Symposium* is subtle and complex, and I encourage the interested reader to experience it for himself or herself. I will touch here on a few of the major points.

As I mentioned previously, this dialogue is set up as a series of speeches by leading Athenians, some more intellectual than others. One of the early speeches is by a physician named Pausanias, who posits that there is a good kind of *eros* and a bad kind. Along the way, he gives us some interesting information about Athenian practices of desire. He begins by discussing the practice in some other city-states:

In particular, erotic customs in other cities are easy to understand and straightforward. But the customs here and in Sparta are elaborate. In Elis, and in Boiotia, and where they are not sophisticated speakers, it is simply the custom that it is good to satisfy one's lover *[erastes]* and no one young or old would say that it is shameful, so that, I think, they don't have to go to lengths trying to convince their young men with words, since they are not good speakers. (*Symposium* 182a–b)

First off, we should note that Pausanias does not think of attraction to boys as a particularly Athenian trait; Athens and Sparta share that idea with other city-states. Rather, what separates Athens from these other cities is that in Athens, it is not *always* considered a good idea for a beloved to satisfy his lover. The social rules, enforced not by law but by matters of public shame, reputation, and the like, make Athens difficult to understand. Moreover, Pausanias attributes this distinctly Athenian flavor to the fact that Athenians are better speakers than their neighbors, and so better able to undergo the rigors of seducing boys who may not be easily convinced.

Pausanias then goes on to explain that Athenians are willing to grant unusual license to lovers: they allow lovers to behave foolishly and without the usual self-restraint. They can sleep all night on their beloved's doorstep (a common trope of the lover), beg, swear oaths, and even put up with "slavery" to their beloved. All of this would quite rightly be considered out-of-bounds in other social circumstances. As for the beloved, however, Pausanias points out that there are numerous safeguards against his giving in too easily or too quickly. These include physical guardians, but also the reproach that the boys will receive from their friends if they are too easily seduced (*Symposium* 183). All of this, Pausanias concludes, constitutes a kind of test for both lover and beloved:

Our custom intends to test, well and truly, these lovers, so that the boy satisfies the good, and flees from the bad. For this reason, then, custom orders the lovers to pursue, and the boys to flee—it creates a contest and tests what sort the lover is, and what sort the beloved. (*Symposium* 184a)

Finally, Pausanias specifies what the real point of all these tests are, namely, that the relationship between lover and beloved be one that benefits the boy. The lover, however avid in his pursuit, must love the boy's mind and not just his body, which is doomed to fade from beauty sooner rather than later (*Symposium* 183e). The boy, likewise, is free to give himself to such a lover if he believes that the lover can improve him by giving him "wisdom or some other virtue" (*Symposium* 184d). Ultimately, then, the boy is expected to satisfy his lover for a quite specific and lofty reason. He should reject reasons of a financial nature, namely, gifts or money, which are not sufficient basis for a relationship. Moreover, he is not expected to actually *want* to have sex with the lover; that is, nowhere in this passage does Plato speak of the beloved's desire. Rather, pleasure is something that the beloved gives to the lover in return for something noble—an enrichment of character, an education into the ways of wisdom and virtue. In Pausanias's view, then, the right kind of *eros* is a desire that brings about good for both lover and beloved.

Now, Pausanias presents this view of the *erastes-eromenos* relationship as if it were standard Athenian custom. While it would be a mistake to assume that Plato's dialogues in general are representative of what the average Athenian thought, in this case, there is some reason to believe that Pausanias is not greatly out of touch with popular sentiment. His speech is less sophisticated and certainly less intellectually challenging than those that follow. Moreover, he appeals to common practice as a basis for his remarks. Pausanias is a friendly armchair sociologist, attempting to make sense of a set of practices that he remarks, rightly, are not always easy to understand.

At the same time, Pausanias's speech sets up that of Socrates in several important ways. Like Pausanias, Socrates will argue that desire in its best form is not desire for a particular body, or even a particular person, but for the good that is inherent in that person. In making this leap, Socrates effectively redefines erotic desire as a force for philosophical inquiry. Again, I can only summarize here a complex masterpiece of philosophic thought, and the interested reader is encouraged to seek out the original dialogue.

Socrates, in giving his speech about *eros,* adds another level of narration to the already complex narrative of the dialogue. He purports to recount a teaching about love that he received, some years previously, from a woman named Diotima. The reasons for the introduction of this secondary character have been much debated. Without discounting the possibility that Diotima was a real person, an educated woman who acted as a teacher to Socrates, it is also fair to say that in "her" discussion of love, the idea of *reproduction* acts as a figure for the product of *eros.* It may be the case that Diotima, the only speaking woman in the dialogue, is introduced because women are involved in physical reproduction in a way that men, especially men whose erotic pursuits are all boys, are not.

In any case, Diotima redefines *eros* in two significant ways. First, she suggests that all desire is desire for something that one does not have, and necessarily for something that is good. This is an important step in the argument; Pausanias had based his speech on the assertion that there is a good and a bad kind of desire (and good and bad type of lover). For Diotima, *eros* is not in itself good since it desires good, and one only desires what one does not have, but neither is it bad; rather, desire is an intermediary step, and one that impels us, ultimately, toward the good. Second, Diotima argues that when we desire something, it is not simply the possession of that thing that we want, but rather the possession of it for all time, that is, some form of immortality. Since we are not gods, this means that *eros,* sexual desire, is always directed toward some sort of reproduction, toward something that will continue indefinitely to the future.

One might think that this line of reasoning is leading toward that taken by conservative thinkers in the modern West, namely, that sex is immoral unless it has the purpose of procreation. Although arguments like that are made at times by Plato, that is not the point of the argument here. On the contrary, Diotima tells Socrates that there are different types of procreation; only those whose creative urge is physical "turn toward women and are erotic in this way, and through the production of children provide immortality and fame and happiness for themselves, as they think, throughout all time" (*Symposium* 208e). People who have different kinds of erotic urges, urges that are clearly superior to these base physical urges, will try to create beauty in another medium. Such people include poets, artists, and the like.

After a brief mention of creative artists, however, the argument takes a somewhat surprising turn back to what we think of as erotic. Diotima argues that the person who is creative in his *psyche* ("soul," or perhaps better, "mind") will search for a person in whom to beget "the good." Naturally, he will seek someone beautiful. Diotima says specifically that "he will never beget in that which is shameful/ugly" (*Symposium* 209b). But even more important than physical beauty will be to find a "beautiful mind, wellborn and noble" (*Symposium* 209b); then the combination of physical and intellectual beauty will be ideal. One of the curious things about this passage, however we may view the likelihood that creative people will experience *eros* as a desire to engage in ennobling conversations with beautiful youths, is that the speaker (Diotima, speaking to Socrates, as recorded by Plato) assumes here that the relationship in question is a male-male one. Women were mentioned just earlier, but having been discussed as an outlet for men whose erotic energy is directed toward the physical, they disappear again from the discussion; rather, it is clear that when Plato discusses trying to "beget the good" in a noble soul, he has a pederastic relationship in mind.

Diotima is still not finished, however. From this set of propositions, she outlines a doctrine that is among the most important in Plato's thought, that of the "ladder of love." Beauty, she says, like other noble abstract concepts, cannot be perceived directly; that is, we cannot see the form of beauty itself; we see only examples of beauty, in imperfect worldly manifestations. The philosophic lover—that is, the Platonic lover—moves from specific instances of beauty toward the apprehension of the form of beauty itself. And so, from the recognition of beauty in one body, he comes to recognize the sameness of the beauty in all bodies. From there, he must recognize intellectual beauty as superior to physical; this in turn will turn him toward the beauty of "laws and institutions" (*Symposium* 210c), and from there the knowledge of beauty in its pure form, which can only be apprehended through philosophical intellection. Diotima summarizes this process of ever-widening generalization as follows:

This is the right way to go about erotics, or to be led to them by another, starting from specific beauties, but always returning for the sake of that one beauty. Using it [beauty] as if it were a ladder, he goes from one to two and from two to all beautiful bodies, and from beautiful bodies to beautiful behaviors, and from behaviors to beautiful learnings, and from beautiful learnings to that one final learning, which is none other than the knowledge of beauty, and he knows, when he finishes this, what beauty is. (*Symposium* 211b–c)

Desire, then, has been completely redefined as a drive for philosophic knowledge. We are now in a position to understand the idea of a platonic relationship in its fullest sense. If we follow the logic of Diotima's teachings to Socrates, then we recognize that fulfillment of desire in its physical sense is the least satisfying, and least complete, form of such fulfillment; rather, Plato's text argues, such desire should be sublimated into the quest for philosophic knowledge. It would, however, be a large and significant mistake to conclude from this that Plato (or Socrates, or Diotima) was opposed to same-sex sexual relationships.[5] Remember that those whose drive to reproduction was purely physical were relegated to the inferior necessity of sex with women. On the contrary, relations with boys are regarded as necessarily of higher philosophic value than those with women because the offspring of such a relationship can only be of an intellectual sort. Plato's reluctance about sex with boys in this text is, in an important way, out of step with the thinking of the average Athenian: the argument presented here suggests that *any* such sexual outlet is less satisfying, less noble, than one of philosophical inquiry.

In the other of Plato's major dialogues on *eros,* the *Phaedrus,* Socrates elaborates on this theory.[6] He outlines an elaborate argument that is part logic, part myth, in which the sight of beauty, in the form of one's beloved, causes wings to sprout in the soul of the lover. These wings allow the lover's soul to ascend to heaven and view the forms in their pure state, that is, to achieve full philosophic knowledge. This dialogue also should be read in its entirety, but here I would like to focus on one of the remarkable aspects of the relationship described in it: the reciprocity between lover and beloved. As we have seen, a typical Athenian pederastic relationship involved a desiring older man and a younger man who was willing, if not eager, to give his lover pleasure in return for general improvements. This, however, is hardly the description of desire that we find in the *Phaedrus* (Socrates speaks):

When he has been doing this for a while and has been with the boy, even touching him at the gymnasium and in other gatherings, then the spring of that stream, which Zeus named "desire" when he made love to Ganymede, begins flowing toward the lover. Part of it flows into him, but the rest, when he is filled up, overflows out. And like a breeze or an echo is carried back from something hard and smooth to the place from which it set out, thus the stream of beauty goes back into the beautiful boy through the eyes, which is the natural route to the soul, and sets him fluttering. It waters the paths of his wings, and urges him to grow wings and fills the soul of the beloved with love in return. Indeed, the boy loves, but does not understand what he loves; and he does not know what he has experienced, nor is he able to say. Having caught something from the eye of another, he is not able to explain, and he does not realize that he is seeing himself in his lover as if in a mirror. And when his lover is present, this abates his pain just as it does the lover's; and when his lover is gone, he longs for him as he is longed for, having an image of desire, a "desire in return" *[anteros]*. But he calls this and thinks of it not as desire but as friendship. And he wants, equally with his lover, though less strongly, to see him, to touch, to kiss, to lie together. (*Phaedrus* 255b–e)

Nearly everything in the preceding passage is remarkable. The idea of one's soul growing wings aside, what is striking about Socrates' description is that the desire that the boy's beauty originates is seen as flowing into the lover, then back into the boy himself; that is, both lover and beloved experience the same thing. We may think of this as fairly normal and indeed necessary for love, but in an Athenian pederastic relationship, it is almost unheard of. Even here, however, Plato recognizes that the experience of lover and beloved cannot be identical; unlike the lover, the beloved experiences this desire with a charming innocence, so that he is unable to understand or articulate what he feels. And though he does want to fondle and kiss his lover (again, shocking), he does so "less strongly." Even so, the desire that he feels, however much he may think of it as "friendship" (*philia*), is the same desire that the lover feels. Technically, it is a kind of echo of that desire.[7] Their experiences are symmetrical to such a degree that Plato can describe the beloved as seeing himself in his lover as in a mirror.

This notion of reciprocity, of a desire that flows back and forth between lover and beloved, represents an important development for Plato's argument about desire as a force for philosophical enquiry. It allows that both lover and beloved are engaged in this form of enquiry—if not exactly equally, at least with equal impetus. This conception of *eros* is what allows Plato to conceive of pederastic relations as of equal value for both partners in a male-male relationship; that is, not only the lover experiences beauty, and through it the contemplation of the form of beauty, but the beloved also experiences the same beauty—his own, reflected back through the eyes of the lover—and so can begin his own journey to the contemplation of the form of the good.

This discussion has taken us a long way from the simple rules and regulations of Athenian sex. That is because Plato was not a typical Athenian thinker, and his concept of desire is not what one would expect to hear from a typical man on the street. On the contrary, sexual desire is, for Plato in these middle dialogues, a form of impetus toward philosophical inquiry. As such, it is simply impossible to map onto Plato's lovers a sense of sexual orientation or sexual identity, unless we are willing to extend the idea of sexual identity to include this new and challenging sexual type of being, the philosopher. At the same time, however, it is instructive to see how thoroughly Plato assumes a *pederastic* relationship when discussing *eros*. That, for him, is the social norm from which to begin his investigations.

SOCRATES AND HIS BELOVED

The *Symposium* ends with a dramatic and lighthearted demonstration of just where the sexual identity of a philosopher will lead him. The setting, the reader will recall, is that of a drinking party. At the end of the dialogue, Alcibiades, a notorious Athenian aristocrat, general, and former pupil of Socrates, stumbles onto the scene, quite drunk. He proceeds to launch into a speech in praise of Socrates. In essence, Alcibiades describes Socrates as a man who seduced him with the sharpness of his intellect and impelled him, through this erotic spell, to a "madness for philosophy" (*Symposium* 218b). In the process, Alcibiades describes himself as an unusually eager, even improper, beloved (*eromenos*) and recounts his attempts to physically seduce Socrates. The passage is worth quoting here at length:

When, men, the lamp was out and the slaves had gone, it seemed to me that it was necessary to abandon subtlety toward him, and to say freely what I thought. And nudging him, I said,

"Socrates, are you asleep?"

"No indeed," he said.

"Do you know what I think?"

"What, exactly?"

"You seem to me," I said, "to be the only *erastes* worthy of me, and you seem to be hesitating to seduce me. But I look at it this way. I think it would be thoughtless not to give you pleasure in this way, and in some other way, or if you needed something from my property or from my friends. For nothing is more important to me than that I become as noble as possible, and I think that there is no one who is a more appropriate assistant in this than you. Indeed, I would be more embarrassed in not giving pleasure to such a one as you—at least before intelligent people—than I would be in giving pleasure before the common and unthinking folk." (*Symposium* 218b–d)

Before I go on, I want to take a moment to recognize this for the remarkable passage that it is. For one thing, it is one of the only times in all of Greek literature that we hear from an *eromenos,* or at least from a person positioning himself as one. As an *eromenos,* Alcibiades is quite unconventional. He literally throws himself at Socrates, and he is at some pains to justify his shocking behavior. The language that he uses is carefully calculated to mitigate his forwardness: he is willing to offer pleasure (*charizomai*) to Socrates in return for moral and intellectual improvement. He is careful not to mention any specific sexual acts, relying instead on euphemisms ("give pleasure") and vague promises ("and anything else"). Even so, he is aware that giving himself in this way may result in some reproach; he anticipates this criticism and argues that *thinking* people will recognize that it would be more shameful for him not to give himself than to give himself, when the recipient is Socrates.

In other words, Alcibiades tries to argue himself into the position of an *eromenos* to Socrates' *erastes,* as the relationship was traditionally idealized. Here, however, Socrates shows himself to be an untypical Athenian. The reader should be aware that Alcibiades was, evidently, possessed of considerable physical charms. But Socrates declares himself unwilling to make the usual pederastic bargain of teaching for sexual favor:

Dear Alcibiades, you are in no danger of being a fool if what you say about me happens to be true, and if I have some power by which you could be improved. You must see some unmanageable beauty in me, and a beauty completely different from your physical charms. If, seeing this, you are trying to strike a bargain with me and exchange beauty for beauty, then you are planning to cheat me, and not by a little. You are trying to gain the truth of beauty in exchange for its appearance, and you think to exchange "bronze for gold" as Homer says. (*Symposium* 218d–219a)

This is a remarkable reversal of the normal order of things. As we have seen in Pausanias's speech, and as nearly all Greek literature makes clear, the lover (*erastes*) is supposed to take the attitude that he is enslaved by his beloved's beauty and willing to beg for the right to enjoy it. The language of such a relationship is weighted on the side of the beloved; it is his prerogative to decide whether or not to "give pleasure" to the lover. Socrates completely reverses this power dynamic and in the process declares that what he has to offer is of infinitely more worth than Alcibiades's renowned physical beauty, that is, beauty itself, in the form of philosophical truth. By refusing to be seduced by Alcibiades, moreover, Socrates incites the beautiful young man to seek out such real beauty.

We should note, finally, that this episode ends with a description that further establishes Socrates as embodying the highest ideal of Athenian manliness. Alcibiades goes on to describe how he continued trying to seduce the philosopher, even crawling under his cloak and spending the night with him. He arose in the morning, however, untouched, as if he had slept with a father or brother.[8] Finally, Alcibiades says, he felt "dishonored" but also felt great admiration for Socrates' "character and self-control and manliness" (*Symposium* 219d). The words I have just translated here are important, and they are words we have seen before. "Character" is the Greek work *physin*, which usually means something like "inborn nature"; "self-control" is *sophrosyne*, often translated as "temperance"; and "manliness" translates *andreia*, that quality of bravery required of men on the battlefield. Socrates, here, embodies the Greek ideal of sexual self-restraint. He has the opportunity to have sex with one of Athens's most celebrated beautiful boys and chooses not to. Such self-control in the face of what Alcibiades calls an "assault" marks Socrates as a man's man, in full command of his own sexual impulses and in possession of unusual bravery. At the same time, this traditional self-control becomes proof of Socrates' unconventional dedication to philosophic, rather than sexual, forms of desire.

CONCLUSIONS

Plato is not a typical Athenian, though he does work within typical Athenian categories of thought when it comes to sex. Even a passage as apparently familiar to us as the myth told by Aristophanes in the *Symposium* does not map, on close examination, onto our modern categorization of sexual identities as gay, straight, or lesbian. Nor does it entirely break free of the idea of sex as an activity in which men are defined by their role as active or passive and in which such roles correspond to particular phases of life.

On the other hand, Plato reconceives sexual desire as a force that each of us can use for personal and moral improvement. Within this persuasive re-definition, he pushes the boundaries of sexual norms on several fronts. He is careful to suggest that there are specific circumstances in which it is not only acceptable, but desirable, and even quite manly, for a boy to give himself to his lover. He goes further, however, in arguing that the *eromenos,* the beloved boy, should feel sexual desire for his lover; he should actively desire him and not merely give him pleasure as a concession for education. Such an idea is necessary for Plato's quite radical notion that sexual desire is, ultimately, a form of philosophic inquiry, an attempt to grasp and reproduce that aspect of the good that we can perceive with our senses, namely, beauty. The pursuit of such good cannot, in the Platonic system, be limited to one partner or the other, but must be sought by both equally. In positing this reciprocity and near-equality of desire, Plato's sexual ethics are both surprising and highly influential.

Seven

Love and Sex in Hellenistic Poetry

Sweet, in the summer, to drink ice-cold water; sweet, for sailors
to see the spring stars come out of winter;
Sweeter, whenever a single cloak hides two lovers,[1]
and both praise Aphrodite.

—Asclepiades, *Greek Anthology* 5.169

In this chapter, I examine a new era and a new city: the Hellenistic period, in which a remarkable center of Greek literature and art flourished
in Egypt. After Phillip of Macedon conquered Athens in the mid-fourth
century BCE, his son Alexander became the undisputed ruler of the Greek
world. Alexander, however, died young in 323 BCE, and on his death, the
Athenian empire was divided among his generals, who proceeded to engage in a series of wars with one another. By about 275 BCE, Greece was divided into four relatively stable kingdoms: Macedon and Greece, Asia, Asia
Minor, and Egypt. Of these, the kingdom of Egypt, ruled by the Ptolemies
in Alexandria, became, over the next century, a leading cultural center of
the Greek world.

Alexandria was a fascinating cosmopolitan city. Though under Greek rule,
the vast majority of its inhabitants were Egyptians, with large populations of
Palestinians and Jews as well. During the 300 years or so traditionally thought
of as the Hellenistic period (323–31 BCE), moreover, the region came increasingly under Roman control and influence. There was, therefore, a heady mix
of cultures and ideas. To give only one example: the second Ptolemy, named
"Philadelphus," married his sister Arsinoë, a custom traditional for Egyptian
pharaohs but initially scandalous to the Greeks living in Egypt. It is also clear
from various historical documents that women in Hellenistic Greece enjoyed greater economic and political freedom than they had in the previous
centuries in Athens. A cultural history of Hellenistic Greece is, unfortunately,
well beyond the scope of this volume. Instead, this chapter will focus briefly
on some of the Greek literature that was produced by the scholar poets of
the period.

From the beginning of their rule, the Ptolemies in Alexandria engaged in a deliberate program of supporting Greek culture. The first Ptolemy (Soter) set up a *mouseion* (literally, a "shrine of the muses") for the study and production of Greek art, literature, and science. At the same time, the famous library at Alexandria was established, in which a series of scholars, some of whom were also poets themselves, studied, copied, and produced editions of masterworks of classical Greek literature. Among other things, the Ptolemy Euergetes (the third Ptolemy of Egypt, ruling from 243 to 222 BCE) "borrowed" the official Athenian copies of the tragedies of Aeschylus, Sophocles, and Euripides, leaving a deposit of 15 talents, a vast sum of money. When he returned copies, rather than the originals, to Athens, he forfeited this deposit but obtained the originals for the library. Tragically, this library was burned in the siege of Alexandria by Julius Caesar in 48 BCE. This is one of the great filter points in the history of Western literature: countless works that were burned in this fire are now lost forever.

The scholars who worked in the library were, in a sense, the first modern classicists. They began the process, continued today, of producing definitive editions of Homer, Hesiod, the lyric poets, and the rest of Greek literature by comparing different copies of these works and determining which readings were, in their opinions, correct. They knew Greek literature, therefore, at a deep and detailed level. This knowledge of the cultural past is reflected in the poetry of the Hellenistic era at every turn. Their poems are witty, polished, and relentlessly learned. References to the literature of fifth- and fourth-century Greece appear on every page, and some poems seem to be the product of a competition to see who can be the most clever, include the most obscure reference, or use the most unusual grammatical construction. This does not always make for great poetry, but it does give us a glimpse into the unprecedented scholarly community that existed in Alexandria at the time.

In addition to this self-conscious literary quality, a particular aesthetic developed in Alexandria. Poets there tended to avoid the long, connected narrative of epic (and even Apollonios of Rhodes's epic, the *Argonautica*, has a significantly different tone than its Homeric precedents). Instead, authors preferred to write poems that strike us as more personal, often exploring emotional or psychological states. We also find, at times, a fascination with an idealized simple life set in the rural countryside. This representation of rustic life is more imagined than real, and the subject matter stands in stark contrast to the sophisticated meter and form of the poetry that portrays it. An emphasis on *eros* and its workings is present everywhere.

This chapter will focus on just a few works, each remarkable in various ways. As always, the interested reader is strongly encouraged to seek out more translations of these Hellenistic authors. Before beginning these analyses, I must provide a warning: because of the self-conscious literary aspects of these poems, it is even more difficult than usual to draw a line between literature and life. When a text demonstrates a certain way of thinking about male-male sexual relations, for example, it is not easy to say if that way of thinking is a reflection of life in second-century BCE Alexandria, or if it is a deliberate allusion to earlier Athenian practices. Hellenistic poetry shows an increased interest in the private conversations of women, but again, it is not easy to know if this is a reflection of greater freedoms in society in general, or simply a result of poetic interest in the personal, the domestic, and characters who are not typically seen as heroic.

THEOCRITUS AND THE EROTIC WOMAN

One of the major authors of the Hellenistic period, Theocritus, is best known for a series of poems that were called "idylls" in antiquity. Three of these idylls are written in the same meter as that used by Sappho; the rest are in dactylic hexameter, the meter used for epic poetry. Most of Theocritus's poems, however, move far from the world of epic. Theocritus is generally credited with the invention of bucolic poetry. This poetry is usually set in the Greek countryside and features speakers who are shepherds, goatherds, and the like. They engage in singing contests, praise the virtues of their rural life, and generally paint an unrealistic and rosy image of a simple rusticism that never was in fact.

Sexually, the poems are of considerable interest. The herdsmen of Theocritus's poems sing endlessly of both heteroerotic and homoerotic love affairs. At times, during singing contests, competing herdsmen will engage in bawdy one-upmanship, resulting in sexual threats and insults worthy of Aristophanes. Also worth noting, however, is the fact that even the descriptions of the landscape tend to drip with a heady eroticism. Theocritus's poetry is sensual in the most literal sense of the word: the poet takes delight in describing the cool shade of a mossy glen on a hot day; the rustling of leaves in a delicate breeze; the taste and smell of honey, wine, cheese, and garlic. Theocritus's poetry, in other words, invites a personal, at times almost physical response.

I will discuss only one of Theocritus's poems here, *Idyll 2*, which the Roman poet Virgil imitated as the second half of his *Eclogue 8*. The poem is remarkable for having a woman as narrator, and one who, moreover, speaks—as if to herself, in private, and not to all the world in an erotic poem—quite frankly about her desire for a young man. In fact, the woman, who is named Simaetha, spends the first half of the poem trying to enact a love charm that will bind her beloved Delphis to her and cause him to return to her side. He has, apparently, been dallying elsewhere, and Simaetha is prepared to use whatever means she can to ensure his return. In the second half of the poem, she pauses from her incantations and tells the brief story of her affair with Delphis, addressing the moon. The poem goes, then, in a reverse chronological order: it begins with the current, disastrous end of the affair and then moves to the story of how it began, before returning, at the end, to the present hopeless state of things. This neat narrative trick has the effect making the story of Simaetha's fling with Delphis all the more poignant.

The poem assumes that we are familiar with the ancient practice of erotic magic and with the image of women as practitioners of that magic. We do know that ancient magic was practiced quite early on in Greece.[2] References are made to it in tragedy, especially in Euripides' *Medea* and *Hippolytus* and Sophocles' *Trachiniae*. We even have the text of a legal case that involves magic in which a woman is accused of having poisoned her husband. She accomplished this poisoning, the prosecutor argues, by convincing a concubine to administer the poison to the defendant's husband and the concubine's lover under the belief that it was a love charm (Antiphon *Against the Stepmother*). We also have some hundreds of scraps of papyri that contain magical instructions on them, hard evidence that the practice of erotic magic was a part of everyday life in the ancient Greek world.

Two elements of ancient Greek magic are particularly important. First, most of the magic that we have evidence for falls under the category of *sympathetic* magic; that is, the way that one causes magical effects to happen is by taking an object that represents the human target of the spell and doing something to it, while suggesting that the same thing happen to the target. So, in *Idyll 2* (28–29), Simaetha says quite early on, "As I melt this wax with the goddess's help, so may Delphis swiftly be melted by desire." Second, the ancient Greeks did not think of being in love as a pleasant sensation; rather, love was regarded as akin to a disease, and the sweat, pain, and inability to eat or sleep was often portrayed in negative terms. The point of much ancient love magic, then, is not necessarily very kind; the magic practitioner wants her target to suffer the same pain and discomfort that she does. Again, to take an example from Theocritus's literary representation of this magic, Simaetha says the following:

Delphis has vexed me. But I burn these bay leaves
for Delphis. And as the leaves crackle loudly in the fire,
and are burned suddenly, and we do not see the ashes of them,
so also may Delphis utterly destroy his flesh in the flame. (*Idyll 2* 23–26)

Simaetha's wish here is double: not only that Delphis melt with desire (picking up on the common image of love as a flame), but that he do so in a destructive flash of brilliant consumption.

One of the most interesting aspects of this poem, of course, is that it presents us with an image of a desiring female subject. Simaetha appears to speak for herself, and she clearly is erotically interested in Delphis. Her desire is her own, and here it is portrayed as aggressive and potentially destructive. We should, however, approach Simaetha with a certain caution. Of the erotic magical papyri that we have, the vast majority of them indicate that the person enacting the spell is male, and usually his target is female.[3] In literature, unlike life, however, we usually see women who are practitioners of magic, their sexual desires posing a threat to otherwise unobjectionable men. The reason for this inversion of actual practice is not entirely clear, but it reflects both fantasy about and a fear of women's sexual desires.

In part, what makes this poem interesting is the implied contrast that it draws between a high literary tradition, to which it alludes, and the relatively mundane events that take place in the poem itself. Simaetha, for example, asks that her magical drugs be no less effective than those of Medea, or Circe, or Perimede (*Idyll 2* 14–16). The third of this trio is something of a mystery; Medea is well known from Euripides' play as a beautiful, seductive Colchian witch who marries the hero Jason. Circe is the powerful demigoddess who turns Odysseus's men into swine in the *Odyssey* (and with whom Odysseus dallies for a year after he defeats her). Simaetha appeals, then, to the grand enchantresses of serious literature, but her own position is rather less exalted. Though she appears to be of solid middle-class stature (she has at least one servant and is herself evidently a citizen), she is an everyday young woman whose love affair has gone sour. She demonstrates, then, a kind of innocence in thinking herself a wronged Medea, and the tension between her real feelings and our perspective of them gives the poem considerable charm. This innocence, or ignorance, comes out more strongly in a later passage from the poem:

Three times I pour a libation, and three times, I say the following:
Whether a woman lies by his side, or a man,
May he forget, just as Theseus, the story goes,
forgot fair-haired Ariadne on the isle of Naxos. (*Idyll 2* 43–46)

Again, the speaker compares her own situation to that of one of the great heroic couples of classical Greek literature. To add to the contrast implicit in this comparison, Simaetha seems not to realize how appropriate her example is; that is, she wishes that Delphis will forget his *new* love just as Theseus forgot Ariadne; she does not see that Delphis is treating her exactly as Theseus did Ariadne, by forgetting her. We, however, make the obvious connection. Simaetha sees her situation from a point of innocence, while we both see her innocence and stand outside of it: we realize that her allusion to Theseus presages the end of her love affair.

Roughly halfway through the poem, Simaetha sends her servant out to knead some herbs on Delphis's threshold (another attempt at a charm, though it is not clear with what intended effect). She then finds herself alone and begins addressing the moon, telling her the story of her affair. As with the lyric poetry from archaic Greece, of course, this is merely a literary trick, creating the illusion that Simaetha is speaking to a third party (or herself), and we are overhearing what presents itself as private. We become voyeurs to her erotic entanglement, which allows her to say, and us to overhear, things that otherwise would not be allowed in public.

The story begins innocently enough: Simaetha went to see a procession as part of a festival of Artemis.[4] When she saw Delphis and a friend at this festival, however, her reaction was swift and devastating:

The moment I saw, I went mad, my spirit was attacked by fire,
I was wretched, and my beauty melted. I no longer noticed the
procession, nor do I know how I got back home.

A burning sickness shook me violently,
 and I lay in bed for ten days and ten nights. (*Idyll 2* 82–86)

Again, we see a strong reaction to male beauty, this time from a young woman. It is worth noting that Simaetha assumes that Delphis might be attractive as an object of desire to men as well as women (see lines 43–46, quoted earlier). In any case, her own reaction is that she is virtually incapacitated. She experiences her erotic desire, as is typical for this kind of poetry, as a debilitating disease, one that burns and shakes the victim. For all the sensual immediacy of this imagery, we should recognize it as a typical *literary* depiction of love.

Indeed, the next section of the poem requires that we read the story of Delphis and Simaetha's affair against a literary tradition. Simaetha tells the moon that she sent her serving girl to the wrestling school to invite Delphis to her, as a "cure" for her "sickness." From everything that we have read, this invitation on her part is, perhaps, a bit forward. Women are not supposed to initiate love affairs, at least not so directly. But in this poem, as we have seen, it is Delphis who is the object of beauty and Simaetha's emotions that are revealed to us, an inversion of the norm in love poetry.

In case we miss this inversion, Delphis himself calls attention to it. On receiving Simaetha's summons, he comes to her house. He goes into a smooth, seductive speech and says that had Simaetha not invited him, he would have come soon anyway:

For I would have come, by sweet Eros I would have come,
with three or four friends, at the start of night. . . .
And then, if you received me, things would have been lovely (for I am called
quick and pretty by all the other boys)
and I would have slept only if I kissed your lovely mouth.
But if you had pushed me away, and barred the door,
Then I would have surely come against you with axes and torches. (*Idyll 2* 123–26)

This speech is a bit humorous. In it Delphis makes reference to the normal approaches that an ardent lover must make of his beloved, hoped-for mistress. If she won't kiss him, he declares, he will be unable to sleep. If she won't let him in, he and his friends will break down the door with axes, a violent correlative to the strength of his desire. But here, Delphis is in a somewhat awkward spot. Not only does he not need to do any of this, but Simaetha has already thrown herself at him. His speech, then, is an attempt to reassure her of his ardent desire, but he can only express this desire in a contrary-to-fact condition: he would have been willing to play the lover, had he been given the chance. The whole situation presents their love affair as an inversion of the usual structure of pursuer and pursued, desiring and desired, with a gentle humor. It is, however, a less than auspicious beginning for Simaetha.

The reversal implicit in such a desiring woman might remind us of the most famous woman of Greek poetry, Sappho. Indeed, the reference to fire in the preceding passage calls to mind Sappho 31, the powerful poem in which Sappho speaks of seeing her beloved (a woman) speaking to a man:

For as I look at you quickly, so I can no longer speak
But my tongue breaks, silently, and thin
fire steals straight under my skin
and there is no sight in my eyes, and my ears hum,
a cold sweat holds me down, a trembling seizes
all of me, and I am paler than grass,
and I seem—to myself—little short of dying. (Sappho 31, 7–16)

The allusion is picked up a little later, when Simaetha describes her response to seeing Delphis approach her home:

I froze completely, colder than snow, and from my brow
sweat poured down like glistening dew,
and I was not able to speak, not even as much as a child,
whimpering, calls for its dear mother in sleep,
but all over my skin froze like a wax doll. (*Idyll 2* 106–10)

Again, a contrast is drawn between the knowing reader and the innocent narrator. Simaetha does not seem to realize that she is quoting Sappho, but the allusion is there for us to catch. Moreover, Simaetha unknowingly quotes a particularly appropriate narrative. Just as Sappho's poem is structured around a love triangle—the speaker is in love with a woman who is in an erotic situation with a man—Simaetha produces her poem at a point when her beloved seems to have run off with some other lover.

   All of this literary background, then, is in our minds when we finally reach the point at which Simaetha describes her sexual encounter with Delphis and the inevitable disaster that follows:

Thus he spoke. And I, trusting him too quickly,
took him by the hand and lay back on my soft bed.
And swiftly flesh warmed upon flesh, and my brow
was warmer than before, and we whispered sweetly.
And so let me not babble too much, dear Moon:
we did the greatest thing, and we both reached our desire.
And he found no fault with me until yesterday,
nor I with him. But the mother of Philista, our flute girl,
and of Melixo, came to me today
as soon as the sun's horses ran into the sky
carrying rosy Dawn from the ocean,
and she told me many things, and that Delphis was just now in love.
And whether desire for a woman holds him or for a man,
She said that she did not know for sure, but she knew this:
he was pouring the unmixed wine of *Eros*. (*Idyll 2* 138–52)

Again, there is a brief echo of Sappho 31 in the "whispering sweetly," and as we might expect, the actual act of sex is mentioned only in a euphemism. The poem is unusual, however, in its description of these events from the woman's point of view and for its depiction of the man, rather than the woman, as fickle, flighty, and inscrutable in his desire.

How should we read this expression of female desire? Is there, in the end, a woman behind this text? In a sense, the answer is clearly no. The poem is little more than an amalgamation of various literary tropes, cleverly written so that the subject of desire is a woman, but without seriously examining what that might mean. As a desiring subject, Simaetha experiences the same symptoms that her male counterparts would be expected to: burning sensations, cold, inability to speak, sweat. Given her somewhat unusual subjectivity, the poem justifies it by having her allude to Sappho and allowing her to speak, in fact, with Sappho's voice. At the same time, the poem is unable to fully let go of a male desiring subject. Placed in the unusual position of having been called to Simaetha's bed, Delphis still makes the speech that a male lover would be expected to, albeit in contrary-to-fact condition. On the whole, this all feels more like a literary game than an exploration of female subjectivity.

On the other hand, the attempt to write a love poem with a woman as the primary speaker and desiring subject is interesting and allows the reader to see a familiar story from another perspective. Rather than sympathizing with a brash young man who presents himself as enslaved by his desire for a beautiful woman, we are invited to think about how the same desires might affect such a young woman. More important, we are encouraged to imagine how she must feel when her young man trades her affections for those of another, unknown rival.

Perhaps most striking of all, however, is the relationship that the poem creates between Simaetha and her reader. Unlike Simaetha, we are able to catch the import of her allusions to Sappho, to Theseus and Ariadne, and so on. The experience of a love affair is represented as a move from innocence to experience; what this poem does is recast that physical and emotional experience in literary terms. As a result, we may sympathize with Simaetha, but we see the inevitable falling off of her love affair in a way that she cannot since we know the end from the start and, furthermore, know the course of things from previous literary experience. This has the effect of making Simaetha's narrative all the more poignant and all the more emotionally effective. We both enjoy the sight of her innocence, of the powerful emotions of first love, and are able to remember, perhaps, the heartrending effect of that innocence coming to an end. In that, the poem does show an original leap of the imagination.

As for questions of sexuality, the poem tells us little directly, though certain assumptions can be deduced. Twice in the course of the poem, we learn that we do not know if Delphis's new flame is a man or a woman (lines 44 and 150). Both times, Simaetha tosses this fact off as if it were perfectly natural to assume that it could be either, which is consistent with what we know of earlier Greek practices. It is significant, however, that in both of these passages, the choice that is presented is a *man* (Greek *anêr*) or a woman, not a *boy* or a woman. In other words, Delphis may be still young enough to be playing the boy with an older male lover. This would be consistent with other evidence that we have seen from the Greek world; that is, a boy is considered to be at the height of his attractiveness when he is just on the edge of manhood (and so able to be the active partner in an affair with a woman). This attractiveness is assumed to appeal to both sexes, despite the fact that the boy/man will play different roles with partners of different sexes.

What about Simaetha's sexuality? There is no suggestion in the poem that she has a sexual identity, or even preference, beyond that of being a woman. As such, she is struck with desire for a beautiful boy. There is, however, an interesting literary aspect to her desire, evident in her evocation of Sappho. When Simaetha describes her own feelings toward Delphis, as we have seen, she echoes Sappho's famous poem 31. In that poem, of course, Sappho is describing her character's feelings for another woman. She is struck numb, cold, and on fire for a desire that, in the frame of the poem, can only remain unrequited. Simaetha, on the other hand, positions herself (unknowingly) both as Sappho and as Sappho's beloved, the woman who sits across from some man and whispers to him as a prelude to lovemaking. Through this complex literary evocation, then, Simaetha both embodies an idea of female desire and experiences the sense of loss that famously accompanies that desire. She is both lover and beloved, though her narrated experience is rigorously heteroerotic.

HERONDAS: TWO WOMEN AND A DILDO

Even less is known about Herondas (also sometimes referred to as Herodas) than about Theocritus. He appears to have lived in the early part of the Hellenistic period; his poems, known as *mimiamboi,* or "iambic mimes," were virtually unknown to modern scholars until a papyrus containing them was published in 1891. Several of these poems have scurrilous subject matter and characters, including prostitutes and pimps, as well as regular middle-class women. Though the speaking characters in his poems are often female, the outlook of the poems themselves is frequently misogynistic.

In poem 6, the subject could hardly be more scandalous. Two women, who are both married and appear to belong to the middle class, meet for a conversation. The subject of their talk is primarily the lovely leather dildo that one of them has obtained. Here, at last, it appears that we are finally going to get a frank discussion of some aspect of women's sexual lives.

Somewhat surprisingly, however, the first thing that happens is that the dildo becomes the subject of an elaborate literary joke. The two speakers are named "Metro" and "Koritto;" Koritto is the owner of the dildo, but it appears that she does not have it with her at the moment. In fact, when Metro asks her about it, Koritto wants to know how Metro heard about it. Metro responds that a woman named "Nossis," daughter of Erinna, had it; she apparently got it from a woman named "Euboule." The names Nossis and Erinna are not, as we might think, merely chosen at random; both are known to us as famous women poets. Scholars have debated since the nineteenth century what the exact valence of this allusion may be.[5] Is Herondas making fun of these celebrated women poets, suggesting that they are no better than his characters and, in fact, sexually voracious? Or is he suggesting that, in taking up the act of poetry, they are merely imitating men, just as women who use a dildo are? Such interpretations seem likely, especially given the response that Koritto has to the news that Nossis has the dildo:

I do not think that I would give her one [of my dildos],
—if I complain more than is just, may Vengeance overlook it—
not if I had a thousand, not even if it were rotten. (*Mimiambos* 6.34–36)

Nossis, here, is the clear object of Koritto's scorn, and we are probably right to read this as an oblique (and small-minded) form of literary criticism.

Whatever the insult against Nossis, however, one thing is amusingly clear from this episode: dildos travel. This dildo, in fact, has already gained a fame that verges on epic. Before its owner gets to use it, it's been borrowed by Euboule (a woman whose name means "good counsel"), who has loaned it to Nossis, who showed it to Metro. The easy transference of this sexual object suggests a close society of women who may be doing sexual things outside the watchful eyes of their husbands and who literally share sexual experiences. In fact, the poem seems designed, in part, to make fun of those men who do not realize what their wives are doing behind their backs. Among other things, the dildo is described as considerably preferable to the husbands themselves. Metro eventually gets Koritto to admit that the dildo was crafted by a cobbler named Kerdon. When she describes seeing the dildo for the first time, she sounds almost overcome with desire:

The workmanship! What workmanship! You would say
it's Athena's work, not Kerdon's when you see it.
And I—for he came bringing two of them, Metro—
when I saw them, my eyes went wide.
Men don't make their cocks so—
it's just us here—straight. And not just this, but it's soft as sleep, and the straps
are wool, not leather. You could search,
but you'd not find a cobbler more kindly disposed to women. (*Mimiambos* 6.65–73)

The dildo is not just an acceptable substitute, it is actually better than a real man.

As a result, the women demonstrate themselves to be quite shameless in their pursuit of this lovely item. Koritto has now revealed that there were two of the dildos; Metro asks why she did not obtain them both. Koritto's response is more than a bit scandalous:

What did I not do [i.e., to get it]?
What sort of persuasion did I fail to bring to him?
I kissed him, I rubbed his bald head,
I poured out sweet drinks, I teased him—
the only thing I didn't give him was my body. (*Mimiambos* 6.74–79)

Metro, however, responds even more enthusiastically:

But even if he asked for that [i.e., her body], you should have given it. (*Mimiambos* 6.79)

Kerdon's name, probably not coincidentally, means "profit," and here he has thoroughly capitalized on the transaction for his handiwork. The women are depicted as so taken with the dildo that they're willing to do anything, even commit adultery, to obtain it. Indeed, at the end of their conversation, Metro suggests that she is going to try her luck with Kerdon in pursuit of the second dildo: "You've said enough. Now I'll go to Artemis, so I can learn what sort this Kerdon is" (*Mimiambos* 6.95–96).

Who, then, is made fun of in this poem? On one hand, the women are depicted as sexually voracious and willing to trade sexual favors on the cheap. This is hardly a flattering portrait. On the other hand, the poem seems to play on men's fears and insecurities. These women's husbands are not as satisfying as a leather stand-in, and their wives will do almost anything to get their hands on a really good piece of leather. The fact that the dildo trades hands so extensively before the poem begins only adds to this sense of paranoia: men are not only replaceable, but their replacement easily trades hands among a community of women who share their secrets about it with one another.

One final point needs to be made about the dildo. At line 71, the speaker mentions the dildo's "straps." The word here is sometimes translated "laces" (suggesting the laces used to sew the seams together). But the word in Greek, *himantiskos,* is derived from a word (*himas*) that always refers to a leather strap that ties one thing to another: a chinstrap on a helmet, the traces attaching a horse to a chariot, reins, the thong on a sandal. It seems reasonable to conclude, then, that this dildo has straps and is designed to be tied on and used with a partner. Though the poem makes no mention of such activity, the poem perhaps hints at same-sex activity between two women. If this reading is correct, it makes the joking criticism of these women's husbands all the more pointed and the understanding of a secret, sexually linked community of women all the stronger. This community may exist more in male fantasy than in reality, but it is helpful to know that men may have been anxious about the possibility.

EROTIC EPIGRAMS

Throughout the Hellenistic period and beyond, authors imitating the earlier Greek poets wrote epigrams,[6] that is, short poems in elegiac meter.[7] The person addressed in the poem is sometimes the speaker's love object, sometimes no one in particular. But the poems are often about love and frequently lament an unrequited love. Quite late in the textual history of Greek literature, a collection of epigrams from the earliest authors of Greek poetry down to the sixth century CE was edited, producing a document that we have come to know as the *Greek Anthology* (also called the *Palatine Anthology*).

Within this anthology, one finds both heteroerotic and homoerotic poems. Book 12 of the anthology, however, is somewhat striking in that it contains 258 poems, nearly all concerning the love of boys. Some of these poems are anonymous; others include poems by several important Hellenistic poets, including Callimachus, Theocritus, Asclepiades, and Meleager. A fair number are by Strato, who dates to the first century CE and who is credited with collecting these verses into a single book.

The art of the epigram is, like much Hellenistic poetry, highly polished. The poem must convey a complex situation and set of emotions in just a few brief lines. Sometimes the poems take delight in rendering an everyday conversation into the careful poetic meter required. Often, the poems contain a twist at the end, a sudden reversal (or a wish for a such a reversal). These are poems designed to elicit a quick response; they are short, funny, literary, and sometimes brutal.

When encountering the poems in the 12th book of the *Greek Anthology,* the reader has the sense that the authors are trying to be more Athenian than the Athenians were; that is, there is a relentless pursuit of the themes that we saw earlier: the virtues of self-control; the cruelty of boy beloveds and the regret that they will experience later; the advantages of boy love over love of women. In particular, a number of poets demonstrate an obsession with the beauty of the boy who will grow too old and rather suddenly be no longer attractive at all. Indeed, this moment of transition seems to have held particular fascination. An anonymous poem puts it rather baldly:

Nicander is burned out, all the bloom has flown
from his body, and not even the *name* of charm is left,
though before we thought him one of the immortals. Realize
that nothing is more than mortal, young men. Hairs exist. (*Greek Anthology* 12.39)

The poem plays on the notion of divinity and beauty: Nicander was once so beautiful that he was thought divine, and the standard word for divine in Greek is "immortal." But alas, his beauty has proven to be the most mortal thing about him. And as the last two words (also the last two words in the Greek original) make clear, the marker of that failing beauty is, simply, the development of pubic hair. Once that line is crossed, beauty is gone.

An early poet in the collection, Asclepiades, explores the experience of the boy who has just crossed the threshold in a brief dramatic monologue:

Now you ask, when fine whiskers creep under your temples,
and sharp hairs appear on your thighs.
Then you say, "This is sweeter for me." But who would say
that rough stalks are better than sweet corn? (*Greek Anthology* 12.36)

Here the appearance of hair is more than a simple visual aesthetic. The descriptive adjectives, particularly the idea of thighs covered with sharp stubble, call to mind an act of sex. More important, though, is the poignancy that the poem creates in the first two phrases: "now you ask." We understand immediately that at an earlier time, the addressee of the poem had been *asked,* rather than *asking.* Now, when it is too late, the young man is interested; his time was shorter than he knew.

The Hellenistic poems, then, demonstrate the development of a poetic rule. Whereas earlier Greek poetry certainly prized young masculine beauty, and occasionally expressed disgust at a beloved who was too old, the Hellenistic epigrams insist that a boy can only be so old, and no older. Whether this reflects a real, social development, or merely the development of a literary idea, is impossible to say, but the number of poems in book 12 of the *Greek Anthology* that deal with this moment is remarkable. Strato, the poet who made the first-century collection on which the later *Anthology* was based, writes a number of poems in this vein. One of the more tightly crafted pieces, though not the most poetic, is explicit about the aesthetic rules:

I am pleased by the prime of a twelve-year-old.
But even more desirable is thirteen.
The one passing twice seven is a sweeter flower of *Eros*
But even more pleasant is the one beginning thrice five.
Sixteen is the year of the gods. But seventeen
is not mine to seek, but rather Zeus's.
And if someone has a desire for still older, he is no longer playing,
but already he seeks one "answering him in turn." (*Greek Anthology* 12.4)

This careful delineation of each year in turn is a bit prosaic, despite the clever poetic names for each number (remembering that in Greek, each line fits a fairly restrictive meter). The poem has a bit of fun, though, toward the end. Sixteen is divinely beautiful, but 17 is evidently a bit *too* beautiful; that is, the poet suggests that a young man at that age is still attractive, even excessively so, but now out-of-bounds for mortals. The real clincher to the poem comes, however, in the last line: if one seeks someone older than 17, then he is looking not only to penetrate, but to be penetrated. This shocking idea is made playful, and palatable, by the fact that the euphemistic phrase indicating the idea ("answering him in turn") is a stock Homeric formula. It occurs hundreds of times in the *Iliad* and *Odyssey,* in a nonsexual context, usually in a sentence beginning "And so he spoke, answering him in turn . . ." Here this otherwise innocuous phrase is used to suggest the one great taboo of Greek sexual rules, the desire to play the passive role.

Some poems also suggest, however, that the rules were not always observed as regularly as they could be stated. The same poet who wrote the preceding poem writes in another epigram about his enduring love for a boy who has passed his prime:

Even if your whiskers, bringing hair, have sprung forth,
and soft blonde curls are on your temples,
Even so I do not flee my beloved. But his beauty
even with a beard, even with hair, is mine. (*Greek Anthology* 12.10)

Here, we should note that the usual rules are mentioned, even if only to indicate that they will not be followed. The vocabulary of this poem is almost exactly that of Asclepiades' poem (*Greek Anthology* 12.36) discussed earlier. It is not known if this poem has any biographical relevance or if it is simply the poet trying out another stance. One should note, however, that this poem is not taking the position that we saw at times in the classical period, that an erotic attraction could flower into a nonsexual lifelong friendship. Even in the last line of the poem, the speaker is discussing his beloved's physical beauty and is stating, perhaps shockingly, that it has not faded with age.

I have given only a small sampling of the poems that deal with this theme, and it is worthwhile to pause for a moment and consider what is lacking from them. Unlike, for example, the poems of Theognis from an earlier era, we do not see in these poems an anxiety over whether it is right for a boy to give himself to his lover. There is no discussion of this or that act being "shameful" or of the boy giving himself for the wrong reason. A lover-centered anxiety seems to have entirely replaced these kinds of concerns. The speaker of these poems is concerned only that he be able to convince the boys to give themselves before it is too late.

Two other important themes from book 12 deserve mention. First, several of the poems lament the commercialization of love. Strato writes of a boy's discovery of profit as the real loss of his innocence:

Alas! Why are you crying again, and why are you downcast,
little boy? Tell me simply, don't be hurt. What do you want?
You held out your cupped hand to me. I am ruined!
You ask, perhaps for payment. Where did you learn this?
Slices of cake are no longer dear to you, or sweet sesame,
or jolly nuts to use for marbles.
But already you've turned your mind to profit. May whoever taught
you this die. He's done away with my only boyfriend. (*Greek Anthology* 12.212)

We saw this theme earlier, but here it is treated with a slight twist. The archaic elegiac poets warned that some boys might give their love for the wrong reasons, that is to say, money. And of course, Plato warned against entering into love affairs for these reasons. Here it is not a question of the wrong sort of boy, but rather of an *erastes* who was enjoying a boy who hadn't yet learned that he could charge money. The lament of the poem, gently ironic, is that now he will have to pay; but it is also more than that. Now that the boy is interested in profit, he is no longer a boyfriend. Though the speaker does not seem to be aware of it, he is being gently chided for his obsession with an innocence that is more coincidental than essential. Less gentle is the following poem, which describes an entirely different dynamic:

Good-bye to you, you falsely noble one, good-bye, you trash,
You who just swore never to give it away.
Now you'll not swear anymore. For I recognized you, and you won't escape;
I know where, how, with whom, and for how much. (*Greek Anthology* 12.237)

Here the issue is not just that the boy is a prostitute (though evidently, he is that); rather, the poem pokes gentle fun at its speaker, who has just learned that he has been turned down by a boy of easy virtue. On the surface, the poem is about the boy, but in a more important way, it shines a light on the speaker's moment of failure, rejection, and anger.

The next recurring theme is another that we have seen before, and that is discussions about the relative merits of love of boys and love of women. Some poems rework old ground, such as *Greek Anthology* 12.192, which contrasts the makeup and false beauty of women with the "natural" appearance of a boy, freshly oiled from the wrestling ring. Others, however, take a more humorous approach to the difference:

A girl has no sphincter, nor a simple
kiss, no natural good scent of skin,
There's none of that dirty talk, nor a straight
come-hither look, and the girl who's been taught is worse.
All of them are cold from behind. But what's bigger than that,
there's no place where you can put your wandering hand. (*Greek Anthology* 12.7)

This poem is amusing precisely because it assumes that the reader has had experience, or at least can imagine it, with boys. Nothing especially indecorous is mentioned, but in the process of reading the last two lines, we are forced to think about our "wandering" hand and what it grabs on to. The whole poem is a masterful exercise in conjuring, without mentioning, a boy's penis.

The poem just discussed is also important, however, for in articulating the differences between sex with boys and with women (or girls), it implies that there is not all that much different. One can desire either, or so the poem seems to suggest. There are advantages, of course, to one, and the speaker clearly prefers boys. But not because he finds sex with women fundamentally repugnant, or even all that different; it certainly would not mark him as a different type of man to have sex with a woman. It's just that when he has sex with a woman, there is no handle to grab on to. He may have a sexual preference, but it hardly qualifies as an orientation, and there is no indication of a sexual identity.

A similar sense of distinction without essential difference is expressed in the following piece, from book 5 of the *Anthology* (i.e., not identified as belonging in the pederastic poems of book 12):

Love of females is the best for mortals,
for those whose mind is serious about love.
But if you are also fond of masculine desire,
I can teach a cure, by which you can stop this bad-loving sickness.
Turn fair-hipped Menophilê over, and imagine
that you have male Menophilus in your arms. (*Greek Anthology* 5.116)

This is an interesting poem, in that it does suppose that the person spoken to has a fairly strong preference for one kind of love over the other; that is, he prefers love of boys to such a degree that he is in need of a mental trick to have sex with a woman. This begins to look like a sexual orientation (within the confines of an always penetrating gender role). The poem also describes his predeliction for boys as a "sickness." Once again, however, we need to be careful not to assume an entire set of modern assumptions about psychological normativity because of that one word. In the terms that the poem sets up, love of women is better because it is more *serious*; that is, a time comes when a man should stop dallying with boys and begin a longer-lasting sexual relationship with a woman. Moreover, the speaker suggests (though here with a bit of light humor) that there's not so much difference, after all, between kinds of love objects.

One other poem suggests a more serious difference in the types of desire and deserves mention here. The poet Meleager, active in the first century BCE, assembled a collection of earlier epigrams as well as writing his own. His poems contain a number of lovely heteroerotic poems, many of them addressed to a woman (or rather, a fictional persona) named "Heliodora." Other poems are explicitly homoerotic. In this poem, he bridges the gap:

I no longer write of beautiful Theron, nor is Apollodotos
fiery bright as before, but now he is a smoldering brand.
I desire a female love. May goat-mounting shepherds
squeeze the hairy-assed male sluts.[8] (*Greek Anthology* 12.41)

The effect of this poem is brought about by the contrast between the two couplets. The first couplet is fairly decorous and uses the regular vocabulary of love poetry. The image of a boy being a source of fire is common enough, and the idea that he has burnt out is one that appears in many gentler poems. With the second two lines, however, everything becomes rude and crude. In the Greek, the word order is something more like, "the squeezing of hairy-assed sluts, let it be for shepherds who mount goats." All the emphasis falls on the end of the line, so that the speaker's insult grows as the line progresses: from insulting men who desire other men to suggesting that such men also enjoy bestiality. The contrast in this poem, then, is between the positive portrayal of boy love that love poetry quite regularly shows and the negative portrayal that inhabits invective poetry.

The interesting thing about the poem is that it presents this move from elegy to invective as a personal transformation. Yesterday the speaker saw boys as love objects; today he finds them disgusting. But again, the terms of abuse are important. Whereas in the first two lines, the speaker seems to be discussing boys—at least, there is no indication that Theron and Apollodotos are past their prime—in the next two lines, he is repelled by the idea of sex with older men. Perhaps it is not the speaker who has changed, but his beloveds, who have grown old. The poem does not say so, but it is clear that he does not say anything negative about sex with boys who are not yet hairy and goatlike. Or perhaps the poem is the result of discovering that the speaker's boyfriend has been sleeping around: as a result, the speaker abuses all boys as "sluts" and denigrates them as hairy as well. Again, does the speaker of the poem possess a sexual orientation? It may be said that he does, in that he now declares himself solely interested in women. But it is not same-sex desire per se that he finds repugnant, but rather sex with hairy, sexually voracious young men.

THE OTHER SIDE OF THE EPIGRAMS

I have dwelt at some length on the epigrams from book 12 of the *Anthology* because it is particularly interesting to see the ways in which the Hellenistic poets took up and subtly modified the Athenian tradition of pederasty. It would be misleading, however, to suggest that the epigrams are primarily homoerotic. Indeed, most of the poems in book 5 (consisting of love poems) are heteroerotic, and they range from the tender and loving to the fairly explicit. Some are appeals to reluctant girlfriends, others are downhearted monologues on having been rejected, and still others depict conversations with prostitutes. As with much Hellenistic poetry, high value is placed on literary reference, on cleverness and wit, and occasionally, on making poems about normally unpoetic subjects. I will close this chapter with a discussion of the most salient features of a few heteroerotic poems.

In the first place, several of the epigrams depict a speaker who is trying to convince a young woman to sleep with him, and the sooner the better. These poems are especially useful as a point of comparison with the homoerotic poems discussed previously. In both, the object of the speaker is roughly the same. The concerns that seem to underlie the heteroerotic poems, however, are quite different. As one might expect, they do not show the same concern with the possibility that the woman will grow old and hairy. As earlier examples have shown, one of the virtues of love of women is that they do not suddenly become out-of-bounds once they pass the threshold of puberty. Perhaps even more interesting, however, some of these poems demonstrate anxiety over the women's virginity that is not as clearly present in earlier literature.

This poem from book 5 of the *Anthology* is attributed to Plato (the philosopher, discussed in chapter 6). A number of epigrams are attributed to him, though most are considered the work of later poets. The speaker urges his female beloved to make haste:

I strike you with an apple. And you, if you [female] love me willingly
then receive the apple, and give in return your virginity.
But if you think what I wish you would not, take this same [apple]
and think how short the moment will last. (*Greek Anthology* 5.79)

This is an entirely different aesthetic than the homoerotic poems addressed to boys. Here, as there, the moment for love is short. But the reason that the moment is short is, simply, vague and undefined. Clearly the poem draws a parallel between the woman's sexual attractiveness and the apple, since the first two lines set them up in explicit exchange, and suggests that the woman's beauty will fade as quickly as the apple will go bad. In this reading, though, there is no suggestion of what will make the woman overripe. There are no thigh hairs threatening to destroy, in one moment, the brilliance of her beauty just before it goes over the edge. The speaker is simply saying that this one moment is the woman's best chance. After this, who knows?

On the other hand, the poem introduces a term into the erotic conversation that the homoerotic poems do not: virginity. The speaker is not only interested in sex with the woman, but is interested in her specifically because she is without sexual experience. This sexual aesthetic is so much a part of the later Western tradition that it may not seem remarkable. But in fact, very little Greek poetry (or prose, for that matter) before the Hellenistic period concerns itself with the idea that a woman possesses a quality of being innocent of sex and that this quality is lost forever with the first sexual act.[9] In the earlier, archaic lyric period, poets like Archilochos and Anacreon place a good deal of emphasis on the innocence of the woman addressed, but they do not insist on virginity as a state of physical and personal being. The preceding Hellenistic poem also posits virginity as an object of exchange: the speaker wants to trade it for an apple. The woman, then, is not merely giving sex, but is being asked to give up this state of being. This is a new and important development in the way the Greeks thought about sex.

Another poem from the same period is even more explicit about this development and expresses a sentiment so familiar that it seems quite modern:

You guard your virginity. And for what? For when you go into Hades,
you will not find a lover, girl.
The pleasures of Aphrodite are among the living. In Acheron,
we will lie bones and dust, maiden. (*Greek Anthology* 5.85)

As Marvell puts it in his "To His Coy Mistress," "The Grave's a fine and private place, / But none I think do there embrace." As in Marvell's poem, the Hellenistic poet looks forward with regret to the day when the pleasures of love will not be possible and argues for making the most of time. Already it appears that what he needs to argue against is specifically the idea that the woman will want to protect her virginity. Her impulse, evidently, is to remain in her current state of innocence. Against this impulse toward the static, the speaker can only throw his most effective argument: time rushes on, anyway. Again, this notion of virginity as a thing, to be protected by the woman and to be overcome by the man, is rarely expressed in earlier poetry. Its importance for the later tradition of Western love poetry can hardly be overestimated.

The *Anthology* also contains a number of poems that I can only describe as playful, such as the following conversation between a young man and a female prostitute (dashes indicate a change of speaker):

—Hello, you. —And hello to you. —What should I call you? —No, what should I call you? —Don't be in a hurry about that. —You neither. —Don't you have anyone?[10]
—I always have a lover. —Would you like to have dinner with me tonight?
—If you like. —Good then. How much will you cost?
—Don't give me anything. —That's unusual. —Rather, as much as would
seem right for sleeping with you, give me that. —You are not unjust.
Where will you be? I'll send for you. —Figure it out. —When will you come?
—Whatever hour you wish. —How about now? —Lead the way. (*Greek Anthology* 5.46)

It is difficult to know what to do with a poem like this one, attributed to Philodemus. Obviously it is not a transcript of a real conversation. Much of its charm comes from the fact that this brief conversation, which frequently changes speaker mid-line, is nonetheless placed in rigorous elegiac meter. No prostitute and john ever spoke quite so prettily. On the other hand, the poem only works if the author can assume that his readers know something, whether from real life or literary depictions, about prostitution.

The poem establishes, then, that prostitutes were a known quantity in Hellenistic Greece. It also tells us a little bit about negotiations between prostitutes and their clients. In this poem, the client asks the woman how much she will cost. Clearly he expects her to name a set price. The fact that she does not is, perhaps, a nod to the literary rules that govern this conversation. It is one thing for the poem to replicate this somewhat sordid negotiation; but as long as the prostitute does not name a price, a certain poetic decorum is preserved. The prostitute's circumspection, however, creates a tension between the content of their conversation and its form. As the client notes, not naming a price is unusual, perhaps the sort of thing that only happens in poetry.

The poem also plays, I believe, with the elegiac form in another way. A large number of the epigrams in book 5 of the *Anthology* are pleas from a lover to his beloved. The speaker begs his girlfriend to pay attention to him, to be faithful, to let him in her door at the arranged hour, and so forth. In some poems, a spurned lover wishes that his girlfriend feel the same pain that he does. Here, however, the elegiac negotiation is neatly evoked, but avoided. The speaker fears a rival, asking the woman if she "has anyone." She responds in the language of elegy, saying that she always has "a lover" (Greek *phileonta*). If she were a girlfriend in elegy, this might be an obstacle. But here, phrased as it is, the woman's statement becomes an invitation. At the end of the poem, even more strikingly, the man asks rather plaintively when the date will be. The answer is one that never appears in more traditional elegy: "whenever you like." Now is good. Rather than reproducing the agonizing tension of a lover who may or may not ever win over his girl, then, this poem simply makes all those problems go away. All one needs to do, this elegiac poem suggests, is find a girl for hire. This is, again, a light and fairly subtle joke, and the laughter is only available to the reader who knows the elegiac tradition already.

One final epigram provides information, in a muted and indirect way, about the possibility of female-female sexual relationships:

Two women from Samos, Bitto and Nanion, do not like to
meet Aphrodite by her own rules.
They desert to the other side, which is not good. Queen Aphrodite,
hate these fugitives from your kind of sex. (Asclepiades, *Greek Anthology* 5.207)

The poem, of course, does not actually say that Bitto and Nanion are having sex with each other (or with other women, for that matter). In a detailed philological analysis of the poem, however, Dover has shown that that is the most likely interpretation of the suggestion that these women have deserted Aphrodite's kind of sex.[11] During the later classical and Hellenistic periods, Aphrodite is increasingly depicted as governing heteroerotic desire, while her son Eros rules over male-male relations. (No god or goddess, apparently, rules over female-female sex.)

The most difficult line of the poem to translate is the second. Literally, it says something like "they desert to other, not good things." The words that I have translated "not good," unfortunately, are *mê kala*, a negative (*mê*) followed by a fairly flavorless Greek word that can have a range of meanings, everything from "good" (in a moral sense) to "beautiful" to "noble." So what are these things that Bitto and Nannion turn to that are either morally bad, or perhaps unlovely, or possibly even not fitting for their station in life? It seems likely that the poet is referring to sex with each other and that he finds this idea morally problematic. The word that I have translated "desert" is used regularly of men when they desert in battle—a particularly shameful act— and later, the women are referred to as fugitives. The language of the poem, then, suggests that these women have strayed from the proper bounds of sexual relations. It does not tell us anything about those relations, and it does not bother to suggest any motivation for the women's actions; it only records the fact that, from the speaker's point of view, the women are now traitorous in love.

It does appear that the women's desertion, if the preceding interpretation is correct, is not merely a single act; rather, these two women have made a lifestyle choice about the kind of sex that they prefer (or so it seems to the speaker, in any case). Does this make them lesbians, in the modern sense? Perhaps, though we have no information about any aspect of their lives other than their sexual practices, and even those are described so euphemistically as to be uncertain; that is, we can say that they have a sexual orientation. It is simply impossible to know if the (imagined) women in the poem would have thought of themselves as a different kind of person because of their sexual practice, or if, as is often the case, their choice of sexual partner would be conceived of as a preference, a choice of appetite, rather than identity.

As always, we are left with all too little information. It seems certain that some women in Greece did have sexual relations with one another. Outside of the poems of Sappho, however, the conditions of these relations are never described. This may be the one sexual thing that Greek men simply did not want to think about. Whether this is because they found the idea threatening or because they wanted all women to be sexually available to men is not specified. It may also be the case that Greek men did not want to think of women as having desires of their own, rather than merely reflecting back their husbands' desires. In any case, as Dover has argued, there is a virtual conspiracy of silence on the subject.

CONCLUSIONS: GREECE

As this study has shown, the Greeks talked and thought about sex in a variety of different ways and in a variety of different contexts. Erotic poetry tells us how they thought about sex in a subjective, emotional way. Legal speeches give information about what was legal, illegal, legal but immoral, or moral but socially frowned on. Philosophic texts provide glimpses of the ways in which leading intellectuals thought about desire as a force for intellectual inquiry and personal improvement. In addition to these variations of context, it is clear that some aspects of sexual life changed over time.

Certain broad ideas about sex, however, appear to be constant in Greek culture, and indeed, many of them are also true of Roman society. The Greeks did not define men's sexual desire by the gender of the love object; that is, a man could love women or boys with equal legal, moral, and social approval.

What he could not do, morally and socially, was desire to be penetrated once he became an adult. Legally, there were no restrictions on homoerotic behavior per se, any more than on heteroerotic behavior, though considerable legal protections existed to keep citizen boys' futures as active adult males intact, just as legal protections prevented men from having sex with citizen women who were unmarried or married to another man. And most important, it does not seem that the Greeks thought of people who preferred one kind of sex over another as *types* of people.

Change over time, however, should not be minimized. Fifth- and fourth-century Athens exhibited an almost paranoid fascination with questions of whom a boy should give himself to, under what circumstances, and for what recompense. The literature of the Hellenistic period shows no such concern. Instead, the highly polished poems of that period focus increasingly on moments of transition, when a boy becomes suddenly unattractive because he has grown hairs on his thigh. This period also demonstrates, if not for the first time then with considerably heightened emphasis, a concern with women's virginity, and these poems present that physical state as a thing to be protected, traded, and lost. Less explicit information exists about legal disputes from this later period, but that may be attributed to a lack of legal sources, rather than to a shift in actual practice.

As I turn my attention to Rome, I will not entirely leave Greece behind. Greek culture and practice had considerable influence on the development of the Roman state, not least because schoolteachers in Rome were commonly Greek slaves. And while Roman ideas about what was acceptable and unacceptable in sex largely share the pattern demonstrated by Greek sources, there are also significant differences. The institution of pederasty, in particular, was viewed with considerable distrust by the Romans. This does not mean, however, that the Romans disapproved of the love of boys; they merely disapproved of the penetration of unmarried citizens of either gender (even if done with decorum). As with any culture, Rome exhibits its own concerns, anxieties, legalities, and constructs around the practice of sex, and these are best understood through an examination of their cultural productions. We turn, then, to Rome.

Eight

Rome and Roman Sex

The history of Rome, and Roman culture, begins traditionally in the eight century BCE and continues, with various interruptions, well into the sixth century CE. Needless to say, I cannot survey every era of this remarkable city-state. To briefly orient my reader, however, I provide here the barest sketch of the different periods of Roman history. As was the case with Greece, sexual practices and attitudes surely changed over the long span of Rome's development as a political state and eventual domination of the West; it will be the task of the following chapters to highlight some of those shifts, changes, and breaks.

According to tradition, Rome was founded in the year 753 BCE. Unfortunately, we have no contemporary sources from the early centuries of Roman civilization; indeed, it is not until some 500 years later, at the end of the third century BCE, that the earliest surviving Latin literature was written, and even then, what survives are the comedies of the Roman playwright Plautus. Nothing like a reliable history of Rome exists from these time periods, and the later historians who do write about it (such as Livy, who is active early in the first century CE) recount the clearly mythical stories of early Rome as if they were historical fact. Though such historical works give us some indication of the military, political, and legal history of the development of Rome, when it comes to issues of behavior, they tend to reflect the attitudes of the time in which they were written. All of this is to say that, for the first 400 years of Roman history or so, we can say almost nothing with certainty about Roman attitudes toward sex and sexual behavior.

My survey of Roman sex, then, will begin with the earliest surviving Roman literature, beginning in the late third and early second century BCE. During this time period, Rome's form of government was a republic, in which two consuls were elected as the preeminent officeholders for each year. Rome's government and society developed significantly over the 400-year period from the beginning of the city to our earliest sources, and interested readers are encouraged to look into these early centuries. At the time that my survey begins, however, it is important to note simply that Rome exhibited a rigorous class structure. Citizens were divided into two separate, though largely overlapping, systems of status. In the first, a citizen was either a patrician or a plebeian; these statuses were a matter of birth, and the patrician families tended to represent what we would think of as old wealth. (Traditionally, the patricians were descended from the members of Rome's first senate, as constituted by the mythical figure of Romulus; what, if any, fact lies behind this idea is impossible to determine.) Patricians controlled the Roman Senate throughout the republic, and initially, only patricians could hold important offices in the government. During the fourth and third centuries BCE, the plebs grew in power and privilege and eventually won the right to their own legislative body, the plebeian council.

At the same time, Roman citizens in the republic were divided into five property classes, based on wealth; of these, the first two classes (the *equites,* often translated "knights") and first class (the "senatorial" class) together held a majority of votes in the *comitia centuriata,* a legislative body that chose the holders of important offices and determined matters of war and peace. (A confusing but important point is that membership in the senatorial class did not equal membership in the senate.) Needless to say, patricians tended to outnumber plebs in these first two property classes, though in the later republic, a class of wealthy plebs became part of the ruling elite.

Even more important than the various divisions of citizens into different kinds of classes, however, was the distinction in Rome between citizens, freedmen, and slaves. Citizens, regardless of class or property status, held certain unalienable rights, such as the right not to be beaten or used sexually by another citizen. Slaves, on the other hand, were legally the property of their masters and literally had no control over the use of their bodies. Freedmen were former slaves who had been manumitted by their former masters; though free, they did not have full citizenship rights and in some cases were thought of as owing deference to their former masters. Their freeborn children, however, were full citizens.

In the first century BCE, Rome entered the period of the late republic; with the dictatorship of Sulla in 81 BCE, a series of challengers threatened the republican government, culminating in the civil war between Julius Caesar and the republican forces of Pompey. This period is particularly rich for the study of sexuality because from it we have the legal speeches and letters of the great orator Cicero as well as the erotic poems of Cicero's contemporary, Catullus. In the 50s BCE, Julius Caesar rose to power, though he was killed by the last guard of the republic in 44. After a series of political maneuvers and battles, however, his adopted son Octavius, later known as Augustus Caesar, established the Roman Empire (with himself as emperor) in 27 BCE.

The era of Augustus is particularly important in the study of sexuality because he enacted a series of laws meant to encourage marriage and to limit extramarital sexual activity.[1] In 18 BCE, he passed the Julian law on marriage (*lex Julia de maritandis ordinibus*). This set of regulations stipulated that citizen men between the ages of 25 and 60 and citizen women between 20 and 50 were to be married. The law provided considerable encouragement to comply. Men who were not married could not inherit legacies outside of the sixth degree of relationship, and those who were married without children could only inherit half of these legacies. More important, men who were married and had produced three children were given increased access to certain political offices and were allowed to progress more rapidly up the ladder of political power. Women who had produced three children in a marriage were allowed to perform legal and economic transactions on their own behalf, without the use of a guardian. All in all, the law provided significant incentives.

The Julian law on adultery (*lex Julia de adulteriis*), passed in 18 or perhaps 16 BCE, made sex with another man's wife a violation of criminal law (rather than being subject to a civil action) for the first time in Roman history. The punishment for violation was significant: both the man and woman were exiled to an island and had their property confiscated. Though enforcement of these laws must have been spotty, it was not unknown. In the year 2 BCE, Augustus banished his own daughter Julia (the elder) to an island after she was convicted of adultery.

It is against this background that we must read the erotic poets of the Augustan period. The poets, including Propertius, Tibullus, Horace, and later, Ovid, all adopted speaking personas who gloried in extramarital affairs with married citizen women, perhaps fictional, perhaps not. In addition, these poets extol the virtues of such affairs, in direct opposition to more traditional Roman male activities, such as participation in the military and management of business. Their poems, then, had the potential to be read as subversive of the moral attitudes of the Augustan regime. Indeed, Ovid eventually pushed the emperor too far, though we do not know exactly how, and was himself banished in 8 CE. Perhaps his poetry simply cut too close to the bone, and the emperor found that he could no longer tolerate the poet's playful undermining of legal sanctions against adultery.

Augustus's reign, which lasted until his death in 14 CE, was by all accounts highly successful. Though social changes did not take place overnight, it is clear that the creation of the Empire radically changed structures of power in Rome. Augustus did not disband the offices or legislative bodies of the republic; part of his genius was to leave these structures in place, while legally having the powers of several important offices conferred on himself for life. What this meant, however, was that a new superstructure of power and influence existed on top of the old Roman republican structures. Closeness to the emperor himself could invest a person with personal influence that could not have been achieved under the republic.

Later emperors showed less restraint than did Augustus, and as the Empire developed, personal, familial structures of power grew in importance. With them grew increasing paranoia about the role of powerful women, especially those in the imperial household. When most readers think of the Roman Empire, they think of the famously corrupt emperorships of figures like Caligula, Claudius, and Nero; and indeed, the period of the first century CE saw the development of a culture of lavish spending and unprecedented personal power. It is also during this period that traditional structures of wealth began to erode. Even some freedmen became quite wealthy as members of a new merchant class, and with their wealth acquired considerable power; such members of a *nouveau riche* come under vicious attack from satirists and moralists such as Juvenal, who express alarm at the unsettling of traditional class structures.

Finally, some of our most important evidence for legal practices comes from the late Empire. These legal sources provide a singular problem because the texts of the laws exist in digests, summaries of laws from all periods of Roman history. These digests were written down in the sixth century CE and later, and it is not always easy to tell at what period a particular law was in effect. As a comprehensive account of Roman law, however, the digests are an invaluable source.

ROME AND GREECE

There can be no doubt that the Romans were different from the Greeks in myriad ways: their social structure was more carefully stratified; their view of themselves as a military state was more pronounced; their clothes, food, and literature were all different from those of their Greek counterparts. Needless to say, then, the Roman's ideas of sex, sexual practice, and sexual identity were not identical to those in Greece. In this chapter, I provide a brief outline of the differences between the two, before turning to individual case studies.

From the start, it is important to note that the line between Greece and Rome is not quite as clearly drawn as it may seem. Greek cities began colonizing Italy in the sixth century BCE, some four centuries before our earliest Latin literature. Greek pottery, moreover, was highly prized by the Etruscans in Italy (a high number of the pots from Greece that depict erotic scenes come from Etruscan graves), and it appears that the Romans and Etruscans were in contact from the earliest era of Roman history. In the time periods for which we have secure historical sources, moreover, Greeks were a constant presence in Rome: Greek slaves regularly served as schoolteachers for elite Roman families, and educated Romans from the early republic onward learned to read and write Greek as well as Latin.

In the matter of literature, moreover, Roman authors explicitly acknowledged their debt to their Greek predecessors. Plautus and Terence indicate in their plays that their dramas are based on the New Comedies of Menander, Diphilus, and other Greek authors. Catullus, the earliest extant writer of Latin lyric poetry, imitates the meters of Sappho and refers to the (fictional, or at least fictionalized) addressee of his love poems as "Lesbia," a clear reference to Sappho. The great Roman orator Cicero studied the Greek litigators and indicates his approval, especially, of Demosthenes. Virgil, whose epic masterpiece the *Aeneid* is among the best-known pieces of Western literature, owes an obvious debt to Homer, but a significant debt to Greek Hellenistic poets as well, especially Apollonios of Rhodes. To study Rome, then, one must always be aware of the weight of Greek tradition, and this makes the analysis of cultural practice particularly tricky. When Catullus writes of his beloved Lesbia, does his poetry reflect Roman attitudes and practices? Or is he, perhaps, merely imitating Greek love poetry? It is not always easy to sort out the strands of one culture from those of another, and we must bear in mind that Roman literature and culture is always an amalgamation of sorts.

Despite this cultural debt to Greece, however, another strand of Roman ideology was particularly concerned with distinguishing Roman practices and attitudes from those of the Greek cities, which Rome formally conquered in 146 BCE. For stern Roman moralists such as Cato the elder (active in the early second century BCE), solid Roman morals and practices were in danger of decline because of influence from the decadent, soft, and unmanly Greeks to the east. This narrative of insidious moral degeneration because of the temptations of a decadent population in one's own midst is one that should be familiar to modern readers; it is mobilized frequently today in our own political discourse. In Rome, the idea of Greekness took on different values at different times and in different contexts, but it was nearly always a bit dangerous to be too enthusiastic about things Greek. For Nero, his admiration of the Greeks and his willing participation in Greek athletic events and poetry contests became further proof of his general unsuitability to rule Rome.

In studying Rome, then, the ideas that I outlined in chapters 1–7 will never be far away. Greece is a constant source of comparison, for the Romans as well as for us. At times, the Romans seem to imitate Greek ideas without complication, and at others, they work hard to distinguish Roman practices and morals from their soft, eastern, conquered neighbors.

GREEK LOVE?

In part because of the strain of rhetoric that presents Greece as soft and decadent, it has sometimes been asserted that homoerotic relations between males were not a part of indigenous Roman culture; rather, the argument goes, the Romans were all normal straight men, until they were corrupted by the Greeks, at which time they fell prey to the insidious culture of pederasty.[2] Adding some weight to this view is the fact that many of the words used to describe male-male sexual relations are loanwords from Greece: *cinaedus* (Greek *kinaidos*) and *catamitus* (probably derived from the Greek name Ganymede) are taken to indicate a Greek origin to same-sex relations.

There are, however, several problems with this line of argument. Most important is the simple fact that Latin literature, from the early comedies through the late republic and well into the imperial period, speak frankly and openly of men's desire for boys as well as women. The sheer pervasiveness of such references as well as the offhand way in which they appear in multiple texts argues against the idea that love of boys is a Greek import.

Warren cup, side A. A man and boy are engaged in lovemaking, while a figure at the far right peers in the door-
way. © Trustees of the British Museum.

It appears that a Roman man could legitimately desire virtually any social
inferior, whether a young slave, an older slave, a noncitizen woman, or his
wife. The Romans did criticize some Greek practices and as will become
clear, they did view the Greeks as suspiciously soft in a variety of ways. But
there is no indication that they thought of the love of boys as particularly
Greek, and indeed, the term *Greek love* (which appears in numerous discussions of this issue) does not appear in any of our Roman sources.[3]

It is true that Roman law did not allow for the Greek practice of pederasty,
in which an older citizen man would cultivate a sexual relationship with a
citizen boy. The reason for this, however, is not that the Romans disapproved
of sexual relations with boys; rather, they disapproved much more strictly
than did the Greeks of sexual relations with *citizen* boys, which they viewed
on par with sexual relations with unmarried citizen women. In an often
quoted passage from a little-read play of Plautus, a slave and his master are
discussing the master's love affair. The two stand before a house, where the
master's beloved resides:

PALINURUS, *the slave.* Be careful where you walk; love what you love with witnesses present.

PHAEDROMUS, *his master* But a pimp lives here.

PALINURUS Nobody prohibits this or forbids it—if you have the money, you may buy what is openly sold. No one prohibits anyone from going on the public street so long as you do not make a path through fenced fields. So long as you stay away from brides, widows, unmarried women, (male) youths and free boys, love whom you like. (Plautus *Curculio* 31–38)

The scene begins with Palinurus worried that his master is in love with a forbidden love object, most likely a free woman. Once he learns that they are standing in front of a brothel, his concerns are dispelled. And in the explication of what is in bounds and out-of-bounds (colorfully indicated through the metaphor of fenced fields), Palinurus provides a full picture of who is a legitimate love object. On one hand, the field is fairly open: women as well as boys and youths are apparently not only thinkable, but fully acceptable. On the other hand, the picture is narrower than in Greece: no category of citizen woman (married, unmarried, widowed) is available, nor any citizen males. Who, then, is left? Only nonfree residents of either sex. The question of whether or not the sex is "openly sold" also has considerable weight in Roman legal texts: a man could not be convicted of adultery if he could prove that the woman he slept with was a prostitute.

Given these considerable legal restrictions, one might expect that the Romans would view the practice of pederasty (in the restricted sense of the love of citizen boys) as particularly Greek. As Williams has shown, however, the Romans simply did not do so.[4] Sexual relations with a citizen boy could be harshly criticized, and indeed harshly punished, but were not viewed as a "Greek" activity. Perhaps more important, when the Romans do speak of Greek softness and vice, it appears that sex of any kind, let alone sex with citizen boys, is only one aspect of that vice, and often not an important one. To take only one example, Plutarch, a Greek writer living in Rome in the second century CE, discusses the pernicious influence of the Greeks:

For the Romans were especially suspicious of the practice of anointing, and they thought that nothing was so great a cause of slavery and softness of the Greeks as the gymnasium and the wrestling ring. These give birth to listlessness and leisure in the cities, and mischief, and pederasty, and to ruining the bodies of the young by sleeping and wandering around, rhythmic exercises, and strict diets. Because of these things, they have forgotten and given up their weapons, and are delighted to be called nimble athletes, and beautiful, rather than noble hoplites and horsemen. (*Roman Questions* 40.274d)

What is Greek here, then, is hardly just pederasty, or indeed any particular attitude toward sex at all; rather, pederasty is mentioned only as one of a list of symptoms of a general disease of improper attitudes. The Greeks are, simply put, wasting their time with idle pursuits that serve no immediate purpose. Rather than taking pride in military activities—the one thing that any good Roman would prize—they would rather play about with sports. Shocking behavior indeed. This idleness, to the Roman mind, is indicative of a more general lack of purpose and has led directly to the Greeks' current state of enslavement. But it is neither caused by, nor indicative of, an especially Greek form of desire; as Craig Williams says, " 'Greek love' is a modern invention."[5]

ROMAN IMPENETRABILITY

Michel Foucault argued that sexuality is a result of the particular discourse that comes out of a nineteenth-century medicalization of sexual behaviors. If this is true, then one should not expect the Romans to hold modern sexual categories as significant, and indeed, they did not. One can find some Romans (though not many) who appear to have held strong preferences for sex with one gender over the other, that is, whom we might identify as having a sexual orientation. But as was the case for Greece, these preferences were not generally thought of as constituting an identity, nor were they in themselves sufficient to mark out a person as perverse. On the other hand, the Romans, like the Greeks, held strongly to the idea that a man's role in sex, whether penetrating or penetrated, was of utmost importance.

In fact, the Romans were much more rigid than were the Greeks about the idea that a citizen man should never be penetrated, even when still a youth. Jonathan Walters has argued that the Roman word for man (*vir,* plural *viri*) is more than an indication of sex, but rather an indication of both gender and class status. *Viri* were men who had the right to penetrate non-men of various sorts. A more class-neutral term, *homines,* was regularly used to indicate men who were not of citizen status and who therefore could be penetrated, at least theoretically, by *viri.* But even more commonly, slaves were regularly called *pueri,* that is, "boys." They were regarded as not full men, and unlike the *pueris liberis* (free boys) mentioned in both legal and literary texts, they were not protected from acts of penetration by citizen men.[6]

Gender in Rome, then, was more than a question of biological sex; it was also a question of citizen status. Only *citizen* men were fully men when it came to sex, and others were relegated to an inferior position. Such a notion of gender was also reflected in the language that was used to talk about males who were penetrated by *viri:* such a man was said to *pati muliebria,* literally, "to suffer womanly things." When it came to sex, then, Rome consisted of two kinds of participants: men and everyone else, a group that Williams has argued is best thought of more or less coherently as non-men. Obviously, within the group of non-men, there were significant differences: a rich citizen woman was not subject to the same kinds of sexual abuse and availability as was a slave boy. But from the point of view of a desiring man, the important thing was that everyone else belonged to this inferior gender/class and that he did not.

This system of gender/class also means that sexual activity had somewhat different permutations of meaning than it did in Greece. In the Greek world, one could lose citizenship rights if convicted of male prostitution, and in that regard, one's sexual behavior had ramifications extending to all aspects of public life. In Rome, a similar situation occurred, though the lines of significance were somewhat different. One of the marks of a free man in Rome was that he could not be whipped or beaten. In most situations, a man who could be beaten would be assumed to be a slave, which meant that he could also be used sexually. A citizen who was beaten or penetrated, then, ran the risk of slipping in the class structure, of being taken, quite literally, for a slave.

There was, however, one important exception to the rule about beatings, and that was the case of the citizen soldier. Soldiers could be beaten by their superior officers; in this one regard, they were at the mercy of another citizen man. Here, however, the context is carefully marked so as not to be confused with other kinds of beating: a centurion could only beat his charges with a vine staff. Moreover, a story that several Roman authors and orators used as a paradigm concerned a soldier who killed his superior officer on the grounds that the officer wanted to violate his sexual integrity. Not only was the soldier not convicted for the killing, but he was honored by the general Marius.[7] A soldier could be beaten, but this did not signify sexual availability in the way that other beatings might.

What of the men who were sexually penetrated? If citizens, the episode carried considerable shame, as later chapters will show. It is also worth noting what kinds of people were subject to this kind of shame, and here again one sees significant differences from the Greek world. In the Roman legal codes, men who had been penetrated (or *pati muliebria*) were often lumped together with gladiators and actors, two professions that evidently carried a considerable stigma. In Greece, of course, no shame whatsoever accompanied acting on the civic stage; it was, in fact, an honor for young citizen men to be part of a tragic chorus. In Rome, by contrast, actors are often asserted to be prostitutes, and in any case, no citizen can appear on stage without experiencing deep disgrace. It is not clear why this should be the case; Catherine Edwards suggests that these three categories of males (actors, gladiators, prostitutes) were treated as analogous because no such person was in control of his own body.[8] In different ways, and with different social valences, each was an object of citizens' desiring gaze and provided pleasure to citizens without being in control of that pleasure. In any case, the shame associated with performing on the Roman stage certainly marks one of the sharpest differences between Greece and Rome.

PENETRATED IDENTITIES?

If, as Williams suggests, the Romans had two large categories for sexual types—men and non-men—then they also had a dizzying array of subcategories with which to describe men who, for whatever reason, were penetrated in sex. Of particular interest are citizen men who *choose* to be so penetrated; a slave was assumed to have no choice in the matter (much like a woman). But some men evidently did enjoy being penetrated, or at least Roman moralists were afraid that some men did, and these men were carefully scrutinized, categorized, and ridiculed.[9]

Although each of the terms used to describe penetrated men has a slightly different emphasis, it is important to note that in general, such terms are terms of abuse, and they have the desired effect primarily through assimilation to the female gender. A typical word of abuse, for example, is *mollis*, or "soft." A man who is *mollis* is probably able to be penetrated, but this is a secondary meaning; at a more basic level, the word simply means that, like a woman, such a man does not demonstrate the solid, even hard (*durus*) qualities that characterize impenetrable men. Such a man would also be assumed, moreover, to be soft in areas that have nothing to do with sex—to have a penchant, for example, for warm baths and delicate clothing.

Similarly, the word *impudicus* (unchaste) is often used for a man who is willing to be anally penetrated. This may seem a more straightforward category of sexual identity than *mollis*, as it clearly contains an inherent value judgment—one might assume, that is, that the Romans saw anal penetration as inherently immoral. But in fact, the word *impudicus* should be understood as closely related to the word *pudicitia*, which, especially for women, often means simply "chastity." A man who is *impudicus*, then, is indeed acting out-of-bounds, but not because of any moral judgment about anal sex (at least, not any judgment about the penetrator), but because such a man is behaving like a loose woman in allowing himself to be penetrated. Significantly, men are not *impudici* for penetrating too many partners; this is a term that is applied only to the penetrated.

Even more clear is the term *pathicus*, which is related to the phrase *pati muliebria* (discussed earlier). To be "pathic" is to have things done to you, rather than to be the one doing them. This is never good for a Roman man and is, again, closely tied to the idea of a feminine gender identity.

Perhaps the most problematic term, however, is the word *cinaedus*, which comes from the Greek *kinaidos*. It has often been assumed that a *cinaedus* is a passive man, and some commentators have wanted to translate it as "passive homosexual" to draw lines of political alliance between ancient *cinaedi* and modern gay men.[10] It is true that *cinaedi* are often assumed to be sexually penetrated. But again, as Williams has made clear in his large-scale study, the characteristics of *cinaedi* extend well beyond the realm of specific sexual acts. *Cinaedi* are described as being particularly sexually voracious in a number of texts, and their behavior is not just passive, but scandalously loose. They are attacked as adopting feminine modes of speech, dress, and walk. And finally, it appears that the word *cinaedus* can have a transferred meaning of simply "sexually immoral." At one point, the poet Catullus refers to a *female* prostitute as *cinaedior*, literally, "more cinaeduslike" (Catullus 10.24–25). A *cinaedus*, then, is best understood as someone who violates the basic rules of gender decorum, rather than as a member of a particular sexuality.

PRIAPUS AND PHALLIC CULTURE

One of the interesting aspects of Roman sexual culture was a particular interest in the size of a man's penis. One sees this fascination in a number of literary sources, some of which are discussed in subsequent chapters: Seneca criticizes a man, Hostius Quadra, who uses magnifying mirrors to enhance the imagined size of a man who is penetrating him; in Petronius's *Satyricon,* one of the characters of the novel is picked up in the bath after a crowd stands around wondering and applauding at the size of his penis. While certain aspects of Greek culture certainly revolved around the phallus as an image of fertility, in Rome, there seems to have been an appreciation of size for its own sake.

One aspect of this phallic culture comes in the form of a Roman god of fertility and gardens, Priapus.[11] Priapus is often figured as a crude wooden statue, in the form of a man with a preternaturally huge phallus. He stands guard over gardens and uses his member as a weapon in that service: would-be thieves are warned that if they attempt to steal fruit from the garden, they will be raped by Priapus himself. A unique corpus of texts by unknown authors, the *Carmina Priapea* (Priapic Poems), provides a series of poems in various meters, in which Priapus is imagined as the speaker. The date of these poems is not secure, but they are generally assumed to be Augustan (i.e., early first century CE). Priapus is imagined as being more than willing to have sex with boys, women, or adult men. Several of the poems suggest a rising scale of humiliation for the person whom Priapus will penetrate, with oral sex being the most humiliating. A few examples here will suffice to give the reader an idea of the flavor of these poems.

Priapia 25 provides a representative sample of the genre. Priapus makes a general threat to a hypothetical thief, who is presumed to be male:

This field is entrusted to me; whoever brings
a thieving hand to it
will learn that I am not a eunuch.
Perhaps he would say to himself, "no one
here, in this remote spot among the fruit trees
will know that I have been buggered," but he'd be wrong.
The deed will be done with serious witnesses/huge balls.[12]

In particular, this poem emphasizes that there is an aspect of shame to being penetrated by this phallic god; thieves are warned against taking comfort in the agrarian countryside, where they might think that no one will see the deed being done. Through a clever pun in the Latin, the god's testicles become the legal witnesses of the man's sexual humiliation.

Poems 13, 28, and 35 all refer to oral sex as a particularly degrading experience for the person performing fellatio:

I warn you: boy, you will be buggered; girl, you'll be fucked.
A third punishment remains for a bearded thief. (*Priapea 13*)

You, who plan evil deeds and do not restrain
yourself from stealing from the garden,
you'll be buggered with my foot-long cock.
But if such a serious and painful punishment
is not effective, I'll try something higher up. (*Priapea 28*)

Once, thief, you'll be buggered; but if again
you are taken a second time, I will screw your mouth.
But if you try a third theft,
then you will suffer both this punishment and that:
you'll be buggered and mouth-screwed. (*Priapea 35*)

The first of these three poems is particularly interesting because it shows the god as not particularly discriminating in his sexual objects. Each kind of person to be screwed has his or her own method. The fact that the bearded man will suffer *irrumatio*, that is, forced to perform oral sex on the god, perhaps reflects the idea that at his age, performing anal sex on him is no longer an attractive option.

It is also interesting to note that in poems 13 and 28, oral sex is clearly alluded to, but in careful periphrasis, as if the god were hesitant to actually say the word. Part of the pleasure of reading the poem comes in figuring out what the god means; our understanding is meant to come with a masculine chuckle. In poem 35, however, the poet clearly has no hesitancy about being explicit, and anal and oral sex are doled out in precise escalation for each violation.

One final poem from the collection deserves mention, and that is poem 51. This relatively long piece (27 lines) begins with Priapus wondering aloud why it is that so many thieves come to his garden when "whoever chances upon me pays the price / and is hollowed out right up to his arms?" (*Priapea* 51.4–5). He then lists all of the qualities of his garden that are not any finer than any other garden and comes to a rather unexpected conclusion:

Although I have all these things in my field,
the neighboring gardens do not produce any poorer.
But you ignore these, and come to the place
guarded by me, most unchaste thieves.
You fly to the punishment which is entirely too well known;
the punishment itself, what I threaten with, attracts you. (*Priapea* 51.22–27)

The poem suggests, with a sly wink, that some thieves might want to be penetrated. In this case, then, this Priapus is particularly ineffective. Instead of preventing thieves from stealing from his garden, he is plagued with a perverted lot who steal specifically to enjoy the punishment. Of course, the humor of this poem stems from the idea that wanting to be penetrated by Priapus should be deeply shameful. By suggesting that if someone steals from his garden, that person is a deliberate pathic, the speaking Priapus accomplishes his goal by other means. The poem itself, by implying deliberate passivity, becomes the deterrent against theft.

Priapus weighs his phallus in front of a bowl of fruit. Though his member is unusually large, this Priapus is more realistic in proportion than many; note as well that he is not shown as fully erect. Casa dei Vettii, Pompeii. First century CE. Photo taken by the author.

Priapus is a country god, rude and crude, but with a sense of humor. His sexual aggression is an object of boast, rather than of actual fact. But his bluster is also typical, in many ways, of Roman ways of talking about sex. Men especially speak of sex in violent terms, as a mode of dominating other males and establishing their own social and political superiority. We will see this attitude toward sex, for example, in several of the poems of Catullus. In the comic work of Petronius, who wrote during the time of the emperor Nero, Priapus acts as a motivating deity. The hero of Petronius's novel, Encolpius, has somehow angered the garden god, and he spends much of the narrative suffering from a humiliating impotence and being forced to undergo bizarre sexual punishments and cures for his condition. In that work, the humorous side of Priapus seems to have come to the fore. Petronius satirizes the Roman male's preoccupation with penetration and reveals the hero's cock in all its ridiculous detail.

WOMEN, NORMAL AND DEVIANT

Women in Rome had a bit more freedom than those in Greece. A Roman wife might eat dinner out with her husband, for example, or initiate loans from her own capital resources. In later periods of Roman history, it is clear that women sometimes wielded considerable monetary power. This is not to suggest that the women of Rome enjoyed anything like full political autonomy. Throughout Roman history, citizen women were legally under the watch of a male guardian: initially a woman's father, later, sometimes, her husband. A father's ability to scrutinize and control the actions of his daughters, known as the *patria potestas* (literally, "father's power"), was wide ranging. It included the right to decide not to raise the daughter after her birth, in which case, she would be exposed to die.

When a woman got married, she might do so in one of two ways. If she married *cum manu* (literally, "with her hand"), then the *patria potestas* transferred to her husband, and she became legally as a daughter to her husband. If she married *sine manu* (without her hand), her father retained legal guardianship over her. For a variety of reasons, marriage *sine manu* appears to have become increasingly popular during the first century BCE. This may well have led to a certain population of upper-class women who exercised greater social and economic mobility during this time. If a woman were married *sine manu,* and her father were to die, she would no longer be under the direct *potestas* of any male. She would still be subject to guardianship, but in some cases, it appears that such a woman was allowed considerable freedom. A woman named Clodia seems to fall into this class, the sister of one of Cicero's great political rivals. Though much in Cicero's attack on her should be read skeptically, she appears to have enjoyed wide discretion in matters of finance as well as sexual liaisons.

At the same time, Roman men viewed this level of freedom as deeply problematic. Women were assumed to be not in control of their sexual desires; left to their own devices, they would, it seems, have sex with virtually any man at any time. Catullus, whose love poetry is often written from the point of view of a lover who wishes to have affairs with a married woman, is nonetheless shocked and dismayed to discover that his beloved Lesbia is not faithful to him. In one particularly angry poem, he suggests that she "takes on three hundred lovers at once, not being truly in love with any, but breaking the groins of all" (Catullus 11). The sexual appetite of independent women cut both ways, it seems.

For more traditional Roman moralists, this sort of sexual appeal had political ramifications as well. The great danger that women posed was that they were considered likely to parlay their sexual attractiveness into direct political power. At one point, the Roman historian Livy reports that the elder Cato made the following speech in an attempt to block the repeal of laws against financial extravagance on the part of women:

Gentlemen, do you wish to create this contest among your wives, so that the rich will wish to have that which no one else is able, and the poor will reach beyond their means, lest they be held in contempt because of it? Once they begin to be ashamed of what they should not, they will not be ashamed of what they should. What she is able to do by her own means, she will procure; what she is not able, she will ask her husband. How wretched he will be, both the husband who is persuaded and the one who is not, since what he himself will not give, he will seen given by another. Now women are commonly making requests of strange men and, what is worse, they demand legislation and votes, and from some men they get them. (Livy 34.4.16–18)

Lurking just below the surface of Cato's concern about women's sumptuous spending is a question of a wife's loyalty to her husband. If extravagance is allowed, then women will ask their husbands for things; if their husbands will not give them, then they will ask "strange men" (*alienos viros*), a phrase that really means "men outside of their family or husband's family." Though sexual infidelity is not spelled out here, the idea of a woman having business dealings with such "strange men" all but means exactly that.

Even normal women, then, were viewed with suspicion when it came to sexual matters. Because of their presumed sexual appetite or, perhaps, their lack of control over sexual desires, they needed to be watched carefully and kept within the social circle of immediate family. As for their sexual role, however, a normal woman was assumed to be passive, in the rather strict sense that she was always to be penetrated. So much describes the expectations of women as a gender; what of the expectations of their sexual behavior within those gender norms? Women could be penetrated vaginally, orally, or anally and still be considered normal. Wives, of course, might object to certain sexual acts and might prefer not to perform fellatio or have anal sex with their husbands. But in terms of sexual norms, a prostitute would be considered normal, as long as she was penetrated.

What of women who are depicted as sexually deviant? The primary word used to describe them is *tribas* (plural *tribades*), a troubling term that is often translated as "lesbian." The origins of the word are of little help: it appears to be derived from a verb that means "to rub" or "to grind," and in fact, it is nearly always used to denote women who have sex with other women. One might argue, then, that in the case of women, the category of sexual deviance is sufficiently close to our own that we should think of them as equivalent, that is, that we should translate *tribas* as "lesbian."

A close reading of the sources in which *tribades* appear, however, makes this identification less easy. As is the case for terms of male deviance (*cinaedus* and the like), virtually all of our sources come from invective. No *tribas* ever self-identifies as such. The terms of the invective, moreover, are telling: in case after case, what is particularly disturbing about *tribades* is that they "take the part of men" or "act like men" in the performing of sex. In a few extraordinary cases, a *tribas* is described as penetrating a *boy* (see, e.g., Martial, 7.67). It may be the case that Martial is exaggerating, taking the *tribas*'s mannishness to an absurd extreme. But even so, the exaggeration shows that what is primarily disturbing about the *tribas* is not that she has sex with another woman, but rather that she is gender-deviant in taking the active role.

To be fair, not all cases of invective against *tribades* are so clear-cut. In one often cited passage, the elder Seneca describes two women who are sleeping together as both being *tribades* (*Controversiae* 1.2.23). This does begin to look more like lesbianism than the purely active-passive distinction on which I have been insisting. But even here, it is not fully clear that the love object is what makes a *tribas* a *tribas*; it seems more likely that, for the Romans, a sexually active woman was the primary form of deviance, and when two women were in bed together, one of them had to be deviant. It was, perhaps, of relatively little concern to distinguish which of them was the real *tribas*, the active partner.

FOUCAULT AND ROME

In many ways, then, the picture that Foucault and his followers have drawn for Greece also holds true for Rome. Foucault has come under considerable criticism, however, for his discussion of Roman texts, which constitutes all of volume 3 of *The History of Sexuality*. In this volume, Foucault argues for two parallel developments: first, he sees an increased concern in the imperial period in Rome with physical and spiritual regimes of moderation, including moderation of sexual activity, as a way to maintain general health. At the same time, he suggests, the Romans placed a greater emphasis on the emotional bonds to be found in marriage, to the detriment of other forms of sexual pleasure. In a passage that has been frequently cited, Foucault argues, "Philosophers condemn any sexual relation that might take place outside marriage and prescribe a strict fidelity between spouses, admitting no exceptions."[13]

Foucault is not entirely wrong in these observations, but I must admit that the picture he draws is significantly incomplete. In the first place, Foucault jumps from the fourth century BCE in Greece (with which he ends volume 2 of *The History of Sexuality*) to the imperial period in Rome, beginning roughly in the middle of the first century CE. To do so is to ignore the first 200 years of Latin literature, including some particularly rich sources for the discussion of sexuality; Foucault loses all of Cicero, and perhaps most important, all of the early erotic poet Catullus. As later chapters will show, Catullus is little interested in the regimes of moderation that Foucault cites and discusses.

Moreover, even within the time frame that Foucault discusses, his selection of texts has much to do with the picture that he draws. Foucault primarily cites philosophers like the Stoic Seneca from the first century CE and medical writers such as Galen from the second century CE. He does not discuss, for example, the early-second-century satirist Juvenal, who attacks, and therefore paints a picture of, Romans who engage in excessive behavior of all sorts. Nor does he deal with Juvenal's contemporary Martial, who is perhaps even more pungent and outrageous than Catullus was 150 years earlier.

If Foucault's picture of developments in ideas about sex in Rome is incomplete, however, it is important to emphasize that it is not entirely wrong. As a reading of Stoic philosophy and of new medical regimes, Foucault's third volume has much to recommend it. Perhaps even more important, Foucault considers at some length the way in which the nature of power changed as Rome became an empire and the long-standing class structure of Rome began to shift. With an emperor overseeing Rome, being a wellborn Roman citizen was no longer sufficient to guarantee real power. Indeed, personal closeness to the emperor came to count for more than traditional structures of authority, and this left Roman senators and upper-class citizens unable to confidently negotiate within the imperial court. The increasingly complex and private network of power embodied in the emperor's household was certainly one cause for the increased popularity of Stoic philosophy, which advocated developing and maintaining a serene inner life, regardless of the political turmoil in which a man might find himself.

CONCLUSIONS

The following several chapters, arranged roughly chronologically, will show the ways in which the Romans thought about sex, sexual behavior, and sexual identities from about 200 BCE to the later Roman empire, about 200–300 CE. As will become clear, attitudes and ideas do shift over this broad expanse of time. As was the case for the study of Greece, however, the kind of evidence that we have also significantly colors the picture that scholars paint for each time period. In the early years of Latin literature, our sources consist of Roman new comedy, which is greatly concerned with the testing and eventual confirmation of the prevailing class structure. A hundred years later, our richest evidence comes from the legal speeches and private letters of the orator Cicero. In the last years of the first century BCE and the early first century CE, we find a wealth of love poetry, addressed to both young men and women. The era of Nero provides us with the wicked satire of Petronius and the somewhat pedantic moralizing of Seneca the Younger. In the late first and early second centuries CE, the invectives of Juvenal and Martial provide a highly critical view of sexual perversions of all sorts. And finally, the later Roman imperial period provides a canonized set of Roman laws that, unfortunately, gives us laws from every era of Roman history in a synchronic digest.

Each of these sources, then, provides a different kind of information about Roman attitudes toward sex. As this study progresses, certain themes will remain clear. First, it does not appear that the Romans thought of people as homosexual or heterosexual, as the modern West does. Second, like the Greeks, the Romans placed a high premium on a man's ability to control his own sexual desires, and especially to avoid falling prey to the temptation to slip into the other gender: to *pati muliebria.* But perhaps most interesting is the fact that the Romans did think of certain sexual appetites as constituting men and women as sexual types, to a greater degree than did the Greeks: the Roman *cinaedus* and *tribas,* though not corresponding to our sexual categories, appear to have both a sexual morphology and, at times, a recognizable sexual identity. Again, the valence of these identities is not the same as that of a modern sexuality, and the legal issues of their definition should not be confused with our own debates about gay rights, but the recognition of sexual types, and perhaps even sexual identities, is important for the study of Roman sexuality.

Nine

Roman Comic Sex

Scholars refer to the comedies of Aristophanes from the Greek world as Old Comedy. As we saw earlier, Aristophanic comedy is characterized by ribald sexual jokes; topical, often political satire; a loose plot that moves primarily from situation to situation without regard for logical development; and an often nonsensical ending that, through more sexual jokes and innuendos, suggests a return to both normalcy and sexual fertility. In this chapter, I will treat the New Comedy of the Roman playwrights Plautus and Terence. Plautus was active during the end of the third century and beginning of the second century BCE. Terence wrote roughly a generation later, and in some ways shows a deeper concern with social institutions and practices than his predecessor.

New Comedy is not a form originated by the Romans; we know that Greek playwrights of the fourth and third centuries BCE wrote New Comedies, although we have only one complete Greek New Comedy, the *Dyskolos* (or *Grouchy Man*) of Menander. Plautus and Terence inherited this genre and often indicate in the prologues to their plays that they have based their works on a Greek original (or originals). It is important to note, however, that even when these plays are set in a Greek city, as they often are, Plautus and Terence have thoroughly Romanized the setting as well as the characters and their social structure.[1] When Shakespeare sets a play in Venice, his characters remain, nonetheless, recognizably English (and none of them speak Italian); a similar transformation should be assumed for the plays of Plautus and Terence.

In form, the plots of New Comedy are largely familiar to modern audiences. In most plays, the action centers around a wellborn young man and wellborn young woman who fall in love. Alas, circumstances conspire to make the marriage of this promising young couple seem impossible. Often at least one of the lovers *appears* to be lower class, or even a slave. If this is not the case, the woman's father may object to the marriage on financial grounds, or the young man's father may interfere because he has made arrangements for his son to marry someone else. In a case that I will treat in some detail, the son's father wants to have an affair with the young woman himself and so proves a stumbling block to his son's marriage. Hilarity ensues. Clever slaves trick their masters. Old men fume and fret. Lessons are learned. Finally, through a series of unlikely events, it turns out that all the impediments to marriage fall away. Often, for example, a set of tokens carried by the young woman prove that she is not a slave, but the wellborn daughter of the young man's neighbor. Order is restored, and the play ends with the happy marriage of the happy couple, or at least the promise of this cheerful and reassuring event.

While the preceding plot sounds, no doubt, insipid, in fact these plays are often quite funny and highly enjoyable. Although every event in the play is fairly predictable, a great deal of skill and ingenuity enters into the arrangement of the plot and the development of comic situations. The most successful of these plays feel fresh and interesting, and much of the pleasure of watching the play comes from the knowledge that the playwright *must* get the characters out of the situation that he has put them in, and the seeming impossibility of doing so. Invention is the order of the day.

The plots of New Comedy are necessarily familiar to modern readers, as New Comedy forms the primary basis for modern romantic comedies, both in print and on film. For this reason we need to be particularly careful. It is easy to see only the parts of a play that are familiar and to overlook the evidence that it presents for social structures that are radically different from our own: the willing mistreatment of slaves, for example, or the suggestion that a husband who "accidentally" rapes his future wife before their wedding are all part of the natural order of things. In the course of this chapter, I will outline those aspects of Roman New Comedy that demonstrate, with particular clarity, what Roman assumptions about sex and sexual practice were in the early second century BCE and how they differed from our own.

YOUNG MEN, OLD MEN, SLAVES

In Roman comedy, both old men and young men are often portrayed as not in control of their erotic desires. Old men fall in love with beautiful young women (in some cases citizens who are thought to be slaves at the time) or prostitutes and, as a result, engage in risky and foolish behavior. They also may express desire for their male slaves. In general, the wife of an old man will act to restrain this sort of behavior, not because it is illegal, or necessarily immoral, but because it does not reflect well on her to have her husband gadding about. The old man's return to proper and restrained behavior—which is to say, limiting his sexual behavior to his own wife—usually comes at the end of the play and is one of the marks of a return to the proper state of things in general.

The young man in comedy (often the son of an older man who is also a character) is usually destined to marry a young citizen woman. He, however, also has erotic desires that may need to be reigned in. In some plays, he is involved in a long-standing relationship with a (female) prostitute, and this relationship needs to be brought to an end before his marriage. In a few comedies, young men have raped young women before the action of the play. Often the raped woman is thought to be a slave at the time, which makes the sexual act legal and relatively unproblematic; when she turns out to be a citizen (as in Terence's *Adelphoi*), the rape creates a social conflict that must be resolved. In Terence's *Hecyra* (discussed at length later), the young man rapes an unknown woman some months before his marriage; this has unforeseen consequences that are only resolved when it is discovered that the woman he raped is the same woman whom he married later.

Obviously, the Romans held views and attitudes that would not work in modern-day comedies. At the root of these depictions of old and young men, however, is a fairly straightforward plot mechanism. Early in the play, the principal male characters are not in control of their own desires. The end of the play brings about social resolution, and at the same time, the men learn to exercise some self-restraint. Marriage, the usual ending to these plays, represents the culmination of both these trajectories: social relationships return to a normal state, in which class lines are clearly defined, and men's sexual desires are curtailed for the foreseeable future to interactions with their wives.

Slaves, on the other hand, are presumed to have no control over the use of their bodies. They might not like what is done to them, but there is little they can do to prevent it. A number of plays include one- or two-line throwaways, in which slaves will taunt one another for having been penetrated by their masters. If one slave wants to be particularly cutting, he might suggest that the other suffered such treatment willingly (cf. Plautus *Captives* 867–68). In a passage from *Plautus's The Persian,* we see the interesting suggestion that a slave might have traded sexual favors for his eventual freedom. Two slaves are arguing with one another (a frequent event in comedies):

SAGARISTIO   I know you—you're already sleeping with your master.
 PAEGNIUM   So I am. What's it to you? At least I'm not doing it for free, like you are.
SAGARISTIO   Pretty cocky.
 PAEGNIUM   So I am, by Hercules. For I know that I will be free, which you can never
                      hope for yourself. (*Persian* 285–87)

Neither suggests that they like being penetrated; but Paegnium suggests that at least he is making a worthwhile trade.

A less easy passage for modern readers takes place in Plautus's *Pseudolus* (*The Liar*) (767–88). In it, a young male slave expresses his fears of his master, a pimp:

When the gods make a boy the slave of a pimp, and on top of it make him ugly, indeed, as far as I can reckon, they give him a big evil and lots of troubles. Consider the servitude I have, where I am propped up by every sort of difficulty, large and small. Nor am I able to find any lover for me, who would love me, so that I'd be cared for and kept just a little more brightly. Today is the pimp's birthday; he threatened us all, from the smallest to the largest, that if anyone did not send a gift to him today, tomorrow that one would die by the greatest torture. Now I don't know what to do with my problems. I'm not able to do *that*, which those who are able are used to doing. But unless I send a gift to the pimp today, tomorrow I'll have to drink fuller's juice.[2] Alas, how small I am even now for *that thing*. But by gum, since now I'm wretched and fear him badly, if anyone should give me something which makes my hand heavier (although they say that doing *that* makes one groan loudly) I think I'll be able somehow, and I'll grit my teeth.

Modern audiences are unlikely to find this passage funny. To understand how a Roman audience *could*, it is necessary to realize that the Romans thought of slaves primarily as property. A Roman man would never be in the position of the slave boy who delivers this monologue; the Roman audience could only think of him as a sexual object and would never have to squirm at the uncomfortable thought of identifying with him. As such, his potential discomfort at the thought of performing anal or oral sex (as I take the reference to fuller's juice to imply) was apparently amusing.

PLAUTUS *CASINA:* PHILANDERING AND CROSS-DRESSING

Several manuscripts of Plautus's *Casina* preserve the following summary of the plot (the so-called argument)[3]:

Two slaves seek a fellow slave girl as wife.
An old man encourages one, his son the other.
The old man wins the lot, but is tricked by a stratagem.
And so a little [male] slave is substituted in place of the girl,
a wretch, who beats the master [i.e., the old man] and his estate manager.
The young man marries Casina, once she is recognized as a citizen.

As a six-line summary of the play, this is pretty good, although the suggestion that the male slave beats his master is not quite right. When one considers that it is written in verse, and moreover, under the constraint that (in Latin) the first letters of each line spell out the name of the play (CASINA), it is remarkable. Obviously, a great deal needs to happen between lines 5 and 6: a slave boy cross-dresses, the old man gets what is coming to him, Casina is recognized as a citizen rather than a slave, and her young man (not his slave) marries her. In the space of a few hundred lines toward the end of the play, then, nearly every imaginable sexual situation has been tried out: an old man and a slave girl, an old man and a slave boy, a young (male) slave and a slave girl, a citizen youth and a citizen girl. Only a comedy could try so many situations in so little time, and settle, finally, on the one that will result in all being right in the world.

Male Desires

The play begins in a world where sexual passion threatens the social order. Lysidamus, who is the "old man" and "master" in the synopsis above, has fallen in love with a slave girl named Casina. This Lysidamus is married to a respectable citizen woman named Cleostrata. Nonetheless, he hopes to set up a sexual affair with the slave girl. His strategy for doing so is to have his personal attendant (a slave), named Olympio, marry her. So long as Casina is the wife of his slave, Lysidamus will have the legal right to have sex with her. His wife, as becomes apparent later, is not happy with this sort of arrangement, but she is also careful about complaining too loudly. At the same time, Lysidamus's son (who does not appear in the play) has also fallen in love with Casina. He also has engaged his personal slave, Chalinus, to try to marry her. His mother, Cleostrata (Lysidamus's wife), for obvious reasons, supports her son's cause. The entire play, then, revolves around this conflict, in which two slaves are competing to marry a (supposed) slave girl; remarkably, Casina does not appear on stage either, and the discovery that she is a citizen so that she can marry the offstage son takes place in a brief narrative passage at the end of the play.

The character of Lysidamus, who is on stage for most of the play, is a good place to begin an analysis of Roman sexual assumptions. As I have mentioned, he is depicted as madly in love with the girl Casina, to the point of being ridiculous. In an early scene, he talks about the personal transformation that his desire has brought about: "I trouble all the perfume sellers, and wherever there is a pleasant perfume, I use it in order to please her; and I think I do please her" (*Casina* 225–26). Whether or not he actually does please Casina, we never find out. But a few lines later, his wife smells the perfume on him and asks where it came from; Lysidamus must try, hurriedly and unsuccessfully, to wipe off the scent with his cloak. The perfume, then, becomes a perfect example of the kind of foolishness that Lysidamus is up to. Left to his own devices, he is wasting money in an attempt to look (and smell) like a young lover; but once in the presence of his wife, his behavior— both the perfuming and the love affair that is its motivation—is revealed as an embarrassment.

To be clear, there is nothing illegal, or even necessarily immoral, about the idea that Lysidamus should have sex with one of his female slaves. But he should not expect his wife to like it, and this is especially so when he has quite lost himself in an infatuation that ill fits his age and station. As Cleostrata puts it,

Oh, you nothing, you white-headed gnat, I can hardly hold back from telling you what I ought,
Do you actually walk around on the streets, wearing perfume at your age, you wretch? (*Casina* 239–40)

The complaint here is larger than just sex. Lysidamus's sexual obsession is only indicative of a broader lack of self-control on his part, resulting in foolish and wasteful behavior. A young man might indulge in such perfumery; an old man should know better.

A little later in the play, there is a suggestion that Lysidamus is also interested in sexual exploits with men, and rather shockingly, with older men. Lysidamus and Cleostrata, unable to agree on whose slave should marry

Casina, settle the matter by drawing lots. As it happens, Lysidamus's slave Olympio wins. Thinking momentarily that he has won the day, Lysidamus begins to show considerable affection for Olympio, while Chalinus overhears:

LYSIDAMUS   May the gods love me, I can hardly restrain my lips, can hardly help kissing you for this, my darling.
CHALINUS   What, kiss? What's this? Your darling?
By Hercules, I think he wants to drill into his attendant's bladder.[4]
OLYMPIO   So now you love me a bit, eh?
LYSIDAMUS   Not a little—by Pollux, I love you more than me. Can I hug you?
CHALINUS   What, a hug?
OLYMPIO   You may.
LYSIDAMUS   When I touch you, it's like licking honey!
OLYMPIO   Hey, you—lover—get off my back. (*Casina* 452–57)

This scene is clearly meant to be broadly comic, and it demonstrates again the lack of control that Lysidamus has over his own sexual desires. What starts out as gratitude to Olympio for having won Casina quickly goes over the top. Lysidamus's affections, once riled, easily transfer to Olympio himself. There is no hint here that such affections are unthinkable or shameful in themselves; rather, what is ridiculous is Lysidamus's lack of moderation.

The scene ends with a throwaway line that is worth mentioning. After Lysidamus and Olympio go back and forth a bit, Chalinus observes,

Today, by Hercules, I think these two soldiers will be sleeping together; indeed, the old man tends to chase after bearded men. (*Casina* 465–66)

The point that excites this comment is not that Lysidamus is interested in a male slave, but rather that here, he appears interested in sex with an older man.[5] In Rome, as in Greece, the ideal of beauty was inhabited by youth; a man with a beard was normally not attractive. Chalinus suggests that Lysidamus is a bit of a pervert in having a preference for older men, easily identified by their full beards.

Female Desires

As often, when one asks what the women of Roman comedy desire, it is difficult to come up with an answer. Cleostrata does not appear to have any particular desire for Lysidamus (not that one could blame her). And of course there, is no suggestion that she should have a desire for a male slave to parallel Lysidamus's desire for Casina. That would be quite improper, and it never happens in Roman comedy. She seems, rather, simply to wish that her husband not embarrass her with external affairs.

One conversation that Cleostrata has with her neighbor and friend, a woman named Myrrhina, is revealing. The two meet on the street and begin with an affectionate exchange:

MYRRHINA   But what is it that now pains you? For whatever is painful to you, the same is worrisome for me.
CLEOSTRATA   I believe it is, for there is no neighbor whom I love more than you, rightly, nor one in whom there is more of what I would wish.
MYRRHINA   I love you, and so I want to know what the matter is.
CLEOSTRATA   I am despised at home in the worst way. (*Casina* 178–85)

The declaration of love just above is translated quite literally but should be understood, probably, in the sense of neighborly closeness. The characters suggest a society of women who, when the men are not around, have close affective ties to one another and who get together to talk about the folly of their husbands. This picture may well reflect reality; we should remember, however, that this is a play by and for men. A certain amount of male paranoia may motivate these kinds of scenes.

Myrrhina and Cleostrata continue their conversation, and Cleostrata explains that her husband has gone foolish over Casina. Myrrhina eventually expresses a view that, presumably, Roman men hoped their wives would hold:

MYRRHINA   Be quiet, silly, and listen. Don't you set yourself against him; let him love, let him do what he wants, so long as you lack nothing at home.
CLEOSTRATA   Are you insane? Just there you speak against your own interests.
MYRRHINA   You fool, you must always avoid one saying from your husband.
CLEOSTRATA   What saying?
MYRRHINA   "I want a divorce." (*Casina* 203–12)

Here Myrrhina expresses the double standard that was, in fact, operative in Rome: husbands could have affairs and do what they liked out of the house without much criticism, so long as the household was not affected. Their wives, so long as they were properly cared for, needed to exercise some caution about complaint. Here, however, the play at least raises the double standard for all to view, and Cleostrata has the temerity to point out that it is not quite fair. Within the comic world of the play, moreover, the community of women represented by these two neighbor wives will not only expose this double standard, but overcome it. In a small way, then, this play may be read as legitimate social criticism of sexual expectations for Roman wives.

By the end of the play, however, the notion of women being on top has become a clear comic inversion of the norm. Indeed, in a scene much later in the play, a mock wedding takes place (discussed at more length later). At the moment of marriage, a slave woman named "Pardalisca" gives a bit of advice to the so-called bride:

Gently, lift your foot above the threshold, my new bride,
begin this journey safely, so that you always stand above your husband,
and so that your power is stronger than his, and you defeat him and are the victor,
and so that your words should rule and your authority; and may your husband
clothe you, but you strip your husband. Remember, I beg you—night and day you
must deceive him. (*Casina* 813–20)

At this moment in the play, the women decidedly have the upper hand, and the playwright depicts them as such. There is more than a bit of paranoia in this characterization, however. In this scene, all women are in cahoots, and all of them are deliberately deceiving (and ruling over) their hapless husbands. The wedding that Lysidamus so urgently hoped for has become the moment of his undoing. Even the language here is clearly from the male realm; the new bride is a *victrix,* a female form of *victor,* often used of the winner of a battle, and when she is urged to "strip" her husband, the word is *despolio,* a word used for stripping armor off a fallen warrior. Marriage has become a battlefield, and the idea that women "defeat" their husbands on this field is the sort of joke that only men secure in their superior social position can afford to make.

Such a scene, however, tells us nothing about what a real bride might really want, or what a young woman might really desire. Here the absence of Casina herself from the entire play becomes especially significant. She simply is not on stage; her wishes, thoughts, and desires are not at issue. What does matter is that she is a citizen (as we learn in an epilogue), an issue that is a concern for her future husband. But her desires are not depicted, discussed, or questioned.

Cross-dressed Revelations

In the course of the play, Lysidamus and Cleostrata agree to decide, by choosing lots, whose slave will be allowed to marry Casina. Much to her regret, Cleostrata loses, which means that Lysidamus's slave Olympio will marry the girl. Cleostrata and Myrrhina do not give up so easily, however, and the two women team up to upset the marriage plans. In a plot device that is quite rare in Roman comedy, they have the slave Chalinus cross-dress *as Casina,* so that he becomes the one getting married to Olympio. As a cross-dressed bride, Chalinus acts in the way that cross-dressed male characters often do in modern comic movies; that is, the characters around Chalinus are apparently convinced by his costume, but "she" has the advantage of masculine physical strength in dealing with them. By crossing the boundary between male and female, then, Chalinus's character exposes the assumptions that are normally made of each gender. The other characters' reactions to "her" also serve to expose their expectations and desires.[6]

The advice given by Pardalisca (discussed previously) was, in fact, given to Chalinus disguised as a bride. In that regard, the use of masculine language, and the suggestion that the bride should be victorious over her husband in all things, is more than generic advice to women; here it prefigures the event of the wedding itself, in which Chalinus literally defeats Olympio in physical terms. A good deal of slapstick humor drives the scene:

OLYMPIO   Oh, what a soft little body, my little wife. What?!
LYSIDAMUS   What is it?
OLYMPIO   She stepped on my foot like an elephant.

LYSIDAMUS   You be quiet. A cloud is barely as soft as her breast.
   OLYMPIO   By Pollux, what a pretty little nipple—oh, wretched me!
LYSIDAMUS   What is it?
   OLYMPIO   She hit my chest, not with an elbow, but with a battering ram! (*Casina* 843–49)

Although Chalinus apparently looks pretty good as a bride—at least, to the men on stage, who keep addressing "her," describing her using diminutive terms, and trying to feel her up—his more-than-female strength affirms the real sex that underlies the costume of female gender.

The bride asserts her masculine gender even more forcefully a few minutes later, after Olympio and Chalinus (disguised as Casina) have gone inside the house, presumably to their marital bed. We do not see what happens in the house; but a few moments later, Olympio runs out of the house, distraught, and describes his attempts to have sex with his bride. He admits to being ashamed, and then comes the moment of revelation. Unfortunately, our manuscripts are damaged just at this point, but enough words remain to make out the main points:

   OLYMPIO   It was enormous! I was afraid she had a sword; I began to search . . . while I was looking for the sword, in case she had one, I grabbed the hilt. But when I think about it, she didn't have a sword, for a sword would have been cold.
CLEOSTRATA   Go on.
   OLYMPIO   I'm ashamed.
CLEOSTRATA   Was it a radish?
   OLYMPIO   No, it wasn't.
CLEOSTRATA   A cucumber then?
   OLYMPIO   By Hercules it certainly was not any vegetable, unless, whatever it was, no disease ever touched it. For, whatever it was, it was huge. (*Casina* 906–13)

The humor here stems from the audience's full knowledge of what it was that poor Olympio was feeling and his inability to conceive of the fact; that is, he is simply unable to imagine that his bride is male, though, again, the suggestion that she has a "sword" points in that direction, in both a literal and metaphorical sense.

One might ask, given the realities of Roman sexual practice, what exactly the problem is with a bride who is male. After all, as various texts show, men can as easily be sexual objects as women, and Chalinus is a slave. What this scene shows, however, is not that sex with men is out-of-bounds, but simply that it is different than sex with women. Chalinus lacks certain qualities that a bride should have: for one thing, he should be light, and delicate, and soft. As Olympio discovered when he tried to treat Chalinus as such, however, he is instead rather hard and strong. More exactly, when Olympio reaches down and expects to find a vagina, he finds instead a penis, and from his description of it, it is an erect penis. Olympio goes on to describe the beating that he has received at Chalinus's hands. All this suggests a full power reversal that is not realized in the play in sexual terms; that is, Chalinus does not try, so far as Olympio tells us, to penetrate Olympio. He does, however, dominate him physically, sending him running ashamed into the street without his cloak. Effectively, Chalinus (dressed as a bride) has rendered Olympio the more feminine of the two.

At this point, the master Lysidamus, who was also hoping to have sex with "Casina," also runs out of the house, missing his cloak and staff. He, too, has been bested and feminized by Chalinus. As he tries to escape, Chalinus comes out of the house and threatens to beat him; Lysidamus replies in complete terror:

I'm lost; this man will depilate my loins with his club. I must run this way, for that way there's a shipwreck waiting for my loins. (*Casina* 967–68)

Lysidamus is, perhaps, so terrified that his language does not make much sense. One does not get depilated with a blunt object. The point, however, is that as a depilated male, Lysidamus would clearly be marked as the penetrated of the two. Again, the positions are radically and ridiculously reversed. Here, however, it is important to note a point of decorum that is observed by the comedy even in this topsy-turvy moment. Although Chalinus has repeatedly beaten his fellow slave Olympio, and although he threatens to beat Lysidamus, he never actually does so; that is, even when the humor is generated through an inversion of power structures—the master fears his slave, the husband fears his bride—it would have been too dangerous to show a slave actually beating his master. Similarly, though Lysidamus can sputter about the possibility that Chalinus will depilate him with his "club" (i.e., his phallus), the play stops well short of suggesting that the slave has actually penetrated his master.

Resolutions

Eventually, Lysidamus is reconciled to Cleostrata. He promises that he will no longer cheat on her and in fact says that if he ever does so, she can string him up and whip him; that is, she can treat him as she might a slave. At the end of the comedy, then, Lysidamus's status as a free, unbeatable man is dependent on his exercising a modicum of sexual control. Once he has agreed to this principle, Cleostrata has Chalinus return his cloak and staff to her husband. At this point, Lysidamus once again has all the things he needs to behave as an adult citizen male. Cleostrata, likewise, declares herself satisfied with her newly mature husband. The household has returned to order.

Almost as an afterthought, the play ends with this remarkable epilogue:

Audience, we will tell you what will happen in the house. Casina will be found to be the daughter of the next-door neighbor, and she will marry our young master, the son Euthynicus. Now it is proper for you to give due reward with earned applause. Whoever does this, will have whatever prostitute he desires, and his wife quiet. But whoever does not applaud brightly, as much as he is able, that man will find a goat perfumed with bilge substituted for the prostitute. (*Casina* 1012–18)

Once again, the audience is transported to a world of male wish fulfillment, where everyone knows what he is supposed to do and everyone, at the same time, admits to what he wants. In this epilogue, Lysidamus's dream in the play is held out as a joking reward for approving the play itself. If, therefore, the audience enjoyed the play, then they are compelled to admit that the play also represents the guilty pleasure that Roman men would have, if only it did not cause so much trouble. They, like Lysidamus, would like to have access to extramarital sex without consequences at home. This is a winking, joking lack of resolution that suggests that Roman men can have their cake and eat it too, even after we have seen the disastrous results of trying to do just that.

TERENCE *MOTHER-IN-LAW*

Terence wrote comedies a bit later than Plautus; his plays are generally thought to date to 170–159 BCE. In quite general terms, his plays are more thoughtful than his predecessor's. They rely less on broad physical humor, and the characters are drawn with more depth. Significantly, Terence's plays do not depict male-male erotic behavior, even between masters and slaves. Though this is significant, it does not appear to be the result of a historical trend; male-male erotic scenes continued in Roman literature for the next several centuries. Terence also appears interested in thinking seriously about large social questions: the best way to raise children, for example, is debated through two characters who represent different schools of thought (and each of whom must raise a young man) in the *Adelphoi*. Terence's comedies, then, encourage the audience to think about their social relations, even while following the improbable plotlines typical of comedy.

The plot of the *Mother-in-Law* (in Latin, the *Hecyra*) is typically improbable. It goes as follows: the young hero of the play, Pamphilus, has married a young woman named Philumena. He has done so somewhat against his wishes, as he was at the time thoroughly besotted with a prostitute named Bacchis; as a result of this affair, he and his wife did not have sexual relations immediately after their marriage. In fact, the marriage was not consummated until five months before the time that the play takes place. When the play commences, Pamphilus is just back from a long business trip. On his return, he discovers that Philumena is pregnant and about to give birth; she has moved back into her father's house. Because of the timing of his sexual relations with her, Pamphilus assumes that Philumena had sex with another man before their marriage. He refuses to allow his wife to come back into his house, though he does agree not to tell anyone about the child. This forms the comic conflict of the plot: the fathers of the young bride and groom do not understand why the couple have separated, and they try earnestly to bring them back together. Various characters assume that they understand what the obstacle is to the harmony of the marriage, but none is able to guess that the problem is (as Pamphilus thinks) that Philumena is pregnant with an illegitimate child, and so all of their attempts to reconcile the couple fail.

The conflicts in the play are resolved in a way that most modern audiences would find problematic, to say the least. We learn that some months before his wedding, Pamphilus had raped a young, unknown woman. Through an ingenious exchange of tokens (discussed later), Pamphilus learns toward the end of the play that Philumena is, in fact, the woman whom he had raped. This means, in effect, that the illegitimate baby whom Philumena has borne is Pamphilus's own. Once this fact has been established beyond a doubt, the couple is reunited, the play can end happily, and life returns to normal. I turn now to several revealing details of the play.

Young Men and Women

To begin with, the character of Pamphilus has been having a long-standing affair with a prostitute (or perhaps a courtesan, given the nature of their relationship), and it appears that nobody finds this unusual. This relationship presents a problem only in that it appears to have been an impediment to his marriage. His father convinced him to get married, according to Pamphilus's slave Parmeno, by using "the standard arguments," that is, that Pamphilus was his only son and he wanted some "security for his old age" (*Mother-in-Law* 115–19). In other words, the kind of relationship that Pamphilus has with Bacchis is all well and good, but it will not provide heirs; for that, he needs a legitimate citizen wife.

It is instructive that later in the play, other characters also speak of this long affair with little or no sense of disapproval: Phidippus (Philumena's father) says the following to his wife, Myrrina, at a point when he thinks that Myrrina is somehow responsible for the rift in the young couple's relationship:

I knew long before you did that he had a girlfriend, Myrrina. But I never thought it a fault in a young man—it's natural. But by golly, the time will come when he will certainly hate himself [i.e., for it]. (*Mother-in-Law* 541–43)

There are several assumptions here, and it is worth unpacking them. Phidippus finds nothing unusual in a young man having such an affair with a courtesan. But he also makes the assumption (wrongly, in this case) that his wife (Pamphilus's mother-in-law) would find such a relationship deeply objectionable. The play, in other words, points to a recognized and perhaps deeply felt difference of opinion between men and women about such relationships.

A bit later, Phidippus makes a still more impassioned defense of Pamphilus's relationship with Bacchis, even to the extent of rationalizing the continuation of the affair after the marriage had taken place:

Perhaps you heard from someone who said she saw him coming from or going to his girlfriend. So what? If he did this discreetly and only occasionally, surely it is more noble for us to pretend not to notice than to make it our business to know about it, so that he might hate us? For if he were able to suddenly pull himself away from her, with whom he had had an affair for so many years, I would not think him a man, nor a suitably stable husband for our daughter. (*Mother-in-Law* 550–56)

Phidippus is trying to reason away the affair, and it is possible that his argument should be seen as somewhat specious; that is, perhaps no Roman father would actually argue that the strength of a man's attachment to his courtesan provides evidence that he will make a good husband. But there is nothing obviously funny about this speech; it does not smack of wild exaggeration, and I think it reasonable to assume that Phidippus's basic attitude is one that most Roman men would share. So long as the affair is kept discreet, and is not out of control, it is best ignored.

On the other hand, such an affair has a clear limit. Later in the play, Laches, Pamphilus's father, has become aware of the birth of the child (he thinks, rightly, but for the wrong reasons, that the child is Pamphilus's). Unable to figure out why, under the circumstances, Pamphilus will not take Philumena back, he assumes that the problem is an ongoing affair with Bacchis:

You're wrong if you think I don't know what's in your mind. In order that you might eventually direct your mind here [i.e., toward marriage], I gave you a long time to love your mistress. How many expenses you paid out for her, and I bore it with an even temper! And I begged you and led you to marry a wife. I said it was time. You married at my insistence. In obeying me you did what was proper. Now you've led your mind back to your mistress, and by obeying her you do injury to your wife. For I see that you've returned again to the same way of life. (*Mother-in-Law* 683–92)

Now that Pamphilus is married, it might still be possible for him to carry on with an affair. But in this case, so it seems to Laches, such behavior is damaging his marriage. At that point, the affair becomes an "injury" (*iniuria*), a source of personal hurt to Pamphilus's wife, and that is precisely the limit at which such behavior must stop. Again, the basic attitude toward a young man's sexual desire is one that values moderation and self-control rather than insisting that a particular kind of behavior is necessarily wrong.

The play also provides considerable evidence that relations between a young man and his wife could be, and should be, marked by mutual affections. In the middle of the play, Pamphilus finds himself in a difficult situation. Because he has promised not to reveal the presence of the child (who has not yet been born), he must invent an excuse as to why he will not take Philumena back. He lands on the desperate dodge that his mother and Philumena have had a falling out and that as a son, he must remain loyal to his mother. Everything about the situation is, in effect, a lie: there has been no rift between mother and daughter-in-law, Pamphilus is covering up the birth of a child, and, unknown to all on stage, the child is not illegitimate. In the midst of all these deceptions and half-truths, however, Pamphilus discusses his relationship with Philumena in terms that are frank and charming:

LACHES   Pamphilus, I heard what you said to me willingly, and I understand that you put your parent before everything. But be careful that you don't go the wrong way because you are pressed by anger.

PAMPHILUS   What anger could push me to be unfair to her now, father, when she has never been guilty of anything against me, never done what I did not wish, and I know that she's often been responsible for things I wanted. I love her and I praise her and I fervently miss her. For I know from experience how carefully attuned she was to me, and I pray that she spends the rest of her life with a husband who is more fortunate than I, since necessity has dragged her away from me. (*Mother-in-Law* 482–92)

There is more than simple affection in this speech. When Pamphilus speaks of his wife being "responsible for the things I wanted," the audience gets a glimpse of a marriage in which there is a mutual give-and-take between husband and wife. And although the first lines of the speech may not ring entirely true, since Pamphilus thinks she has done something against him in being unfaithful, the end of the speech goes beyond what he needs to say to convince his father. The playwright has crafted a careful monologue, in which Pamphilus's true affections for his wife, and real heartbreak over her loss, come out in the end. How real such a portrayal is remains an open question, no less than such scenes in modern romantic comedies. But apparently, this kind of mutual affection was capable of striking a chord with Terence's Roman audience, at least as a representation of an ideal.

The Curious Case of the Prostitute Who Saved the Day

Perhaps the most remarkable thing about the *Mother-in-Law*, in the midst of all this domestic dispute, is Terence's manipulation of the character Bacchis, the courtesan. Early on in the play, as some of the earlier discussion has shown, Bacchis is assumed to be responsible for breaking up the marriage between Pamphilus and Philumena. As events come to light, it turns out that she *has* come between the two young lovers, but in a way that confirms and validates their marriage, rather than interfering in it.

In many Roman comedies, the heroine begins the play as a slave, or at least lower class. She was abandoned as a baby and raised by a poor but well-meaning couple who find her. Crucial to the plot, when she was abandoned, her mother left with her certain tokens—a piece of jewelry, a swatch of cloth—that are brought out later in the play to establish the young woman's true identity as a citizen woman and the daughter of one of the older couples in the play. Through this device, the genre of comedy suggests that class is simultaneously a natural and inborn state and one that is, paradoxically, easily manipulated by external signs; that is, the girl who has the right ring becomes the wellborn citizen who really should marry the hero of the play.

In the *Mother-in-Law*, there is a similar use of tokens for identification, but in this play, Terence (or his Greek model) has made a remarkable shift in the use of the token. Philumena (who never appears on stage) is understood to be a respectable citizen woman from the start, so her identity as such is never at issue. What is central is the question of who raped her before the start of the play, and therefore who is the father of her child (born offstage during the play). Here's how it works: in the backstory to the play, it turns out that when Pamphilus raped this unknown young woman some months before his marriage, he took a ring off her finger in the dark of night. Later on, he gave this same ring as a gift to the courtesan, Bacchis. At the very end of the *Mother-in-Law*, the audience hears from Bacchis directly that Myrrina (Philumena's mother) saw Bacchis wearing the ring and recognized it as belonging to her daughter. She asked where Bacchis got the ring; once the story was told, the ring establishes that Philumena was raped by none other than Pamphilus. The ring, then, becomes a medium of communication: it establishes that the woman Pamphilus had raped is his own wife, and that Philumena's son is also his own. A happy resolution to the play proceeds swiftly after this revelation.

There are, however, several points that we should note about this remarkable instance of recognition. Earlier in the play, Philumena's father argued that Pamphilus's strong attachment to Bacchis was evidence for his being a stable husband for Philumena. Remarkable though that argument is, it is borne out even more incredibly by the plot of the play: it is quite literally Pamphilus's relationship with Bacchis that saves his marriage. Even more improbable, it is the fact that he gives Bacchis gifts (presumably in exchange for sex) that leads to the changing hands of the critical ring. In other words, it is specifically her role as a courtesan that allows Bacchis to validate and save Pamphilus's marriage to Philumena.

As a courtesan, Bacchis is able to cross lines that other characters in the play are not. She is the only character in the play, for example, who has scenes both with other courtesans and with the upper-class families around whom the plot revolves. The fact that she is the medium through whom the ring is communicated, moreover, is a direct result of the fact that she is someone who has sex with men who are not her husband. Her flexibility in sexual matters translates into an equal flexibility in social matters; she becomes a go-between on multiple levels.

For Bacchis to play this crucial role, however, she must be willing to act against her own interests. The play opens, in fact, with a conversation between two other courtesans, who lament the fact that Pamphilus has not remained faithful to her. When Bacchis tells the audience about the revelation of the ring to Myrrina, she comments on this apparent conflict of interest:

Just now Myrrina saw that I had the ring on my finger. She asked where I got it; I told her everything. From this, she realized that Philumena was raped by *him,* and that the son who was born is his. I am pleased that these joys have reached him because of me, even if other prostitutes would not wish this. For it is not in our interest that any lover be pleased in his marriage. But by golly, I will never behave badly for the sake of profit. (*Mother-in-Law* 830–36)

Bacchis, it turns out, is the most altruistic person in the play, a clear inversion of her social function: as a prostitute, the usual assumption would be that everything she does is for profit or gain. It is this unique and comically fantastic attribute of altruism *while a prostitute* that allows her both the social mobility and the personal motivation necessary to resolve the plot.

Though Bacchis's actions result in the reunion of Pamphilus and Philumena, however, toward the end of the play, there is a surprising suggestion
that things may not change significantly between Pamphilus and Bacchis.
Pamphilus sees Bacchis and goes to her to thank her for the revelation that
she has made:

PAMPHILUS   Bacchis, my Bacchis, my savior!
   BACCHIS   You're welcome—it was my pleasure.
PAMPHILUS   You're as good as your deeds, and you still have your former charms;
             meeting, conversation, visits with you will always be a pleasure, wher-
             ever you are.
   BACCHIS   And you by golly have your former ways and manner; no man will ever
             live who is more charming than you. (*Mother-in-Law* 856–62)

A curious ambiguity hangs over the entire scene. Formally, Pamphilus is saying good-bye to Bacchis and thanking her for saving his marriage, but he
does so with reference to future meetings and future pleasures. Now that his
marriage is secure, it appears that he might be able to return without penalty
to the Roman model of a wife at home and a mistress, within reason, elsewhere. All of this, however, is made possible by Bacchis's good behavior; she
is "as good as her deeds," so that she, again paradoxically, becomes a model
for proper female behavior.

One final aspect of the play also argues against a neat resolution to all the
conflicts of the previous 850 lines or so. In the final lines, Pamphilus and Bacchis agree that they will not tell the fathers about the revelation of the ring.
In a moment that almost breaks out of the comic frame, Pamphilus gives
instructions:

Be completely silent. I'd rather that it not happen here like it does in comedies, where
everyone recognizes everything. Those who needed to know, know. Those who don't
need to know should not find out or know. (*Mother-in-Law* 866–68)

Of course, among those who now know are the audience; we are left with
a complete knowledge of how things have worked out and also the aware-
ness that the old men in the play are now going to be manipulated, the only
characters left who are in the dark about the true nature of Pamphilus and
Philumena's former relationship. This is disquieting, at least, and suggests
that the forced resolutions of the play should not sit entirely easily.

What, then, does all of this tell us about sexuality? Perhaps the most striking thing about the remarkable plot and its manipulations is what it does not
address. Once again, the woman who is at the center of all the relationships
in the play, Philumena, neither appears nor gives voice to any desires. We
hear about her behavior only through other characters. Even more notable,
however, is the fact that no character in the play seems to find it disturbing
that Pamphilus is now discovered as the rapist of his (then) future wife. The
only anxiety that this violent and, one would think, emotionally disturbing
act stirs up is the concern that is produced about the patrimony of the baby

who is born during the play. The rape that started the entire plot is simply swept under the carpet and never addressed. It is difficult to know if the Roman audience would have found this disturbing, or to what degree.

On the other hand, the various manipulations of the plot before the identity of the rapist is known show us quite a bit about what was expected of Roman men, at least Roman men in comedy, in terms of sexual behavior. The general rule, as we have seen so often before, is simply one of moderation. So long as Pamphilus does not stray too much, does not allow his affections for Bacchis to affect his marriage, does not overspend or embarrass his wife, all will be fine. Seen in this light, the significance of the rape becomes clearer: though it happens before the time of the play, it represents a moment of excess that threatens to completely overturn the social order, dissolving the marriage and resulting in Pamphilus not recognizing his own son. Only the remarkable altruism of the go-between Bacchis, as charming as she is noble, is able to restore this social order, by demonstrating the kind of self-control that Pamphilus should have had in the first place. She is willing to give him up when his marriage requires it.

COMIC CONCLUSIONS

None of the preceding discussion should be taken as a transparent model of everyday behavior. Comedies are meant to be funny; much of their humor stems from an inversion of social norms, as when clever slaves get the better of their masters, or as when an old man acts foolishly like a young one. At the same time, the list of topics that the Romans found acceptable as fodder for comedy does reveal something about attitudes toward sex and sexual behavior. In modern times, the movie *Arthur* (starring Dudley Moore) has quickly become dated and is no longer very funny because the plot revolves around the main character's uncontrolled alcoholism. If the beating of slaves created the same sort of chilling reaction for Romans that jokes about alcoholics do for modern Americans, most of Roman comedy would not work.

I have discussed only two comedies in depth, and each of them has unique characteristics. The cross-dressing scene in *Casina* is quite unusual, and the centrality of Bacchis in the *Mother-in-Law* is also not typical for these kinds of comedies. In these unique characteristics, *Casina* and the *Mother-in-Law* provide us with particularly useful evidence for Roman attitudes toward sex. It is certainly true that sex with slave boys is not fully identical with sex with a woman who will be one's wife. The comedy of the cross-dressing scene in *Casina* depends on the fact that one can only marry women, and Chalinus is demonstrably not one. At the same time, much of what is funny in that scene is the power reversal, which is a result of gender inversion: Chalinus physically overpowers his would-be husband, in a way that wives, we presume, normally did not.

The *Mother-in-Law*'s lack of shock and anxiety about an act of rape, even if it did happen offstage and before the time of the play, also tells us about Roman sexual attitudes. Had Pamphilus raped a slave woman, it is likely that there would have been no consequences at all. Because he has raped a citizen, however, the familial system that Roman marriage is meant to uphold is thrown into disarray; the irony of the play is that the marriage Pamphilus has endangered by this excessive and troubling act is his own.

Equally important in this analysis are the kinds of relationships that are not shown. The only same-sex relationships in Roman comedy are those that are unproblematic in Roman society, between a master and his slave. There is no indication in our extant plays that a master's desire for his slave would have been considered questionable, nor any strong suggestion that such love relationships were considered Greek. But neither is there anything that looks like pederasty in these comedies; that is, there are no close affective relationships between an older man and a younger citizen with a sexual component.

As always, the women's reaction to all of this, and the expression of women's sexual desires (beyond a few muted statements by the courtesans) is simply not a part of comedy. Comedy's subject is masculine society: it is the men's marriages that are central, their families that are threatened, their desires that must be regulated and finally brought under control. The women in the plays are generally smarter than the men, and through secret cooperation with one another, they manage to keep their husbands in line. But beyond forcing their husbands to behave, the choices that are open to them, as we saw with Cleostrata in *Casina,* are always severely circumscribed.

Ten

Legal and Illegal Sex in Ancient Rome

This chapter treats two different kinds of evidence: first, I present a brief discussion of some of the comments about sexual behavior in the corpus of Cicero, the most famous Roman orator of his day. Most of these comments come from his speeches, though Cicero also wrote rhetorical treatises and philosophical works (as well as poetry, most of which is now lost). In the case of Cicero's speeches, we know exactly when they were delivered and usually know with considerable precision what the context is. On the other hand, because of the way Roman courts worked, we cannot take everything that Cicero says literally; when he gives a legal speech, he must attack his opponents, and sexual slurs and innuendos were fair game in such attacks. While it is likely that Cicero exaggerates when describing the vices of his great enemies, Gaius Verres, P. Clodius Pulcher, and the notorious Clodia, these diatribes are nonetheless useful. Even if what Cicero says about Clodius is not true, it is helpful for us to know what sorts of sexual rumors would be considered particularly damaging.

The other set of evidence is both more objective and less precise: in the second half of this chapter, I discuss some of the texts of Roman laws that impose penalties for certain kinds of sexual behavior. These laws come to us in the form of digests, that is, encyclopedic compilations of the Roman legal code. The most important of these digests, that of Justinian, was written in the mid-sixth century CE, though it drew on the works of second- and third-century jurists Ulpian and Paulus. In some cases, we have good information on the historical context of specific laws; in others, it is not clear exactly when they were passed or under what circumstances. The digest, then, can be taken as giving useful information about the legal situation in the later Roman Empire, but we cannot always assume that the laws in it applied to earlier periods.

CICERO

Before discussing the sorts of things that Cicero said about his enemies in public speeches, it will be worthwhile to review the contexts of those speeches. In brief, Cicero's speeches fall into two broad categories: legal speeches, delivered in a court of law, and political speeches, usually delivered before the senate. In both cases, we should imagine that the speeches were delivered before a crowd of people. Criminal cases in the late republic took place in the Roman forum, before a jury of people from the senatorial class, and potentially with an audience of passers-by and interested parties.

In terms of content, these legal speeches are somewhat freer than what one would expect in a modern courtroom. Although ultimately, any criminal case came down to a question of whether or not the accused had broken a law, the kinds of evidence that were considered acceptable were quite broad. A prosecutor was generally at pains to attack the character of the accused to establish that she was the kind of person who might have performed the crime. What is more, if we take some of Cicero's comments seriously, this kind of evidence was considered more persuasive and more reliable than the evidence provided by witnesses, whose testimony could be influenced or bought.

A word is also necessary about these witnesses. Citizens, if witnesses, provided evidence much in the way that modern witnesses do: they provided sworn testimony, either in person or in the form of signed statements. If a slave was to provide testimony at a criminal trial, however, he or she was subjected to physical torture. The Roman conception of slaves was such that their testimony was considered of no value unless extracted in this way.[1] Here also there was room for manipulation. A person accused of a crime might manumit his or her slaves before coming to trial; once freed, such slaves could not be forced to testify under torture. (In his speech on behalf of Caelius, Cicero implies that Clodia has done just this.)

When we consider political speeches, the procedure is different, but the content may not be. Speeches before the senate might be in favor of a new law, but they might also consist of personal attacks. In a celebrated series of speeches in the year 44 BCE, for example, Cicero launched a public attack on Mark Antony, who had been Cicero's lifelong enemy and a supporter of Julius Caesar before his murder. Officially, Cicero's speeches had the aim of urging the senate to declare that Antony was an "enemy of the state." In practice, this meant that Cicero was declaring open season on his opponent, and he wasted no opportunity to defame Antony in both personal and professional terms. Among these speeches, needless to say, are some choice remarks about Antony's sexual behavior; and so this sort of rhetorical performance can also provide us with information about what was, and was not, considered acceptable. The slurs against Antony may or may not be true, but even if not true, they inform us of attitudes and assumptions of the time.

Cicero's speeches, both legal and political, then, contain any number of brief, sexually charged attacks on his enemies, and I will discuss a few of these brief comments before turning to a more carefully contextualized discussion of his *Pro Caelio*. A few patterns are worth noting: first, as we have seen before, there is no invective against men who are attracted to boys (*pueri*) per se. Cicero does often criticize his opponents for a lack of self-control in such attractions. On the other hand, any action that could be interpreted as womanish, including being the penetrated partner in a love affair, was fair game. We should also note that Cicero does not assume any sort of exclusivity in sexual desires: men who are criticized for having profligate affairs with women are also subject to charges of being effeminate themselves, or to being slaves to their desires for boys. Cicero's rhetoric, then, strongly supports Williams's notion that Rome is divided into men and non-men, the former characterized by impenetrability and self-control, the latter by effeminacy and no self-control at all.[2]

Cicero's prosecution of Verres provides us with some early examples. Verres had been the governor of Sicily in the 70s BCE; during that time, he had engaged in "corruption." As a provincial governor, Verres' power in Sicily was virtually unchecked, and he used his position to extort money from local Sicilians by a variety of schemes. Once his governorship was ended, Cicero brought a suit against him on behalf of the Sicilian people. The speeches against Verres are lengthy and convey a wealth of information about Roman provincial government in general. At various points, however, Cicero is particularly keen to attack Verres' character. At the end of his second speech, he engages in some pointed speculation about what Hortensius, the defending counsel, will say on Verres' behalf:

But now what will Hortensius do? Will he minimize the charges of avarice by praising his [Verres'] restraint? But he is defending the most immoral, the most lustful, the most despicable man. Or will he divert your attention from his notorious worthlessness by calling attention to his bravery? But it is not possible to find a man less inclined to action, more lazy, more a man among women or more a dirty little woman among men. But [he might say] that his manners are pleasant. Who is more rude? Who less civilized? Who is more cocky? But perhaps these qualities do not harm anyone. Who has ever been more harsh, who more treacherous, who more cruel? (*Against Verres* 2.2.92)

Clearly Cicero is not interested in limiting himself to a single mode of attack. It is not enough that Verres has one or two bad qualities. The prosecution provides a series of such qualities, affecting nearly every aspect of public and private life.

Among this panoply of insults are two that are of particular interest for this study: Verres is *libdinosissimus,* "the most lustful," of men. His lack of control over bodily lusts fits in with his other forms of immoral, cheating, cruel behavior. Even more specific, however, is the comment that Verres is "a man among women and a dirty little woman among men." The phrase "a man among women" begins as something of a surprise. Cicero uses here the term *vir,* a word that normally indicates a proper Roman man, as opposed to *homo,* a more derogative word for "man" that Cicero normally uses when describing his enemies. As Santoro L'Hoir points out about the word *homo,* "its use in reference to slaves, freedmen, foreigners, and even the dimmer lights of the municipal aristocracy, renders it a likely word for political invective. To call a member of the upper classes, who would normally be termed a *vir,* a *homo,* is an effective way of diminishing his status."[3] But it turns out that the use of *vir* here is deliberate: Verres is a *vir* "among women," which is to say, not so among men. There may even be a suggestion that he is too sexually active with women. The real point comes, however, in the next phrase. The suggestion that Verres is a woman among men must suggest that he has been penetrated by other men in sex, and the distaste that this is meant to engender in Cicero's audience is indicated by the adjective *impura,* "dirty," and the diminutive form of the word for woman that Cicero employs; that is, Verres is not even a woman among men: he is a *muliercula,* a "little woman." His character as a Roman man has been completely demolished.

In the preceding example, clearly Cicero is not using modern categories of sexuality to attack Verres. The point is not that he has sex with men (though that is implied) since he also has sex with women in the same sentence; rather, we should take both parts of the sentence as insulting, and both parts as impugning his manhood. The gender of his sexual partner does not matter so much as the fact that in both sexual situations, he is less than a full Roman *vir.* We might want to speak of Verres' implied passivity as a sexual identity, but again, it is important to read that passivity in terms of a larger pattern of lacking self-control. This is made even more clear by a later passage, in which Cicero details some of Verres' lavish spending of Sicilian plunder:

In this place he, praetor of the Roman people, guardian and protector of the province, spent his summer days in daily dinner parties with women, no men present at the table except Verres himself and his young son—and rightly, I could have said that there were no men present, without exceptions, since it was only those two. Sometimes the freedman Timarchides was added; the women were all wellborn and married, except for one daughter of the actor Isidorus, whom he had abducted from a Rhodian flute player because of his passion. There was a certain woman named Pipa, the wife of Aechrio of Syracuse, about whom several verses were quite popular throughout Sicily, dealing with his desire for her. (*Against Verres* 2.5.81–82)

Here Verres is clearly active in sex and clearly involved with women. But the description is nonetheless scandalous on several fronts. The expense involved in continuous dinner parties is inappropriate. Worse is the fact that Verres' passion for the daughter of Isidorus leads him to two outrageous behaviors: first, her abduction, and second, introducing the daughter of a mime actor into the company of noble married women. All of this indicates a man out of control, which leads to the crack that "no men were present" since Verres, by his behavior, has shown himself not a *vir.* This is better understood as gender deviance than as sexuality.

A later speech, Cicero's prosecution of Cataline for conspiracy against the Roman government, is peppered with descriptions of Cataline's character. In another context, Cicero says that he himself was initially taken in by Cataline's charms (*Pro Caelio* 5.12), but in the speeches *Against Cataline,* his portrayal is of a man who uses those charms for evil and disgraceful ends:

Indeed, what seductive charms were ever present in any young man as much as they were in him? He loved some men most foully, and he was a slave, most disgracefully, to the passion of others. To some he promised the enjoyment of their lusts, to others the death of parents, not only by encouragement, but even by assistance. (*Against Cataline* 2.8)

Cicero suggests that at times, Cataline was penetrated in sex—at least, that is how I take the phrase "was a slave to the passion of others." But again, this behavior is not particularly more disgraceful than other aspects of his behavior, including his seduction (and implied penetration) of young men. As with other such examples, the point of this invective is not that having desires for young men is in itself disgraceful, but in penetrating these *citizen* men, he is destroying their manhood, an act that should be seen as parallel in intent and effect to the one that follows, offering to help kill their parents. Cataline's lusts, and his seductive charms, know no bounds, and both lead to the destruction of the most basic limits of Roman moral behavior.

A passage just a page later describes the effect of Cataline on the crowd who follows him. After the stock accusation that they have squandered their inheritances (another sign of lack of self-control), Cicero lets out the rhetorical stops:

[These men] reclining at banquets, embracing unchaste women, debilitated with drink, stuffed with food, crowned with garlands, smeared with scented oils, made feeble with illegal sex, they talk drunkenly in their conversations about the slaughter of noble men and the arson of Rome. (*Against Cataline* 2.10)

Cataline's men are the very picture of depravity, engaging in every appetite to excess while they plot the downfall of the Roman Republic. This is not sexuality per se; rather, sexual misbehavior is one part of a picture of general moral dissolution.

Such examples could be multiplied from Cicero's speeches almost endlessly. I provide here only one other extended passage, from Cicero's brutal speeches against Antony, made in 44 and 43 BCE, shortly before Antony came to an agreement with Octavian (the future Augustus Caesar) and had Cicero put to death. In this passage, Cicero narrates a story of Antony's sexual life, beginning with his boyhood. Again, what is remarkable about Antony's sexual proclivities is how unrelentingly they are indulged and how, even when a man, Antony is mastered by his passions, rather than master of them:

Do you wish, then, that we should examine you from boyhood? Yes, I agree; let us start from the beginning. Do you remember that while still in boy's clothes you went bankrupt? You will say, "that is my father's fault." I give you that point. For it is a defense full of filial devotion. . . . You took up a man's clothing, which you immediately rendered a prostitute's toga.[4] From the first you were a common whore, with a set price for your disgrace, and not a small price. But soon Curio intervened, who led you away from your prostitute's profession and, as if he had given you a citizen woman's robe, he set you up in a stable and secure marriage. No boy ever bought for the sake of lust was ever under the rule of his master as you were under the rule of Curio. (*Phillipics* 2.44–45)

As often in Cicero, there is such a density of insults here that the sense almost turns against itself. First, it seems, Antony himself played that part of a prostitute. There are several mutually reinforcing implications to this statement: first, that Antony was the penetrated partner; next, that it was well known that he was sexually available; and finally, the fact that he did this at least in part from venial motives. The price to have sex with him was, evidently, not cheap. All of this is unacceptable behavior and speaks to a combination of depravity and poor financial management on Antony's part.

Antony's phase as a prostitute, however, came to an abrupt end when he fell in love with Curio. Now, Curio was a so-called boy, a young man who should have been the passive partner in a relationship with the young adult Antony. We might think that this would be an improvement, but in Cicero's hands, it is simply another opportunity for abuse. Antony's relationship with Curio is likened to a marriage, and it seems that Antony is the wife. This relationship is a full inversion of what Antony, as an adult man, should be doing, namely, entering into a marriage with a woman. Though Cicero does not specify who is the passive partner in this relationship, he implies it through his description of the power in the relationship. Antony should be a master of whatever boy he is in love with. But in this case, because Antony has no control over his own lust, Curio has become *his* master. There is a strong implication here that even the sexual roles in this affair were reversed. If Antony is under Curio's control, perhaps he is still playing the penetrated role. The entire description of Antony's life is an inversion of gender norms and shows Antony to be less than a man: first because he could not manage his estate, then because he was a prostitute (and presumably penetrated), and then because he had no control over his lust for a citizen boy.

That, however, is not all. It appears that Curio had, in the course of this relationship, put up a small fortune in money on Antony's behalf, and moreover, that Curio's father disapproved of his relationship with Antony (as well he might). Cicero here presents himself as the savior of the young man:

Curio himself, burning with desire, assured me that he would go into exile, since he was not able to bear the longing for you, if you were parted from him. What a great evil of the most prosperous family I mitigated, or rather, bore myself. I convinced the father that he should pay off his son's debt, that he should redeem through the family's resources this youth, full of promise and spirit and intelligence, and that he should prohibit the young man through his authority and power as a father not only from intimacy with you [Antony], but even from meeting with you. (*Phillipics* 2.45–46)

Here we see quite clearly the Roman concern with an improper lover's effect on a good (if misled) citizen boy. Curio, here, is not held to be at fault. He is not of age and not fully responsible for his behavior. If Antony has corrupted him through an improper passion, then it is the job of Curio's father and other concerned members of the adult community to protect him and to redeem him for the sake of his future as an adult male.

Antony, then, has played every reprehensible part possible in this review of his youth and early manhood. He has been so passive, and so venial, in his affections as to be likened to a prostitute. He has fallen madly in love with a citizen boy, to the extent that the boy completely rules over him, inverting the natural order of power. And in this relationship with a citizen boy,

Antony has played the part of an active, adult partner, but a bad one. He has so corrupted the youth that Curio is at risk of destroying his entire future as an adult male. Curio can only be rescued by concerned onlookers and the firm hand of his father.

Can we say, then, that Antony possesses a sexuality? In modern terms, he might look from some parts of the preceding passages like a homosexual. But elsewhere Cicero chastises the same man for his slavish devotion to the Egyptian queen Cleopatra as well as mocking him for an adulterous relationship with Fulvia. It is not that he only loves boys, then. Is he, in Roman terms, a passive? At times, and in the suggestion that Curio has made him a wife, it seems that he continued in this role for too long. But even here, the distinguishing mark of his sexual behavior is not that he adopts one role or the other, but that he is never in control. It is difficult to map this characteristic onto any modern notions of sexuality. If, however, we accept the essential quality of Roman manhood as that of being in control, it is easy to understand this portrayal of Antony as a gender deviant.

THE *PRO CAELIO* AND THE SEXUAL LIFE OF CLODIA

In 63 BCE, while consul, Cicero had exposed the conspiracy of Cataline and had put Cataline himself to death. The legality of this execution was, at the least, open to question, and in 58 Cicero's political enemy Publius Clodius Pulcher succeeded in having Cicero exiled from Rome. Over the next two years, however, Clodius engaged in a series of increasingly violent threats against noble Roman men, and the senate recalled Cicero from exile in 57.

In the meantime, a young protégé of Cicero named Marcus Caelius had strayed from Cicero's circle of influence, begun renting a flat from Clodius, and entered into an extramarital affair with one of Clodius's two sisters (both of whom would have been known as Clodia under the Roman system of nomenclature). This Clodia had previously been married to a stern Roman politician named Quintus Metellus Celer. Metellus had died under somewhat suspicious circumstances in 59—Cicero suggests that Clodia poisoned him—and after his death, Clodia appears to have become a rather independent woman. She was possessed of considerable wealth, and although legally she was under the guardianship of her natal family, here likely represented by her brother Clodius, Cicero paints a picture of a woman who is largely independent.[5]

The love relationship soured at some point, and it appears that Clodia arranged to have Caelius prosecuted. The case was brought to trial by a young man named Atratinus, but in Cicero's defense speech (we do not have the speeches of the prosecution), Cicero implies that the real hand behind the attack is that of Clodia. Five charges were brought against Caelius; Cicero, who spoke last, defended his friend and former pupil against the last two, of which only the last is fully understood. It appears that Caelius was charged with trying to obtain poison for the purpose of killing Clodia, and that he had done so to avoid repaying a loan which Clodia had made to him. The speech is remarkable in many ways, but perhaps most important is that it launches an all-out attack on Clodia as a sexually profligate, unrestrained citizen woman. We have seen how capable a verbal assailant Cicero can be, and we have seen as well that he is not above exaggeration for rhetorical effect. Nonetheless, his portrayal of Clodia gives us some insight into the real fears that Roman men had about unrestrained female sexual behavior.

In attacking Clodia for her affair with Caelius, however, Cicero is on tricky ground. He must make Clodia seem morally reprehensible, while portraying Caelius as innocent of any serious violations. He accomplishes this by arguing, first, that Caelius has been the target of slander because of his uncommon good looks (*Pro Caelio* 3.6). Later, he argues in several places that whatever minor lapses Caelius may have had, they can be ascribed to youthful indiscretion. Indeed, Cicero suggests, Caelius has been up to no more hijinks than many another noble Roman:

And there have been many men of the highest order and most famous citizens, judges, both in our time and in that of our fathers and ancestors, who, when the passions of youth had simmered down, have been outstanding in their more stable years for virtue. I prefer not to mention any of them by name; you yourselves remember them. For I do not wish to tarnish the greatest praise of a brave and noble man with mention of even the smallest fault. (*Pro Caelio* 18.43)

This is not to say that anything goes for the youth. Cicero is, in fact, quite clear about what the limits of such behavior should be, and this again provides us with a clear map of Roman moral concerns:

True and upright reason need not always prevail; let desire and pleasure sometimes defeat reason, so long as in this sort of thing the following rule and limit is held: a youth should protect his own sexual temperance, and not destroy another's; he should not squander his patrimony, nor should he be ruined with debts; he should not attack the home and reputation of another, nor bring shame upon the chaste, stain upon the pure, or scandal upon the good; let him not threaten with violence, nor take part in conspiracy, and let him avoid crime. (*Pro Caelio* 18.42)

This list is a virtual catalogue of the limits that I have been discussing. The signs of someone who is truly out of control are that he squanders his patrimony and that his sexual adventures are harmful to his own reputation or to others'. So long as he remains within these limits, there is no real problem.

If young men are to be allowed some sexual freedom, however, this is not true of recently widowed women. At several points, Cicero defends Caelius's affair with Clodia by arguing that Clodia has, in fact, acted like a prostitute. Her sexual license thereby becomes absolutely inexcusable, at the same time that it provides an excuse for Caelius's peccadilloes. The most stunning of these passages comes about midway through the speech. Cicero pretends that he is not talking about Clodia, but by the end of the speech, it becomes clear that he means exactly her:

Here and now I will explain the situation, though I will not name any woman. So much I leave unsaid. If there were a woman, not married, who opened her house to the pleasures of all, and who openly situated herself in the life of a prostitute; who became accustomed to attending the dinner parties of men outside her family; if she did this in the city, in the gardens, in the crowd at Bath; if at last she carried herself not only with the step of a prostitute, but with the decorations and companions of one; if not only in the openness of her looks, not only the freedom of her speech, but even in the embraces, kisses, beach parties, boat parties, dinner parties, she showed herself not just a prostitute, but a forward and brazen prostitute; if a young man by chance were with such a woman, which would you say, Lucius Herrenius—is he an adulterer? Or a lover? Is he destroying [her] chastity, or is he satisfying desire? I pass over the wrongs you have done me, Clodia, and I put aide the memory of my grief; the things that were done against my family in my absence, I pass over; may these things which I have said not be said against you. (*Pro Caelio* 20.49–50)

Again, it is important to remember that what Cicero says Clodia has done should not be taken as objective fact. But what he says she has done, fundamentally, is that she has violated the principle that women should remain private, within the sphere of their families. Even the fact of attending a dinner party, specifically a dinner party hosted by men outside the family (*alienissimi viri*), becomes an indication of sexual misbehavior and cause for reproach. Every aspect of Clodia's manner is a sign of her sexual availability: the way she walks, dresses, looks, kisses, embraces, talks—all is too public and not appropriate for a Roman matron.

On the other hand, when we look at this picture without the lens of moral disapprobation, it provides considerable information about Clodia's economic and social freedom. Dinner parties, beach parties, and boat parties all cost money. Evidently, Clodia has the wherewithal to provide such entertainments and is able to do so without the interference of her formal guardians. Cicero's not-very-veiled accusation is important specifically because it links this kind of economic and social freedom with an assumption of wild and profligate sexual freedom; in the high-blown rhetoric of the passage, it is not even enough to call Clodia a prostitute. She becomes a forward and brazen prostitute, a woman who is not bound even by the modesty of normal whores.

Earlier in the speech, Cicero indulges in a bit of mock theater to attack Clodia. He reproaches her in the voice of two of her relatives: the first, an ancestor, the famously stern Appius Claudius Caecus, who represents old-fashioned Roman morals. There are few surprises here: Appius Claudius reprimands Clodia, again, for having relations with men who are outside of the circle of her family and suggests that she has not lived up to the example of her famous ancestors. Her sexual misbehavior, then, is a betrayal of her class status:

Woman, what did you have to do with Caelius, with this young man, with this man outside the family? . . . When you had married into a most famous family from a family of the highest rank, why were you so connected to Caelius? Was he a kinsman? related by marriage? a friend of your husband? None of these. What then was it, unless some sort of boldness and lust? If the images of the men in our family did not influence you, did not that descendent of mine, that is Quinta Claudia, inspire you to be a competitor in the contest of womanly glory for praise for our house? Did not that Vestal virgin Claudia, who embraced her father as he was celebrating a triumph and did not allow him to be dragged from the chariot by a hostile tribune of the plebs inspire you? (*Pro Caelio* 14.34)

It is interesting that Appius Claudius has little to say about Clodia's general activities. He does not go on at length about her beach parties and boat parties. The fact that she has strayed outside of the family circle is evidence enough for him that improper behavior is going on. Moreover, for Appius, Clodia's behavior is conceived of primarily as a crime against her family. Her activities hurt the reputation of the family, she does not increase the "praise for our house," and so on. Perhaps most telling, she does not live up to the example of her ancestor the Vestal virgin (also named Clodia), whose act of bravery is specifically one of filial devotion.

Less concerned with family name is the next speaker whom Cicero impersonates, namely, Clodia's brother, and Cicero's great enemy, Publius Clodius Pulcer. This Clodius was a constant target for Cicero; earlier in his career, he had evidently dressed as a woman to infiltrate an all-women's festival and visit Caesar's wife there, and Cicero made frequent mention of this bit of cross-dressing.[6] In this speech, he also suggests several times that Clodius and Clodia had engaged in incestuous sexual relations, an insult that was apparently a matter of rumor in Rome.[7] So it is not surprising that Clodius is described in terms that are less than virile:

From your relatives, then, I will choose someone, and in particular your little brother, who is the most urbane of that crowd; who loves you very much and who, for some reason or another—maybe it was fear and those empty night-time terrors—when he was little, always used to sleep with his older sister. (*Pro Caelio* 15.36)

In addition to the not very subtle implication of incest, the fact that Clodius is "urbane" carries a somewhat negative connotation. He is a bit slick and worldly and not tied down by old-fashioned Roman values.

That being the case, it is something of a surprise when Cicero imagines that he, too, would be critical of Clodia's behavior. The terms of his criticism, however, are entirely different than those of the earlier Appius Claudius:

You saw a young neighbor boy; his beauty, his height, his face and his eyes struck you; often you wished to see him; you were often in the same gardens; as a noble woman, you want to keep this young man bound by your favors, this young man with miserly and cheap father; you are not able; he kicks, he rejects you, he does not think your gifts to be so great; so—find someone else. You have gardens on the Tiber, deliberately set up in that spot, where all the youths come to swim. From there you can make arrangements any day. Why are you so bothered by this one who rejects you? (*Pro Caelio* 15.36)

Needless to say, the real Publius Clodius would never have made this speech. Part of its rhetorical effect comes from the fact that it makes Clodius morally reprehensible at the same time that it uses his overly liberal moral stance to criticize Clodia. In brief, "Clodius" suggests that Clodia spends her time buying boys anyway. If she is going to be a sexual libertine, why get emotionally attached to any one of her toys? The audience members are meant to take exception both to Clodia's behavior—she should not be making "arrange-ments" daily on the Tiber with young aquatically talented youth—and to the amoral attitude toward sex that "Clodius" espouses.

Equally damning in the preceding speech of "Clodius," though, is the sug-gestion that Clodia wants to use her own riches to separate Caelius from his miserly father. Clodia is figured here as an inversion of the proper wife, a woman who draws sons out of their fathers' houses, rather than being a daughter who leaves her own house to join that of her husband. The fact that she does so by means of economic largesse makes the behavior all the worse; her sexual promiscuity is matched, and here made possible, by an equally liberal attitude toward financial resources. She is the very picture of an out-of-control woman, sleeping around, buying boys, engaging in plea-sure with no regard for traditional familial values or limits.

Some other passages illustrate the way that Clodia's sexual improprieties spill over into other areas of social behavior. At one point in the argument, Cicero must discuss whether or not Caelius has conspired with Clodia's slaves in the alleged attempt to poison her. Cicero raises an important ques-tion: what kind of slaves would these be?

But to what kind of slaves [did he entrust his fortunes]? For this matters a great deal. To those slaves, whom he knew were not used to the normal state of servitude, but were accustomed to live more easily, more freely, in greater intimacy with their mis-tress? For who does not see, judges, or who does not know, that in a house of this sort, in which the mother of the family lives in the manner of a prostitute, in which nothing happens that can be made public, in which strange lusts, expenditures, finally every unspeakable vice and outrage happens—who does not know that here the servants are not servants, to whom everything is entrusted, through whom everything is car-ried out, who take part in these same pleasures, to whom secrets are entrusted, who even benefit a certain amount from her daily expenditure and extravagance? (*Pro Caelio* 23.57–58)

It is not enough that Clodia has inverted gender norms by herself pursu-ing young men, and that she poses a threat to those young men's families. Her sexual behavior is assumed to also necessarily erase the boundary be-tween free and slave. The suggestion is just below the surface that Clodia engages in sexual activities with her slaves. This, however, is perhaps too shocking a suggestion for Cicero to make explicitly. But again, in Clodia's household, according to Cicero, there are no social limits at all. This is com-plete chaos.

Finally, and perhaps most threatening of all, Cicero suggests that Clodia, through her sexual charms and considerable financial capabilities, has cor-rupted some of the male Roman nobility. Apparently, the prosecution has claimed that Caelius had arranged for a friend, Lincinius, to hand over the poison to Clodia's slaves in the public baths. Clodia, alerted to the plot, ar-ranged for some men to hide in the baths and capture Lincinius at the mo-ment of transfer. Cicero makes a good deal of fun of this imagined scene and of the men who, allegedly, will provide their testimony about it:

Indeed I was eagerly waiting to hear the names of these noble men *[viri]*, who witnessed the poison being handed over; for so far they have not yet been named. But I do not doubt that they are very serious men, since, in the first place, they are intimate with such a woman, and second since they have undertaken this assignment, to stuff themselves in the baths. This is a task that she could never have assigned to anyone but the most honorable and most full of dignity, no matter how powerful she is. (*Pro Caelio* 26.63)

The line about Clodia's power is paramount here; the point is that these men have been directed to do something more than a bit embarrassing by Clodia, and evidently, they were happy to do so. As Cicero has already explained, for this group of men to hide in the baths, they would have had to remove their clothes. There is more than a hint of sexual impropriety, then, in "stuffing" themselves naked in the baths to lie in wait, and the audience is predisposed to realize that they are anything but "most honorable" and "most full of dignity."

A bit later, Cicero again makes clear that these men are, shockingly, at the beck and call of Clodia, a woman. They become a parody of good Roman soldiers:

I can hardly wait to see these distinguished young men who are, first, intimate with this rich and wellborn woman, and second, strong men who were positioned by their female commander in an ambush in the garrison at the baths. From them I will ask, how did they hide themselves, and where? Was it a bath tub, or a Trojan horse, which hid so many invincible men, men waging this womanly war? (*Pro Caelio* 28.67)

The military language in the passage only serves to emphasize how unmanly these men are. Rather than fighting a real battle, they are in a garrison at the baths; they are ruled by a female commander, an *imperatrix*. Even the form of battle that they undertake is an ambush, a cowardly and effeminate mode of conflict. The point of all this rhetoric is, however, not just that these men are effeminate and ridiculous. Because they have willingly submitted themselves to Clodia, whose character Cicero has already established as that of a prostitute, they have essentially jettisoned their status as Roman men. As such, their testimony, which has not yet taken place (and may not, after Cicero's speech) is of no value.

Cicero presents Clodia's sexual activity, then, as breaking down the social order on several fronts. Clodia herself does not behave as a proper woman should: her aggressive pursuit of young men, her use of economic resources to seduce them away from their families, makes her into an uncontrolled, sexually voracious prostitute. Her household, Cicero says, makes no distinction between slaves and free Romans. And the men over whom she maintains a seductive influence, either through money or through her own charms, have themselves been emasculated, made into the sexual soldiers of this "female commander." In Clodia we see the Roman man's worst fears about female sexuality: not only that women are sexually voracious, but that that very quality of sex out of control will spread through all registers of society—social, economic, cultural, military—and destroy the boundaries by which that society defines itself.

If we believe Cicero, Clodia does have a sexual morphology; that is, her walk, dress, and manner demonstrate her sexual character. Is there, in Clodia, a notion of sexual identity? Only in the broadest definition of that term. Clodia's sexual tendencies are not different in kind from those of other women; rather, what makes Clodia a threat to Cicero is the fact that there is no man to keep those sexual drives and desires under control. Her sexuality, then, is simply that of being a woman. It is her social position—still young, still attractive, widowed, rich, and surrounded by useless and corrupt male family members—that makes her sexual desires and activities dangerous.

LAWS REGULATING SEX

In none of the examples discussed previously is Cicero accusing anyone of sexual behavior that is against the law. He may go so far as to suggest that both Antony and Clodia acted like prostitutes, but unlike the examples from Greek oratory in the previous section, he does not suggest that their sexual behavior is illegal; rather, he uses their perversions of gender norms to launch broad attacks on their characters and render them unconvincing to the Roman juries, or in Antony's case, to the Roman Senate. While this sort of attack was as frequent as it is interesting, it does not tell us what, if any, sexual acts were considered illegal in Rome. In the following discussion, I will talk about just that. The reader should know that much of what I say in the next section is still highly controversial; I have made decisions about what I think is correct, but other scholars disagree with me.

Stuprum

Stuprum is a general term in Roman law for sex with any illegitimate partner, that is, anyone other than a man's wife, or slave, or paid prostitute. The word can be used in a more general sense, meaning simply "disgraceful sex," applied, for example, to sex with prostitutes; but when used in a legal sense, it always involves sex (sometimes forced) with a male or female citizen.[8] As such, *stuprum* was considered a crime against the *pudicitia*, "sexual integrity," of a married woman, an unmarried woman or girl, a man, or a boy.

It has sometimes been argued, however, that a particular law against *stuprum*, the *lex Scantinia*, outlawed same-sex *stuprum*, and that this therefore indicates a distinction in Roman law between homosexual and heterosexual illicit sex. The controversy surrounding the *lex Scantinia* is quite complex, not least because we do not have the text of the law, only scattered references to it. The issue is further complicated by the fact that the law is often cited in conjunction with another law, the *lex Julia de adulteriis coercendis* (Julian law concerning adultery). The argument has been that if the *lex Julia* covered adultery, which is only possible with women, then the *lex Scantinia* may have been distinguished from it by addressing specifically *stuprum* with boys.

This argument fails, however, on several counts. The most important is that *stuprum* was clearly already illegal before the *lex Julia* was passed during the Augustan period, and the vast majority of references to *stuprum* speak of violations against "wives and children" and fail to distinguish in any way an offence against a citizen boy and an offence against a citizen girl or woman. Indeed, the Justinian *Digest* records the law against *stuprum* as follows:

> Whoever has convinced a boy who has not assumed an adult cloak to allow *stuprum* or another crime, after having abducted or bribed his attendant; or who has solicited a woman or girl, or done anything for the purpose of corrupting her sexual integrity *[pudicitia];* or who has offered a gift or given money by which he might convince her to do it; if the crime has been carried out, he is punished by death; if not carried out he is deported to an island. Attendants who have been corrupted are subject to the ultimate punishment [i.e., death]. (*Digest* 47.11.2)

There is no reason to suspect from this statement of the law that *stuprum* with a boy is conceived of as legally different from *stuprum* with a girl or woman. The question, then, is why the *lex Julia* needed to be passed; that is, how was this law distinct from the *lex Scantinia* against *stuprum*?

Williams has argued, I think correctly, that the *lex Julia* was distinct in that it singled out the offence of *adultery*, which is to say, sex with another man's wife. This is an especially pernicious subset of *stuprum* because it could result in illegitimate children; that is, it could corrupt the bloodlines of Roman families. The penalties for such behavior were evidently quite harsh, and significantly also contained provisions for punishing the woman involved in the adultery: "If convicted, the guilty party faced banishment, loss of property, and permanent social disabilities: a woman could never again marry a free-born citizen, and a man was deprived of certain basic legal rights, becoming *intestabilis* and *infamis*."[9] The *lex Julia*, then, appears to have been a more specific law concerning a subset of infractions that would have been considered *stuprum;* but what distinguishes it is not that the object of *stuprum* is female per se, but that she is already married to another man.

This picture is complicated by the fact that, in some cases, it appears that some later authors will refer to the *lex Julia* when talking about *stuprum* with a woman and the *lex Scantinia* when discussing *stuprum* with a boy or man. The most pointed of these, Juvenal's second satire, has been used as evidence that the *lex Scantinia* referred specifically to *stuprum* with males.[10] In that poem, however, the narrative distinctions are not entirely clear. A speaker, identified as a *cinaedus*, accuses a woman named "Laronia" of adultery. He does so by naming her with the law itself: "Where, *lex Julia*, are you sleeping now?" Laronia responds by saying, "If laws and rights are going to be called up, the Scantinian ought to be cited first" (Juvenal *Satire* 2.36–44). Since the man Laronia responds to has been identified as a *cinaedus,* and therefore potentially sexually passive, indeed the law that might apply to him is the *lex Scantinia;* Williams has further suggested that the *lex Scantinia* might have meted out punishments for the passive partner as the *lex Julia* did for the adulteress. But in any case, the gist is that the *cinaedus* calls Laronia an adulteress, using the *lex Julia* to refer to that crime; that she responds by citing the *lex Scantinia* on *stuprum* does not prove that that law referred only to sex with men, and multiple other sources suggest that it did not.

Such a reading is further supported by the definition of *stuprum* preserved in the Justinian *Digest* and attributed to the third-century CE jurist Modestinus:

That man commits *stuprum* who keeps a free woman for the purpose of an affair rather than for marriage, excepting, of course, a concubine. Adultery takes place with a married woman; *stuprum* happens with an unmarried woman [*vidua*, which can mean "widowed" or "unmarried"] or a maiden [*virgo*], or a boy [*puer*]. (*Digest* 48.5.35)

Adultery, here, calls for a specialized definition, and one that might be legally a bit tricky. One can keep a concubine for the purposes of sex, even if she is a citizen. The distinction there is that she is known to be available for this sort of a relationship; that is, she has already forfeited the citizenship status that the other women in the citation have not. But the category of *stuprum* is defined to include all possible types of partners other than married women: unmarried older women, unmarried girls, or boys. There is no indication here or elsewhere in the *Digest* that *stuprum* with boys is thought of as qualitatively different from *stuprum* with unmarried women or girls.

Penalties for Passivity?

The Justinian *Digest* does contain some provisions that punish men specifically for being passive in sex, at least if they do so willingly. (There are no laws against active homoerotic behavior per se, though obviously, any act of *stuprum* was illegal.) Of particular concern in recent years has been the question of whether taking the passive role in sex could result in a significant loss of citizenship rights. As we saw in the previous section of this book, being passive in sex did not automatically lead to loss of citizenship rights in Greece, though it could subject one to accusation of being a prostitute. A person who was proven to be a prostitute in Athens experienced *atimia,* a loss of civic rights. The relevant term for Roman law is *infamis;* falling under the category of *infames* was not in itself illegal, but it could result in substantial civic restrictions, with different repercussions for people of different classes. A member of the senatorial class might be removed from that class, while members of lower classes could lose voting rights. If marked with *infamia,* a man could be prevented from representing himself or others in court, could be prevented from bringing legal actions in court, and could be declared unable to create a will. The penalties for *infamia* are quite broad.[11]

As with many aspects of Roman law, there are more ways than one by which a man could be marked with *infamia*. Originally, it appears, the distinction was made by a group of Roman magistrates known as censors. These censors were charged with maintaining the rolls of people who belonged to the senatorial and equestrian classes, and if they "noted" a person with *infamia* (by literally marking their name on the list), then such a person became *infamis*. The censors made such notations on the basis of a wide variety of moral lapses and, in theory at least, reviewed the rolls of *equites* (the class of Roman "knights," second in status only to the senatorial class) each year in a public ceremony. Somewhat later in the Republic, another group of magistrates known as praetors further developed legal definitions of *infamia*. The praetors oversaw the functioning of the courts in Rome and published a yearly edict, which had the force of law. At some point in the late Republic, the praetors' edict defined what kinds of people should be considered *infames;* Amy Richlin argues, quite plausibly, that this edict reflected the general practice of censors making such decisions.

So much is agreed on by scholars of Roman law. The issue becomes more controversial, however, when we try to determine if being passive in sex could have resulted in a man being "noted" with *infamia*. Here is a literal translation of Justinian's *Digest,* section 3.2.1, the first section "Concerning Those Who Are Noted with Infamia":

The words of the praetor say: He is noted with *infamia:* who has been discharged from the army because of disgraceful conduct, either by his general or by someone who has authority to act in this matter; who has gone onto the stage either for the purpose of acting or for declaiming; who has acted as a procurer; who has been convicted in court of having brought an action for the purpose of false accusation or for collusion; who has been convicted, or settled a charge [with guilt] of theft, of robbery with violence, of injury, of trickery and fraud in his own name; who has been convicted in his own name in a case of partnership, tutelage, mandate or deposit, with no contrary judgment; who, after the death of a son-in-law, when he knows the son-in-law to be dead, during that time when it is customary to mourn for a husband, has given in marriage a woman who was under his authority; or who has married such a woman knowingly without the order of him, under whose authority she was; or who has allowed anyone who is under his authority to marry such a woman as is described above; or who in his own name and not under the orders of someone who had authority over him, or in that of one, male or female, whom he had under his authority, has at the same time held two betrothals or two marriage agreements.

Needless to say, there is a considerable level of specificity in this law, particularly regarding marital contracts, and it is quite interesting to note the protections offered to recent widows. What is conspicuously lacking from this detailed specification, however, is any indication that particular sexual activity results in a notation of *infamia,* other than acting as a procurer. We might suspect that the idea of discharge from the army for disgraceful conduct (*ignominia*) hides some illicit sexual activity, but in fact, the gloss of Ulpian on this passage does not mention any such activity. It does specify that anyone convicted of the *lex Julia* (i.e., convicted of adultery) is automatically marked with *infamia* because such a conviction results in an automatic dishonorable discharge (*Digest* 3.2.2.3).

My reader may be confused as to why I have gone on at this length about something that is not there. I have done so because scholars have, at times, suggested that men who accepted the passive role in sex (in Roman terms, *pati muliebria*) were, under the praetor's edict, marked with *infamia*.[12] Their argument is based, however, on a reading of the previous section of the Justinian *Digest*, that is, not section 3.2.1, but section 3.1.1.6, which continues a discussion of those people who are subject to a particular restriction, that they cannot make an application to the court on behalf of others. Because the interpretation of this text hangs on the repeated appearance of a single word, I provide here the Latin text as well as a literal English translation:

Removet autem a postulando pro aliis et eum, qui corpore suo muliebria passus est. si quis tamen vi praedonum vel hostium stupratus est, non debet notari, ut et pomponius ait. et qui capitali crimine damnatus est, non debet pro alio postulare. item senatus consulto etiam apud iudices pedaneos postulare prohibetur calumniae publici iudicii damnatus. et qui operas suas, ut cum bestiis depugnaret, locaverit.

He removes from bringing action on behalf of others also that man, who with his body has suffered womanly things. But if anyone has been raped by the violence of robbers or enemies, he ought not be [so] *noted*, as Pomponius also says. And that man who has been condemned of a capital crime ought not bring action on another's behalf. Likewise the man condemned of false accusation *[calumnia]* in the public court is prohibited from bringing action by order of the senate, even to the lower courts. Also that man who has hired himself out to fight with beasts [i.e., in gladiatorial combat].

The difficulty here is simply that the writer of the *Digest* uses the word *noted* (*notari*) to discuss this case, and this word calls to mind the structure of the definition in the following section, where certain kinds of people are noted with *infamia*. In fact, an early and influential discussion of the *Digest*, that of A.H.J. Greenidge in 1894, treats this passage as meaning "noted with *infamia*."[13] The only problem is that this is not what the Latin says; this passage occurs in a list of people prevented from a particular civic right, whom the praetor has found "*notable* for their foul behavior" (*personas in turpitudine notabiles*).[14] Notable indeed, but this need not mean "to be noted as *infamis*." In brief, there is simply no evidence from the *Digest* that states that men who have "suffered womanly things" (*pati muliebria*) are subject to declaration of *infamia*.

That having been said, the objection can still be raised that men who have "suffered womanly things in their bodies" are, in fact, prevented from full participation in Roman political life. They cannot bring actions to court on behalf of another person, and in this regard, they are made parallel to gladiators, those condemned of a capital crime, women, and persons who are blind. The fact that people who have been raped are not so disqualified indicates that the law is concerned with the intent of the person who is being so penetrated. Clearly, then, the Romans considered those who are willingly penetrated by another man to be, in some respect, incapable of full participation. We may see, as Catherine Edwards has, a similarity in the categories of actors, gladiators, and men who are sexually passive in that they are all men whose bodies are used by other men for pleasure and who therefore are not in full control of their bodies.[15] But Williams argues about this particular restriction that it is surprising specifically in being so narrowly limited; men who have been penetrated retain nearly all their rights as Roman citizens. Unlike the modern category of homosexual, moreover, there is little evidence here that men who are passive in sex are demonized or thought of as medically pathological.[16]

CONCLUSIONS

Neither the legal codes nor the references in Cicero's speeches indicate that any particular orientation or attitude toward sex was considered illegal in ancient Rome. What was illegal was the penetration of Roman citizens (whether boys, girls, or women), with a particular emphasis on the illegality of adultery. The law, then, seems primarily occupied with protecting the integrity of Roman bodies and maintaining the purity of Roman family bloodlines. In this regard, Roman law is sharply different from most modern Western codes of law, which have, variously in various areas and various times, made the practice of sodomy a criminal offence.[17]

On the other hand, it is clear from the use that Cicero makes of his opponents' sex lives that the Romans had clear sexual norms for men and for women. Men were expected to exercise rigorous self-control, and an essential part of this entailed maintaining their gender identity as masculine. That meant dressing, moving, eating, spending, and generally behaving appropriately, but perhaps the surest way to attack a man's manhood was to suggest that he was passive in sex. For added piquancy, Cicero could suggest that not only was the man in question passive, but that he also sold himself as a sexual object. Women, as the attack on Clodia makes clear, were not to pursue men and were to keep their sexual relations strictly private and their social relations within their natal or marital family groups. A woman who ventured outside of these social boundaries even for events not obviously sexual, such as dinner or boating parties, could be attacked as acting like a prostitute.

A curious asymmetry rules over this understanding of gender roles. If a man was passive (and is said therefore to "suffer womanly things" in sex), then this became a marker of his lack of self-control, of his unlimited and decadent appetite for sex. Antony, in the preceding discussion, provides a characteristic example. Women, then, were assumed to be similarly without limits and in need of masculine control. When, however, a woman like Clodia began to act like a man—by actively pursuing her own erotic life, by exercising her own economic transactions—she was not portrayed as possessing masculine self-control; rather, she became a kind of hyperfeminine figure, even more voracious and uncontrolled than a so-called normal woman. The default position, then, and one that all Romans (but especially men) had to constantly guard against, was that of giving in to sexual desire. Masculinity was won after a hard fight by limiting desire, controlling sexual activity, and controlling the sexual activity of women under one's authority.

For a boy, or a young man like Caelius or Curio, the great danger was that he would be seduced into a feminine role of uncontrolled appetite. If he had a strong friend like Cicero to save him, he could be molded into a proper Roman man. If, however, his companion was a thoroughly feminized man like Antony or Cataline, the dangers were very great. The signs of his debauchery would be clear: a wasted patrimony, a tendency for luxurious dress and behavior, and a virtual enslavement to his erotic desire. These themes are taken up with a vengeance, and interestingly transformed, by the erotic poets of the Republic and early Empire, who provide the bulk of material for the next chapter.

Eleven

Roman Poetry about Love and Sex

In this chapter, I will focus primarily on Catullus, a writer of the late Roman Republic who was contemporary with Cicero. Catullus's erotic poetry was highly influential on a series of poets who came after him, including Horace, Tibullus, Propertius, and Ovid. These poets continued the tradition of writing relatively short, highly personal poems depicting erotic experience.[1] Most of their poems describe, or assume, heteroerotic relations, but not all. These later poets celebrated in particular the idea of the (male) lover who was entirely enslaved to his beloved, unable to control his passion for her. Their poems develop a persona of the lover, familiar to us from a later romantic tradition, who presents the practice of love as an alternative to the traditional pursuits of Roman men. After a thorough discussion of Catullus, I bring in a few examples from Propertius and Tibullus, but as in other chapters, any full treatment of the Roman erotic poets is beyond the scope of this book, and the interested reader is strongly encouraged to read their poems in translation herself.

I give more room to Catullus in this chapter than to the other erotic poets because he provides the most varied range of emotional positions when it comes to sex. In addition to poems to boyfriends and girlfriends, he writes about boyfriends and girlfriends to other men—friends, rivals, and enemies. In one poem, he appears the hapless, soft, and dominated lover, in the next, the aggressive potential rapist of his critics. While the other elegiac poets are particularly rich subjects for the study of gender relations (especially the role of women in Augustan Rome), Catullus provides the most complex example of masculine sexual subjectivity.

CATULLUS

At about the same time that Cicero was attacking Clodius, Clodia, and Cataline in the Roman courts, a small group of poets was thriving in Rome. Among the most celebrated, and the one whose poems have survived in greatest number to the modern era, was Gaius Valerius Catullus. According to tradition, Catullus was born in Verona in 84 BCE; though little is known with certainty about his life, he lived and wrote in Rome during the 60s and 50s BCE. His poems are charged with aggressive and erotic energy. Like the Greek lyric poets whose work he knew and sometimes imitated, they present the reader with a poetic persona, the autobiographical "I" of the poems, who feels the tortures of love keenly and expresses the joys of those torments with precision and elegance.

The temptation for scholars has been to read Catullus's poems as the unalloyed expression of a personal life, to construct, in effect, a biography of Catullus from the poetry that he wrote. This tendency must be avoided. Each of Catullus's poems is carefully crafted to create a specific moment in a complex set of relationships between the speaker, another person in the poem, and the reader of the poem. Some poems are written as if a monologue, addressed to a "you" who is named "Catullus"; but most allow us, in the lyric tradition, to overhear what appears to be an intensely private conversation between lovers, or about lovers. This fictional relationship gives this kind of poetry its peculiar charm, but it should not be mistaken for real life. Indeed, as the speaker tells us in poem 16, the poems are not the poet.

At the same time, certain historical temptations exist for the reader of Catullus's poetry. Catullus addresses poems to both male and female beloveds; the most frequent woman to appear in his work is named, in the poems, "Lesbia." This is surely a nod to Sappho, the poet from Lesbos who so effectively wrote of personal love and anguish. Indeed, two of Catullus's poems, 11 and 51, are written in Sapphic meter, and 51 is in part a direct translation of Sappho's brilliant fragment 16. What complicates this picture, however, is that in his *Apology,* Apuleius tells us that the woman addressed in Catullus's poems as "Lesbia" was, in fact, Clodia—the very same Clodia Metellus who had an affair with Cicero's young friend Caelius and whom Cicero attacked in open court (discussed in chapter 10).

There is some support for this identification, even though Apuleius was writing a good 200 years after the time of Catullus. For one thing, the names "Clodia" and "Lesbia" are metrically equivalent; that is, they scan the same in a line of poetry. Even more important are the first two lines of Catullus's somewhat cryptic poem 79. Because the identification rests in part on a pun in Latin, I give both the original and a translation:

Lesbius est pulcer: quid ni? quem Lesbia malit
quam te cum tota gente, Catulle, tua.

Lesbius is pretty; why not? Lesbia prefers him
over you, Catullus, with all your kin. (Catullus 79)

If Lesbia is Clodia, who would Lesbius be, other than Clodius? And when we remember the jokes that Cicero made about Clodia sleeping with her brother, the line about Lesbia "preferring" Lesbius begins to look suspicious. But the kicker is a complex pun, contained in the first three words: Lesbius is "pretty" *(pulcer).* The full name of Cicero's enemy, brother of Clodia, was

Publius Clodius *Pulcer.* It is difficult not to identify Lesbius with Clodius, and by association, Lesbia with Clodia.

Once we accept that identification, then it becomes all too easy to read each of Catullus's poems as a chapter in his personal life. Poem 77, addressed to "Rufus," accuses this man of having "burned away my intestines and stolen away everything I had that was good" (4–5). Some scholars have seen this as indication that Marcus Caelius Rufus has stolen Clodia away from Catullus and, on the basis of this, created a relative chronology of the two men's affairs with that woman. Simply put, this sort of speculation is entertaining and fascinating, but the poems themselves do not give adequate evidence for such elaborate reconstructions. We do not even know if "Rufus" is the same person as Caelius. (The Roman system of nomenclature allowed that he could be addressed by either name.) More important, Catullus did not write biography, and his characterizations of people are always tied to the erotic and poetic situations of each individual poem. The fiction of erotic poetry is such that it appears to be highly personal, for both reader and writer; the extent to which it reflects the real life of the author is never clearly known.

With that as a warning, the speaker of Catullus poems often addresses himself as simply "Catullus." For the sake of simplicity, in the discussion that follows, I will often refer to the poem's speaker as Catullus (as Catullus does himself). The reader should realize that this speaker is nothing more than the fictional narrator of an individual poem, a part of the created world of the poem, and not necessarily identical to the historical person.

If Catullus's poetry cannot be used as direct evidence for what Catullus the person (or Clodia the person) was like in bed, Catullus's poetry gives us good evidence for what the Romans viewed as normal, abnormal, risqué, and degrading when it came to sex. When Catullus addresses his enemies, for example, and tells them how he will abuse them in explicit sexual terms, we can be sure that these obscenities are meant to express a power relationship between the two men. When he suggests that a rival's lips are white because he has been performing fellatio, we can be fairly certain that the accusation is meant to shock the reader and that such behavior was not considered normal for Roman men. Catullus's careful delineation of sexual power relations and of deviant sexual behavior is invaluable for understanding the Roman erotic landscape.

Even here, however, some caution is required. Part of the program of Catullus's poetry is to redefine Roman manhood. In the course of his book of poetry, the speaker of individual poems is presented as a personal, erotic subject. This subject, the person who appears to speak, often does not value the things that a good Roman man ought to: his abilities as a soldier, his self-restraint, his control over both his person and his erotic desires. The person who speaks as the "I" in Catullus's poems valorizes, in sharp contrast, the experience of being overwhelmed by desire, of being tormented and in anguish because of the strength of his passion. In staking out such a position, the poet must simultaneously define such pursuits as acceptable and even masculine. Part of the fun of reading Catullus is in recognizing the sly subversiveness of this position within the wider world of Roman social expectations.

Finally, a word on obscenity: Catullus is quite possibly the most obscene author discussed in this book. In particular, when he is writing about his rivalries with other men, he uses blunt and aggressive language. It is worth noting, however, that he is not always obscene; he is rarely so when addressing Lesbia, though he is at times when speaking to other men *of* Lesbia. He is never sexually crude when addressing his male beloveds, Juventius or Veranius. In the discussion that follows, I translate Catullus's obscenities bluntly, without euphemism. In so doing, I hope to make clear that Catullus uses obscenity pointedly, and particularly when he wants to establish his own authority. Understanding when he is, and is not, obscene also helps us to understand his erotic persona.

Several unstated rules govern the practice of Catullus's erotic poetry. First and foremost, the erotic and the sexual occupy different worlds in the Catullan corpus. Catullus never discusses explicit sex with a beloved (though he does with prostitutes), and sex is nearly always an expression, not of love, but of physical and political domination. Eroticism, on the other hand, suggests a mutual give-and-take and the apparent elevation of the beloved to a position of power. Unfortunately for the speaker of Catullus's poems, the erotic also generally supposes that the speaker's desires are unfulfilled, or at least held off until some unspecified future. I begin by discussing some of Catullus's erotic poetry addressed to a female beloved (usually, Lesbia, when named).

Catullus and Women

When Catullus addresses his beloved, he never uses obscene language; rather, he engages in a program of erotic persuasion, and he generally does so from an apparent position of powerlessness. We can see this quite clearly in two of his most famous poems, those numbered 5 and 7 in the traditional corpus.[2] In the first, Catullus asks for kisses from his beloved, and his entire attitude is one of optimism and hope. Significantly, this poem gives us no indication of Lesbia's response:

Let us live, my Lesbia, and let us love,
and let us count the all gossip of serious old men
as worth a single penny.
Suns can set and rise again;
but for us, once the brief day has come to an end,
we must sleep one continuous night.
Give me a thousand kisses, then a hundred
then another thousand, then a second hundred,
then still another thousand and a hundred,
and then, when we have made many thousands
we will mix them all together, so that we do not know [i.e., how many]
or so that no evil person will be able to give the evil eye
when he knows how many kisses. (Catullus 5)

The poem is framed as an appeal to the beloved and in its very structure suggests that love is something that cannot be understood by traditional economies. The gossips of old men are given a definite value—a small one—but the kisses themselves are to be so numerous and so varied that one literally cannot know their number. Between Catullus and Lesbia, then, there is a request for an erotic experience that extends beyond the world of mundane business.

Outside of the two lovers, however, the poem hints at the darker realities of a world that pries into their relationship. It is not merely that these two lovers must enjoy love while they can (a poetic commonplace in later English love poetry). The world outside is actually hostile; the old men who see them together are assumed to be busy with gossip (*rumores*). The point in the last three lines, moreover, seems to be that if someone knew exactly how many kisses Catullus and Lesbia shared, he or she would be then be able to use that knowledge to cast a curse on them. And indeed, erotic magic from the ancient world often does work in this way. By invoking specific knowledge about a person, one is able to enact a curse. Making their love into something so unbounded that it cannot be counted, Catullus suggests, will allow it to escape both criticism and curse.

Catullus's poem 5 takes the form of a polite request, and we have no indication of how Lesbia has responded to that request. Lesbia appears, however, to be the one in control of this erotic relationship, a point that becomes clearer with poem 7:

You ask, Lesbia, how many of your kisses
are enough for me, or too many.
As many as the grains of Libyan sand
lie in sylphium-bearing Cyrene,
between the oracle of sweltering Jove
and the sacred tomb of ancient Battus;
or as many as the number of stars, when the night is quiet
that look on the stolen loves of men;
so many kisses are enough or too much
for crazy Catullus to kiss you,
kisses that neither the inquisitive will be able to count,
nor an evil tongue bewitch. (Catullus 7)

Once again, we see the concern with an overly nosy external world, a landscape of neighbors who would try to interfere with Catullus and Lesbia's affair. Catullus's response to this threat is, again, to make their love literally uncountable. But the attitude in poem 7 has shifted a bit from that of poem 5. In poem 7, the speaker begins with a question that Lesbia has evidently asked: how many kisses are enough? The reader is invited to reconstruct a conversation between Lesbia and the speaker of the poem, and it does not sound as if it is going all that well for the speaker; that is, if Lesbia were entirely in agreement with Catullus, if she were as giving of her kisses as he would like, she would not be asking how many are enough. Moreover, in the 10th line of the poem, the speaker refers to himself as "crazy Catullus." Where does the adjective *crazy* come from? It seems entirely possible that

Lesbia has used it of Catullus in the offstage conversation between the two poems; in any case, poem 7 is written as if the speaker of poem 5 has met with some resistance, and he must try again, and harder, to convince his mistress.

The woman's apparent control of the love relationship became a standard trope of Roman erotic poetry, but we should recognize it for the fiction that it is. As with the Greek lyric poets, the speaker of these words, and therefore the person in control of them, is the fictional poet within the poem. His declaration of abjection before the beloved is at least partly a rhetorical device in attempt to win her love; as Ellen Oliensis puts it in her discussion of Propertius and Horace, "the poet plays the slave within a fiction of his own masterful making. In this sense, the power of the beloved is always his gift, and dependent on his willingness to keep playing."[3]

This position of relative helplessness is explored in considerable detail by Catullus, but perhaps it is most precisely articulated by poem 8. In this short piece, the speaker writes from the position of a lover whose affair has gone sour. It is important to note that he never names his beloved in this poem; we do not know if the poem's narrator (again addressed as "Catullus") is speaking of his affair with Lesbia or with someone else, and it would be stretching the point to place poem 8 immediately after poem 7 in a reconstructed biography. But in any case, poem 8 begins with the speaker encouraging himself to return to a state of self-control after having been rejected by his beloved:

Wretched Catullus, stop being a fool,
and realize that what you know to be lost is lost.
Once bright suns shone for you,
when you used to go where your girlfriend led,
she who was loved by you as no one will ever be loved.[4]
Then there were many happy games,
For which you were willing and she was not unwilling,
Truly bright suns shone for you.
But now she does not wish; so you, impotent,
do not chase after her as she flees, nor live wretched,
but hold out with a determined mind; harden yourself. (Catullus 8.1–11)

In much of Catullus, the moment of being in love seems never to be in the present; it is always something requested for the future or, as here, a moment that is irrevocably lost. Though the speaker can reflect on happier times, his advice to himself is to buck up and stop chasing the phantasm of his past love. More important, Catullus's vocabulary here calls to mind solid Roman masculine values. For him to continue to dote on this girlfriend leaves him a wretch (*miser*), a state of personal debasement indicating a lack of control over one's circumstances. The opposite of this is to "become hard" (*obdura*) and to carry on with a "determined mind" (*obstinata mens*). This is what a Roman man generally should do. At this point, then, the experience of being in love is presented as diametrically opposed to traditional masculinity.

The poem continues, however, and amid his protests that he is recovered from the affair, the speaker begins to feel the inescapable pull of the experience of being in love:

Farewell, girlfriend. Already Catullus grows hard.
He will not seek you nor ask you, while you are unwilling:
but you will be sorry, when you are not asked for at all.
Wicked woman, off with you. What life remains for you?
Who now will come to you? To whom will you appear lovely?
Whom will you love? To whom will you be said to belong?
Whom will you kiss? Whose lip will you bite?
But you, Catullus, determined, grow hard. (Catullus 8.12–19)

In the repeated assertions of his newfound self-control, we already suspect that Catullus is not as successfully over the love affair as he would like to believe. In the last five lines, moreover, his attempt to dismiss the girlfriend goes beyond sour grapes; he not only wants her to be lonely, he begins to wonder, who will her next boyfriend be? The particular specificity of "whose lip will you bite" especially makes it impossible not to picture the event happening and to realize that the speaker is already jealous of this unspecified future rival for the woman's affections. In light of these lines, the final line speaks against itself; he may wish to "grow hard," but we are painfully aware that he has not yet become fully "determined."

Taken as a whole, then, the poem subtly undercuts the traditional view of Roman masculinity, with its valorization of self-control. The speaker of the poem may desire to be a fully independent man, "hard" of mind, but in the advice he gives to himself, we see the irresistible experience of erotic desire. Who, given the choice, would rather give it all up than live in that moment when "bright suns shone for you"? This valorization of a specific erotic subjectivity, the subjectivity of being not fully in control, is a hallmark of Catullus's poetry and one that his successors imitated and developed.

At the same time, this erotic subjectivity hearkens back to the Greek lyric poets, and especially Sappho. Just as Sappho wrote with precision and control about the experience of being uncontrollably in love, Catullus is in complete control of his poems about his own helplessness; that is, there are (at least) two Catulluses in the preceding poem: the Catullus who cannot help his own feelings for Lesbia and the Catullus who recognizes that helplessness and, standing at a distance from it, turns it into poetry. The poem presents an erotic dialogue between these two Catulluses. By representing both the attempt at personal control and its failure, the poem recreates the contradictory forces that make up the experience of being in love. The poem, in other words, does what it describes: invokes the masculine ideal of self-control but shows that position losing out to the erotic ideal of one overwhelmed by desire.

When Catullus writes to others about a Lesbia who has spurned him, his characterization of her changes dramatically. No longer the beautiful, sensuous partner of stolen loves, no longer the girl who made bright suns shine, Lesbia becomes both untrustworthy and sexually voracious. In this context,

Catullus does not hesitate to use obscenities when describing her; again, however, it is important to note that he does not address Lesbia with obscenities. Only when he is talking to other men does he use overtly foul language.

In poems addressed to Lesbia, Catullus speaks of her betrayal of him in fairly polite terms:

Once you used to say that you knew only Catullus,
Lesbia, and that you would not prefer to hold Jove over me.
I loved you then not as the common man loves his girlfriend,
but as a father loves his sons and sons-in-law.
Now I have recognized you; and while I burn even hotter,
you are nonetheless much more cheap, and tawdry.
How is it possible? you ask. Because this sort of injury forces a lover
to love more, but to wish well less. (Catullus 72)

Once again, we see Catullus draw a sharp distinction between what he thinks and what he feels. Rationally, his thoughts toward Lesbia are no longer so beneficent, even if his passion for her is somehow increased. Lesbia has injured him in such a way that she appears debased. But nothing in the poem tells us specifically what Lesbia has done; there is only the barest suggestion that her infraction was in some way sexual.

In poems in which the speaker imagines that he is addressing other men, however, Catullus is quite explicit about what has happened, and he does not hold back. In poem 11, written in Sapphic meter, Catullus begins by asking Furius and Aurelius to carry a message "to his girlfriend." The poem as a whole is quite extraordinary, but the part that concerns me is primarily in the last two stanzas, as follows:

Let her live and be well with her adulterous lovers,
whom she holds, embracing, three hundred at once,
loving none truly, but repeatedly busting the balls
of all of them.
And may she not look, as before, for my love,
which fell by her fault like a flower
at the edge of a field, after it has been touched
by a passing plow. (Catullus 11.16–24)

Lesbia is not named in this poem; it is perhaps a bit unfair, then, to link it with the other poems in which Catullus speaks of her betrayal of him. But regardless of who the woman in question is, the terms here are quite explicit. The image of the woman that he conjures up is the nightmare of sexual voracity that Cicero painted of Clodia Metellus. Not content with her one lover, the girlfriend addressed here has sex with, and does physical damage to, 300 men, identified by the legal term for adulterers, *moechus*. Once out of the circle of Catullus's desire, women become an uncontrollable sexual force.

I will return to the image of women as voracious in a moment. But first, I also want to point to the remarkable reversal of imagery in the last stanza of the preceding poem. Catullus describes himself as a flower, crushed by a plow. In most of Greek and Roman literature, women are associated with flowers, and it is not uncommon for men to be likened to plows, especially when describing sexual intercourse. Catullus describes himself here, then, in feminizing terms. It is not his love affair that feminizes him, however, but the loss of it: when the woman in the poem exercises her subjectivity in such a way that Catullus is hurt, he expresses that hurt in terms that suggest that he has been sexually violated.

Of course, the speaker has not really been so violated, and this is another example of the phenomenon that we saw earlier. Catullus writes as if all the power in the love affair lies with the beloved: she can bestow kisses (or not), she can make the sun shine (or not), and she can crush him like a plow. In all of this, Catullus still controls the words of the poem, still decides to whom he is speaking and in what sort of language. One of the remarkable and subversive aspects of Catullus's poetry is the invocation of a subject position of (apparent) powerlessness, of being unable to control one's own emotional response.

Finally, we should note that when Catullus feels himself to have been hurt by a woman, his response is to insult her with the charge of sexual profligacy (as earlier). In another famous short poem, addressed to "Caelius" (probably Marcus Caelius Rufus of Cicero's *Pro Caelio*), he contrasts Lesbia's own behavior with an implied vision of what Rome should be:

Caelius, my Lesbia, that Lesbia,
the Lesbia whom alone Catullus loved
more than himself and all his friends and family,
now at the crossroads and in the narrow doorways
she peels the descendents of greathearted Remus. (Catullus 58)

The most remarkable word in the poem, "peels" (*glubit*), apparently refers to drawing back the foreskin of a man's penis. The poem, then, is highly obscene, and it makes its point through the contrast of the first three lines with the last two. In the first three lines, all is fidelity and high-minded devotion. In the last two lines, we move to crossroads and narrow doorways, both places appropriate for prostitutes, and read about Lesbia's sexual acts in precise and anatomical terms. Even the phrase "descendents of greathearted Remus" is designed to emphasize the difference between what these people should be doing and what they are. By contrast, consider how Catullus speaks when writing a poem to a real prostitute:

Please, my sweet Ipsitilla,
my darling, my charming one,
order me to come to you for the afternoon.
And if you do order me, I also ask this,
that no one bar the door,
nor may it please you to be out.
But may you stay at home, and prepare for me
nine continuous fucks.
But, if you're going to do anything, order me at once:
for I'm lying down after lunch, and satiated on my back
I'm poking through my tunic and my cloak. (Catullus 32)

This poem is able to be light and lighthearted because, in brief, there is nothing at stake. No fraught emotions, no risk of real rejection looms over the scene. Moreover, Catullus here has no particular moral objection to Ipsitilla being a prostitute or to his making use of her. Nor does Catullus need, in this context, to show restraint, either over his language or his sexual desire. What is objectionable to Catullus, rather, is when his girlfriend, a noble Roman woman, behaves like a prostitute, which, in Catullus's rather overwrought and quick-to-temper poetry, may mean nothing more than that she takes up with another man.

Finally, I should note a few things that are lacking from Catullus's poems about women. First, the women themselves almost never speak; occasionally, we are able to discern their words, reported in indirect speech. But in none of Catullus's poems does he take on the persona of Lesbia. Ultimately, these poems are about Catullus and his reactions to his own erotic experience; the women's experience remains on the margins. Equally important, there is almost no discussion of female desire, other than the characterization of it as fickle with regard to Catullus and insatiable with regard to others. We do not hear what Lesbia wants. Nowhere does Catullus explore the idea that women might desire other women. Again, that kind of female subjectivity simply is not in the Catullan corpus.

Catullus and Boys

Catullus by no means limits himself to female sexual beloveds. In several poems, he addresses two young men, Veranius and Juventius, sometimes asking for sexual favors, sometimes merely criticizing them for carrying on with other men. Because I have discussed poems 5 and 7 previously, it will be useful to look at poem 48, addressed to Juventius:

If I should be allowed, Juventius
to continue kissing your honey-sweet eyes
[I would kiss] up to three hundred thousand kisses,
nor would I ever seem to be sated,
not if the harvest of our kissing
were thicker than the dry grain.

Once again, there is no obscenity here, no violence or dominance. Indeed, the whole poem takes the form of a condition, perhaps best thought of as a highly polite request. As in the poems addressed to Lesbia, the speaker desires numberless kisses and characterizes his own desire as boundless. Of the beloved, we can discern little beyond the speaker's desire for him. Nothing about the poem presents Catullus's feelings for Juventius, or his relationship with him, as problematic. Since it has sometimes been asserted that the Romans viewed male homoerotic behavior as Greek, we should also note that nothing in the poem suggests that Catullus's experience is foreign, decadent, effeminizing, or in any other way non-Roman.

That having been said, nowhere in Catullus's poetry does he ever mention a sexual act with a boy beloved. He is perfectly willing to threaten to screw his immediate rivals, but this has less to do with sex than with assertion of dominance. Once, in poem 56, he declares that when he found the "little boy" of his girlfriend masturbating, he "killed/screwed him with my rigid member in place of a spear" (Catullus 56.6–7). But it is quite possible that this anonymous little boy was a slave. When it comes to Veranius and Juventius, he does not talk about having sex with them. The closest that he comes is in poem 15, in which he entrusts an unnamed boyfriend to Aurelius. In so doing, he requests that Aurelius keep the boy *pudice,* "chaste," for Catullus. He does not fear others, he says, "but I am afraid of you, and your cock / a danger to both good and bad boys" (Catullus 15.9–10). Even here, however, Catullus does not explicitly say that *he* wants to have sex with the boy, just that he wants him kept safe and "intact" (*integellus,* line 4). It appears that although desire for boys was, for Catullus, entirely unproblematic, he was fairly circumspect about suggesting—even in poetry, even if the poet is not the poems—that he has penetrated them.

Boys as well as women are capable of destroying the fragile Catullan erotic ego. Though poems to his boy beloveds are less frequent than those to women (especially Lesbia), Catullus expresses hurt and surprise when his attentions are not requited by his boys. Among the most striking of such poems is poem 99, in which Catullus describes Juventius's response to Catullus stealing a kiss from him:

For no sooner was it done than you washed your little lips
with many drops [of water] and brushed them with your soft little fingers,
so that not any remnant of my mouth should remain,
as if it were the disgusting spittle of a common prostitute.
In addition, you did not delay, but betrayed wretched me,
to a harmful love, and tortured me in every way,
so that the little kiss already was changed from ambrosia for me
to something more bitter than bitter poison.
Since you have placed this punishment on my wretched love,
never again after this will I steal kisses. (7–16)

As before, there is nothing in the poem to suggest that there is anything wrong in principle with Catullus stealing a kiss from his favorite boy; nor does Juventius's response appear to be motivated by a rejection of such advances in general. Rather, what is particularly painful to the speaker is the Juventius rejection of *him* in particular and the way that rejection makes him feel. What Juventius thinks, we cannot know. But the speaker thinks that Juventius treats him as if he were a common prostitute; that is, the speaker is stripped of status by the way Juventius wipes him off his lips.

As in his relationship with Lesbia, Catullus is not able to tear himself away from desire for the boy. The boy tortures Catullus, we are told, in every way. This torture, however, is only possible because Catullus is emotionally attached to him. It is the strength of Catullus's affection that turns the kiss bitter as much as it is the boy's rejection. And though the speaker claims that he is done with stealing kisses, we may suspect that this is a position more wished for than realized.

Catullus does not, however, write a vicious poem to his friends describing Juventius's outrageous behavior, and in this his relation with the boy is different from his affair with Lesbia. In part, this must be because of the different nature of the beloveds as sexual objects and sexual subjects. In the case of Lesbia, there is a constant possibility that she will, of her own choice, move on to another lover. Though Catullus also worries about other men stealing away Juventius (see especially poems 15 and 81), Juventius is not imagined as sexually aggressive in the same way. The danger is that he will be seduced away, not that he will go off and bust 300 lovers' balls. As a result, when Catullus has a complaint, it is entirely within the context of his relationship with Juventius: Juventius has not shown him the proper affection and respect.

Catullus and Masculine Control

We should not assume, however, that Catullus never speaks bluntly about sex; rather, in Catullus's poetry, the erotic is generally separated from the sexual, which more often is a declaration of personal power and dominance. This is nowhere more clear than in poem 16, which makes deliberate reference to the poetic persona in poems 5 and 7, and perhaps to poem 48. It is important to note that the person addressed in the following poem is not Catullus's beloved, nor (as in poem 8) Catullus himself, but rather, two other men. This shift of addressee is significant; when the poet imagines that he is speaking to other men, everything about his attitude and self-presentation changes (let the reader be warned: poem 16 is among the most obscene in the corpus):

I will fuck you up the ass and I will fuck you in the mouth,
passive Aurelius and *cinaedus* Furius.
You have thought that I was not decent enough,
from my little verses, because they are a little soft.
For a dutiful poet ought to be chaste
himself, but it is not necessary for his little verses;
which only have salt and wit,
if they are a little soft and not quite decent,
and are able to rouse what itches
I don't say for boys, but for those hairy ones,
who are not able to move their stiff limbs.
You, because you have read many thousands of kisses,
you think me not masculine enough?
I will fuck you in the ass and I will fuck you in the mouth.

The first thing to notice about this poem is the prior relationship that Catullus has with Furius and Aurelius. In the situation that is imagined by the poem, these two men have been criticizing Catullus *himself* because of some of the poems he has written. But what, exactly, is the tenor of their criticism? They apparently feel that he has been a bit immodest, a bit unchaste, but they do not seem to object to the poems on the grounds that they are immoral; rather, the imputation is that Catullus may not be fully a man.

It is not, however, Catullus's poems that address boy beloveds that have left him open to these criticisms: in line 13, it is specifically the "many thousands of kisses" that have gotten Catullus in trouble. It is true that this phrase occurs in poem 48 as well as in poems 5 and 7, but nothing in poem 16 marks the kissing of *boys* as the problematic kisses; rather, it seems to be the kisses themselves, whether of women or boys, that inspire criticism. Foremost, then, is the understanding that writing this sort of lovey-dovey mush might mark a man as not quite a man.

Catullus responds to this charge with three distinct but overlapping strategies. First, he says, the poet is not his poems. Catullus the person may be quite masculine but may nonetheless write some fairly tender stuff to his beloved. Next, he argues that his poems are for a specific audience; they are not intended for young boys, but rather, for old men. There is a backhanded insult here. Even as Catullus claims the safe ground of writing for adults, so that he cannot be charged with corrupting the young, he makes it clear that these older men are "hairy" (*pilosus*) and therefore no longer attractive themselves, and stiff not with sexual energy, but with old age. (The suggestion that they cannot move their stiff limbs may be a suggestion of sexual impotence as well.) But the most obvious and most effective strategy lies in Catullus's simple declaration of sexual dominance. He calls Aurelius a "passive" and Furius a *cinaedus* and threatens to use them both sexually. No poem from the ancient world makes the importance of the active-passive dichotomy more clear. Catullus is accused of being insufficiently masculine because of his love poems to Lesbia; he responds by threatening to screw his critics.

As poem 16 makes clear, Catullus often sees himself in competition with other men and, in that competition, uses the language of penetration (whether in the ass or the mouth) to establish his position in that contest. Elsewhere, he mocks a father and son for their theft of bath clothes and, in particular, paints the son as a pathic:

Best of all bathhouse thieves,
Vibennius the father and his *cinaedus* son,
(since the father has a filthier right hand,
and the son has a more voracious ass):
why don't you go into exile and off to vile shores,
since the father's thefts are known
by the people, and you, son,
can't sell your hairy ass for a penny. (Catullus 33)

Here the two men's crimes are almost equated; and just as the father shows no bounds in the act of theft, the son shows no restraint in his hunger to be penetrated. Within the insult, however, is a further insult: just as the father can no longer steal with impunity, since his behavior is too well known, the son has also reached a limit to his crime. His buttocks, now hairy, are no longer even attractive. In neither of these poems, of course, is Catullus actually exploring the life choices of men who have self-identified as *cinaedi*. These targets of his should not be taken as examples of an emergent premodern sexuality; rather, to call a man a *cinaedus* is a way to establish social dominance over him, particularly if it is coupled with the suggestion that he wants to be penetrated.

In another poem, Catullus does attack another man's sexual behavior as deviant, and here there is some suggestion that the man's behavior is deliberate, and even secretive. If there is anything that is more degrading in Rome than wanting to be penetrated anally, it is being willing to perform fellatio on another man. In poem 80, Catullus characterizes Gellius as soft in various ways, a nice demonstration of the unmanliness of these characteristics. But the idea that he might perform fellatio is skillfully held until the end of the poem and revealed as something almost unbelievable:

How is it, Gellius, that those rosy lips
become whiter than wintry snow
when you get up in the morning and when the eighth hour
rouses you from a soft rest in the long day?
I don't know for sure; but surely not what rumor whispers,
that you swallow the large stretched tendon from a man's middle parts?
Yes, it is certain; the busted loins of the wretched conqueror cry out
and your lips marked with milked sperm.

Before we get to the act of fellatio, Gellius looks a bit suspicious; both the rosy lips and the idea of being whiter than snow are ideas often associated with women. The fact that he is sleeping late, in a rest described as "soft," also suggests a life of indolence and effeminate extravagance. As it turns out, however, these are only general signs of a more specific degradation. The sequence of exposure, which is entirely under Catullus's control, is highly effective: there are rumors; I don't believe them; yes, it's true. All of this marks the act as particularly despicable.

Even more interesting is the fact that the active partner in the fellation (a position for which there is no word in English, but which exists in Latin as *irrumo*) is not portrayed as a particularly lucky fellow. There is no doubt that he is dominant since he is referred to as *victor,* which I have translated "conqueror."[5] But not unlike the unnamed 300 adulterous lovers of Lesbia, his sexual experience leaves him with "busted loins" and results in his being labeled *misellus,* the diminutive form of *miser,* "wretch." It seems that the act of male-male fellatio is so distasteful that even the active partner, at least in this implied willing couple, is depicted as not really enjoying it.

There is another aspect to Catullus's criticisms of other men, however, and one that needs a bit more exploration. In several poems, Catullus mocks other men for failing to keep their wives under proper scrutiny. This, too, should be understood under the rubric of control that defined Roman manhood: men should control their wives just as they control their own desires. Thus, in poem 17, in which Catullus asks the town of Colonia to throw a certain man in that town off the town bridge into the muck and mire below, the reason for Catullus's anger is at first puzzling. It does not seem that this man has done anything to Catullus:

The man is completely stupid. He does not know as much
as a two-year-old, sleeping in the shaking arms of his father.

For he has a girl in the greenest flower for a wife—
and she is more delightful than the most tender little goat,
and should be guarded more carefully than the ripest grapes—
he allows her to play as she wishes, and he doesn't care a whit,
nor does he raise himself on his own behalf, but lies like an elm tree
in a ditch, chopped down by a Ligurian axe,
paying just as much attention as if she did not exist at all;
In this way, the pure idiot sees nothing, hears nothing,
doesn't know or not know who he is, or whether he is or not. (12–22)

The description of the old man's wife makes it clear that she is not only charming, but highly attractive. Though we may not think of baby goats as sexy, goats were often associated in antiquity with sexual behavior, and with a certain friskiness. The likeness to ripe grapes, likewise, indicates that this woman is just sitting there, waiting to be picked by some passer-by.

Why, though, is Catullus so upset at this old man? The answer is that this is the other side of the culture of spying and probing and continuous competition that Catullus so vehemently defends himself against in his attacks on Furius and Aurelius. The culture that Catullus describes is one of constant surveillance, and as a result, real men are supposed to watch over themselves, and their own, lest they be subject to some action by their neighbors. The old man in this poem is utterly failing to work within this societal expectation: he is just setting himself up to become a cuckold, and Catullus can barely stand to watch such incompetence at work.

In a similar way, Catullus declares complete contempt for Lesbia's husband in poem 83:

Lesbia insults me a great deal with her husband present:
These insults are a great pleasure for him—the fool.
Mule, you understand nothing. If, forgetting me, she were quiet,
she would be healthy; now because she grumbles and abuses,
not only does she remember but, what is a much sharper point,
she is angry. That is, she burns, and she speaks.

The speaker may or may not be correct in his assessment of Lesbia; it is possible that we are meant to read his own desperation in finding signs of love even in abuse. But more important, the speaker's main criticism is of Lesbia's husband for not realizing that her abuse *might* be a cover for a deeper and more damaging emotion. He is not adequately savvy, not performing scrutiny at an acceptably crafty level.

The picture drawn in the past three sections is one that may initially seem inconsistent, but is not so if we bear in mind that Catullus speaks differently to different audiences and in different circumstances. His discussions of love and sex adhere to certain principles: first, love and sex are separate issues. When Catullus speaks of love, and especially when he speaks to his love object, he refers to sex only obliquely, if at all; rather, his poems are self-aware models of erotic persuasion, and he positions himself as powerless in the face of his desire in a rhetorical attempt to convince his beloved to satisfy that desire. On the other hand, when Catullus does speak of sex, it falls into two categories. Either he threatens to perform sexual acts against other men as a form of social dominance, or he abuses his rivals or his former lover. His attacks on men take the form of rendering them passive; his attacks on women (especially Lesbia) paint them as insatiable, sexually voracious, and out of control.

Finally, and most important, in all of this Catullus assumes that there is a watchful and at least partially hostile audience.[6] This means that the speaker of Catullus's poems is always on his guard and always seeking a way to place his erotic activity outside of the realm of social criticism. At the same time, Catullus plays an active part in this game of scrutiny, criticizing others' sexual practices and ridiculing those who are not, for their own part, sufficiently watchful. This double-edged approach to sexual activity marks Catullus's erotic persona and shows him as successfully negotiating the gauntlet of Roman manhood.

Does the speaker of Catullus's poems have a sexual identity? He does not have a clear sexual orientation. Catullus, like most Greek and Romans, seems to have been equally interested in boys and women. (He does not express overt desire for men over the age of 18 or so.) While we can certainly see him adopting the role of active—that is, masculine—in poems addressed to his rivals, Catullus also carves out for himself a relatively new sexual identity: that of the elegiac lover, who revels in the position of being so much in love that he cannot completely control himself. This erotic subjectivity should not be mistaken for passivity—we know what Catullus would say to any man who suggested as much; rather, within the strictures of Roman masculinity, Catullus expands on the idea of being hopelessly in love as an acceptable sexual position. The subversiveness of this position is best explored in a few poems that overtly contrast the erotic male self with his political counterpart.

Catullus and Politics

In some of the poems I have already discussed, Catullus takes on a role that is not entirely masculine. When, at the end of poem 11, he compares himself to a flower crushed by a passing plow, he seems almost to have abandoned all notions of manhood. Yet Catullus does not embrace a feminine gender orientation. On the contrary, Catullus's poetry is engaged in a subtle game of jockeying, in which he threatens to redefine the masculine order.

In several poems, Catullus writes scathing attacks against a man named Mamurra, an *eques* who had served under both Pompey and Julius Caesar in the early 50s BCE. His chief criticism seems to be that Mamurra spent his time in the military getting rich at others' expense. Catullus depicts him in terms that are by now familiar as the diametrical opposite of proper masculinity: he has devoured not one, but three, patrimonies, and he is voracious in his appetites, sexual and otherwise. In poem 29, Catullus launches his most explicit barrage against Mamurra and suggests that Caesar and Pompey, who have put him in a position of power, are to blame for the results. In making this political argument, we should note that Catullus relies almost entirely on the language of sexual depravation:

Who can look at this, who is able to suffer it,
unless he is unchaste and voracious and a gambler:
Mamurra has what Gallic Comata used to have,
and has what farthest Britain had?[7]
Cinaedus Romulus,[8] will you see this and bear it?
And now he, haughty and overflowing,
will make a circuit of everyone's marriage bed,
like a white dove or an Adonis?
Cinaedus Romulus, will you see this and bear it?
You are unchaste and voracious and a gambler.
Single ruler, was it for this reason
that you were in the far islands of the west,
so that this debauched prick of yours
should consume twenty or thirty million? (1–15)

What is easy for the modern reader to overlook is that what Catullus is describing is essentially a political appointment: Mamurra has been made governor of a province. But his abuses are described in terms of insatiability of every kind: just as Mamurra is insatiable in matters of money, he is evidently insatiable in sex. The detail that he will now feel free to invade other men's marriage beds (*cubilia*) only marks his sexual appetite as more uncontrollable.

Even more important, however, is the suggestion that by appointing him to this province, Caesar has become tainted with the same vices. Mamurra is referred to in line 14 as "your prick" (*vestra mentula*), suggesting that he is literally a part of Caesar's body. (Elsewhere in the Catullan corpus, Mamurra is referred to simply as "Mentula"; see poems 94, 105, 114, and 115.) Somewhat paradoxically, this "prick," which we might think of as inherently masculine, instead represents an unmasculine lack of control. His overeager consumption becomes, by an extension of this metaphor, Caesar's own consumption. And in the logic of the first few lines, if Caesar is willing to watch this happen, he, too, is unchaste (*impudicus*, a word that can suggest that he has been penetrated anally), and voracious, and a gambler; that is, by allowing Mamurra's political behavior, Caesar is showing himself, like Mamurra, to lack self-control, sexual and otherwise. As a result, he is branded with the word *cinaedus*, which is to say, a gender deviant marked by exactly this sort of lack of control.

At the same time that Catullus renders the political world with a few deft sexual metaphors, he also uses the language of politics to describe his relationships, especially that with Lesbia. This is particularly noticeable in some of the poems later in the collection, which are written in elegiac meter. Two brief examples will suffice here:

No woman can say that she was loved as much, truly,
my Lesbia, as you were loved by me.
No faith in any contract was ever so strong,
as was found, for my part, in love for you. (Catullus 87)

The word translated "faith" here is *fides,* a fundamental Latin concept of trust; Cicero urges the judges to live up to their responsibility to *fides* in the *Pro Caelio* (21). The word for "contract," *foedus,* is even more explicit: this word is used to denote legal contracts and treaties. The point of Catullus's poem, then, is that his erotic bond to Lesbia was stronger, more substantial, than the legal contracts that made up the world of Roman business. Her implied destruction of that bond becomes, then, a violation of the concept of trust itself.

This metaphor reaches its fullest expression, however, in poem 76:

If there is any pleasure for a man in recalling prior kindness,
when he thinks that he has done his duty,
and thinks that he has not violated his trust *[fides],* nor in any contract *[foedus]*
made use of the power of the gods to trick men,
many pleasures wait in a long life for you, Catullus,
from this ungrateful love.
For whatever good men are able to do or say for anyone,
this has been said and done by you;
all of this, entrusted to an ungrateful mind, has perished. (1–9)

The language here is all based on the Roman system of exchange of goods and favors. A man does good for another, not only out of kindness, but on the understanding that there will be reciprocity. The word that I have translated "ungrateful" is *ingrates* (applied first to the love itself, then to his lover's mind), and it speaks directly to this point. Catullus has done everything that anyone could, but recompense in kind is not forthcoming. On one hand, applying this language of business to a love affair is something of a bold metaphor, and it supports the program discussed earlier, in which Catullus is trying to carve out a niche for the erotic subject in the world of Roman masculinity. His love affair, by means of these common metaphors, takes on the legitimacy of more typically manly pursuits, especially the practice of *negotium,* that is, the business of contracts and social compacts.[9]

At the same time, of course, it turns out that love is not business, that sometimes one's favors are not returned. The poem documents the speaker's response to learning this hard fact of life, and he suggests that perhaps another contract is in effect; that is, instead of receiving the love that he deserves, the speaker can derive pleasure from looking back on his own good behavior. This is, perhaps, not recompense in kind, but it may be all the resolution that a lover can expect, as the speaker realizes by the end of the poem:

I don't ask for this, that she love me in return,
or, since it isn't possible, that she be chaste;
I hope to be well, and to put down this harsh sickness.
Gods, give me this in return for my adherence to duty *[pietas].* (Catullus 76.23–26)

Reciprocal desire is apparently out of the question; a second option, that his lover not enter into affairs with others, is rejected. What is left for the speaker, then, is to ask the gods for repayment for his proper behavior. His prayer, in the last line, takes on the form of a contract, as was regular for prayers in ancient Rome. What began, then, as a failed contract with his lover is resolved at last in a request for reciprocity from the gods.

In poems like these, the poet engages in a radical and subversive program. Catullus is speaking, after all, of his love affair with a woman who is married to someone else. In this affair, he is technically a *moechus,* an "adulterer," punishable by law and certainly considered to be doing something immoral. For him to describe his actions in this affair as adherence to *pietas* (from which we derive the word *piety)* turns the world of Roman ethics on its head. Within the logic of the erotic persona, however, it makes a kind of sense. Catullus is valorizing the experience of being in love and is importing into that experience the values of traditional Roman society.

Catullus in Love, for Real This Time

Catullus's poems to Lesbia are fraught with failure, lost opportunity, wishes for a better future, and regret over a failed past. His poems to the boys Juventius and Veranius similarly look to some other time when love will be, or has been, experienced. As for Sappho, love for Catullus is almost never here and now. There is one poem in the corpus, however, that is almost unique in its expression of erotic satisfaction, though it, too, ends with an expression of longing. The poem is unique in another way as well: it is addressed to another man, also a poet, who appears to be Catullus's social, intellectual, and amatory equal. I close my section on Catullus with a brief discussion of poem 50, the most erotic poem in the Catullan corpus[10]:

Yesterday, Licinius, on a day of leisure,
we played many games on my tablets.
Since we had agreed to be luxurious *[delicati]*
writing little verses, one of us
would play now with this meter, now with that,
giving back in turn with jokes and wine.
And from there I went away on fire
with your wit, Licinius, and your cleverness,
so that neither food was pleasing to wretched me,
nor did sleep touch my eyes with rest,
but I tossed all over the bed, raging with fever,
desiring to see the light,
so that I could speak with you and be with you.
But after my limbs were exhausted with this work,
and were lying half-dead on my little couch,
I wrote this poem for you, delightful one,
so that from it you could see my suffering.
Now, be careful not to be proud, and do not, I pray,
reject my prayers, sweetheart *[ocellus]*[11]
lest Nemesis extract a punishment from you.
She is a violent goddess: take care not to offend her.

The absolutely striking thing about the poem is its insistence on mutuality, and on reciprocal affection. Everything in the poem goes back and forth. The two men exchange verses; Licinius evokes strong, erotic feelings from the speaker; the speaker looks forward to future exchanges; he writes (and sends) the poem that we are reading to Licinius, thus both continuing the previous day's activity and sharing his current state of longing. The poem ends with a lighthearted invocation of vengeance (Nemesis), suggesting that if Licinius does not respond to Catullus's feelings in kind, he may be struck with unrequited love himself. No other poem of Catullus describes such mutual affection, and in no other poem are the lover and beloved described as so equal in status and ability.

The poem works, however, on another level. There is no actual sex in this poem. But Catullus depicts himself clearly as a lover. His symptoms are those that have become standard: he is unable to eat, unable to sleep, obsessed with longing. What evokes this remarkable state of being in love, however, is not Licinius's physical features, but rather his wit, his cleverness—in brief, his ability to answer Catullus verse for verse. In this poem, then, it is the writing of poetry that becomes an erotic act, and in this respect, the poem represents Catullus's program. All of his poetry is, in a sense, about reproducing the state of being in love: about seeing in another person a version of oneself, about simultaneously enjoying the moment of fulfillment and longing for its endless repetition.[12]

There is a subtle subversion of the rules here: Catullus's poem is remarkably erotic for an exchange between social equals. The kind of eroticism expressed here is not possible when Catullus addresses Lesbia, or Juventius, because in those cases, the lover expresses desire for someone who is socially unequal. Because the speaker and his addressee in poem 50 are so evenly matched, the reciprocity that Catullus sought, but could not find, in his relations with Lesbia becomes possible. The poem is written, as nearly always, from a moment of longing, when the wish for reciprocal desire may be answered, and may not. But in presenting that desire as possible, even likely, Catullus invents here a new kind of erotic self, an erotic, if not exactly sexual, desire for one who is his match. Catullus would not call this "homosexuality," nor should we. For one thing, there is not any sex; for another, there is no constitution of a new kind of self through particular desire, unless we are willing to think of the persona of "poet" as a kind of sexuality. But it is a moment in which the Roman poet imagines a type of erotic exchange that goes outside of the normal roles of powerful and powerless, man and boy, male and female, free and slave.

A LITTLE PROPERTIUS

The poetry of Propertius, one of Catullus's chief successors in the field of erotic poetry, describes heteroerotic desire almost exclusively.[13] Propertius was born in the last years of the Roman Republic (49–47 BCE) and was writing during the reign of Augustus. The political developments of the last decades BCE form an important backdrop for Propertius's poems. Not only did Augustus enact important legislation regulating extramarital sex, but his reign was a time when Rome prided herself on military conquests. To be a great Roman was to be a soldier, a definition of masculinity that Propertius rejects on several levels.

Propertius wrote extensively of his uncontrollable passion for one "Cynthia" and developed and expanded on the idea of being helpless in the face of his desire. Where Catullus spoke primarily of being unable to curb his emotions, Propertius often used the image of enslavement to describe his position in regard to his beloved. To give only one example, in poem 1.5, Propertius warns Gallus about the dangers of taking up with Cynthia:

And if, somehow, she does not oppose your prayers,
how many thousands of troubles she will give you[14]
Soon she will not allow you to sleep, will not give up your eyes;
she alone, ferocious, ties men up with her spirit.
Ah, once rejected how often you will run to my door,
when your strong words fall to sobs,
and trembling and fright will rise up in sad tears,
and fear will introduce ugly lines to your face,
and whatever words you wish for will flee, as you complain,
nor will you be able, wretch [miser], to know who you are or where.
Then you will be forced to learn heavy slavery to my girlfriend,
and [learn] what it is to go home, shut out. (9–20)

The entire poem is predicated on the fiction that, should Gallus try to enter into a love affair with Propertius's Cynthia, he will be treated just as Propertius has been. The experience, even more than in Catullus, is one of complete domination: the word *slavery* (*servitium*) becomes, in the work of Propertius and his contemporaries, a trope for the experience of being in love. So while Catullus talks primarily of losing his self-control, Propertius fairly wallows in the details of that debasement and translates it into the social register. To be in love is to no longer be a free man.

With the later elegiac poets, moreover, the idea of love being a replacement for the normal pursuits of a Roman man also takes on a new force. In particular, Propertius and his contemporaries propose their erotic activities as an alternative to the practice of military conquest. This theme comes up repeatedly; early in the first book, Propertius explains to Lucius Volcacius Tullus why he cannot go on campaign with him:

I am not afraid to discover the Adriatic sea with you,
Tullus, nor to spread the sail before the Aegean;
I could climb the Rhipaeon mountains with you,
and wander beyond the halls of Memnon.
But the words of a girlfriend as she embraces me hold me back
and her serious prayers and oft-changing color. (Propertius 1.6.1–6)

So far it is merely a question of Propertius declaring willingness for one activity, rather than the other. He makes it clear that it is not fear of the rigors of campaign that holds him back, even though Tullus should go to the ends of the earth. But he cannot go against his girlfriend.

Later in the poem, the contrast between the two men becomes more fundamental. We might say that Propertius internalizes the role of lover, as opposed to soldier:

For your youth has not ever slowed down for love,
but your concern was always for your fatherland at arms;
May that boy [i.e., Eros] never bring you my labors,
and everything that is marked by my tears. . . .
Allow me, whom fortune always wanted to lie down,
to give up my last breath to this folly.
Many have perished freely in a long-lasting love;
may the earth also cover me up in their number.
I was not born fit for praise, nor fit for arms;
the fates want me to undergo *this* sort of military duty [i.e., that of love affairs].
(Propertius 1.6.21–30)

Here, the love affairs that Propertius prefers to actual warfare are called a kind of *militia*, quite literally, "military duty." This is a radical redefinition of Roman masculine subjectivity, and it marks the program of the elegiac poets at its most subversive. Moreover, Propertius describes it as a kind of inborn quality. Some men, like Tullus, are born to war; Propertius is destined, instead, to be an unhappy lover. This is not, again, exactly a sexual identity, but it is a valorization of the erotic, emotionally overwhelmed subject of love poetry specifically against the image of a Roman soldier.

This valorization takes an even more explicit form in the first poem of Propertius's second book. The poem begins with a provocative question:

You ask, why is it that all the loves written by me,
why is it that my book arrives soft on the lips. (Propertius 2.1.1–2)

The word *soft* (*mollis*) is, of course, a standard term of abuse for men. Catullus writes poem 16 in response to critics who found his poems "a little soft." To be soft is to be penetrable, and potentially feminine. Propertius's poems are soft "on the lips," perhaps recalling those thousand kisses that got Catullus into trouble. The answer that Propertius provides is that his poems are inspired by his girlfriend herself (line 4); though he does not quite say so, the poet implies that his poems are soft because they must reflect their subject.

Later in the poem, however, the poet again indicates that he writes these kinds of poems because of the kind of person that *he* is:

nor is my heart suited to preserve the name of Caesar
among his Phrygian ancestors, in hard verse.
The sailor talks of winds, the farmer of bulls,
the soldier counts wounds, the shepherd, sheep.
I, by contrast, write poems about battles in a narrow bed;
let each one spend his day doing what he is able. (Propertius 2.1.41–46)

Here the poet explicitly rejects the kind of "hard verse" that would be necessary to describe the military glory of Caesar (in this case, referring to Augustus Caesar). That in itself is a little risky. When the poet refers to the battles that he does describe, however, those that take place in bed, the subversion is complete. Not only is Propertius unwilling to write of the military conquests of the new emperor, but he gives his love poetry an equivalent validity by describing his affairs as "battles" (*proelia*). Like Catullus before him, Propertius champions an alternative model of manhood, and it is one that runs increasingly counter to the military ideals of the Roman Empire.

A BIT OF TIBULLUS

Tibullus was also contemporary with Propertius, though we know little of his life. He seems to have been born in about 54 BCE and to have died young in 19 BCE or thereabouts. In his first book of poetry, he writes primarily about the narrator's relationship with a woman named "Delia." In poem 1.4, however, he asks the god Priapus for advice on how to seduce boys, and poems 1.8 and 1.9 deal with the narrator's relationship with a boy named Marathus. There is no reason to take any of this as biography or to assume that the narrator of the poems to Delia is the same fictional persona as the narrator of the poems about Marathus. But it is significant that Tibullus apparently sees no conflict in writing about a relationship with a boy in the same form and using similar terms as in his imagined relationship with a woman.

Poem 1.8 is of particular interest because it posits an unusual love triangle. The narrator begins by addressing Marathus, who, it appears, has become completely smitten with love for a woman named Pholoe. The poet tries to give the boy some advice on how to manage his passion. The poem then purports to record a monologue by Marathus about Pholoe. Finally, the narrator returns and addresses the last part of the poem to Pholoe herself, pleading with her on Marathus's behalf. The narrator, of course, is not a completely disinterested party, and lurking just behind his "advice" to Pholoe is his own passion for Marathus. The erotic and narrative situations are unique to Latin love poetry, and among other things, the poem demonstrates the ambiguous beauty of the boy, who is just on the cusp of manhood: he is attractive as a beloved to the narrator and as a lover to his would-be girlfriend.

There are several interesting reversals of norms in this poem. To begin, we discover that Marathus, once acting as lover, rather than beloved, is trying to enhance his beauty artificially:

What good does it do you now to adorn your soft hair,
and to try new hairstyles continuously,
or to decorate your cheeks with shining rouge,
or to get a manicure from the learned hand of an artist?
. . . she is the one who is pleasing, although she comes with unadorned face
nor has she arranged her shining hair with careful art. (Tibullus 1.8.9–16)

The adornments that Marathus is attempting all carry a sense of softness, of femininity; his hair is even described as *mollis,* one of the standard words used to describe men who are feminine. This is not inappropriate for Marathus, as a young man and the beloved of the poet. But it is surprising to find him engaging in the practice of makeup and artifice to look good. As we have seen, one of the standard tropes of love poetry is that boys are naturally beautiful, where women have to use artifice to be so. Here, because Marathus is now in the position of the pursuer, he is the one who must try to look good. There is also a touch of irony in the beginning of line 9: when the poet asks "what good does it do *now,*" he creates an implied contrast with his own relationship with Marathus when, as the pursued, rather than pursuer, Marathus did not need any of these artificial enhancements.

The poet goes on to ask Pholoe not to be hard on Marathus, to reserve her hard ways, in fact, for old men (Tibullus 1.8.49–50). Here, again, we see a careful distinction between women as love objects and boys: women like Pholoe can be pursued by beautiful young men, like Marathus, or by old men, like Marathus's former lovers. The poem argues, then, that Pholoe should be smart about this choice and enjoy the love offered her by a boy who, in another context, is considered the height of beauty.

It appears, however, that Pholoe is not doing this, and the poet quotes Marathus's monologue about her neglect of him at some length. Once again, his complaints fall with a gentle irony:

"Why do you neglect me," he says. "The guardian could have been defeated.
The god himself makes those who desire able to deceive.
Stolen love is known to me, how the breath may be taken lightly,
how kisses may be taken which give no sound.
I am able to sneak out, although at dead of night,
and silently relock the door with no sound.
. . . or when she promises, but suddenly, falsely, does not fulfill,
I must spend the night awake with many evils.
While I imagine that she is coming, whatever moves,
I believe to be the sound of her feet." (Tibullus 1.8.55–66)

In brief, the lover Marathus complains that his new beloved does not practice the arts that he learned when he was a beloved. Just as he was able to sneak out at night to meet his lovers (perhaps including the poet), he expects that Pholoe should do the same. And yet, of course, the standard complaint of lovers about their boys is that they are fickle. Marathus wants his lover to be crafty: he wants her to deceive her guardian, to sneak out and enjoy "stolen love" with him, but then he is surprised when she is not constant in her affections. From our position of relative knowledge, his innocence is a bit charming and amusing.

Finally, the poem ends with a warning from the poet to Pholoe:

This Marathus once toyed with wretched lovers,
not realizing that a vengeful god was right behind him;
often he was said to laugh at the tears of the sorrowful,
and kept a lover waiting with false delay.

Now he hates all pride, now he is unhappy
with whatever hard door is barred closed against him.
But punishment waits for you, unless you cease to be proud.
How you will wish then to call back this day with prayers. (Tibullus 1.8.71–78)

Now the full irony of the situation is laid out. Marathus, it turns out, is suffering no worse than he doled out. Though our sympathy for him may therefore be somewhat diminished, the narrator of the poem maintains the difficult position of one who is still besotted with Marathus. Although he apparently no longer has any chance with the boy, then, he cannot help appealing to Marathus's new love on his behalf. The notion of turnabout, here, is perhaps a bit artificial. As I have argued, the period of time during which a boy was considered beautiful was severely constrained. Presumably, Pholoe, who is figured as able to toy with old men even while she satisfies young ones, will have a longer period of being desirable. But within the careful literary construct of the poem, retribution for spurning love is never far away. What the poet does not say, but we understand, is that Marathus is also here criticized for his fickleness; but in this poem, unlike so many others, the poet shows us the situation after the lover's wished-for vengeance has, in fact, come to pass.

The figure of Marathus, then, is particularly interesting because he occupies, in the space of a single poem, the full range of options available to a young man just on the cusp of manhood. He has been a teasing, delightful boy. He is still, evidently, attractive enough, or at any rate beloved enough, to engage the poet's sympathy and affections. At the same moment, he is a lover, now himself frustrated by the beloved; but his beloved, because of the affections of the poet, is being warned that she should enjoy this youth while he is still so beautiful and pleasing and reserve her teasing ways for the old.

CONCLUSIONS

The genre of Roman erotic poetry is an unusually rich source for the study of sexuality in the ancient world. In the personas created by Catullus and Propertius, one can see a playful attitude toward the rigorous rules of sexual roles that we have seen elsewhere. Catullus, in particular, presents a masculinity that, in certain circumstances, and when talking to certain kinds of people, valorizes a personal softness and a willingness to be emotionally overabundant. In a series of poems that are slyly subversive of the political order, both he and Propertius redefine the erotic realm as an adequate and even preferable substitute for Roman politics, warfare, and business. As Catullus makes abundantly clear when talking to men, however, he is always ready to reassert his sexual dominance should his masculinity be called into question.

Tibullus also adopts the persona of the lover who shuns masculine duty, although that is not the focus of the preceding poem. But Tibullus's lover is one who is able to see, with a certain distance, the various roles that a boy beloved will play and to enjoy the irony of going from the position of beloved to that of lover. Here, too, there is a celebration of the hopelessness of love, of the way in which a lover is always doomed to desire more than he is fulfilled. Tibullus's erotic subject is tormented no less than Catullus's or Propertius's, and to read his poetry is to enjoy the position of being so tormented.

One aspect of all three poets that is important for the study of sexuality is the degree to which they describe the lover as a sexual self who has internalized a certain view of the world because of his erotic desires. Neither Catullus, Tibullus, nor Propertius can be properly said to have a sexual orientation (though Propertius does not write poems to boy beloveds). But all three might be thought of as having a sexual identity, namely, that of the lover. They declare themselves unable to perform the manly duties of soldiers, or even to write poems that celebrate those manly duties; rather, they have internalized the somewhat softer persona of the lover and at times celebrate his lack of control over his desires.

At the same time, these poets attempt to redefine masculinity, referring to their erotic and poetic activity in the language of warfare, military duty, and business. In that regard, the Roman elegiac poets reject a notion of gender inversion implicit in dedicating themselves to love. How fully this subversive attitude would have been accepted by everyday Romans is a matter of speculation; it has the feel of an elite, and elitist, literary convention. But in any case, their poetry shows us how the persona who speaks in love poetry does so against the ideological ideals of military valor and erotic self-control.

Twelve

Excursus: Lesbians in Ovid's *Metamorphoses*

Ovidius Publius Naso (Ovid) lived during the Augustan period and somehow ran afoul of the emperor Augustus himself. In the year 8 CE, Ovid was exiled from Rome; in the same year, Augustus's granddaughter Julia—whose mother, also called Julia, had been exiled in 2 BCE—was also exiled. Though scholars have speculated endlessly about the cause of Ovid's punishment, he tells us only that he was banished because of "a poem and a mistake." Even the "poem" in question has not been securely identified.

One thing is certain, however: Ovid thumbed his nose at Augustus and his marriage legislation more brazenly than any of the erotic poets in the generation just before him. Ovid's *Art of Love* (*Ars Amatoria*) is a three-book poem explaining to men, in the first two books, how to succeed in seducing married and unmarried girlfriends. Book 3 of the same poem, written some time later, is addressed to women and gives them advice on how to get picked up. Such bold levity could not sit well with the emperor's program of moral reform and his legislation against extramarital sex, even if the poems were not meant to be taken seriously.

Ovid is best known, however, for his extraordinary long poem, the *Metamorphoses*. This ingenious, constantly brilliant work strings together much of Greek mythology, linking story after story through an endless variation of narrative devices. Within these retold Greek myths, there are a number of stories that deal with various sexual situations, including tales of transgender change, of incest, of bestiality, and, needless to say, of same-sex love. One of the most striking of these is the story of Iphis and Ianthe in book 9, a story of impossible love between two women. Given that the Romans rarely discuss female-female erotic love in any context, this story provides us with evidence that cannot be ignored.

The episode in the poem tells us of a relationship between two young women—though one is disguised as a boy—and of the unusually equal passion that they share for one another. The story ends happily, at least within the conventions of typical romance, when the young woman named Iphis is transformed into a boy, allowing the two star-crossed lovers to marry. This mutually successful ending makes the story unusual in the *Metamorphoses*. But what makes this story unique, not only for Ovid's poem, but for extant Latin literature, is that it presents same-sex passion between two women and treats that passion with considerable empathy. Iphis does deliver an over-wrought and despairing monologue in which she explores and regrets the unusual nature of her passion. Unlike the invectives of Martial or Juvenal, however, Ovid's narrator does not condemn either of the young women in his story for wanting to sleep together. The story presents this untypical love not as a moral failing, but as a thorny and near-tragic problem for a young woman who is, in every other regard, admirable.

As virtually the only text in the extant Latin corpus to treat in such de-tail and with such empathy the subject of female-female relations, the story has naturally attracted the attention of scholars working on sexuality in the ancient world.[1] In general, however, the analyses of this passage have taken Iphis's monologue at face value and have argued that it represents a typical Roman attitude toward female homoeroticism, an attitude that we might label homophobic. Here lies the interesting problem of this unique text. Iphis's condemnation of her own love for Ianthe would seem to fly in the face of the idea that the Romans did not think of sexual actors as either heterosexual or homosexual. When we read the story in its full literary and social context, however, it supports the view that the Romans were not con-cerned with homosexuality (male or female) per se. The story does indeed aid our understanding of Roman sexual categories and practices, but not in the straightforward and unmediated way that has often been assumed.

THE REMARKABLE TALE OF IPHIS AND IANTHE

The story in brief: a poor man in Crete, Ligdus, informs his pregnant wife, Telethusa, that they cannot afford to raise a girl, and orders her, if her baby is born female, to expose the infant. A dream comes to Telethusa, however, in the guise of the goddess Isis, who tells her to raise the infant no matter what. She does so, disguising the young girl as a boy. As luck would have it, Ligdus gives the girl the name Iphis from his (Ligdus's) father, a name that can apply to either sex. And Iphis, too, seems to partake of a bisexual nature, with good looks that would fit either a boy or a girl:

Her father paid his vows and named her after her grandfather,
Iphis had been her grandfather, and the name made her mother happy,
since it could go either way, and she would deceive nobody with it.
Begun from this deception, the pious lie lay hid:
Her clothing was a boy's, and her form, whether you gave it to a girl
or a boy, either one was beautiful. (*Metamorphoses* 9.708–13)

Iphis is, at this point, 13, and somewhat surprisingly, by Roman standards, the time has come for her (still disguised as a boy) to marry. She has been betrothed to Ianthe, a beautiful but poor girl, and they are madly in love. The day of the wedding comes. Iphis is beside herself with anxiety, and here she speaks her famous monologue, which I discuss in detail later. Finally, she and her mother go to the shrine of Isis, loosen their hair, and pray for help. The statue moves: a sign of acceptance. And as Iphis and her mother leave the temple, Iphis becomes, miraculously, a boy:

Not yet sure, but happy with the favorable omen,
her mother leaves the temple and Iphis follows as her companion
with a longer stride than she was accustomed; nor does her pale complexion
remain, and her strength increases, and her face becomes sharper,
and the measure of her loosened hair shorter,
and she has more energy than she had as a woman. For you who
were just now a woman, are now a boy. (*Metamorphoses* 9.785–91)

In this passage, Iphis acquires the signs of masculine gender: her step lengthens, color darkens, hair grows shorter, and so on. And so the two are married, and for once, at least, as most scholars take it, we have a happy ending.

In the middle of this episode, Iphis presents the reader with a remarkable monologue. I will treat it in two major sections. In the first, Iphis draws on parallels from the natural world to declare the impossibility of her love:

Holding back tears with difficulty, "what escape is there for me," she said,
"me whom an unheard-of heartache holds, a monstrous
heartache of novel Love? If the gods wanted to spare me,
they ought to have spared; if not, and they wanted to destroy me,
at least they ought to have given a natural destruction, a customary one!
For love of cows doesn't burn cows, nor love of mares, mares.
The ram follows the ewe, and his own female follows the [male] deer,
So even the birds come together, and among all the animals,
no female is caught by love for female.
I would that I were not [a woman]![2] In order that Crete should bring forth
every sort of monster, moreover, the daughter of the Sun loved a bull,
at least a female after a male: mine is a more rabid love than that,
if I confess the truth; at least she followed
a hope of Love, at least she, by trickery and the shape of a cow
suffered a bull, and he who was deceived was an adulterer!" (*Metamorphoses* 9.726–40)

Iphis's speech is indeed unparalleled in Roman poetry: she tells us explicitly that the problem is that she, a woman, is chasing after a woman. The careful juxtaposition of gendered terms, "cow for cows," "female for female" (in Latin, *vaccam vaccae, femina femineo*), emphasizes this crucial lack of difference. This "monstrous" (*prodigiosa*) new love is demonstrated to be contrary to nature by means of several examples. And finally, we are told that even Pasiphae's love for a bull was less remarkable: at least there we had a male and a female. Later, toward the end of the soliloquy, Iphis tells us that only nature stands in the way of her desire (*Metamorphoses* 9.758–59). It is hardly surprising that modern scholars have read this as a "damning denunciation of homosexuality."[3]

It is important, however, to step back and consider whether our own understandings of sexuality might be affecting the way we read this story.

Several scholars have read the preceding passage as homophobic because they see Ovid himself as opposed to same-sex relations. I make no argument here about Ovid's personal sensibilities; I do not take it as given that, even if Ovid's narrator were homophobic in one poem or section of a poem, he would necessarily be so elsewhere. But I should discuss briefly one of the passages that is frequently cited in favor of this view. In the second book of his *Art of Love,* Ovid declares a preference for heteroerotic relationships: "I hate that sleeping together which doesn't satisfy both parties: / this is why I am touched less by love of boys" (*Art of Love* 2.683–84). Of course, this statement of sexual preference does not constitute a sexual identity; rather, Ovid (or better, the narrator of the *Art of Love*) is commenting on his particular likes and dislikes from among the available options.

More important for the story of Iphis and Ianthe, the narrator of the *Art of Love* bases his judgment on the lack of mutual desire in man-boy relations, which tells us something about how he thinks about male-male relationships that follow the pederastic model of an older man who pursues a young, beautiful, but not desiring boy. But this inequality of desire is explicitly lacking in the story of Iphis and Ianthe, as becomes clear later. Thus the story of Iphis and Ianthe does not seem to fit the denunciation of homoerotic love that Ovid makes in the *Art of Love.* Nor is it clear that Ovid thinks of female homoeroticism and male homoeroticism as fundamentally the same kind of thing. We should be careful before assuming that he has a notion of homosexuality *in general.* But what of the more specific question? Can this be a denunciation of specifically *female* homoeroticism? Is that a category the Romans thought with? The equality of Iphis and Ianthe's love will prove to be of some importance in answering this question.

IPHIS'S MONOLOGUE: SOME LITERARY ASPECTS

It has long been recognized by feminist critics that Ovid is a problematic source for information about the lives of women in the ancient world.[4] His narrators are shifty, his poems highly literary and stylized, and Ovid's own views are as difficult to discern as they are unlikely to be representative of the thoughts of everyday Romans. This story, however, has regularly been taken at face value, as a straightforward expression of homophobia.

We should note the difficulty that arises when we assume that Iphis's story is a comment on the social reality of female homoeroticism per se. What, exactly, is Iphis's problem? What is all this talk about new, revolutionary, unheard-of love? Ovid's audience had heard about women who enjoyed sex together, though generally they are labeled and criticized as *tribades,* which is to say, women who are active in pursuing their sexual desire. What is particularly curious about this story is that *tribades* are never mentioned. Nor, in fact, is Iphis's love for Ianthe structured as "tribadic." On the contrary, their desire for each other is characterized by an unprecedented equality and mutuality. Tribadism is apparently completely beyond the horizon of possibilities. What Iphis finds unthinkable here is not the typical Roman

category of tribadism (to say nothing of lesbianism), but a romance of equal
partners. Whatever else this story is, then, it is not a transparent representation of everyday Roman attitudes. Instead, Iphis lives in a curious literary world, a world in which love between women is not so much morally
reprehensible as imaginatively impossible because there is no asymmetry of
power between the two lovers.

Ovid has gone to some trouble to create this mutuality and equality, and
the result is that some seams are left showing. In the first place, the two lovers are the same age. We might well ask why Iphis, if presumed a boy, is marrying at the age of 13, rather than the age of 25 or 30.[5] To some extent, of
course, we can answer this by pointing to the comic structure of the story: a
young man, poor but noble, overcomes obstacles to marry the woman who
is his match. Like a good comic couple, they are said to have an *aequum
vulnus,* something like an "equal passion" for one another. This comic reading presumes, however, that Iphis is already destined to play the man's role.
Moreover, what Ovid has done in writing this comic motif is to transform the
very thing that attracts the two lovers—their similarities—into their greatest difficulty. This is a fairly common technique in the *Metamorphoses:* in a
later story, a young woman named Myrrha complains of the one thing that
keeps her from sexual love with her *father* (*Metamorphoses* 10.339–40): "Now,
because he is already mine, he is not mine; and closeness itself is my destruction."[6] Similarly here, Ovid has made these two lovers even more than usually
equal and is playing with the difficulty that this absolute equality creates.
To take this comic twist as a straightforward comment on Roman attitudes
toward female homoeroticism is more than a bit naïve; rather, Ovid's Iphis
creates a humorous melodrama in the context of a fantastic construction of
female homoeroticism—fantastic because nonhierarchical.

We should further recognize here Ovid's penchant for playing with categories of thought in rhetorical display. Iphis's reliance on the natural world to
describe the impossibility of her love is something of a *topos* in love poetry.
A little bit later in the epic, in fact, we find a surprisingly similar argument,
used this time by Myrrha:

... the other animals have intercourse
with no discrimination, nor is it considered disgraceful for a heifer
to carry her father on her back; his own daughter may be a wife for a horse,
and the goat goes into whatever [female] goats he has created, and the bird
conceives from the [male] bird from whose seed she was conceived.
Happy, those to whom these things are allowed! Human worry
has given spiteful laws and, what nature allows,
jealous laws forbid. (*Metamorphoses* 10.323–31)

In this passage Myrrha uses the animal world to argue in favor of father-
daughter incest. It is a funny world indeed, if we take Myrrha's and Iphis's
speeches at face value: sex between two women is so unnatural as to be
unthinkable, but incest is just a matter of human convention. Indeed, even
within Iphis's speech, we learn that bestiality is more acceptable than the
female-female union she contemplates (*Metamorphoses* 9.735–40). Clearly

the rhetoric is excessive here, and Iphis's bombast is meant to be taken as amusing, coming as it does from a 13-year-old.

To say all this, however, does not alter the fact that Iphis seems to be thinking with modern categories: she seems worried specifically about the homosexuality that her situation requires. But is she? Even in the remarkable statement that Pasiphae's love for a bull was less crazy than Iphis's for Ianthe, we see evidence of a passive-active typology of sex. As Iphis puts it, "she, by trickery and the shape of a cow / suffered a bull, and he who was deceived was an adulterer!" (9.739–40). Though Pasiphae was possessed by a desire for a bull, when it comes to the act of sex, she "suffers" it as a woman should: the verb here in Latin is *patior,* from which we derive the English word *passive.* It is not just that the bull is male, then, but that he is *masculine:* active to Pasiphae's passivity. We should note, furthermore, that Iphis's love is "more rabid" (*furiosior*) than Pasiphae's, not for reasons of moral reprehensibility, but because at least Pasiphae had some hope (*spes*) of fulfilling her love (*Metamorphoses* 9.737–40). Iphis's desire for Ianthe is not so much immoral as impossible.

I suggest that one of the reasons Iphis has been taken as representative of lesbianism, moreover, is the very equality of her and Ianthe's passion for one another. Though the proper social form of modern lesbianism is highly contested, one of our narratives about it is that it consists of an equal, mutual desire uninterrupted by the violence of gender difference. It is exactly this sort of narrative that we see in Iphis's relation to Ianthe: contrary to all Roman erotic expectation, nearly everything about their love is marked by equality:

Their ages were equal, their beauty equal, and they learned the first
skills, the basic curriculum, from the same teachers,
From here love touched the simple breast of each, and gave
an equal wound to both. (*Metamorphoses* 9.718–21)

Though their social status, physical status, and even their education is strikingly equal, however, we must recognize that Iphis and Ianthe's passion is not, in modern terms, lesbianism, or even female homoeroticism. The continuation of lines 718–21 reads as follows:

. . . but their hopes were unequal:
Ianthe hoped for marriage, and the day of the promised wedding
and whom she thought to be a man, she believed would be *her* man.
Iphis loved one whom she despaired of ever enjoying, and this itself
increased the flames, and the maiden burned for maiden. (*Metamorphoses* 9.721–25)

Despite the supposed equality of their upbringing, Iphis's passion and Ianthe's are marked, even at this stage in their relationship, by difference. Ianthe loves Iphis *as a man,* and her desire is carefully feminine, concealed behind a hope for marriage and wedding torches. More important, what Iphis despairs here is not the shame of unnatural homoeroticism, but specifically the fact that she is not a man. As Stephen Wheeler points out, the verb translated "enjoying" (Latin *fruor*) here is a standard erotic term for a man's role in sex.[7] The passage does, to be sure, find female same-sex relations unthinkable. Not, however, for the usual reason, that *tribades* are unnatural, nor for the reasons of morality espoused by modern critics of homosexuality, but because, in the highly literary romance that Ovid has constructed, there is no active (masculine) partner.

Finally, we should note that Iphis ends her soliloquy in exactly these terms (*Metamorphoses* 9.762–63): "Why, Juno of marriages, why Hymenaeus, would you come to these / rites, at which he who leads is missing, and where both are veiled?" It is inappropriate for Juno and Hymenaeus to attend a wedding where there is nobody who leads—that is, no *man*—and both parties are to play the passive part. Indeed, the word *leads* (*ducat*) at line 762 suggests the man's role in a common Roman wedding formula, "to lead a wife" (*uxorem ducere*). Similarly, *nubere* in the last line is a verb nearly always used of women and seems to have as its original meaning "to be veiled." In brief, this is not a question of sexuality, but of gender. The conundrum facing the reader of Ovid, then, is not how two women can sleep together (for which, in any case, the Romans had an answer in the figure of the *tribad*), but rather, what do two passives do in bed together?

This reading is further supported by a close reading of the second half of Iphis's monologue. Iphis here is not so much opposed to same-sex love as she is psychologically transgendered; that is, she is a woman who wants to play a man's role. At the end of her monologue, Iphis says,

> Will you not gird your spirit and get a hold of yourself, Iphis,
> and put out these stupid fires, lacking in counsel?
> Look at what you were born, lest you deceive even yourself,
> and seek what is allowed, and love what a woman ought.
> It is hope that would seize love, hope that feeds love.
> The matter itself denies her from you: no guardian keeps you
> from her dear embrace, nor the care of a cautious husband,
> nor the harshness of a father, nor does she deny herself to you as you ask,
> but nonetheless she will not be had by you, nor, even if everything should happen,
> are you able to be happy, not though the gods and humans work [for it].
> Indeed now no part of my prayers are in vain,
> and the gods easily have given whatever they wished
> and what I wish, my father wishes, and she wishes, and my future father-in-law wishes,
> but nature does not wish it, nature more powerful than all these,
> nature who alone harms me! (*Metamorphoses* 9.745–59)

Judith Hallett sees here "revulsion at female homoerotic passion" on the part of Iphis as well as "self-condemnation,"[8] particularly in lines 747–48 and in Iphis's earlier wish that she were dead (line 735). But this straightforward reading overlooks the elegiac overtones of the passage. When Iphis asks, "Will you not gird your spirit and get a hold of yourself, Iphis, / and put out these stupid fires, lacking in counsel?" she positions herself squarely as a (male) elegiac lover, urging herself to buck up in the face of failure.[9] In the following lines, then, she expresses herself in typical elegiac form, caught in a passion she cannot control. Like any lover, she is at a loss for what to do: her love is "insane" (*furiosus*), and so she tries to bring her passions under control and direct the energy to more productive pursuits. Iphis may despair of the impossibility of her love, but if she expresses self-condemnation, it is the ironic self-abasement of a lover at his mistress's door, not the stereotyped self-condemnation of a closeted homosexual.

Here we see Ovid at perhaps his trickiest. The feature that makes Iphis into a conventionally moral woman is the fact that, as a woman (despite her desire for another woman), she remains thoroughly passive. She never acts on her desire, never contemplates becoming a *tribas;* she simply regrets the fact that she does not have the equipment to "enjoy" (*fruor*) her beloved. But now we are left to wonder: is her passivity that of a conventional woman or that of the ironically self-abased, somewhat feminine elegiac (male) lover? There is a triple layering of gender here: Iphis is a woman and is cultured as a man and as a male lover, taking on a feminized role that is generically and literarily appropriate. This, I suggest, is the culminating example of Ovid "[having] it almost all ways."[10]

The image of Iphis as elegiac lover continues in the rest of the passage. At 750 and following, Iphis runs through a catalogue of things that are *not* keeping the two lovers apart: no guardian, husband, father, nor the bride herself, and so on, all common tropes of elegiac poetry. Thus, although at line 744, Iphis suggests—briefly—the possibility that *Ianthe* could change genders, in this long catalogue, Iphis clearly figures herself in the masculine role in this relationship. When she complains of the impossibility of her love, then, she does not despair of an internal sexual identity, an impossible sexuality, but rather despairs of being able to play the masculine gender. Iphis finds herself in the traditional position of a man, but she is not stopped by the impediments that usually obstruct such men; rather it is nature that impedes her—not, as most modern readers have taken it, a nature that objects to female-female sex per se, but a nature that requires an asymmetry in sexual relations. Iphis's role as failed elegiac lover both prefigures her eventual transformation and posits its necessity.

Some comparative material from the *Metamorphoses* will help to establish this consistency. *Tribades* do not appear in the pages of Ovid's epic. That is not surprising, given the generally elevated tone of the work. We can look, however, at passages that hint at female-female relations and that confirm the general understanding of sex as predicated on an asymmetry of active-passive. On several occasions, gods find it handy to take on the form of a mortal or immortal female to get close enough to rape an unsuspecting young woman. Jupiter rapes Callisto after winning her trust disguised as Artemis (*Metamorphoses* 2.424–38); Sol rapes Leucothoë after appearing as her mother (*Metamorphoses* 4.218–320); Apollo rapes Chione still cloaked as an old woman (*Metamorphoses* 11.310), and most famously, Vertumnus tries to win the favor of Pomona by appearing to her as an old woman and singing his own praises (*Metamorphoses* 14.654–766).

In each of these cases, the god appears as a woman older than the love object, and in the case of Callisto, holding great power over her. The disguise as a woman allows the god in each case carefree access to the object of his lust, suggesting something like a community of women, a regularity of homosocial bonds between members of the same sex. The sexual act that follows in each case, however, destroys that community, indeed marks the difference between female-female relations and male-female relations. While still disguised as Artemis, for example, Jupiter kisses Callisto: "He kissed her, / not quite modestly, nor as a maiden kisses" (*Metamorphoses* 2.430–31). Jupiter's true sex is hidden in those immodest kisses, and it will be fully revealed momentarily when he rapes Callisto. Similarly, Vertumnus, disguised as an old woman, kisses Pomona: "To her, praised, he gave a few kisses, such kisses as / never a true old woman gave" (*Metamorphoses* 14.658–59). Again, there is no lesbianism here, particularly in that sense that sees lesbians as partaking in a love unmarked by hierarchy and difference; rather, in these female-female scenes, the disguise hides—imperfectly—exactly the one thing on which the Roman sexual scheme is predicated: gender difference.

FROM SYMMETRY TO DIFFERENCE

This bit of comparison brings us back to the aspect of Iphis and Ianthe's relationship that is, in fact, so unique: their mutuality. In a sense, as I have argued, this story *is* about homoeroticism. But it is not about female homosexuality as a known and derided sexual identity; rather, it is an exploration into the fantastic conundrum presented by two lovers who are not different. This, then, is the feature that Ovid makes Iphis describe as a "monstrous heartache of novel love" (*Metamorphoses* 9.727–28).

This reading has received support in a recent article by Stephen Wheeler, treating wordplay in this story.[11] Wheeler notes that Ovid has taken the story from Nicander (preserved in the mythography of Antoninus Liberalis),[12] but in the process, he has changed all the names of all the characters. Most significantly, Wheeler sees the name "Iphis" as a bit of wordplay on the Latin word *vis*, "strength," which, as he notes, "calls attention to the missing element of male sexual potency."[13] *Vis* is often used in the *Metamorphoses* as a marker of rape; to take one of the examples I just described, it is what Vertumnus prepares, but does not have to use, when all seems lost in his bid for Pomona (*Metamorphoses* 14.769–70). Iphis does not have *vis* before her transformation; that is why she cannot be a real man, a *vir*. (Wheeler also notes here that wordplay on *vis* and *vir* is frequent in this story.) Iphis is not a *tribas*, and still less a lesbian; she is "a man marked by the lack of virility advertised by her name."[14]

Once Iphis undergoes her magical sex change, this problem is solved, and she obtains a fully masculine identity. What is fascinating about this masculinity, however, is that it has less to do with biological *sex* than social *gender*.

Unlike his predecessor Nicander, Ovid never mentions the growth of male genitalia; rather, we are drawn to the distinguishing marks that guarantee masculinity in the public street of Rome: a longer stride, shorter hair, sharper features, and the like. This is of some importance because the Romans viewed masculinity as an embattled position—not a biological fact, but a hard-won social position that had to be continually bolstered and reinforced. This re-inforcement took place via a series of external signs meant to represent a never-quite-stable biological identity.

In the course of our story, then, Iphis changes his gender; whether or not his sex changes is not specifically addressed. In fact, Ovid has carefully changed the narrative in such a way as to maintain this perhaps disquieting silence. In Nicander's version of the story, the deity responsible for the sex change is Leto *phutiê*, which seems to mean, in this context, "Leto who helps grow genitalia." And indeed, in Nicander's version of the story we learn that Leukippos—on whom Iphis' character is based—grows male genitalia in the course of the miracle. Here, Leto has been replaced by Isis, much to the con-sternation of modern editors and critics. Why these changes?

I see an answer in the shifty relation of gender—a set of arbitrary, cultur-ally determined external signs—to sex, the biological fact that is supposed to underlie gender. In Egyptian mythology, Isis's consort Osiris is ripped apart after death, and his body parts are scattered over the globe. Isis spends her eternal life looking for bits and pieces of him. Alas, one part, eaten by fishes, is never found: his penis. And so, as Plutarch tells it, Isis creates a copy, around which the Egyptians hold a festival "even today."[15] In Ovid's text, Osiris is de-scribed as "never fully found Osiris" (*Metamorphoses* 9.693), a periphrastic reference to this story. Here, with characteristic brilliance, Ovid presents the marks of gender with near-total silence about what that gender is supposed to represent. Even the reference to Osiris's missing part fails to name that part. But at the same time, he hints at the signified—that is, male genitalia—by bringing in a goddess whose story represents its lack. Isis is the perfect emblem for the ideology of gender, an external pointer to something that is never quite there, that can only be represented by an indirect reference to the search for it.

CONCLUSION: THE CATEGORY OF THE *TRIBAS*

As we read Ovid's narrative, it can tell us something about how the Ro-mans organized their thought about women's sexual practices. It also tells us something important about how modern Western society relates to the ancient world, engaging as we do in the activist project of interpreting those sexual practices. Over the past 15 years or so, one of the central preoccu-pations of those scholars who would like to locate sexual identities—and individuals identified by those identities—in ancient Rome has been "the materiality of the *cinaedus*."[16] Good reasons exist for seeking out the mate-rial *cinaedus* and for trying to discover what his life was like. Good reasons also exist for wanting to see, in the invective against *cinaedi,* the roots of modern homophobia. But in all this talk of materiality, there has been a stunning silence about the materiality of the *tribas.* We are not so impelled, it appears, to prove that women identified as *tribades* really existed in Rome; rather, when it comes to women who were sexually deviant, scholars have tried to conceptualize them as lesbians (in the modern sense) and to see the category of *tribas* as part of the oppression of that deviance. In other words, *cinaedi* look to us like oppressed gay men; *tribades* look like a masculine fantasy that reproduces patriarchal hierarchy.

As example after example demonstrates, however, the category of the *tribas,* of an active, penetrating woman, is the one that Romans used to conceptualize female-female sexual relations. That is the way that they thought about women who were sexually deviant. For Iphis, a nonhierarchical love, a love between two *equal* women with no person there "who leads," is not just monstrous, but utterly unthinkable. Iphis literally cannot imagine such a thing. Her dilemma is solved not through sexuality, but through gender, when she takes on the active traits of a man much as, in the world of invective poetry, a *tribas* does. Tribadism is not a denial of reality, any more than an ahistoric lesbianism is reality; it is merely contrary to a modern (perhaps idealized) view of female-female relations. Only by seeing the *tribas,* or "active woman," as *the* category of female sexual deviance in Rome and recognizing its curious absence in this story, then, can we understand what makes Iphis's love a violation of "nature." Hers is not the love that dare not speak its name; it is a love that has no Roman name to speak.

Thirteen

Imperial Sex: Nero and Seneca

In the years after Augustus's death, the Roman Empire prospered. The introduction of an emperor into the system of government, however, irrevocably changed the nature of politics and society in Rome. The various assemblies in Rome continued to meet, two consuls were elected every year, and the senate continued to offer advice. But nothing could change the fact that the emperor held vast personal power and that ultimately, the only way to effectively oppose the emperor's will was to stage an outright revolt and try to replace him through a military coup.

In addition, the office of the emperor meant that forms of power had changed. The previous republican system of political power was largely driven by social class and the exchange of political favors in the public realm. Under the Empire, power with no specific legal authority could be wielded by members of the emperor's family or social circle, moving outside of the regular circuits of political power.[1] Under the rule of Tiberius, for example, a remarkable member of the *eques* class named Sejanus rose to be commander of the praetorian guard, a special military force charged with protecting the emperor. From this position, it appears that he exercised considerable personal influence over Tiberius, eventually vying with Tiberius's son Drusus for the emperorship. According to the Roman historian Tacitus, Sejanus seduced Drusus's wife, Livilla, and with her help, succeeded in poisoning Drusus.

Sejanus eventually overstepped his influence, and though the exact sequence of events is not well known (the section of Tacitus which would have described his fall is lost), he evidently fell from grace. He was called to the senate in 31 CE, ostensibly to receive tribunician powers; instead, Tiberius transferred leadership of the praetorian guard to Macro and, in a letter, denounced Sejanus before the senate. He was arrested, imprisoned, sentenced to death, killed, and his body torn to pieces by an angry crowd, in short order.

This brief story of Sejanus sketches in its extremity what would be, off and on for the next hundred years or so, the main characteristics of imperial power in Rome: personal influence, familial intrigue, wives and mistresses brought into the political arena, dangerous feuds over succession, and beneath it all, an unruly mob of citizens who might erupt in violence. At the same time, the emperor himself wielded almost unthinkable power, so long as he remained popular and maintained the support of the praetorian guard.

When we think of the Roman Empire, it is most commonly the emperors of the first century that come to mind, and their names are synonymous in the modern imagination with an idea of Roman extravagance, decadence, and decline: Tiberius, Caligula, Domitian, Nero. An aspect of this imagined picture that is nearly always present, but not always articulated, is the idea of a confusion of the political and the private. We picture emperors involved in wild sexual orgies, while their mothers or wives wield influence behind the throne. We imagine vast public gladiatorial games, which the emperor watched and where he was watched by his ambivalent crowd of citizens. And above all, we picture the Roman Empire as a time of sexual decadence, in which the emperor used his political power to overstep every imaginable sexual taboo and satisfy his uncontrolled lusts.

This picture is not entirely false, though the reality was no doubt somewhat more tame, at least some of the time, than the picture made popular by sword-and-sandal movies of the last 75 years. In this chapter, I look at attitudes toward sex at a particular historical moment, that of the emperor Nero, who ruled Rome from 54 to 68 CE. This time period provides us with an unusually rich set of evidence, both because Nero himself seems to have had some difficulty distinguishing between appropriate public and private behavior, and because during Nero's reign, the great moralist and philosopher Seneca the Younger was alive and writing. Seneca was, in fact, Nero's tutor and advisor during the early years of his reign.

In what follows, then, I look first at some writings of Seneca in which he describes appropriate modes of self-regulation, sexual and otherwise. I then turn to the historiographical tradition and its treatment of Nero himself, looking especially at the authors Tacitus, Suetonius, and Cassius Dio, all of whom lived and wrote some time after Nero, but all of whom appear to have had access to accounts contemporary with the emperor.

SENECA THE YOUNGER

Lucius Annaeus Seneca "the younger" is so named to distinguish him from his father, a famous rhetorician with the same name. Of his early life we know very little, beyond the fact that he was born shortly before the end of the first century BCE, probably in Spain, and that he moved to Rome while still a child. He was a popular orator and teacher in Rome, but he fell out of grace with the emperor Caligula, who reportedly contemplated having him put to death. In 41 CE the emperor Claudius, apparently under the influence of his wife, Messalina, had Seneca exiled to Corsica . During his eight years of exile, Seneca wrote numerous letters and philosophical essays. He was eventually recalled from exile in 49 CE, probably at the suggestion of Claudius's new wife, Agrippina, and appointed tutor to her son Lucius Domitius Ahenobarbus, who would later become the emperor Nero.

Our historical sources agree that when Nero become emperor in 54, Seneca and the leader of the praetorian guard, Sextus Afranius Burrus, advised the young emperor and largely kept his overambitious appetites under control. Over time, however, it appears that Nero grew increasingly independent of the two senior politicians, perhaps coming under the pernicious influence of his mother, Agrippina (though the historians' attacks on her character should not be taken at face value). In 59, Nero had his mother killed, and in 62, Burrus died under mysterious circumstances. At this point, Seneca seems to have retired from public life, but in 65, accused by Nero of taking part in a conspiracy against the emperor's life, he committed suicide. Nero would continue as emperor for three more years, eventually committing suicide himself in 68, when it became clear that he had lost the support of the praetorian guard.

During Seneca's life, he ascribed to the philosophy of Stoicism, which had no small influence on his view of sexual matters. Classical Stoicism holds that a man should live in accordance with nature and concern himself exclusively with virtue. Knowing how to be virtuous is a problem to be solved by the application of reason since nature herself is organized according to rational principles. The world will, of course, cause a person considerable discomfort, and even pain, but these are to be dealt with by developing sufficient self-control so that such discomfort can be effectively ignored. The Stoic Roman, then, was not uninvolved in the world. He could participate in politics and do his best to make the world better. But faced with the capricious will of an uncontrolled emperor, say, he would not be concerned with the consequences to his person; rather, he would learn to control his own desires and emotions and continue to strive for virtue.

It is important that this striving for virtue is not passive; a Stoic learns self-control, and the ability to manage his emotions, through a series of active exercises, to be taken daily. It is this development of a regime, or *askesis,* that Michel Foucault found indicative of a new set of sexual mores in his third volume of *The History of Sexuality.* The Stoic philosophers demonstrated an increased emphasis on self-control as a mode of personal being, as a way of living in the world. This idea applied not only to sex, of course, but as one of the appetites that needed to be controlled, matters of sex come frequently into Seneca's discussions of proper and improper morality.

The Stoics also placed, as Foucault pointed out, an increased emphasis on the relationship of marriage and advocated "a strict fidelity between spouses, admitting no exceptions."[2] In part, this privileging of marriage appears to stem from an understanding of marital relations as "natural," insofar as they lead to legitimate procreation. But the Stoics went beyond what some modern proponents of marriage do; Musonius Rufus, an important Stoic thinker, argued that procreation could be the result of any number of sexual relations, not merely those within marriage. More important than procreation, then, was the development of mutual affection between husband and wife, which resulted from proper behavior within marriage.[3] Staying within the marital relationship and having sex only with one's wife, then, became part of the Stoic program of self-restraint and proper control of desires.

Seneca on Sexual Behavior

In a work called the *Natural Questions*, Seneca writes a series of short essays about various aspects of the natural world and endeavors to show that nature, if understood and used properly, leads us to a life of virtue. In a section on the use of mirrors, however, he goes on at length about a man named Hostius Quadra, whose life appears to be a virtual textbook on improper sexual behavior. Indeed, Seneca claims that "his obscenities were reproduced on the stage," that is, in a risqué mime performance (*Natural Questions* 1.16.1). Hostius was evidently notorious.

Among the vices of Hostius, Seneca does discuss the fact that he has sex with men (or boys) as well as women. But like most of the other texts I have discussed, it does not appear that the homoeroticism of his sexual activity is particularly what is distressing. Early in the discussion, for example, he writes, "He was not deviant only with one sex, but he was as lustful for men as well as women" (*Natural Questions* 1.16.2). This one sentence carries a wealth of information. Seneca does not characterize his relations with women as acceptable and those with men as less so; rather, Hostius is described as "deviant" (*impurus*) with both. The fundamental problem is not homosexuality, or bisexuality, but rather deviance, which is augmented by the fact that he practices it with all kinds of partners.

Later in the description of the same man, Seneca describes in more detail the sort of *impurus* behavior that Hostius gets up to, speaking in the voice of Hostius himself:

"At the same time," he said, "I am passive to a man and to a woman. Nonetheless, with that part of me that is entirely unoccupied I behave like a man, debauching someone else. All of my organs are involved in adultery *[stuprum]*; let my eyes take part in this lust, and let them be witnesses and supervisors of it." (*Natural Questions* 1.16.7)

This fairly rare description of a ménage à trois (or rather, ménage à quatre) is surprisingly graphic, and it is interesting that Seneca suggests that Hostius himself described it as such. The sudden shift into direct quotation at the beginning of the passage breaks with the paragraph before it and is not signaled by any transition in the text. It has the effect both of distancing Seneca from the description and of making the actions that Hostius describes a part of his internal character. *He* is the one describing these behaviors and his desire to experience them.

What can we say is particularly disturbing about Hostius's behavior? The fact that men are involved may be part of it, but a rather small part. First and foremost is the fact that Hostius describes himself as passive (*patior*). Unlike a typical degenerate adult male, however, Hostius exponentially increases this passivity by experiencing it with a man and a woman *at the same time*. I confess that I do not even know what this means with certainty. My best guess is that one of Hostius's partners is performing anal sex on him and that he is performing fellatio or cunnilingus on the other. Even this, however, is not enough: as long as he is at it, Hostius uses his penis to perform illegitimate sex on another person (of unspecified sex). The word he uses to

describe this act is *stuprum,* the standard Roman legal term for sexual violation of a Roman citizen. In this way, even the act of sex in which Hostius is
the active partner—which would otherwise be normal—is also specified as
outside of the law and of social norms. Hostius represents, then, the exact
opposite of the Stoic ideal, pursuing a superabundance of pleasures in direct
disregard of all social and natural rules.

Even the orgy scene, however, turns out not to be the primary object of
Seneca's description of this bizarre and unbelievable character. The chapter
in which Hostius is described falls in a section of the *Natural Questions* in
which Seneca is investigating the characteristics and proper use of mirrors. As
a philosopher of nature, Seneca wishes to know why nature (which he views
as wholly rational) provides men with visual reflections; what purpose do they
serve? Later on, he will give a series of answers, all of them suitably Stoic:

> Mirrors were discovered so that a man could know himself, deriving many [good]
> things from this: first, knowledge of himself, then, in some situations, advice. If he is
> beautiful, so that he can avoid scandal; if he is ugly, so that he knows that whatever
> his body lacks must be made good by his virtues; if he is young, so that he can be ad-
> monished by his youth that this is the time for learning and for daring brave deeds; if
> an old man, so that he can put aside things that are not suited to his gray hair, and so
> that he can think a bit about death. For these reasons nature has given us the ability to
> see ourselves. (*Natural Questions* 17.4)

Mirrors, then, have practical and entirely moral uses. In seeing our own reflections, whatever our situation in life is, we should see something that will
either urge us to improvement or prevent us from disgracing the abilities
that we have.

As one might imagine, this is not at all what Hostius has been using his
mirrors for. The list of Hostius's ocular perversions is extensive and dizzying.
Immediately after the sentence quoted previously, in which Seneca describes
Hostius as "deviant" (*impurus*) with both men and women, the moralist goes
on to describe a particular perversion of nature involving trick mirrors:

> . . . and he made mirrors of that sort I just mentioned, the ones that give back images
> greatly larger [than the original], in which a finger exceeds the measure and thickness
> of an arm. He used to place these such that, when he was being passive with a man,
> he could see all the motions of his stallion opposite, and then he would be delighted
> with the false size of his partner's member as if it were the true size. (*Natural Ques-
> tions* 1.16.2)

Again, there is a relentless insistence on the passivity of Hostius. One might
think that, given the sort of mirror that he has lying around, he might imagine the exaggerated size of his own penis. But no, Hostius is particularly interested in the size of the penis of the man who is penetrating him. For Seneca,
however, this passivity is perhaps subordinate to Hostius's manipulations of
nature itself. He uses these mirrors not, as one should, to learn about one's
true nature, but rather to manipulate the image of his own perversion and
thereby to increase his own illegitimate pleasure.

Related to this distortion of nature is the fact that Hostius, in wanting to see the man who is penetrating him from behind (as well as various other sexual acts), is also violating that law of nature that suggests that certain acts should naturally be hidden from public. Seneca notes that even prostitutes demonstrate some measure of shame and draw a curtain when they are engaged in sex. Not so Hostius:

> He did not fear the day, but he himself showed those portentous couplings to himself, and he approved them for himself; you would not think that he did not wish to be painted in the very act. . . . Except that that monster made his own lewdness a spectacle and showed those things to himself which no night is dark enough to conceal. (*Natural Questions* 1.16.5–6)

Hostius's perversion here is doubled: not only does he not conceal his sexual acts from others, but again, he wishes to see them himself. He acts as both the sexual subject and the voyeuristic subject of his own objectified lusts.

Finally, Seneca makes clear that Hostius's perversion is a personal opposition to Nature herself. In the passage in which he imagines that Hostius is speaking directly, Seneca quotes him as saying the following:

> Let even those things be seen by means of a mechanism which the position of our bodies removes from sight, so that no one thinks that I do not know what I do. For Nature was miserly in that she gave such poor helpers to human lust, and in that she gave better couplings to the other animals; I will discover some way to both cheat my disease and to satisfy it. (*Natural Questions* 1.16.7–8)

Hostius, then, is the very definition of perversion. He recognizes that his lusts are "sick"—he uses the word *morbus*, "illness," to describe them—and he recognizes further that the way to satisfy them is to use a trick, a mechanism or device, which exceeds the provisions of nature. Everything about his satisfaction of desire is a deception, and the depth of his self-deception is equally a measure of his lack of self-control.

Hostius, it should be pointed out, can hardly be taken as a sexual type. Seneca singles him out for abuse in a way that few such characters, real or imagined, ever are. But because he is such an extreme example, he provides a useful boundary condition for acceptable sexual behavior. For Seneca, again, I should point out that what is acceptable does not particularly seem to be drawn on gender lines. Hostius is criticized for his sexual activities with men, but primarily in terms of his excess of sexual behavior, and secondarily in terms of his relentless passivity. What is perverse about Hostius is his blatant disregard for nature, both in his distortions of the size of body parts and in his willful violation of the norms of privacy.

Indeed, much of Seneca's writings are concerned with violations of nature, and while some of the transgressions about which he talks have to do with improper sexual behavior, most do not. The improper control of one's sexual desires is just one of many ways that a person can move outside the boundaries of proper activity, or that a man can move outside the boundaries of proper masculinity. In one of Seneca's epistles (*Moral Epistles* 122), the philosopher expounds on a wide variety of unnatural acts. He begins by criticizing those men who exchange day for night, that is, who stay awake at night eating, drinking, and engaging in social activity, and then goes on to criticize such varied activities as seeking roses in winter, growing fruit trees on the tops of walls, and swimming in artificial, heated pools. As Seneca argues, his reader should not be surprised that there are so many ways of being unnatural:

> You ought not to be amazed, if you find so many particular forms of wickedness; they are various, they have numberless forms, and all the types of them cannot be classified. Having care for what is right is simple; for what is dissolute is complex, and contains as many new deviations as you like. (*Moral Epistles* 122.17)

Within this long catalogue of personal perversions, however, Seneca does provide us with a few sentences that describe what is unnatural for men when it comes to sex[4]:

> Does it not seem to you that those who exchange their clothing with women live contrary to nature? Do not they live contrary to nature who attempt to make their boyhood shine, once the time has past? What could be more cruel or more wretched? Will he never be a man, so that for too long he is able to be passive to a man? And when his sex ought to have snatched him away from such ill-treatment, will not even his age snatch him away? (*Moral Epistles* 122.7–8)

Several things are worth noting here. First, Seneca again links the idea of feminine dress with being willing to take the passive position in sex. As often, passivity is allied with an internal and external femininity. Beyond that, however, is the problem that this hypothetical person is passive beyond the normal age for such behavior and, indeed, appears to seek it out, by artificially maintaining a look that imitates youthful splendor. Though this passage, like most of our evidence, takes the form of invective, it suggests that some men in Rome might have enjoyed passivity and tried to continue such behavior into manhood.

As Williams has pointed out, however, the passage contains another surprise, at least for the reader familiar with typical Roman expectations and sexual norms. It is normal for Seneca to suppose that the man's age would remove him from the disgrace (*contumelia*) of being penetrated by another man. But in the first clause of the same sentence, he seems to be saying that to be penetrated is disgraceful for any male, regardless of age. As we have repeatedly seen, being penetrated, while not exactly celebrated, was not regarded as a particular disgrace for a boy, so long as he did not seek it out, and so long as he had not yet reached the age of manhood. But here, as Williams argues, "Seneca is suggesting that maleness in itself is ideally incompatible with being penetrated."[5] Seneca does not dwell on the moment, nor does he go on to elucidate all the ways in which such activity might be considered contrary to nature. But it is a moment in which the impenetrability of males, even when still boys, is proposed.

Again, however, perhaps the most striking thing about epistle 122 is the brevity with which it deals with sexual matters. Seneca is, here, much more concerned with a general sense of luxury that seeks to violate nature (which here, as often, means "social norms") for the pure sake of doing so:

In addition, luxurious people want their lives to be gossiped about while they are alive; for if there is no gossip, they think their efforts to be wasted. And so they take it badly whenever they do something that escapes notoriety. Many men consume their goods, and many keep mistresses. If you want to have a reputation among such men, you need not only to do something luxurious, but remarkable; in such a busy crowd, plain wickedness does not result in common gossip. (*Moral Epistles* 122.14)

Such men, in Seneca's eyes, do not violate nature because they cannot control their urges, or to gain ordinary pleasure, but specifically for the pleasure of having been noticed as outrageous or scandalous. And though elsewhere (as we have seen) some sexual behavior may fall into this category, it is far from prominent here.

Another of Seneca's *Moral Epistles* is worth attention because it draws a link between character and the way that one presents oneself, not only in appearance, but even in manner of speech. As often, a lack of sufficient self-control is linked, in part, to effeminacy:

The style of a man's ability cannot be different from that of his soul. If the latter is healthy, if it is orderly, serious, temperate, then his ability is dry and sober; but if his soul is corrupted, his ability is also infected. Do you not see, if a man's soul becomes lazy, his limbs drag and his feet move with difficulty? If it is womanish [*effeminatus*], in his very walk softness appears? If it is sharp and fierce, that his step is made quicker? (*Moral Epistles* 114.3)

The idea that one's character is evident by his external appearance is not new with Seneca, of course. But he places a greater emphasis on the integrity of a person's inner character and his outer person and raises this correspondence to a general principle. A man who is degenerate in one way is likely to be so in another, and this leads Seneca to describe individuals in ways that begin to sound like our notion of a sexual identity. After all, if one's lack of sexual self-control is visible even in one's walk, then what Seneca is describing is a sexual morphology as well as an idea of sexual character that infuses every aspect of a person's life.

Indeed, in the next section of the same letter, Seneca begins to describe Maecenas, a wealthy Roman from the Augustan period who acted as a patron to several of the great poets of that age, including Virgil, Horace, and Propertius. Apparently, Maecenas was known for his effeminate style, which manifested itself in his manner, dress, and speech:

How Maecenas lived is too well known to require description—how he walked, how delicate he was, how he desired to be seen, how he did not wish to hide his vices. What then? Was not his speech loose just as he himself was unbelted? Surely his words were not more noticeable than his manner, than his company, than his house, than his wife? . . . And so you will see the eloquence of a drunken man, twisting, wandering, and full of license. (*Moral Epistles* 114.4)

Seneca's larger point is that Maecenas's entire character is marked by a kind of looseness, and that this manifests itself in every aspect of his character. Evidently, Maecenas took to going about with no belt around his cloak, and this lack of a belt (described by the Latin adjective *discinctus*) becomes a metaphor for everything about him. His walk is loose, his house is loose, his wife is not under his control, and finally, even his manner of speaking is unacceptably ornate and delicate.

There is almost nothing explicitly sexual in Seneca's description of Maecenas, and this should give the reader pause. When we discuss modern notions of sexuality, we generally think of sexuality as the key, the single source of a person's character from which all the other signs of deviance spring. In Maecenas's case, it is rather the opposite. His looseness of character is fundamental, and this leads to the kinds of behaviors that Seneca describes in preceding extracts. In fact, only one explicitly sexual comment comes out in Seneca's description. After he has given several examples of Maecenas's speech, he returns to Maecenas's person:

Does it not occur to you, when you read these words, that he is the one who always went about the city with his tunic untied? . . . Or that this was the man, when the citizens were embattled with civil war, and the city distressed and under arms, who was accompanied in public by two eunuchs, more men nevertheless than he was? (*Moral Epistles* 114.6)

Maecenas, once again singled out for his flowing form of dress, is less a man than the eunuchs who accompany him. Once again, what marks his lack of manliness is specifically a lack of discipline and control, a willingness to allow every aspect of his being to run loose.

In descriptions of people like Maecenas, then, the Stoic philosopher Seneca approaches, in some ways, our notions of sexual identity. Maecenas is not simply a regular guy who prefers a different kind of sex than other men; his sexual character runs deep and is visible in various aspects of his being and of his behavior. On the other hand, it is important to note that the source for all of this effeminacy, looseness, and delicacy is never identified as his sexual behavior per se; rather, what is known (and not specifically said) about his sexual life is merely a symptom of a more generalized effeminacy. As is often the case, it makes more sense to think of Seneca's version of Maecenas as a *gender* deviant than a *sexual* deviant. Seneca may describe his lack of masculinity as degenerate, but to call this a *sexuality* is to think with our categories, rather than with the Romans'.

NERO

When dealing with a character like Nero, it is difficult to separate fact from fiction. Nero became a figure, even during his lifetime, for imperial excess.

The historians who wrote about him may well have exaggerated details about his personal life, or may have accepted common rumors and gossip about him as true. The historiographical tradition about Nero, then, is important not because of whether or not he actually did what he is alleged to have done, but rather because of the fact that these allegations were made; that is, when faced with the task of characterizing the sexual life of this most volatile of Roman emperors, how did the historians go about it? The behaviors, passions, and violations of norms that the historians ascribe to Nero become a useful index of sexual activity that is out of bounds, that exceeds in all the ways that Nero himself is a figure for excess.

There are three major sources for the life of Nero: Tacitus was a masterful historian of Rome, who was born during Nero's reign in 56 CE but wrote about him some 40 or 50 years after the emperor's death, in a work called the *Annals.* Suetonius was an upper-class Roman who served as an imperial official during the reign of Trajan (98–117 CE) and who wrote biographies of the Roman emperors, including Nero. Finally, Cassius Dio, who lived in the latter half of the third and first half of the fourth centuries CE, wrote a massive history of Rome in Greek. The books that covered Nero's reign are unfortunately lost, but we have so-called epitomes (i.e., relatively colorless summaries) of these books, compiled by Byzantine monks in the eleventh and twelfth centuries CE. Though none of these historians is exactly contemporary with Nero, Tacitus and Suetonius appear to have had access to earlier works, including official documents of the senate and private letters from the emperor's household.[6]

When the modern reader thinks of Nero, certain images come immediately to mind, most notably the old story that Nero "fiddled while Rome burned." There is, in fact, a biographical tradition that the emperor took to the stage while Rome was burning and performed a song about the sack of Troy, though the historian Tacitus treats this as a rumor, not a fact (Tacitus *Annals* 15.39). We also hear of his outrageous abuses of Christians (Tacitus *Annals* 15.44), and we think of Nero as an overweight glutton. Part and parcel of this common image are Nero's sexual deviances; as Edward Champlin summarizes what many people "know" in his highly readable study of Nero,

Nero also slept with his mother. Nero married and executed one stepsister, executed his other stepsister, raped and murdered his stepbrother. In fact, he executed or murdered most of his close relatives. He kicked his pregnant wife to death. He castrated and then married a freedman. He married another freedman, this time himself playing the bride. . .[7]

To be sure, Nero's sexual adventures are an essential part of the narrative of his excess. It is far from clear, however, that the Romans of the first century CE found Nero's sexual behavior as the most problematic aspect of his character. I would argue, in fact, that the Romans were much more concerned with Nero's love of Greece (so-called philhellenism) and his interest in appearing on the public stage.

An interesting feature of Suetonius's work is that it does not proceed strictly chronologically; rather, he begins by listing the things that Nero did that were worthy of praise (chapters 1–19); he then announces that the rest of his treatment will be concerned with Nero's "shameful deeds and crimes" (chapter 20). The beginning of this list of crimes deals almost exclusively with Nero's appearances on stage, his dramatic performances, and his trips to Greece, in which he caused the Olympic games to be held in an off year (67 CE) and introduced a singing competition, which he entered and, to no one's surprise, won. Perhaps the most astonishing aspect of this victory, however, is that Nero treated it as if it were a military conquest:

Having returned from Greece, he entered into Naples (since that was where he first appeared on stage) on white horses, at a breach in the wall, as is the custom for winners of sacred games; similarly at Antium, Albanum, and then Rome; but at Rome he arrived in that chariot in which Augustus had once held a [military] triumph. He was wearing a purple robe decorated with gold stars, a Greek cloak, and an Olympic crown on his head; in his right hand was the Pythian crown, and there was a crowd going before him bearing the other crowns, with texts indicating where he had won and whom he had defeated in a contest of song or of drama; and following his chariot were "applauders" performing a ritual of ovation, and declaring that they were Augustiani and the soldiers of his triumph. (Suetonius *Nero* 25)

Nero, in this depiction, violates several norms, but none is more important than the confusion of Greek Olympic victory, in a nonstandard competition of songs and drama, no less, with the military parade that the Romans used to honor a general returning from victory in battle. Augustus defeated enemies of Rome; Nero won a singing contest and claimed the same honors.

All of this adds up to a picture of imperial excess and, in keeping with Nero's philhellenism, softness on the part of the emperor. To be sure, these aspects of Nero's character are also demonstrated in the realm of sexual behavior. Because he has arranged his material thematically, rather than strictly biographically, Suetonius lumps all of Nero's sexual misdeeds together. They are discussed in dizzying brevity:

In addition to his "teaching" freeborn boys and sleeping with married women, he raped the Vestal virgin Rubria. He was little short of making Acte, a freedwoman, his wife in legal marriage, making use of some men of highest consular rank who swore falsely that she was descended from royal stock. He cut off the testicles of a boy named "Sporus," and even tried to transform him into a woman; he had this boy led to him with a huge crowd in attendance, in place of a wife, with dowry and veil celebrating the rites of marriage; there was a rather clever joke by someone or other, that it would have been a good thing for humanity, if Domitius [Nero's father] had had such a wife. This Sporus, decked out in the jewels of an Augusta and carried in a litter, he accompanied around the Greek markets and meeting places, and later around the Sigillaria in Rome, kissing him repeatedly. No one doubted that he wanted to sleep with his mother, but that he was frightened away from doing so by her critics, lest this fierce and powerless woman become overpowering by this sort of favor; especially after he received among his concubines a prostitute who was famous for her resemblance to Agrippina. At one time, whenever he traveled by litter with his mother, they say that his incestuous lusts were made public by his stained clothing.

He prostituted his own chastity to such a degree that, when nearly all of his limbs were contaminated, he thought up a completely novel sort of game: covered by the skin of a wild animal, he would come out of a den and attack the groins of men and women who were tied to stakes and, when he had had enough of being a wild animal, he would be run through by his freedman Doryphorus. To this man [Doryphorus] he even got married, just as Sporus had to him, imitating the cries and the laments of virgins suffering rape (*patientes vim*). (Suetonius *Nero* 28–29)

These sexual misbehaviors did not, as one might think from Suetonius, all happen at once. Indeed, the marriage to Doryphorus (who, in other sources, is called Pythagoras)[8] takes place in the year 64, long after Nero's near-marriage to Acte and the death of his mother in 59. Using Suetonius as a kind of outline, then, let me discuss in turn each of Nero's modes of sexual deviance.

Marriages and Class Status

Let me begin by first discussing Nero's marriages. Tacitus is at pains to show how Nero was under the control of various women in the course of his life and marriages. It is worth remembering that Nero was extraordinarily young when he became the most powerful man in the Western world; when Claudius died, and Nero ascended to the emperorship, he was all of 17 years old. It is, then, perhaps not surprising that he does not seem to have held his desires in particular check. In any case, although he was married to Octavia, the daughter of the previous emperor Claudius, he quickly began a dalliance with a freedwoman named Acte. Some time later, he apparently fell madly in love with the wife of Otho, a woman named Poppaea Sabina. Nero appointed Otho to the province of Lusitania so that he could have an affair with Poppaea unobstructed, perhaps with Otho's tacit consent. Eventually, Nero divorced Octavia, citing barrenness, and married Poppaea. She bore him a daughter who, tragically, died a few months later. A year later, when Poppaea was pregnant with a second child, Tacitus reports that Nero kicked her, resulting in her death (Tacitus *Annals* 16.6).

This brief and tumultuous history suggests nothing particularly out of the way in Nero's sexual life, other than his willingness to use his political power to obtain satisfaction of his lusts. It appears, however, that Poppaea was a highly intelligent woman, and she is portrayed as exercising a considerable personal influence over the emperor. She persuaded Nero to end his dalliance with Acte, which perhaps would not have upset many Romans. But at the beginning of book 14 of his *Annals*, Tacitus portrays Poppaea as being in direct conflict with Nero's mother, Agrippina, for his affections. Tacitus characterizes the sorts of things Poppaea said to Nero:

. . . Nero burned with love for Poppaea more and more each day, and she, hardly daring for marriage for herself or divorce for Octavia so long as Agrippina was safe, reproached the emperor often with accusations, occasionally with wit; she called him a kept boy, who relied on the orders of others and who not only did not control the Empire, but even his own liberty. . . . No one hindered these attacks, or ones like them, made effective with tears or with the arts of adultery; for everyone desired the power of the mother to be broken, and no one believed that the son's hatred would endure to the extent of the murder of his mother. (Tacitus *Annals* 14.1)

The picture that begins to emerge is one of a man very much under the control of competing women, and the language that Tacitus uses is significant. Agrippina is credited with *potentia,* power. Poppaea's attacks are described as *penetrans* (literally "penetrating") by means of tears and adultery. Even Poppaea's characterization of Nero seems to fit the situation: he does seem, here, to be controlled more than controlling. This is a significant inversion of gender norms, even if Nero were not a man who wielded terrific political power.

With Tacitus's characterizations as background, let me now return to Suetonius's depiction of Nero's sexual deviances. Although it may not resonate strongly with modern audiences, it is significant that Suetonius begins his list of Nero's crimes with two class-related violations. First, he reports that Nero engaged in adultery with married women and in *paedagogia* with freeborn boys. The term *paedagogia* may or may not involve sexual violation, though in the context of this paragraph, it is difficult not to infer a sexual transgression. Literally, a *paedagogium* was a Greek training school for slaves. The phrase, then, literally means that Nero treated freeborn boys like slaves (perhaps including sexual penetration of them), just as he violated the marriages of Roman women. Both are violations of the impenetrability of freeborn Romans. Moreover, the conjunction of the two sexual acts clearly indicates Nero's lack of discrimination when it came to sex. He violated both kinds of Romans: boys and women, and a Vestal virgin thrown in for good measure.

In the very next sentence, Suetonius expatiates at some length about Nero's near-marriage to Acte. Nero's affair with Acte is well documented in Tacitus's account, though that historian does not suggest (as Suetonius does) that Nero tried to marry her. Had Nero done so, it would have been a serious violation of protocol. Indeed, Tacitus's comments make it clear that one might expect some concern over an affair between the emperor and a woman so far below him in rank. He comments specifically that Nero's senior advisors did not oppose the affair, as it harmed no one, and because, "should he be prohibited from this lust, it might break forth in *stuprum* [adultery] with wellborn women" (Tacitus *Annals* 13.12). He goes on to report that Agrippina, however, showed no such practical restraint, referring to Acte as "her rival the freedwoman" and "her daughter-in-law the servant girl" (Tacitus *Annals* 13.13).

In other words, the first level of Nero's violation of sexual norms is a disregard for the lines of class. As an emperor, it was acceptable for him to have sex with a freedwoman. But when he began to treat her like a social equal, perhaps to the extent of manufacturing a royal past for her, then Nero showed an alarming disregard for the structures that defined Roman society.

The Violation of Sporus's Masculinity

Suetonius mentions two instances in which Nero marries other men. If we assume that the person named as Doryphorus in Suetonius's account is the person named as Pythagoras in Tacitus's and Cassius Dio's versions, we should note that Suetonius has reversed the historical order of the marriages. The reason for this reversal will become clear shortly.

There are several problems with Nero's marriage to Sporus. As Williams has argued, however, the fact that Nero is attracted to a boy is not among them.[9] After all, such desire is hardly out of the Roman norm, and as emperor, Nero could certainly command sexual favors from a freedman. But there are more disturbing elements to this affair. First and foremost, Nero has Sporus castrated, and in Suetonius's text, there is a hint that he is interested in further surgery to transform the boy into a woman. In other words, Suetonius portrays Nero as forcing a gender change onto Sporus. Cassius Dio, even more disturbingly, tells us that Nero is the one who called him "Sporus" after castrating him (Cassius Dio 62.28). *Sporus* is the Greek word for "semen"—and so, as Champlin observes, this is a rather grim joke.[10]

Moreover, it appears that this transformation of Sporus goes beyond the physical. Suetonius notes that Nero married the eunuch with the full trappings of marriage, and Dio adds the detail that Nero's freedman assistant gave the "bride" away (Cassius Dio 63.13). It appears that this event took place shortly after the death of Nero's great love Poppaea Sabina, and that Sporus was a sort of replacement for her. Cassius Dio's explanation is as follows:

> He called Sporus "Sabina," not only because he had castrated him because of his similarity in appearance to her, but also because he married him, as he had her, in Greece, by contract, with Tigellinus giving him away, as the law required. (Cassius Dio 63.13)

The various pieces of the puzzle come into place. It is not just that Nero liked to have sex with boys; rather, his obsession with Poppaea extended beyond her death, and in a desperate maneuver, he replaced her with a castrated freedman who looked like her. The marriage to Sporus, then, is more than just a perversion of normal marriage practices. It reads like a grim parody from start to finish.

Nero as Passive

Even less acceptable, however, is the suggestion that Nero got married to another freedman, this time playing the part of the bride. In Suetonius, this marriage comes near the end of the list of Nero's sexual peccadilloes, as we have seen. In the history of Cassius Dio, however, it appears that Nero had already made this marriage when he married Sporus: in his description of the marriage to Sporus, the historian says, "And after this, there existed for Nero *at the same time* [emphasis mine] Pythagoras as a husband, and Sporus as a wife" (Cassius Dio 63.13). Why, then, has Suetonius reversed the order of these two marriages? Though I cannot say conclusively, I believe that it is because Suetonius has arranged events so that they culminate in the most perverse. What Nero did to Sporus was bad enough, but this other marriage, in which he literally plays the woman, is absolutely opposed to Roman norms. For Suetonius, then, it must come last in the list. Dio, on the other hand, employs a different rhetorical strategy. He points out that Nero has both a husband and a wife at once, thus emphasizing again his tendency to excess.

There is an element of grotesque playacting in Nero's marriage to Pythagoras, moreover. Suetonius tells us that during the marriage Nero imitated the cries of a virgin being raped; Nero, in other words, is portrayed as having reveled in the idea of playing a young woman newly married, relatively powerless, and physically hurt by the act of first penetration. The contrast with Nero's own sexual experience and debauchery could hardly be made more stark.

One should also note, however, that this aspect of theatricality is not unconnected to the historians' critique of Nero's sexual activity. In fact, Nero was criticized repeatedly, and in many different contexts, for his penchant for appearing on stage as an actor, something that, in an earlier era, proper Roman citizens simply did not do (Tacitus *Annals* 15.13). This aspect of Nero's marriage to Pythagoras is particularly clear in Tacitus's description of the event. He begins, in fact, by suggesting that the entire event was something of a show, and he criticizes Nero specifically for confusing the public and private spheres. It is worthwhile to quote Tacitus's description at length:

> He began, in order to obtain belief that nothing was ever so joyful for him, to serve banquets in public places and to use the entire city as if it were his home. And the most famous dinners with regard to luxury and gossip were those prepared by Tigellinus; I will discuss them as an example, so that I need not repeatedly narrate the same extravagances. He constructed, then, in the pool of Agrippa, a boat, on which was placed a banquet, which was towed by other boats. The boats were decked out with gold and ivory, and the oarsmen were prostitutes arranged by age and by their knowledge of sexual activities. He had collected birds and various wild animals from the earth and marine animals from the distant Ocean. (Tacitus *Annals* 15.37)

Everything here is a perversion of nature of exactly the sort that Seneca (who would commit suicide in the following year) would have abhorred. Not only is the banquet taking place on a lake rather than on land, but the lake itself is artificial, stocked with animals from other regions of the world. Perhaps most perverse is the idea of using male prostitutes as oarsmen for the boat and arranging them according to their *scientium libidinum,* or "knowledge of sexual activities." On a real boat, of course, the oarsmen would be arranged according to their skill as oarsmen; here their erotic skills parody what would be required on a real boat on a real lake.

The description continues in this vein and culminates in a description of Nero's wedding to Pythagoras, again emphasizing the improper display of private events:

Nero himself, fouled by legitimate and illegitimate lusts, left no disgrace by which he could become more corrupt, except that a few days later he got married, in the manner of a solemn wedding, to one of that crowd of degenerates named Pythagoras. The veil was drawn over the emperor, witnesses were sent, a dowry, wedding couch, and nuptial torches were present—everything, at last, was seen which night covers over even in the case of a female bride. (Tacitus *Annals* 15.37)

Again, the author emphasizes the aspect of public parody. This is not a real wedding, but a public display. Ironically, this so-called wedding, which carries all the trappings of legitimate matrimony, becomes the act that caps Nero's display of lusts; nothing else remains. But unlike a real wedding, Nero made public those aspects that are supposed to remain behind the closed doors of the nuptial chamber, an oblique reference, I believe, to Suetonius's tale of Nero crying out like a virgin being deflowered. Nero has moved beyond the normal state of having, perhaps, some unusual sexual desires: he not only enjoys being penetrated, he takes pleasure in displaying what should be hidden. In this regard, he is exactly like Seneca's Hostius Quadra, who uses mirrors to see those things that should not be seen and wants his deviances to be visible to himself and the world.

CONCLUSIONS

Though Nero's sexual behavior was clearly out-of-bounds, we can understand it best in terms of a thorough violation of Roman *mores* in a variety of social spheres. Indeed, for the Romans, Nero's tendency toward theatrical display was more disturbing than any particular sexual proclivity. Earlier, in fact, Tacitus indulges in a diatribe against Nero for introducing a theatrical competition "in the Greek style" in Rome (Tacitus *Annals* 14.20). This, much more than any sexual activity, represents the real threat of Nero as a lover of Greek manners:

In addition, the ancestral morality which had been slowly forgotten was overturned at its foundation by this imported vice, so that whatever at any time was able to be corrupted or to corrupt should be seen in the city, and so that the youth should degenerate into foreign tastes, taking part in gymnasia and leisure and foul loves, by the authority of both emperor and senate, who not only gave license to these vices, but even summoned them, so that Roman noblemen should be polluted on the stage, on the pretence of giving a speech or song. (Tacitus *Annals* 14.20)

Part of Nero's difficulty in Rome stemmed from the fact that he loved things Greek. It is worth noting, then, that nowhere in Tacitus's discussion of his marriage to Pythagoras, or in Suetonius's discussion of his marriage to Sporus or Doryphorus, does either author attribute this sexual behavior to Nero's philhellenism. "Greek love" was not Nero's problem. When Nero tried to institute Greek theater, however, then he was portrayed as falling foul to foreign vice, as failing to uphold proper Roman mores.

The historic depiction of Nero's character, in short, extends far beyond anything we might call a sexual identity or a sexuality. It is a tendency for excess in all things and a willingness to overturn every aspect of that part of cultural expectation that a Roman like Seneca would call "nature." He violated lines of class as well as lines of gender. More important, he publicly exposed those things that normally would have taken place indoors, both sexual and pertaining to other kinds of appetites. He showed no particular predilection for boys or women, unless we ascribe his love of Sporus to an obsession with the dead Poppaea. Less conventionally, he seems to have been willing to be penetrator or penetrated in a sexual relationship, and this, if we accept the chronology of Cassius Dio, at the same time. Nero simply fails to fulfill any of the requirements of his social role, as noble, as emperor, as Roman, as man. The characterization of Nero by later Roman historians reveals not so much a sexual identity as a full-body disregard for all social norms and expectations.

Nero was, moreover, the emperor. The emphasis that the historians place on his behavior, especially that behavior that was excessive, serves the rhetorical purpose of demonstrating the dangerous tendency towards excess that characterizes imperial power. Emperors, in a tradition that has deep roots in the West, are generally laid low by their own violations of social norms. What the historians' accounts of Nero show us, then, are not the normal sexual predilections of normal Romans, but rather the kinds of trouble that an uncontrolled, youthful, impetuous and all-powerful Roman might discover. He becomes a scare-figure for the Romans, a parable of a man with large appetites, no self-control, and no one powerful enough to exert external control over him.

Fourteen

Sex in Satire and Invective Poetry

CATEGORIES OF CONCERN IN THE ROMAN EMPIRE

Though Nero's sexual proclivities resist, in the end, a neat categorization, his behavior helps mark out the boundaries of acceptable sexual activity in the Roman Empire of the first century CE. As this century progressed, social critics began to write satires about, among other things, the decline of sexual morals in Rome. Their writings give us the impression that groups of men identifiable as *cinaedi* (i.e., men of a particular sexual type) were walking the streets, offending the sensibilities of normal men and women. It does not appear to be the case that new categories of sexual beings were created at this time, but when we read the works of Juvenal or Martial, we see an increased emphasis on *cinaedi* and *tribades* as a social threat.

An idea of hypocrisy is crucial to these authors' critiques. The problem, it seems, is not merely that there are men who enjoy playing a feminine role in various aspects of life (including the sexual), but that such men also pretend to be something that they are not, hiding their effeminacy behind a hypermasculine swagger. The exposure of this kind of pretense is the main goal of satiric writing, and in this chapter, I will treat two of Rome's great practitioners of satire, Petronius and Juvenal. I also discuss a few of the poems of the poet Martial, roughly contemporary with Juvenal, whose short poems often have a sharp satiric or critical edge.

THE SHIFTING GROUND OF SATIRE

Satire as practiced by ancient authors is a genre that is rarely seen in the modern world. To explain the mode in which Petronius and Juvenal write, I draw a distinction between *satire* and *parody*. In parody, such as the well-known skits of a television show like *Saturday Night Live,* the general mode is to take something serious and render it ridiculous. So Dana Carvey performed uncanny imitations of the first President Bush, and by recasting his speech patterns into a recognizable but exaggerated format, created a humorous caricature of him. Darrell Hammond's portrayal of Bill Clinton operated on a similar premise.

In satire, at least the satires of Petronius and Juvenal, the operation works in part in the reverse order. These are authors who take something ridiculous (say, the impotence of a loutish character) and, through a process of exaggeration and diatribe, suggest that such behavior is, in fact, deadly serious. At the same time, the object of the ancient satirists' poison pen is often more serious social critics, such as Seneca and his Stoic cohort. The ancient satirist exposes the triviality of those who take themselves seriously as well as the seriousness of an apparently trivial figure. As a result, even when it can be brutally funny, ancient satire often leaves the reader feeling more uneasy than amused. We may be happy to see a figure mocked, but we also find it a bit difficult to side completely with the person doing the mocking; there is more at stake than entertainment, and the satirists leave us with little comfortable ground on which to stand.

An example of what I mean can be found in a brief passage from Tacitus's description of a man named Petronius, now generally taken to be the same person who wrote Petronius's *Satyricon*[1]:

Concerning Petronius a few things ought to be said. For he spent his days in sleep, his nights transacting business and the entertainments of life. As others had risen to fame through hard work, he reached it through idleness, but he was not considered a wastrel or an overspender, as are most of those who consume their estates, but possessed of learned excess. And to the extent that his words and deeds were rather free and showed a certain neglect, they were received more easily in a form of simplicity. Nevertheless, as proconsul of Bithynia and later as consul he showed himself energetic and capable of business. (Tacitus *Annals* 16.18)

It is not simply that Petronius turns the world on its head, then, by spending nights as days and days as nights, one of the unnatural practices of which Seneca was particularly critical. The point is that though Petronius does this, he *also* takes seriously the things that should be taken seriously. His is a kind of reverse hypocrisy: instead of pretending to be serious, moral, and upright, while hiding a secret vice, he pretends to be easygoing and devoted to excess, while actually managing affairs with quiet efficiency.

Even Petronius's death appears to have been performed as a satire. Like Seneca before him, Petronius fell into disfavor with Nero. When it became clear that he was going to be killed, Petronius committed suicide in the customary way, by opening his veins and getting into a bath. With his friends gathered around him, they discussed, Tacitus says, "not the immortality of the soul, or the principles of wise men, but light songs and clever verses" (*Annals* 16.19). Though he appeared not to take his own death seriously, Petronius did take some things seriously in his last moments:

Not even in his will, as did many who were dying, did he praise Nero or Tigellinus or anyone else of the powerful; but he wrote the disgraceful deeds of the emperor under the names of [male] prostitutes and women, and explained the novelty of each act of *stuprum;* then he sent it, under seal, to Nero. (Tacitus *Annals* 16.19)

Unlike Seneca, then, who spent his last moments contemplating noble thoughts of philosophy, Petronius took care of business. In his final act, he let Nero know that he knew what the emperor had done, and with whom, and how. A more devastating social critique is hard to imagine.

PETRONIUS'S *SATYRICON*

This same Petronius seems to be the man who wrote the *Satyricon,* a work that unfortunately exists for us only in fragments. Of an original 16 books, about 100 pages remain, apparently from the latter half of the work. The story mixes long prose narrative with bits of verse (something fairly unusual from the ancient world) and follows the story of a schoolteacher named Encolpius. Encolpius is besotted with love for a boy named Giton, though he has several rivals for Giton's affections, most notably one Ascyltos. These three have, in one of the lost sections of the novel, offended the Roman phallic god Priapus, who seems to be tormenting them through much of what we have left.

Petronius's work is particularly interesting because it portrays, somewhat fantastically, the ridiculous adventures of a pompous and naïve lowlife. As a hero, Encolpius appears to have neither class status nor much wealth, and so his misadventures take him into the seamy underbelly of an imagined Rome, replete with witches, prostitutes, slaves, wealthy but tasteless freedmen, and a Priapus cult. Though the work is fragmentary, the remaining pieces treat a remarkable variety of sexual oddities, including a beloved boy who is all too willing, a forced rape by a eunuch and then a *cinaedus,* a mock wedding between children, and a hilarious bout with male impotence. We should not imagine that Petronius's elaborate tale bears much relation to real life; but through the portrayal of his narrator as a hypersexed dolt, the author reveals the kinds of behaviors that were open to censure and ridicule.

Let me begin with a self-contained episode from relatively late in the novel. At this point, Encolpius has encountered a self-satisfied poet named Eumolpus. Eumolpus tells Encolpius an amusing story about a time when he was engaged to watch over a young boy in Pergamum. He explains that he was attracted to the boy because of his beauty, but he won the trust of the boy's father by responding with overzealous anger whenever the subject of pederasty came up. Over time, he says, the parents, and especially the mother, came to view him as "one of those philosophers" (*Satyricon* 85), playing on the common claim—often ridiculed—that the philosophers spent time with beautiful boys, not for sex, but for nobler pursuits.

Over time, Eumolpus became closer and closer to the boy. After a party one night, when the two were sleeping in the same room, Eumolpus made his move. Sensing that the boy was awake, he whispered (so that the boy would hear), "Mistress Venus, if I can kiss this boy so that he does not feel it, tomorrow I will give him a set of doves" (*Satyricon* 85). Now, the point of this prayer is perfectly clear. Although in form it pretends to be addressed to Venus, the real recipient of the prayer is the boy himself, which is why he, and not Venus, will get the doves the next day. All he has to do is pretend not to feel Eumolpus' kiss. Eumolpus's request, then, lays bare every aspect of this erotic relationship. It is acceptable for him to desire the boy; it is acceptable for the boy to accede to this desire, although it is better for both parties if he pretends not to do so knowingly; and the boy, as becomes clear later in the story, is motivated at least partly by greed.

Needless to say, Eumolpus gets his kiss, and on the subsequent night he promises fighting cocks for a more explicit sexual favor. Finally, on the third night, he promises a Macedonian stallion in return for "the full coming together that I hope for, with this one stipulation: that he not feel it" (*Satyricon* 86). Eumolpus gets his wish but realizes the next day that he cannot keep his end of the bargain. At this point in the story, which has begun to look more and more like a joke, the reader receives the first punch line:

> You know how much easier it is to buy doves and fighting cocks than a stallion and, in addition, I was afraid that such a large gift would render my generosity suspect. So, having walked about for a few hours, I returned to the house and did nothing other than to kiss the boy. But he, looking around as he put his arms around my neck said, "Where, sir, is the stallion?" (*Satyricon* 86)

Of course, the boy was not supposed to know about the stallion, and so in asking, he explodes the conceit of Eumolpus's prayers. Though he asks the question innocently enough, the boy's willing acquiescence to his teacher's sexual advances is now open to the reader's view.

The story, however, does not end quite there. Though the boy is now angry with Eumolpus, the teacher continues to pursue the boy sexually. He tries to convince the boy to sleep with him, to which the boy responds, significantly, "No, go to sleep already, or I'll tell my father" (*Satyricon* 87). Eumolpus persists, and eventually convinces the boy, and here again, we are given a somewhat typical view of what was upsetting to the boy:

> But he, not uncharmed by my naughtiness, after complaining for a while that he had been deceived and that he had been laughed at and mocked by his fellow students, to whom he had boasted of my generosity, said, "You see, I am not like you. If you want something, do it again." (*Satyricon* 87)

The boy demonstrates exactly double standard that has been explored by modern scholars of sexuality. It is acceptable for this beautiful boy to give in to his older male lover. But in public, he has to be prepared for a certain amount of ribbing from his age-mates, especially when it becomes apparent that the older lover is not as good as his word. Here, however, we have something of a titillating story, in that the boy appears to be willing to go through with sex even after his lover has shown himself untrustworthy; there is just a suggestion that the boy enjoys the sex.

That suggestion becomes the point of the second punch line to the joke. Eumolpus and the boy have sex and fall asleep. A bit later, the boy wakes Eumolpus up and offers to do it again; Eumolpus is happy enough to comply. When he wakes Eumolpus a second time, however, his own insatiability becomes the object of the joke. Here's the final sequence in Petronius (beginning with the second act of sex):

And so he woke me up from sleep and said, "Don't you want anything?" And it was not such a troublesome gift. He received what he had wished for, although worn down with panting and sweating, and again, exhausted with joy, I fell into sleep. After less than an hour he began to poke me with his hand, and said, "Why don't we do it?" Then I, having been aroused so many times, became really angry, and I gave his own words back to him: "No, go to sleep, or I'll tell your father." (*Satyricon* 87)

The joke is funny because the speaker has found, to his surprise, his own lust returned back to him by a boy who, at least in the Roman ideal, should not have felt such lust. And ironically, Eumolpus's defense is to call the boy on this violation. Just as the boy's father would have disapproved of Eumolpus having sex with his son, he will surely disapprove of the boy's willingness to be penetrated. The double role reversal—the boy wants sex, his lover has had enough—gives the humor its amusing punch.

Trouble with *Cinaedi*

As the preceding story indicates, the general rules that I have discussed in this book apply to the world of Petronius's *Satyricon* as well: adult men are assumed to be attracted to young boys, who can be the object of serious erotic competition. The boys themselves are assumed not to be interested in sex, though, as Petronius's humor makes clear, sometimes this erotic ideal was probably observed in the breach. Because the characters in the *Satyricon* occupy a less than savory world of back alleys, brothels, and the like, the story also has things to say about some types of people who do not exactly fit the Roman sexual norm. The story is also marked by grotesque exaggeration and derives much of its humor from the narrator's (Encolpius) naïveté in the face of excess, sexual and otherwise.

Early in the fragments, Encolpius, the boy Giton, and Ascyltos attend a dinner with a woman named Quartilla, her maid, and a young girl. It appears from their conversation that the men have done something to offend Priapus, and Quartilla demands that they administer a cure to her for the fever that she has experienced since then. There are a number of gaps in the text, but it appears from one fragment that Encolpius may also be experiencing impotence: "She rubbed my genitals, already frozen with a thousand deaths" (*Satyricon* 20). Eventually, the scene devolves into a sort of orgy, but one that is particularly unpleasant for the person narrating it.

At two points in this episode, *cinaedi* appear, and their behavior provides a fantastic image of what Romans must have found most disturbing about this sexual identity. The first time, Encolpius, Ascyltos, and Giton appear to have been rendered immobile, perhaps by means of an aphrodisiac that they have drunk. The *cinaedus,* contrary to our expectations, rapes them:

Finally a cinaedus arrived, decked out in a myrtle cloak and wrapped with a belt. . . . First he grabbed our flanks and fell on us, then he stained us with greasy kisses, and finally Quartilla, holding a whale-bone military staff, and with her skirt tied up high, ordered a discharge to be given to unhappy us. (*Satyricon* 21)

As I discussed earlier, the *cinaedus* is a character generally associated with sexual passivity, but in this case, it is fairly clear that the *cinaedus* is penetrating our hapless narrator. This passage provides some support, then, for the idea that a *cinaedus* is not identifiable by a preference for a particular kind of sex, but rather for his general inversion of gender norms. Here the *cinaedus*'s myrtle cloak identifies him as effeminately dressed. More important, though, is his generally disgusting character, most clearly demonstrated through his "greasy" kisses. The *cinaedus* is, from the point of view of Encolpius, simply disgusting. At the same time, the fact that the men have been anally penetrated is clearly a disgrace, and it may be that it is even more of a disgrace that they have been penetrated by a *cinaedus*.

A little later in the evening, another *cinaedus* appears, and we are presented with what looks like a variation on the theme. The *cinaedus* begins by calling for *cinaedi* to join him in a few lines of verse and then essentially rapes Encolpius, though this time, Encolpius is the penetrator. I quote the text here at some length:

When he had finished his verses, he slobbered me with the filthiest kiss. Next he came over the bed and stripped me, though I refused with all my strength. He ground himself on my genitalia for a long time, and a lot, in vain. Streams of sweaty hair-dressing flowed down his face, and so much chalk was among the wrinkles on his cheeks that it looked like a wall, crumbling in the rain.

I could no longer hold back my tears, but was led to a final state of grief. . . .

At this order, the *cinaedus* switched horses, and once the transition was made, wore down my companion [Ascyltos] with his flanks and with kisses. Giton stood in the middle of all this and deflated [discharged?] his own genitals with laughter. (*Satyricon* 23–24)

It is not an easy thing, perhaps, to have a passive partner rape an active one, and Petronius has gone to some length to create conditions that make it possible. It appears that Encolpius and Ascyltos are still immobile, and it may be that they have erections because of an aphrodisiac that Quartilla has given them. In any case, the overriding impression that we get of the *cinaedus* is a far from pleasant one. The fact that he is heavily made up is, no doubt, a reference to the need for a sexually passive man to appear younger than he is. In this case, however, the makeup that preserves his youthful appearance only adds to the impression of decadence and even decay.

Again, we should note that what the narrator finds unpleasant about this situation is not simply the fact that the *cinaedus* is male—elsewhere in the narrative, Encolpius is quite enthusiastic about his sexual encounters with Giton; rather, the aspects that make the *cinaedus* disgusting are related to his age. His sloppy kisses indicate an enthusiasm that is inappropriate for an adult male, and his makeup is singularly unsuccessful in replicating the attractiveness of youth. Encolpius cannot be said to be homophobic, though we might think of him as *cinaedophobic*.

Another brief passage from the story indicates that being a *cinaedus* was not the only option for a man who, although adult, preferred to be penetrated, rather than penetrating. At one point, Encolpius and Ascyltos part ways, largely because they are competing for Giton's affections. Later Encolpius meets up with Eumolpus, who tells him a story about being at the bath and running into Ascyltos. We learn, at this point, that Ascyltos is unusually well endowed. Even more important, however, is the crowd's reaction to his physical gifts:

And as the boys were making fun of me with their impudent imitations, as if I were insane, a huge crowd gathered around him, and applauded and admired fearfully. For he had such a weight of genitalia, that the man was just the border of his penis. What a hardworking youth! I think he would start one day and finish on the next. And so he quickly found help; for someone, a Roman *eques,* as they say, disreputable, put his cloak around him and took him home where, I believe, he could enjoy his good fortune on his own. (*Satyricon* 92)

Apparently there could be considerable admiration for such a well-endowed man. Equally important, there is no suggestion that the upper-class Roman who took Ascyltos home was a *cinaedus*. He does have a poor reputation (Latin *infamis*), no doubt for sexual passivity. But unlike the oily, sloppy, made-up, and disgusting *cinaedi* from the earlier chapter, he does not wear his femininity on his sleeve.

The Beautiful Boy

A constant character in the plot is the boy Giton, and his character deserves some direct analysis. It is not entirely clear how old Giton is, though he seems to be on the young end of the range for an acceptable boyfriend. When brawls break out, he does not get directly involved; indeed, he stands to one side during most of the significant action of the plot. He is, however, evidently quite beautiful. Encolpius must defend his claim on the boy against other men (Ascyltos as well as Eumolpus), and against other women, who also find Giton irresistibly charming. Again, we see that youth in men is thought to be attractive to women as well as men.

At one point in the story, Encolpius and Ascyltos have a falling out and decide to part company. They set about dividing up their mutual possessions. Ascyltos suggests that they divide up Giton as well, and Giton stops the ensuing argument by threatening suicide. Eventually, it is agreed that Giton should choose between them. Much to our narrator Encolpius's dismay, Giton chooses Ascyltos without a moment's hesitation. (Later, he will tell Encolpius that, faced with two armed men, he chose the stronger out of self-preservation; it is not clear, however, if we should believe him as easily as Encolpius does.) Abandoned by both his companions, Encolpius indulges in a monologue in which he abuses them both:

And who has imposed this solitude on me? A youth [Ascyltos] defiled by every lust and, by his own admission, worthy of exile; a freeborn, a native-born given to *stuprum,* whose years were dedicated to dice; even those who knew he was a man rented him as if he were a girl. And what of the other? On the day of adulthood he [Giton] put on a dress rather than a man's toga, he was persuaded by his mother that he was not a man, he did womanly work in the prison, and after he disturbed and turned up the earth of his own lust, he gave up the name of long-standing friendship and—for shame!—as if a female nymphomaniac, sold everything for the touch of a single night. Now the lovers lie intertwined all night long, and perhaps when they are worn out with mutual lust, they joke about my solitude. (*Satyricon* 81)

Clearly Encolpius is not an objective witness at this point. Even so, the terms of his abuse are instructive. First, he accuses Ascyltos of the things that young men usually are accused of: committing *stuprum,* spending too much at gambling, playing the part of a woman sexually. But Giton, whose affections Encolpius has been all too happy to receive previous to this moment, now comes in for singular criticism. He is too effeminate, on several counts, and now his desires are described as perversions. More important, though, is the fact that, having abandoned Encolpius, he is now treated as completely lacking in self-control and is compared to a nymphomaniac (Latin *mulier secutuleia,* literally, a "woman who pursues"). The same feminine charms that are so attractive when offered to the narrator become negative attributes when given to someone else.

Giton is equally attractive, it seems, to women. Early in the existing fragments, Quartilla arranges for Giton to "marry" a seven-year-old girl and then watches through a chink in the door as the new couple engages in (unspecified) sexual activity (*Satyricon* 26). This might be simply taken as voyeurism, but a woman later in the novel, Tryphaena, makes it clear that she is interested in Giton herself.

In this episode, Encolpius and Giton, aided by Eumolpus, have stowed away on a ship. Unfortunately, the ship is owned by a man, Lichas, and his wife, Tryphaena, whom Encolpius has somehow offended in another of the lost segments of the narrative. The two shave their heads, making themselves look like slaves, in a vain attempt at disguise. In a rather lighthearted bit, Lichas runs over and recognizes Encolpius by running his hands over his genitals.[2] Eventually, a fight breaks out, but Giton, recognizing that he is the erotic motivation for the tension, manages to stop the mock battle in a singular manner:

Then bravest Giton held a dangerous razor over his genitalia, and threatened that he would cut off the cause of so many miseries; and Tryphaena prevented this great crime by means of a genuine surrender. I quickly placed a barber's knife over my throat, though I was not planning to kill myself any more than Giton was about to do what he threatened. (*Satyricon* 108)

The funniest thing about this scene, of course, is Encolpius's own sense of self-importance. It is fairly doubtful whether anyone in the scene would have cared if he had cut his own throat. Moreover, he makes this gesture only after Tryphaena has already given up. Giton's genitalia, on the other hand, have the capability to bring everyone to a dead stop. Significantly, it is Tryphaena who declares the truce.

After some negotiations, the two parties agree to a treaty. Tryphaena is not to complain of wrongs done to her by Giton, nor is she to force unwilling sexual favors from him, unless she pays for them. Lichas is not to insult Encolpius "nor to ask where he sleeps at night" (*Satyricon* 109). It is not clear what this last phrase refers to, unless Encolpius has previously been Lichas's beloved, and he is now jealous of his affections. In any case, however, the treaty does not work out quite as Encolpius had planned since it only prevented Tryphaena from making *unwelcome* sexual advances on Giton:

For the rest, Tryphaena, resting in Giton's lap, now was filling his breast with kisses, then she was rearranging his wig on his bald head. I was grim, and chafed by this new treaty, did not eat or drink, but glared at them both with angry eyes. Every kiss wounded me, every whisper, whatever that lustful woman contrived. Nor was I sure, whether I was angrier at the boy, because he stole my girlfriend, or at the girl, because she seduced my boyfriend. (*Satyricon* 113)

We see here not only the ambiguity of a handsome boy's beauty, but the full ambiguity of his sexual attractiveness. Poor Encolpius, who seems never to get lucky in this novel for long, has to watch two of his former sexual beloveds enjoy each other, so that he does not know who has stolen whom from him.

The Impotent Hero

Finally, Petronius makes a great deal of fun of male impotence—more so, and more explicitly, than any other ancient author. Toward the end of the extant fragments, Encolpius encounters a woman named Circe and her maid, Chrysis. Circe's name is significant: in Homer's *Odyssey*, Circe is a demigoddess who turns Odysseus's men into pigs and who tries to do the same to Odysseus through a combination of seduction and magic. Though she does not succeed, she and Odysseus do have sex, and in fact, Odysseus dallies on her island for a year, sleeping with her at night.

Petronius's Circe is described as wildly beautiful, and Encolpius falls madly in love with her. Circe recognizes that Encolpius already has a boyfriend (Giton) but suggests that there is no reason for Encolpius not to have her as a girlfriend as well. Encolpius is so enamored that he volunteers to give up Giton. What looks like a classic seduction scene follows, with Circe and Encolpius lying down on the ground; a brief poem evokes book 14 of Homer's *Iliad*, in which Zeus makes love to Hera; and then, "Lying on this grass side by side, we played with a thousand kisses, seeking a stronger pleasure" (*Satyricon* 127).

There is then a break in the text, and when the fragment returns, it appears that Circe is speaking. All is not well:

"What is it?" she said. "Does my kiss offend you? Does my breath smell from hunger? Am I sweaty, having neglected my armpits? I think, if it is none of these things, perhaps you fear Giton?" A blush ran through me, as clear as if I had a fever; I died, as if limp with my whole body. "Please, mistress," I said, "do not add harm to my misery. I have been poisoned." (*Satyricon* 128)

Circe's list of possible reasons for Encolpius's evident difficulties are revealing. She clearly sees Giton as a potential rival and one who might exercise an exclusive claim on Encolpius's affections. It is not the case, though, that Encolpius only has trouble getting it up with Circe; in a slightly later fragment, he seems to have the same difficulty with Giton (again played for laughs). Giton speaks first and is answered by Encolpius:

"Well, for this reason at least I owe you thanks, that you love me with a Socratic devotion. For Alcibiades did not lie on his teacher's couch as untouched as I am."

"Believe me, brother, I do not know myself to be a man, nor do I feel like one. That part of me which once made me an Achilles is dead." (*Satyricon* 128–29)

Though we do not know exactly how or why, it appears that Priapus, the phallic god of Roman gardens and fertility, has taken a particularly apt vengeance on Encolpius. He simply cannot get himself erect.

This sad state of affairs is played for broad laughs over the succeeding chapters. Circe writes a particularly scathing and sarcastic letter to Encolpius, in which she inquires how he managed to walk home with no sinews in his body, and warns him to beware of complete paralysis. Encolpius responds with a letter in which he confesses his "crime"—ironically, that of not having sex with her, where a more serious author would regard having sex with a freeborn woman as a crime—and compares himself to a soldier who had no weapons (*Satyricon* 129–30). In brief, the typical metaphors and conceits of love poetry are here used in the negative. Circe continues to think of Giton as a rival, and she suggests at the end of her letter that if Encolpius will "sleep for three nights without your little friend," he will be cured of his current malady (*Satyricon* 129). Modern readers might be tempted to read this passage as an ancient attempt to cure homosexuality. But the significant thing about Circe's request is that she does not suggest that there is anything fundamentally different about Encolpius's desire for Giton and his desire for her; rather, she seems to base her advice on the idea that Encolpius is enervated because of too much sex with his boy partner at home and so has nothing left for her.

One final passage on this topic deserves mention, both because it is highly entertaining and because it reveals the real object of Petronius's humor. Encolpius, after having been humiliated with Circe once again, contemplates chopping off his genitalia. When his penis withdraws in terror, he decides to address a speech to it:

Making myself erect on my elbow, I chastened the stubborn thing with something like this speech: "What do you have to say," I ask, "you disgrace of all the gods and men? For it is not allowed even to name you in a serious discussion. Did I deserve this from you, that you should drag me to the underworld when I was up in the heavens? That you should trample on my youth, blooming with first strength, and place a torpor on me like that of last old age? I ask you, give me a reasonable response." As I poured this out, angry, it held its eyes turned groundward, nor was its face moved by the speech any more than gentle reeds, or poppies on a tired slope. (*Satyricon* 132)

There is something inherently amusing in Encolpius's address to his penis as if it were a sentient being, made all the more funny by his penis's lack of a response, which is depicted in highly poetic language. What makes Encolpius particularly ridiculous, however, is the importance that he places on his ability to perform sexually. Earlier he referred to his penis as that part that made him an Achilles; here his flaccid member is addressed as if it has destroyed every aspect of his masculine valor. The mirror image of Encolpius is not hard to see here: Petronius stops just short of saying that masculinity is little more than a hard-on, a puffed-up sense of self that emanates from an enlarged member.

There is much more to Petronius, and most of it is highly amusing. The work as we have it pokes fun at a wide variety of social pretenders, not least the extravagantly rich but tasteless freedman Trimalchio. For the purposes of

Ithyphallic bronze *tintinnabulum:* gladiator figure fighting his own phallus in the form of a wildcat. This amusing piece perhaps suggests the difficulty that men feel in keeping their desires in check. Scala, Museo Archeologico Nazionale, Naples, Italy/Art Resource, NY.

this study, though, it is enough to say that Encolpius stands as a satire of typical Roman masculinity. He thinks of himself as extremely manly, in every situation, and is particularly proud of his physical endowments. But these fail him, repeatedly, with attractive members of both sexes. Moreover, in nearly every situation in which he has a romantic rival, he loses out. Ultimately our narrator is a buffoon, and his masculinity is nothing more than the delusions of his egotistical self-presentation. His apparent lack of manhood, however, is not defined by his preference for partners of one gender or the other, but by his inability to perform with splendid Circe or the beautiful boy Giton.

THE EROTIC EPIGRAM: MARTIAL

Martial lived and wrote several generations after Propertius; his poetry comes from the years 86–103 CE, during the reigns of emperors Domitian, Nerva, and Trajan. His poems are primarily written in the same meter as those of Propertius (i.e., the elegiac), but rather than longish attempts to woo a woman, they are generally short, often witty, and sometimes abusive. In attitude, Martial shares several qualities with his contemporary satirist, Juvenal; his epigrams also share some of Catullus's amusing invective, and at times, he directly invokes Catullus as a literary precedent. Martial wrote vast numbers of poems, and again, I will not attempt a comprehensive treatment. Of particular interest, however, are several poems in which he attacks women as *tribades,* a term designating women who take the penetrating role in sex, usually, though not always, with other women.[3]

As I discussed earlier, Catullus often uses terms of sexual abuse simply as a way to insult men who have, in one way or another, offended him; that is, though he threatens to orally rape Furius, and refers to Caesar as a *cinaedus,* it does not appear in those instances that he is actually concerned with Furius's and Caesar's sexual behavior. In the case of Martial, sexual behavior as such comes in for mocking abuse, and if Martial's targets have offended him personally, he does not say how. Not surprisingly, the roles that we have seen before are those that are most often attacked: men who are penetrated in sex, particularly if they seem to enjoy it or seek it out; men who perform fellatio; women who are particularly sexually active. On the whole, Martial does not seem concerned with active (penetrating) men who are oversexed, who show a general lack of self-control. A particularly frequent theme, however, is that of hypocrisy. Men or women who pretend to be something that they are not are the constant target of Martial's pen.

Two poems are worth mentioning at the start because they demonstrate Martial's appreciation and, indeed, invocation of Catullus. Poem 1.35 is a clear reworking of Catullus 16 (and is even written in Catullan hendecasyllabic meter):

Cornelius, you complain that I write verses
not stern enough, nor those which a teacher
would recite in school; but these little books,
like husbands for their wives,

are not able to be pleasing without a cock.
What if you were to order me to sing wedding songs
but not to use the wedding song words?
Who puts clothes on a strip show, or allows
whores to have well-dressed modesty?
This law is given for amusing verses:
they may not please, unless they itch.
So give up the stern demeanor,
spare my jokes and games, please.
Do not wish to castrate my little books.
Nothing is more foul than Priapus made a eunuch.

The vocabulary that Martial uses is almost entirely Catullan, and the use of the diminutive "little book" (*libellus*) is a direct tip-off to the reader. The word that I have translated "itch" (*prurio*) is also borrowed from Catullus's poem. The tone of Martial's poem, however, is less aggressive than that of Catullus: he does not threaten to rape Cornelius, for a start. But at the same time, he insists that his poetry should be allowed the same kind of masculine persona that Catullus claims for himself: they must be allowed to have a cock. The god referred to in the final line, Priapus, was always portrayed as having an enormous phallus. Here, Priapus stands as an image for Martial's book of poems. In brief, then, the poem insists on the right to be a bit sexually explicit and attaches that right to a phallic, penetrating masculinity.

There is another shift, however, from Catullus, and this also changes the way the poetry works. In Catullus's poem, it was Catullus himself who had come in for criticism from Furius and Aurelius. They thought that *he* was "not masculine enough" because of his poems, and his response was that he would respond in person. Here, Martial's concern is that his *books* will be "castrated." All the cocks in this poem are owned by pieces of literature, not men. Catullus's personal investment in his poems is, no doubt, a fiction, but Martial has abandoned that fiction for one of his own, in which what is at stake is only the effectiveness of his poetry.

The poem immediately before this in the standard collection of Martial's poems also hearkens back to Catullus, in that it is addressed to Lesbia. This is a somewhat different Lesbia than that of the Catullan corpus, however:

Lesbia, you always do your deeds with an unguarded
and open door, nor do you hide your illicit acts.
The one watching delights you more than the adulterer,
nor are your pleasures welcome to you if they are hidden.
But a prostitute drives away a witness with a curtain, and with a door-bolt,
and it is a rare crack that appears in Summemmius's brothel wall.
Learn modesty from Chione or from Ias,[4] if from no one else;
tombs hide even filthy whores.[5]
Perhaps my restrictions appear too harsh to you?
I prohibit you from getting caught, Lesbia, not from getting fucked. (Martial 1.34)

Again, the attitude of the later poet is entirely different from that of Catullus. Martial does not pretend to be in love with Lesbia. He is not personally concerned with her sexual behavior; she can have all the sex she wants.

What Martial finds offensive, and perhaps hypocritical, is the openness of this "Lesbia's" behavior, which, ironically, he suggests is less temperate than even that of prostitutes. This exposure of upper-class life is characteristic of Martial. Where Catullus suggested that Lesbia was *like* a prostitute, "peeling" men in narrow doorways, Martial goes one better and argues that prostitutes have better manners than a woman like Lesbia. But Martial's interest in Lesbia appears to be more literary than personal. This is not the fiction of love poetry, but the realm of social critique.

Many of Martial's poems criticize men for willingly seeking out anal sex (as the penetrated partner). One particularly pungent example links this desire with a general lack of control over financial matters:

Often, when you have only one quarter in your money box,
Hyllus (and that one is rubbed smoother than your ass),
even so the baker won't get it, nor the tavern owner,
but whoever is magnificent with a huge cock.
Your unhappy belly watches the dinner parties of your ass;
the former, wretched, is always hungry while the latter gulps it down. (Martial 2.51)

The difficulty here is not just that Hyllus is passive, but that that passivity is linked with a complete lack of self-control. Even when starving, he would rather pay for sex than food. There is a nice touch in the first two lines: the last coin in Hyllus's box is rubbed smooth from being handled so often. This smoothness, suggesting that the coin has been around for a while, is likened to Hyllus's anus, which is similarly smooth from having been rubbed so often. The effect of the metaphor is to translate the desperation inherent in this last, smooth coin to Hyllus desperate sexual hunger. He becomes, then, ridiculous on three interlocking points at once: he is passive, he is habitually so, and he has no control over his sexual hunger, even to the detriment of his physical health.

Worse than being passive, however, is being passive but pretending otherwise. Martial and Juvenal are particularly concerned with passives who try to hide their sexual preferences, and in this regard, the passive begins to look like a premodern sexual identity. In book 7, Martial attacks one Hamillus for trying to hide his sexual passivity with an overabundance of activity:

With doors open you screw large [young men], Hamillus,
and while you do this, you want to be caught
so that neither freedmen, nor your father's slaves,
nor a dark client will tell a story, with hinting gossip.
Whoever gives witness that he is not penetrated, Hamillus,
does that thing often which he does without a witness. (Martial 7.62)

Hamillus shares a feature with Lesbia (discussed earlier): he performs sex with doors open. But unlike Lesbia, who does so because she receives a thrill from being watched, Hamillus takes care to penetrate his partners when people are watching, so that lower-class people who might be privy to his private life will not reveal his real preference. The last two lines have a particularly legal sound to them, using words for witnesses and giving testimony. Nothing is illegal about being passive, but the legal metaphor puts Hamillus's passivity in the category of a furtive act. The kicker, of course, is in the last line: what he does without witness is what he does often. In this way, Hamillus's insistence that he is active becomes evidence for his passivity.

All of this does begin to sound rather like the way that the modern West has constructed homosexuality. Hamillus has a secret, which he tries to hide by acting the opposite of what he really is. For the analyst in the know, Hamillus's insistence that he is active only confirms his essential passivity. Although we can see this as a premodern sexual identity, however, we should note the differences it has from a modern sexuality. First and foremost, it is not defined by the sex of Hamillus's partner, but by which role Hamillus plays in sex. More subtly, it is not clear from Martial that Hamillus's preferred mode of sex is indicative of a psychic secret, a specific kind of desire that constitutes Hamillus as a particular kind of person. Hamillus has a sexual role but is not described, here at least, as possessing a sexual morphology or a sexual identity. All we really know about him is that he prefers to be penetrated and tries to hide that fact.

Again, the reader should not assume that Hamillus is unique in Martial's poetry. Examples of similarly hypocritical sexual types are not hard to find. In poem 9.27, for example, Martial addresses Chrestus and points out that this person is always talking about the ancient Romans who served as moral exemplars, threatening, and speaking badly of modern mores. And yet, at the end of the poem, we learn about Chrestus's mores:

If, during all this, some athlete runs up,
already free from his tutor and whose huge cock
the smith has already unpinned[6]
you call him with a nod and lead him off, and I'm ashamed,
Chrestus, to say what you do with your Catonian tongue.[7] (10–15)

Once again, the point of the poem is that the person under attack pretends to be one thing—in this case, a stern, old-fashioned moralist—but in practice is another. As a fellator, Chrestus uses his tongue for exactly the sort of thing that Cato, a famous moralist from a previous era, would have attacked in speech. Moreover, the poem is written from the point of view of a person who, not unlike Catullus, professes shock and modesty about Chrestus's behavior. The poet, then, maintains his innocence, his sense of decorum, even while exposing the immoral sexual activities of his subject.

Martial is especially critical of men who perform oral sex (as Catullus was in poem 80), and there is good reason to think that performing cunnilingus or fellatio was regarded as particularly degrading for men.[8] In book 2, he attacks Sextillus and coyly implies that he is either a fellator or a cunnilinctor, or both:

Laugh out loud, Sextillus, when someone calls you a *cinaedus*
and give him the middle finger.
But you are not a pederast, Sextillus, nor a fucker [i.e., of women][9]
Nor does the hot mouth of Vetustina please you.

You are none of these, Sextillus, I admit it. So what are you?
I don't know, but you know that there are two things left. (Martial 2.28)

Again, the poem has the structure of a joke. Sextillus may react with derision when someone calls him a *cinaedus,* a clear insult. But if he is not a *cinaedus,* what is he? The poem runs through the other possibilities with anatomical precision: he does not make sexual use of boys, or women's vaginas, or a prostitute's mouth. The only two things left for him to do sexually are to perform fellatio or cunnilingus—both of which, it seems, were considered far worse than the implied passivity of being a *cinaedus.*

Thanks to the poet, Sextillus might have been better off accepting the first insult. Once again, however, the poet maintains his own sense of propriety by claiming not to know what Sextillus is and therefore not saying the words. Of course, since we readers also know what Sextillus is, we are partly the object of the joke: we know which two things are left, and so we must admit to a knowledge of those activities. We find ourselves on the side of knowledge against the poet's professed innocence. Best not to deny it; if we have read Martial, we know that such denials only make the accusation worse.

The *Tribades*

Roman poetry and prose occasionally discuss women who have sex with other women. The standard Roman word for such women is *tribas* (plural *tribades*), a word that at its root appears to have to do with rubbing. The word is often translated "lesbian," though, as will become clear, using that modern term is a misunderstanding of how the Romans thought of *tribades.* In brief, when we see two women in bed together in a Roman poem, we generally assume that the thing that determines their sexual identity is a preference for same-sex love. But in fact, as Martial and others portray *tribades,* this same-sex activity is primarily a result of another distinguishing characteristic, namely, that these are women who prefer to take the active, and even penetrating, role in sex.[10]

Although the word *tribas* does not appear in it, Martial's poem 1.90 provides one of the clearest characterizations of a masculine-behaving woman:

Because I never saw you joined with men, Bassa,
and because no rumor suggested that you had an adulterous lover,
but a crowd of your own sex always surrounded you,
performing every duty, with no man present;
because of this, I confess, you seemed to me a Lucretia.[11]
But you, for shame, Bassa were an adulterous fucker.
You dare to bring together two cunts between themselves,
and your enormous clitoris pretends to be a man.
You have contrived a portent worthy of the Theban riddle:
Here where there is no man, there is adultery.

To be sure, Martial notices that Bassa is sleeping with other women. In fact, that is what he initially finds confusing: given that Bassa spent all of her time with other women (as most Roman women ideally would have), he assumed that she was living a chaste and appropriate sexual life. Again, the poet feigns an innocence of irregular sexual procedure to reveal it in mock-shocked tones to his amused reader.

When it comes time to defining what it is that Bassa does, however, Martial does not languish on the fact that her sexual activities are same-sex; rather, what comes in for detailed description is what he finds most remarkable about her. He calls her, first, a *fututor*, a word usually used to describe men who have vaginal sex with women (see the application to Sextillus, discussed previously) and which I have overtranslated "adulterous fucker." He then engages in an unusually anatomical description of their sexual act, in which the phrase "between themselves" (*inter se*) indicates some sort of vaginal interpenetration. And finally, he suggests that Bassa's clitoris is so large (*prodigiosa*) that it imitates (literally, "falsifies," *mentior*) a phallus. The problem with Bassa is not that she loves women; it is that she imitates men, in their penetrating and insertive role. The fact that she does so with women is a side effect, not a defining term or what we would call a sexual orientation. Finally, we should note that the last word of the poem (*adulterium*) carries considerable weight: it is not only that Bassa has sex in this way, but that in doing so, she commits adultery as a man might. Her sexual activity is both contrary to gender and illegal.

This same idea is explored in a brief and often mistranslated epigram from book 7:

Tribas of the very *tribades*, Philaenis,
the one you fuck you rightly call your girlfriend. (Martial 7.70)

Once again, the point is not that Philaenis is having sex with a woman, though the word for "fuck" (*futuo*) does usually refer to vaginal sex with women; rather, the point is that in screwing like a man, she takes on a masculine role. As a result, the person who is receiving her sexual activity becomes feminine and is appropriately called what men call their sexual partners: "girlfriend." Now, we don't know who the partner is in this poem. It may be another woman, in which case, the object of the joke is purely Philaenis and her appropriation of masculinity. But if Martial is referring to a boy whom Philaenis is screwing, then the poem has a double punch. Just as Philaenis has become masculine, her boyfriend has been feminized.

One other poem deserves our scrutiny, and it again revels in the confusion of gender roles that results when a woman takes the active role in sex. This is the longest and most explicit of Martial's poems about Philaenis:

The tribas Philaenis penetrates *[pedico]* boys
and more harsh than the lust of a husband,
hacks at eleven girls a day.
Indeed, tied like an athlete she plays with the shot put,
gets yellow with sand, and with an easy arm
swings weights heavy for athletes.
Filthy with the sludge of the wrestling ring

she is massaged by an oiled trainer.
She does not eat or lie down before she
has vomited seven pints of wine,
to which she thinks it acceptable to return
when she has eaten sixteen chops.
After all this, when she gets her libido up,
she does not fellate—she thinks this unmanly—
but completely devours the middles of girls.
May the gods give you your own mind, Philaenis,
you who think it manly to lick cunt. (Martial 7.67)

Here again, Philaenis is satirized as a woman who tries to be masculine. In so doing, she rather comically oversteps the bounds of gender and, as a result, becomes a caricature of masculinity, rather than actually becoming manly. Her physical attributes are described as impressive, but instead of being celebrated for her athletic beauty, her efforts in this area only make her filthy. Furthermore, in an attempt to imitate men's larger appetites, she tends to overindulgence, which, paradoxically, is in men a sign of a lack of self-control. She cannot even successfully drink, but ends up vomiting what she has consumed.

Finally, the last lines pick up her sexual behavior, with which the poem opened. Here we find a surprising reversal. Though it makes a certain sense that Philaenis would not perform fellatio, why does she perform cunnilingus? Some scholars have seen this as the *least* virile of sexual acts, even less manly than fellating another man. It is also possible, though, that Martial's point is more subtle. As a cunnilinctor, Philaenis is adhering strictly to the rule that, as a masculine figure, she should not be penetrated. What she does not realize, however, is that such an act is nonetheless regarded as disgraceful for the one performing it; that is, sex does not follow quite the strict logic that Philaenis might wish, and given the unusual gender role that she has taken on, there is really no sexual act that is both appropriate and, for her, adequately masculine.

Whatever the logic of the final two lines, it is clear that Philaenis is better understood as a gender deviant than as possessing a minority sexual identity. She violates the rules of gender in several respects, not merely those that involve sexual behavior. More important, her deviance has more to do with her appropriation of masculinity than with sexuality as we would define it. She may look to us like a butch dyke, but within this comic portrayal, she is so masculine that she even penetrates boys. In a world that divides sexual identity into homosexual and heterosexual, Philaenis makes no sense. In a world that divides sexual behavior into active and passive, she simply takes the logic of that world to the extreme.

Can we, finally, read Philaenis and men like Sextillus as possessing a sexuality? They certainly have a preferred mode of sexual behavior, and like modern homosexuality, their preference is sometimes construed as a secret, something that has to be disclosed by a clever analyst. In several ways, then, we might see such people as belonging to something like a sexuality.

Two aspects, however, remain different from modern sexual categories: first, there is nothing in Martial to indicate that this sexual preference constitutes an overriding personal identity, separate from those signs that mark such individuals as gender deviant. (In modern society, for example, a man can be gender deviant by being a cross-dresser, while still being sexually straight.) And perhaps more important, one must remember that these poems are invective. Martial attacks Philaenis and Sextillus as gender deviant, but we have no evidence that such people self-identified as such. Terms of abuse do not automatically constitute a category of person, though, as Foucault argued, discursive practice can result in such categories being internalized and mobilized by the persons so abused.[12]

JUVENAL

Juvenal was probably born about the time that Petronius and Seneca died, in the early 60s CE. His literary career is generally taken to have spanned from the 90s to the 120s or perhaps 130s CE, though these dates are deduced entirely from references within the poems. He is mentioned three times in the poetry of Martial, and scholars again generally agree that Juvenal's career was beginning as Martial's was ending. Like Martial, his poetry attacks people whose sexual behavior reveals a deeper personal failing. In this regard, Juvenal's critique bears a striking resemblance to homophobic diatribes in the modern world; for Juvenal, at times, the sexual is the key to the moral whole. As we will see, however, even in Juvenal's most pointed attack, the categories of sexual misbehavior are not quite our own.

Juvenal is an inveterate critic of contemporary mores. The persona who speaks in his poems is cranky, irascible, sharp-tongued, and never happy. For all that, there is considerable wit in his presentation, and although few would, I think, wish to be on the receiving end of his satiric poems, he also seems wryly aware of the limitations of his own narrative persona. I am primarily concerned with Juvenal's second satire, in which he lashes out at various degenerate sexual practices. This poem has generated considerable scholarly interest and has, in fact, been used to argue for the presence of a fully understood sexual identity in Rome at the end of the first century and for the presence of a pathic subculture.[13] While on the whole, I disagree with these readings, it is instructive to see how fully Juvenal describes certain kinds of men as possessing a sexual identity.

First, however, I briefly discuss Juvenal's ninth satire, which also provides considerable information and criticism about sexual life in Rome. The ninth satire is, in form, an odd sort of dialogue. The primary speaker of the poem (who is not clearly identified) has a brief conversation with an aging prostitute named Naevolus. Naevolus's principal complaint is not that he does not have enough business, but rather that the men whom he has serviced have not paid him adequately for his performance; now that he is growing older, as a result, he finds that he does not have enough funds to live comfortably. The speaker's attitude toward Naevolus is, curiously, fairly sympathetic. His real target is not the prostitute, but the men who make use of such a person.

Interestingly, one of Naevolus's unnamed fictional clients has made use of the prostitute in two ways. Naevolus complains, on one hand, of the miserly attitude of the man whom he penetrates:

What greater monster is there than a greedy softy *[mollis]*?
"I gave you this much, then I gave you that; later, you got even more."
He calculates, and he wiggles his ass. Bring in the counter, and the boys
with the records. Five thousand sesterces,
for the whole thing. Thus my work is accounted paid.
But is it easy and straightforward to drive a proper cock into his guts,
and there to run into yesterday's dinner?
That slave who plows his field will be less wretched
than the one who plows his master. (Juvenal 9.38–46)

It is clear that the reader is meant to feel disgust at this sexual act, but what is interesting about the poem is the way that our sympathies are manipulated. Because we side with the prostitute, it is his experience that we find unfortunate; we are forced to imagine what it is like to be him. As for the man he screws, he is disgusting on at least two levels. As an adult man, he is passive. As the poem makes clear a few lines later, he is no longer a beautiful boy, so by continuing to seek out penetration, he creates the unhappy situation of prostitutes like Naevolus. But the satirist also encourages us to look askance at his miserly ways: surely such a man should at least pay handsomely for such services and not tot them up with neat precision.

Naevolus also, however, services this man in another way: he has had sex with the man's wife, thus providing him with illegitimate heirs, whom the client passes off as his own children:

But although you pretend otherwise, though you pass over other services
how do you put a price on this, that if I were not dedicated to you,
a devoted client, your wife would remain a virgin? . . .
Is it of no value, ingrate and deal-breaker, none,
that a little son or daughter is born because of me? (Juvenal 9.70–83)

Here there is no indication that Naevolus's sexual acts have been unpleasant for him. But his argument is one that turns Roman values on their heads. From his point of view, what is disgraceful about all this is that his client has not paid him sufficiently for providing the client with heirs and for allowing the client (in accordance with Augustan marriage laws) to acquire full rights as a father. From our point of view, however, the shocking thing about this situation is the open acknowledgment that Roman citizens and heirs are being produced by male prostitutes.

How real is all of this? It is, of course, difficult to say. Juvenal's poems read like rants, and though there is no doubt a kernel of truth to them, they also contain a healthy dose of exaggeration. It is unlikely that most Roman men used male prostitutes to father their children. We can see this element of exaggeration most clearly toward the end of the poem, where the speaker suggests that the entire society of Rome has degenerated to the point that prostitutes such as Naevolus will never lack for business:

Do not be afraid, you will never lack for a pathic boyfriend,
so long as these seven hills of Rome stand. From everywhere they come,
in chariots and in ships, all of them
who itch their heads with a single finger.[14] (Juvenal 9.130–33)

Rome, it seems, has become not only the home of innumerable pathics, who will provide a constant stream of business for Naevolus, but is pictured as a kind of pathic haven, a place where such people come on purpose to seek penetration. Juvenal is making a point here, not just about sex, but about Rome. Rome itself, he wishes to say, has become pathic and therefore degenerate. To take this sort of political statement as evidence for a growing subculture of pathics at Rome is, I would argue, to misunderstand the point of Juvenal's exaggerated characterization of society at large.

Nonetheless, another of Juvenal's satires does give us a picture of a *cinaedus* which suggests that such an identity is both deeply personal and something that affects every aspect of a person's body and life. This is Juvenal's second satire, in which a Stoic philosopher has an imagined conversation with a (female) prostitute named Laronia. As in the ninth satire, the point of this conversation is to demonstrate that, however reprehensible we might think Laronia is, there is a class of men in Rome that even she can criticize. This class of men is, in particular, the secret passives.

At the start, the narrator describes this class of men. Though it is true that the speaker clearly disapproves of their sexual behaviors, what is more disturbing to him is the fact that their characters are hidden behind a veneer of moral rectitude, in the form of Stoic philosophy:

There is no trust in faces; what neighborhood is not full
of serious-looking degenerates? Do you criticize foul behavior, when you
are the most infamous furrow among the Socratic *cinaedi*?
Hairy legs and stiff bristles on your arms, indeed,
suggest a ferocious soul, but swollen figs are cut
from your smooth ass by a laughing doctor. (Juvenal 2.8–13)

Once again, the point is the difference between outward appearance and evident behavior. The word for "figs" (Latin *mariscae*) is a common euphemism for anal piles, vocabulary that Juvenal shares with Martial, generally taken to be a sign of anal passivity. The Stoic philosopher here ridiculed, then, exhibits one sort of self to the outside world: stern, hairy, and manly. These external signs should be evidence for an equally rigid internal self (*animus*), but in fact, an examination of his anus reveals that this man is passive.

When, therefore, the narrator imagines that such a man has criticized the prostitute Laronia, she responds in kind. Her response has led various commentators to suggest that pathics in Rome formed a close-knit and secretive community, but as I see it, this is an overreading of the contrast that Laronia draws. Here is what she is imagined as saying:

. . . consider first,
and scrutinize men. For they do many things, but their numbers,
and their phalanxes joined at the shield protect them.
There is much agreement among softies *[molles]*. There will never be
an example so contemptible among my sex.
Media does not lick Cluvia, nor does Flora lick Catulla;
Hispo goes under youths, and is sick with both diseases.[15] (Juvenal 2.44–50)

In the first place, Laronia is not drawing a contrast simply between female prostitutes and male passives; that is, her general target is *men*. Her point is that men misbehave as much as women, but because men are the dominant gender, an idea reinforced by the military imagery of the phalanx, they do not come under criticism the way that women do. She does say that "there is much agreement *[concordia]* among softies," and this line in particular has been taken as evidence for a passive subculture. In context, however, this line primarily picks up the military imagery in the line before. Men may misbehave, but they stick together, and so are not punished; women, she suggests, never misbehave in this way.

This last point requires some consideration. Laronia's argument, again, is that women (like her) may be committing adultery, but they are not performing sexual acts that are in themselves considered disgusting. She goes on to deny, rather flatly, that there are women who perform oral sex on other women. This may or may not be the case, of course; one imagines that there probably were women who performed cunnilingus (and indeed, Martial suggests as much). But to make her rhetorical point, Laronia is contrasting women who have normal sex outside of marriage with men like Hispo, who perform sexual acts that are considered in themselves degrading.

That this is the real point of the contrast is made clearer by the following lines from Laronia's speech:

Do we [women] ever bring legal cases, do we study civil law?
Or do we disturb your forum with any yelling?
A few are wrestlers; a few eat athlete's rations;
you card wool and carry back the finished fleece in baskets;
you turn the spindle, pregnant with slender thread,
more skillfully than Penelope, more deftly than Arachne. (Juvenal 2.51–56)

I suspect that there is some sort of sexual pun going on in lines 54 and 55, though I am not certain. In any case, however, the argument that Laronia makes is that women have not infiltrated the social arenas of men. They do not speak in court, and they do not try to inhabit the forum. Men, by contrast, have taken over women's tasks, of which the preeminent example was weaving and spinning. By extension, what Laronia is saying is fairly straightforward: women do not act like men (in sex), but men, by being passive, have taken over the women's role. The argument, then, is not that "there is a subculture of men who stick together and who are disgusting," but rather, "women do not do what men do, but you men do what women do, and then stick together so as to avoid criticism."

The rest of the poem is filled with attacks, particularly on men whose behavior marks them as passive. Once again, however, we should note that much of what makes this behavior unacceptable is the fact that such men are behaving in a way that is inappropriately feminine. Once Laronia's brief diatribe is done, the primary narrator makes the following comment:

Fabulla is an adulteress,
and even Carfina can be so condemned if you like; but so condemned,
they would not wear such a cloak (as yours). "But July is hot,
I'm burning." So plead nude; this madness would be less disgusting . . .
What would you not say, if you were to see such a robe
on the body of a judge? I ask, would a see-through be appropriate on a witness?
(Juvenal 2.68–76)

The object of the speaker's scorn, one Creticus, is simply not dressed in a sufficiently manly way. At stake here is not just sexual style, but manhood itself. Juvenal goes on to suggest that dressing in these sorts of light, no doubt comfortable clothes will lead inevitably to an all-out inversion in which Creticus and his cohort will take part in a perverted ritual of the Bona Dea. This festival was one to which men were strictly forbidden; Juvenal imagines a complete reversal, a festival of Bona Dea occupied only by effeminate men, with real women banished from the proceedings (Juvenal 2.82–90). But this is fantasy in the service of critique; we have no evidence that such festivals actually took place.

Finally, Juvenal turns his attention to one last perversion of nature, the practice, apparently historical, of men marrying one another. (The versions of the life of Nero provide further evidence for this practice, at least by the emperor.) Here again, much of what the narrator finds distressing is the fact that in celebrating such an affair with marriage, the men are perverting the purpose of that institution, which is to produce children:

One says, "I must attend a ceremony tomorrow,
early in the morning, in the Quirinal valley."
"What is the reason for the ceremony?" "Why do you ask? A friend
takes a husband; not many are invited." Should we live long enough,
it will come to be that these things are done openly;
they will want them reported in the daily news.
Meanwhile one great problem remains for these brides:
they are not able to give birth, and so keep the affection of their husbands.
But it is better, that nature does not give jurisdiction over their bodies
to these souls: they die sterile. (Juvenal 2.132–40)

To be sure, there is something about this relationship that is, in itself, not acceptable to Juvenal; in any marriage of two adult men, one of them must be passive. It is important that the person criticized in the preceding passage is explicitly the one who plays the role of the wife: the word I have translated "to take a husband" (Latin *nubere*) is used of women in Roman marriage. But what he really seems to mind is the fact that these affairs are being made public and granted the kind of acceptance that comes with the institution of marriage.

Once again, it is difficult to know how common such practice was in imperial Rome. There is enough evidence to suggest that it must have gone on, however much critics may have ridiculed the men who took part. But it is somewhat misleading, I believe, to tie this criticism too closely to the sort of debates that currently surround the issue of homosexual marriage in the modern world. Juvenal does not suggest that men getting married to one another will somehow destroy the institution of marriage, as modern critics have. Nor does he portray desire for another male of a suitable age as inherently wrong; rather, as Williams suggests in his perceptive chapter on this topic, Juvenal sees male-male marriage as incompatible with the function of matrimony: the birth of children and, through them, the establishment of a stable family.[16] Such men are ridiculous, even contemptible. But they are neither considered incomprehensible nor are they demonized.

CONCLUSIONS

Petronius, Martial, and Juvenal, then, provide considerable comic invective about the sexual foibles of men and women in the early Roman Empire. Perhaps the most important aspect of their work is the fully fleshed depiction, however motivated by invective, of the *cinaedus,* the *mollis,* the passive, and the *tribas* as sexual types. In both Juvenal and Petronius, men who deliberately engage in the passive role in sex are depicted as flaunting this deviant sexual preference in behavior, in their manner of clothes, in their makeup, and even in their walk. We have, at this point, a complete sexual morphology, not of a homosexual, but of a gender deviant, of a man who prefers to play the role of a woman in sex as well as in other aspects of self-presentation.

Even more interesting, however, is the idea that there are some *cinaedi* in Rome who attempt to hide this essential feature of their characters. Here the fact that Juvenal's particular target is not just *cinaedi,* but rather stern moral philosophers who pretend to a life of sexual uprightness complicates the issue. Juvenal does criticize their sexual passivity; but his real venom is reserved for their hypocrisy. The figure of such a hypocrite suggests that there were men in Rome who had a preference for a particular kind of sex— they preferred to be penetrated—but who attempted to hide this preference through a veneer of brusque, hairy masculinity. Such men are, in Juvenal, revealed through medical examination of their backsides, which becomes an indication of their real characters.

The idea of man whose real nature is revealed by his (hidden) sexual preference comes closer than anything else in this book to the modern notion of the homosexual. And so long as we remember that what is remarkable about the Roman pathic is not his desire for same-sex contact, but rather his desire to be penetrated, it is useful to think about such men as revealing the truth about themselves through their sex. It remains an incontrovertible fact that we have no firsthand accounts from *cinaedi,* no evidence of pathic pride parades. Our only evidence for the existence of these men comes from invective, which regularly derives its effect from exaggeration and parody. Nonetheless, Petronius, Martial, and Juvenal give us our best literary evidence for the existence of deliberate gender and sexual deviance—what we might call a minority sexual identity—in Rome.

Fifteen

Epilogue

THE ANCIENT NOVELS AND CHRISTIANITY

I began this book by discussing the *Erotes,* a text ascribed to Lucian from the third century CE. We have now come full circle and arrived back at the second century in Rome. There is no particular reason to stop here, except that this book is already long enough. I hope that I have shown that while certain fundamental ideas about sex did not change drastically during the Greek and Roman periods, different aspects of sexual life were highlighted at different periods of history. While both Cicero and Juvenal appear to view self-control as paramount for a Roman man, for example, Juvenal shows a concern with the sexual type of the *cinaedus* that finds no clear parallel in the late republic. As the Roman Empire grew, became Christian, and eventually succumbed to successive attacks from without, ideas about sex continued to shift, change, and develop. In this brief chapter, I outline a few of the major changes of the succeeding centuries.

From the second to the fourth centuries CE, a new form of literature flourished in the form of long prose romances in Greek. These romances, which are generally referred to as the ancient novels, are in some ways surprisingly familiar to modern audiences.[1] They generally tell the story of a young man and woman who are close in age and who fall madly in love with one another. The lovers are prevented from marrying, however, by a series of untimely events, including kidnapping by pirates, amnesia, long journeys around the Mediterranean, mistaken identities, temporary madness, and the like. Throughout most of the novels, even when the young lovers are traveling without a chaperone in strange and distant lands, the heroine maintains her virginity. Sometimes the hero remains a virgin as well. The story generally ends when hero and heroine are restored to their families, given blessing by the heroine's father, and allowed to marry. In all, the novels look much like modern romantic comedies.

Michel Foucault ended his third volume of *The History of Sexuality* with a brief and tantalizing discussion of these novels, in which he found a culmination of some of the trends that he saw developing in the Roman Empire.[2] In brief, Foucault postulated in these novels the development of a new erotics, which was characterized by "the existence of a 'heterosexual' relation marked by a male-female polarity, the insistence on an abstention that is modeled much more on virginal integrity than on the political and virile domination of desires; and finally, the fulfillment and reward of this purity in a union that has the form and value of a spiritual marriage."[3] While there is much in this assessment that is true, it also overlooks some of the ways in which the ancient novels maintained continuity with the picture of sexuality that I have been discussing in the course of this book.

Though it may not seem so to modern audiences, the form of the ancient novels is quite surprising. As Winkler points out, in virtually all Greek and Roman literature before this, the presence of *eros*, "erotic desire," generally signals trouble for the protagonists. Erotic desire was considered an overwhelming force, one that led to foolish, sometimes risky behavior, and one that resulted, as often as not, in humiliation or death.[4] In the novels, by contrast, *eros*, at least that experienced by the hero and heroine, becomes a positive force, one that leads to a celebration of their mutual love for one another. This form has, of course, become our own tradition, and as a result, it is easy to miss how unusual it is in the history of Greek and Roman literature. Winkler suggests that, in the context of their cultures, these novels presented a "fantasy of the significantly impossible."[5]

There is good reason, then, to see these novels as marking a shift in emphasis, if not the full-fledged birth of a new erotics. At the same time, the novels fall far short of giving birth to a radically different conception of sexuality. For all that the novels focus on the hero and heroine, male characters who enjoy pederastic relationships do appear and are not treated as being a different species of individual. In Achilles Tatius's *Leukippe and Kleitophon* (1.7–14), for example, there is a brief tale of an *erastes-eromenos* relationship, that between two minor characters, Kleinias and Charikles.

The story of Kleinias and Charikles is tragic: Charikles (the *eromenos*) announces to Kleinias that his father has just arranged a marriage for him; Kleinias, distressed, launches into a brief diatribe against women and marriage. Charikles reassures him that the wedding is still some days off and then announces that he will go riding for the first time on the horse that Kleinias has given him. Alas, in the course of this first and only ride, Charikles is thrown from the horse and trampled to death. In the subsequent paragraphs, Kleinias and Charikles' father are described as competing in their lamentations for the dead boy (*Leukippe and Kleitophon* 1.14).

On one hand, the tragic nature of the brief tale is significant. The death of Charikles takes place instead of his marriage, which the boy (and his lover) had been thinking of as a disaster in itself. The brutal and violent nature of the boy's death becomes a much worse disaster, and in fact the death stands in for the marriage, at least in the father's eyes: "Oh, these wretched torches! Your marriage torches have become the torches of your funeral" (*Leukippe and Kleitophon* 1.13). At the same time, the competition of the two men in mourning points out, in high rhetorical style, the ambivalent nature of a young, beautiful boy like Charikles. To his father, he is a son to be married, to his lover, a beloved boy whose marriage means the end of their erotic relationship. The tradition of Greek pederasty, with its concern over the fleeting nature of a boy's beauty, is not only still present, but it gives the author an opportunity for a high rhetorical display.

Moreover, the fact that Kleinias offers a vicious diatribe against marriage when he hears that Charikles is to be married should be taken in context. It may be the case that Kleinias has a marked sexual preference for boys, but the novel does not indicate that desire for boys and desire for women are fundamentally different. In a brief passage between the announcement of Charikles' marriage and the news that the boy has died, the hero of the novel, Kleitophon, turns to Kleinias for advice on how he should manage his affair with Leukippe. Not only is Kleinias, in this case, highly sympathetic, but he posits that love of boys and love of women tends to work along the same lines:

> Say nothing about sex to the maiden; rather, search out a way for the deed to happen in silence. For a boy and a maiden are the same in their sense of shame: even if they have some knowledge concerning the pleasure of Aphrodite, they do not want to hear about what they experience. For they think that modesty lies in words. (*Leukippe and Kleitophon* 1.10)

In other words, Kleinias does not conceive of his desire for a boy, and Kleitophon's for Leukippe, as different *kinds* of desire; indeed, he suggests that both objects of desire have a similar sense of modesty and shame. Kleinias' outlook is a bit jaded, in that he thinks both boys and women are more ashamed of notoriety than of the act of sex itself, but nothing indicates that he thinks of them as essentially different love objects.

Why, then, does Kleinias launch on a diatribe against women and marriage earlier? Context is important. When Kleinias complains bitterly about marriage, he is afraid of losing his boyfriend to a wife, and indeed, part of his complaint is rendered in terms of the loss of the boy's natural beauty:

> By the gods, do not, Charikles, become a slave, do not destroy the flower of your youth before its time. For in addition to the other disadvantages, this is the misfortune of marriage: it wastes away your peak of beauty. (*Leukippe and Kleitophon* 1.9)

Charikles' marriage, then, seems destined to destroy his status as an *eromenos,* even as it removes him from that kind of relationship. It is one thing when marriage threatens Kleinias's affair with the beautiful Charikles, and something quite different when his friend asks for advice about his desire for Leukippe. His diatribe against marriage should be understood as an attempt to keep his beloved's affections; Kleinias's apparent misogyny is less a matter of principle than of rhetoric.

It would be misleading, however, to treat this brief passage as typical of the novel as a whole. Like the other Greek novels, *Leukippe and Kleitophon* waxes poetic over some hundreds of pages about the exquisite love relationship between the beautiful hero and heroine. It is also important, as Foucault noted, that the heroine of these novels remain a virgin until the very end.

Her marriage to the hero must be her first sexual experience, and in this the novels appear to transform the idea of self-control into a principle of purity.[6] Even here, however, it is important to note that the novels' authors are working in a tradition that valorized masculine self-control. One brief example will suffice, from Heliodorus's *An Ethiopian Tale.*

Heliodorus's novel, which dates to the third or fourth century CE, is remarkable in many ways, not least in that both hero and heroine remain virgins throughout the novel. Their dedication to a state of bodily integrity becomes, in Foucault's words, "a lofty form of existence that the hero chooses out of the regard that he has for himself."[7] At one point, the hero and heroine (Theagenes and Charikleia) have been imprisoned together, and they take careful solace in one another's company:

And immediately having fallen into forgetfulness of everything, they embraced each other as tightly as if they had become one, having their fill of a chaste and inexperienced love, pouring into one another wet and hot tears, and mixing only in their pure affection. For if Charikleia perceived Theagenes being somewhat too excited and acting manly, she held him back with a reminder of their oaths; and he with no difficulty pulled himself back, and easily was restrained to chastity, being the slave of love, but the master of pleasure. (Heliodorus *An Ethiopian Tale* 5.4)

We see here the construct that Foucault argued for through much of volume 2 of *The History of Sexuality,* namely, that true manhood depends on nothing so much as control over one's desires.[8] And so Theagenes is both ideal man and ideal romantic hero. Charikleia, however, appears here to do Theagenes one better. Though she shares the wet, hot tears with her beloved, the narrative suggests no internal struggle for self-control on her part. On the contrary, her self-control appears a given, and moreover, she exerts a form of control over Theagenes' masculine libido. If he is an ideal hero, she is the heroine who provides his temperance through a gentle reminder of their oaths. Her virginity becomes the impetus for his self-restraint.

The novels, then, work within the general sexual system that I have described over the course of this book. But in their emphasis on sexual purity of the heroine (and sometimes the hero), and their surprising elevation of erotic desire as a positive force in the characters' lives, they point to shifts in the sexual landscape. The story of how this romantic ideal became the dominant form of comic narrative in the West is long and complex, and I cannot trace it out here. The ancient novels, however, are clearly one of its early and important sources.

At the same time that the novels appeared, Christianity found its foothold in the Greek and Roman worlds. There is no denying that the advent of Christianity during the second to fifth centuries CE resulted in fundamental changes in the way that people thought about, and experienced, sex. Even Christian texts, however, maintain some of the threads that I have traced throughout this book, and one can justifiably see a concurrence, if not a direct correspondence, between the practice of daily exercises of self-control by the Roman Stoics and the development of Christian asceticism.

At the same time, there is evidence that the Christian tradition introduced two strong breaks in the history of sexuality: first, Christian teachings supported the idea that desire *in itself* was sinful, potentially damaging to the one desiring and in need of being rooted out from one's very soul.[9] This notion of desire as damaging in itself led, over the course of many centuries, to the development within the church of the practice of confession. If, as Foucault argued in the first volume of *The History of Sexuality*, the profession of psychoanalysis has its roots in this Christian practice, then this development is a crucial step in the history of sexuality as a modern category of thought.

Second, Christian doctrines opposed to same-sex sexual activity resulted, eventually, in serious criticism of, and legal punishments for, even the penetrating partner in male homoerotic activity. The writings of Paul in the Christian Bible clearly condemn homoerotic activity and specify that both active and passive partners are at fault.[10] After the Roman Empire became officially Christian with the emperor Constantine, moreover, Roman legislation showed increasing hostility toward homoerotic activity in general.[11] In 342 CE, a constitution published by Constantius and Constans declared the following:

When that crime takes place which it is better not to know about . . . we order that the laws rise up, that the laws be armed with an avenging sword, so that those who are disreputable *[infames]* may be given to the chosen punishments.[12]

The "crime which it is better not to know about" is referred to in a previous clause of the same declaration, namely, "when a man is married in the manner of a woman," and Eva Cantarella has argued convincingly that the word for "to be married" here refers to being passive in sex. Similar declarations were made in the following decades, and in 438 Theodosius II published the Theodosian Code, in which passive sexual behavior by men is explicitly condemned:

All of those who are accustomed to the disgrace of condemning a masculine body, arranged in feminine manner, by means of the passivity of the other sex, and who are seen to have nothing different than women, will pay for this sort of crime through the vengeance of flames, with the people watching.[13]

It is interesting that at this point, the object of these laws is still clearly the passive partner in such sexual relationships. Nonetheless, there is no denying that these laws show a sharply different sensibility than the earlier Roman laws regarding men who "suffered womanly things" (*pati muliebria*). Rather than being deprived of the right to represent others in court, as is specified in the Justinian Digest, the Theodosian Code proscribes death by fire.

With the publication of Jutinian's *Institutions* in 533, however, the active partner in male homoerotic relations became the subject of legal punishment. The law is curiously parenthetical, considering the significant break that it seems to make with previous practice; it falls in a section in which the jurist is discussing the Julian law on adultery passed by Augustus:

Likewise the Julian law on adultery, which not only punished with the sword those who violated other men's wives, but even those who dared to exercise their shameful lust with men. (4.18.7)

As it happens, the Julian law on adultery made no such provision, and it appears that Justinian is drawing on it somewhat disingenuously as a source of authority for what is, in fact, a change in legal standing.[14] From this point on, both active and passive partners in a male homoerotic relationship were subject to legal action and potentially could be condemned to death. At this moment in history, it appears that sexual acts were defined in the legal code not according to gender roles—that is, not according to penetrating or penetrated—but according to sexual ones. This is a significant step in the development of a notion of sexual orientation and, eventually, sexual identity.

ANCIENT SEXUAL SYSTEMS AND MODERN HOMOSEXUALITY

Even after the publication of the Justinian *Institutions,* however, it is far from clear that an idea of homosexuality in the modern sense existed in the West. The legal codes of Christian emperors outlawed homoerotic sex, to be sure. But that is not the same thing as assuming that people who engage in sex with a partner of the same sex experience a different, usually exclusive, form of desire than those who engage in sex with members of the opposite sex. Still less does it prove that a man who preferred to have sex with boys or other men was considered a different kind of person, whose fundamental character was determined by his particular libido. For those developments, I believe that Foucault was largely correct: they stem from the medicalization of desire that comes about with the development of psychoanalysis in the late nineteenth century.

At the same time, we should realize that the social understanding of modern homosexuality (male and female) is still being shaped in important ways by the social and cultural expressions of sex that we can find in ancient Greece and Rome. Homosexual men may be strikingly different from Socrates and Alcibiades, or Encolpius and Giton, not least in that modern homosexuality does not distinguish as rigorously between the active and the passive partner. But it is also true that many homosexual relationships (again, both male and female) are structured along gender lines, with one partner marked as more masculine and the other as more feminine.[15] In a male-male relationship in which one partner is regularly penetrated, he is likely to be considered by the outside world as the more feminine of the two.

Still more to the point, one does not have to look very far or very hard to discover pockets of modern society in which men penetrate other men but do not think of themselves as gay because they are not the penetrated partners. In a recent book, Halperin discusses a letter to sex columnist Dan Savage by a man who describes himself as a "200 percent straight guy" but who, nonetheless, has found himself going to a male masseur and receiving blow jobs on a regular basis. He closes by asking, "I wonder if the guy who gets the blow job is as guilty as the one who does it."[16] No doubt many readers of this letter will analyze the writer using our own modern categories and come to the conclusion that he is a closeted homosexual. Another way to see his situation, however, is to realize that the categories of active and passive are still alive in our own sexual modes of thought, even if most people do not give them the preeminence that they once had. It is moreover worth pausing, at least for a moment, to realize that in ancient Greece or Rome, the letter writer would have been thought of as normal, if indeed he was remarked on at all. If criticism were leveled at his behavior, it would probably have been on the basis of wasting his money on frivolous pleasures and not exercising adequate control over those pleasures or his finances.

Sexuality is, and will be, fundamental to the way we think of ourselves. Although we can be aware of sexuality as a modern construct, as a product of a series of developments evident in legal, religious, and medical texts, we cannot think ourselves free of our own conceptual categories. Nor should we necessarily try to. But when we think of ourselves as occupying a particular kind of sexual identity, when we see in that identity a fundamental way of being in the world, it is useful to realize not only that the Greeks and Romans did things differently, but that they thought of being in the world with a different set of values and categories than ours.

Notes

CHAPTER ONE

1. Each Greek and Latin text is conventionally referred to by a system of numbering that is idiosyncratic to that text. Throughout this book, I have referred to ancient texts by using these conventional numbering systems. By doing so, I hope to allow the reader to easily find the work referenced in any standard text or translation. Unless otherwise noted, all translations of Greek and Latin literature are my own.

2. Thomas Hubbard, ed., *Homosexuality in Greece and Rome: A Sourcebook of Basic Documents* (Berkeley: University of California Press, 2003).

3. The argument that follows is heavily indebted to David Halperin, *How to Do the History of Homosexuality* (Chicago: University of Chicago Press, 2002), chapter 3.

4. Translations from pseudo-Lucian's *Erotes* are all taken from M. D. Macleod, *Lucian,* Loeb Classical Library 8 (Cambridge, MA: Harvard University Press, 1967).

5. This passage deliberately echoes a passage from Plato's *Phaedrus,* which I discuss in chapter 6.

6. The bibliography on this topic is vast. Among the most relevant works are Amy Richlin, "Foucault's *History of Sexuality:* A Useful Theory for Women?," in *Rethinking Sexuality: Foucault and Classical Antiquity,* ed. D.H.J. Larmour, P. A. Miller, and C. Platter (Princeton, NJ: Princeton University Press, 1998), 138–70; Richlin, "Zeus and Metis: Foucault, Feminism, Classics," *Helios* 18 (1991): 160–80; Marilyn Skinner, "Zeus and Leda: The Sexuality Wars in Contemporary Classical Scholarship," *Thamyris* 3, no. 1 (1996): 103–23.

7. A variety of discussions can be found in D.H.J. Larmour et al., eds., *Rethinking Sexuality.* In defense of Foucault, see Halperin, *How to Do the History of Homosexuality,* esp. chapter 1.

8. Michel Foucault, *The History of Sexuality,* vol. 2, *The Use of Pleasure,* trans. R. Hurley (New York: Random House, 1985), 187.

9. Michel Foucault, *The History of Sexuality,* vol. 1, *An Introduction,* trans. R. Hurley (New York: Random House, 1978), 65.

10. This is no longer held to be the case by mainstream medical practitioners. In 1974, the American Psychiatric Association removed homosexuality from the *Diagnostic and Statistical Manual of Mental Disorders.*

11. I borrow these distinctions from Halperin, *How to Do the History of Homosexuality,* chapter 4.

CHAPTER TWO

1. There is a Greek society before Homer about which we know a fair amount; I refer to the so-called Mycenaean culture that reached its height in 1600–1200 BCE. Our sources for this civilization consist of archaeological remains (buildings, frescoes, tools, weapons, pottery) and a set of tablets written in Linear B. The Linear B tablets, however, were primarily a record-keeping system. We have no Mycenaean literature. Though scholars have ingeniously mined the Linear B tablets for all sorts of social, religious, and cultural information, nothing on them will reveal anything so personal as sexuality. Interested readers are encouraged to read John Chadwick, *The Mycenaean World* (Cambridge: Cambridge University Press, 1976).

2. All translations of Homer are taken from Richmond Lattimore, *The Iliad of Homer* (Chicago: University of Chicago Press, 1961), with minor modifications for clarity.

3. All translations of Hesiod are from R. M. Frazer, *The Poems of Hesiod* (Norman: University of Oklahoma Press, 1983). I have modified some passages for clarity.

4. Translation that of Peter Bing and Rip Cohen, *Games of Venus: An Anthology of Greek and Roman Erotic Verse from Sappho to Ovid* (New York: Routledge, 1991), modified. All subsequent translations of Theognis come from this collection. Theognis's poems come to us in a manuscript in which the divisions between individual poems were not marked; modern editors, therefore, have decided where each begins and ends, and the poems are referred to by their line numbers in the continuous text.

5. All translations of Anacreon are my own.

6. On this point, I have benefited particularly from Eva Stehle, "Sappho's Private World," in *Reflections of Women in Antiquity*, ed. H. Foley (New York: Gordon and Breach, 1981), 45–61.

7. Translations of Sappho are my own.

8. Recently, a new papyrus was published that allows us to complete the lines of an earlier known papyrus. This scrap is now referred to as the new Sappho and probably presents us with a second complete poem. Scholars disagree, however, as to whether the poem is complete, and if so, where it ends.

9. Among the most important works are Yopie Prins, *Victorian Sappho* (Princeton, NJ: Princeton University Press, 1999); Joan DeJean, *Fictions of Sappho 1546–1937* (Chicago: University of Chicago Press, 1989).

10. Denys Page, *Sappho and Alcaeus: An Introduction to the Study of Ancient Lesbian Poetry* (Oxford: Clarendon Press, 1955), 144–46.

11. A highly influential, and in my view correct, work on this question is Holt Parker, "Sappho Schoolmistress," in *Re-reading Sappho: Reception and Transmission*, ed. E. Greene (Berkeley: University of California Press, 1996), 146–83. See also the useful discussion of Eva Stehle, *Performance and Gender in Ancient Greece: Nondramatic Poetry in Its Setting* (Princeton, NJ: Princeton University Press, 1997), chapter 6.

12. This much has been suggested by Kenneth J. Dover, "Two Women of Samos," in *The Sleep of Reason: Erotic Experience and Sexual Ethics in Ancient Greece and Rome*, ed. M. C. Nussbaum and J. Sihvola (Chicago: University of Chicago Press, 2002), 222–29.

13. John J. Winkler, *The Constraints of Desire: The Anthropology of Sex and Desire in Ancient Greece* (New York: Routledge, 1990), 179.

14. Anne Carson, "The Justice of Aphrodite in Sappho 1," in *Reading Sappho: Contemporary Approaches*, ed. E. Greene (Berkeley: University of California Press, 1996), 226–32.

15. The poem here contains an untranslatable ambiguity. The word in the last line, *another,* does not specify another *what,* though the gender is unmistakably feminine. The easiest translation, then, is "another girl." Scholars have suggested, however, that the girl in question despises the speaker to look at another *head of hair,* which is also feminine in Greek. There is simply no way to objectively decide which the poet means.

CHAPTER THREE

1. This is all brilliantly discussed in Edith Hall, *Inventing the Barbarian: Greek Self-definition through Tragedy* (New York: Oxford University Press, 1989).

2. Translation is that of Robin Waterfield, *Herodotus: The Histories* (New York: Oxford University Press, 1998).

3. There are many good books on the subject of women in Athens. A particularly balanced view is presented by Sue Blundell, *Women in Ancient Greece* (Cambridge, MA: Harvard University Press, 1995). See also the useful discussion in Bella Vivante, *Daughters of Gaia: Women in the Ancient Mediterranean World* (Westport, CT: Praeger, 2007), chapter 6.

4. The question of whether or not women attended the dramatic festivals is a particularly vexed one. I tend to believe that they did, but I must admit that there is no solid evidence either way. For a good discussion, see Jeffrey Henderson, "Women and the Athenian Dramatic Festivals," *Transactions of the American Philological Association* 121 (1991): 133–47.

5. My discussion of hoplites and *kinaidoi* is heavily indebted to John J. Winkler, *The Constraints of Desire: The Anthropology of Sex and Gender in Ancient Greece* (New York: Routledge, 1990), 46–54.

6. For a good discussion, see Karen Bassi, "The Semantics of Manliness in Ancient Greece," in *Andreia: Studies in Manliness and Courage in Classical Antiquity,* ed. R. Rosen and I. Sluiter (Leiden, Netherlands: E. J. Brill, 2003), 25–58.

7. Kenneth Dover, *Greek Homosexuality* (New York: MFJ Books, 1989), 35–36.

8. See especially D. Halperin, "The Democratic Body," in *One Hundred Years of Homosexuality and Other Essays on Greek Love* (New York: Routledge, 1990), chapter 5.

9. Dover, *Greek Homosexuality,* 91–100. There are a few pots that show penetration of boys (and even men), though it appears that these are deliberately transgressive. See H. Allan Shapiro, "Leagros and Euphronios: Painting and Pederasty in Athens," in *Greek Love Reconsidered,* ed. T. Hubbard (New York: Wallace Hamilton Press, 2000), 12–32.

10. James Davidson has recently argued against this view. In his view, penetration is not problematic, but being indiscriminate about giving in to such pleasures is. See James Davidson, *Courtesans and Fishcakes: The Consuming Passions of Classical Athens* (New York: St. Martin's Press, 1997); Davidson, "Dover, Foucault, and Greek Homosexuality: Penetration and the Truth of Sex," *Past and Present* 170 (2001): 3–51; Davidson, *The Greeks and Greek Love* (London: Weidenfeld and Nicolson, 2007). In my view, Davidson ignores a good deal of evidence, particularly that of Aristophanic comedy, in order to make his argument.

11. Robin Osborne, *Archaic and Classical Greek Art* (New York: Oxford University Press, 1998), 133–35. Dover, *Greek Homosexuality,* also provides a good introduction to the sexual images on Greek pots, with numerous black-and-white images.

12. See Halperin, "Democratic Body."

13. Interested readers are strongly encouraged to see Halperin, "Democratic Body"; Edward Cohen, *The Athenian Nation* (Princeton, NJ: Princeton University Press, 2000), chapter 6; and Leslie Kurke, *Coins, Bodies, Games and Gold* (Princeton, NJ: Princeton University Press, 1999), chapter 5.

14. See Demosthenes *Against Neaira* 67–68.

CHAPTER FOUR

1. This is not the same Kleisthenes who introduced democratic reforms in 508–507, discussed in chapter 3.

2. The definitive work on obscenity in Aristophanes is Jeffrey Henderson, *The Maculate Muse* (New Haven, CT: Yale University Press, 1975). Much of my discussion of Aristophanes is indebted to Henderson.

3. This is a sexual joke; for a woman to be "split" in Greek slang was to be penetrated sexually.

4. Probably a gross exaggeration; typically, a Greek girl did not have sex before menstruation, which would not normally take place before 12 or 13 years of age.

5. Kenneth Dover, "Two Women from Samos," in *The Sleep of Reason: Erotic Experience and Sexual Ethics in Ancient Greece and Rome,* ed. M. C. Nussbaum and J. Sihvola (Chicago: University of Chicago Press, 2002), 222–29.

6. Jeffrey Henderson translates his name as "Rod Balling," which works well.

7. Another sexual joke; "riding bareback" here translates a word that can mean "to ride" in sexual terms. Here, however, the Kinsman is referring to Eurpides *Hippolytus,* in which Phaedra falls in love with her stepson, named "Hippolytus." Hippolytus's name means "destroyed by horses," so the horse imagery is doubly appropriate for a Phaedra.

8. Remember that the Kinsman's costume probably includes a strap-on phallus; when the Scythian points to his "cunt," then our attention is drawn to this phallus.

9. See, e.g., Thomas Hubbard, "Popular Perceptions of Elite Homosexuality in Classical Athens," *Arion Series 3* 6, no. 1 (1998): 48–78.

CHAPTER FIVE

1. Aeschines *Against Timarchos* is discussed at length in Kenneth Dover, *Greek Homosexuality* (New York: MFJ Books, 1989), 19–59; David Halperin, *One Hundred Years of Homosexuality and Other Essays on Greek Love* (New York: Routledge, 1990), chapter 5. Technical points of the law on prostitution, especially the question of whether citizens were prostitutes, are discussed by Edward Cohen, *The Athenian Nation* (Princeton, NJ: Princeton University Press, 2000), chapter 6.

2. There is, in fact, some evidence that Misgolas, Timarchos, and Aeschines were all about the same age (despite the fact that Aeschines apparently looked older than the other two); see Edward Harris, "When Was Aeschines Born?" *Classical Philology* 83 (1988): 211–14. This does not change the assumption behind Aeschines' assertion, however: for Misgolas to have hired Timarchos as a prostitute, he should have been the older of the two.

3. This speech has also received considerable scholarly attention; see esp. Debra Hamel, *Trying Neaera: The True Story of a Courtesan's Scandalous Life in Ancient Greece* (New Haven, CT: Yale University Press, 2003).

4. Lysias's speech *On the Murder of Eratosthenes* (Lysias 1) deals with just such an issue.

CHAPTER SIX

1. See, e.g., John Thorp, "The Social Construction of Homosexuality," *Phoenix* 46 (1992): 54–61.

2. These words are discussed well by Jeffrey Carnes, "This Myth Which Is Not One: Construction of Discourse in Plato's Symposium," in *Rethinking Sexuality: Foucault and Classical Antiquity,* ed. D.H.J. Larmour, P. A. Miller, and C. Platter (Princeton, NJ: Princeton University Press, 1998), 104–21.

3. Kenneth Dover, "Two Women from Samos," in *The Sleep of Reason: Erotic Experience and Sexual Ethics in Ancient Greece and Rome,* ed. M. C. Nussbaum and J. Sihvola (Chicago: University of Chicago Press, 2002), 222–29.

4. For a thorough discussion of Diotima and the importance of her teachings here, see David Halperin, "Why Is Diotima a Woman?," in *One Hundred Years of Homosexuality and Other Essays on Greek Love* (New York: Routledge, 1990), chapter 6. For an alternative view of her character, see esp. Mary Ellen Waithe, ed., *Ancient Women Philosophers, 600 B.C.–500 A.D.* (Dordrecht, Netherlands: Martinus Nijhoff, 1997), 83–116.

5. We should note that in some later dialogues, Plato does appear to oppose same-sex relations (see, e.g., Plato *Laws* 838–39, in which the speaker opposes all sex that is not for the purposes of procreation). It is a tempting and common mistake to assume that Plato must have held a consistent position on this question throughout his life and to attempt to reconcile contradictory propositions in different dialogues.

6. My discussion of the Phaedrus is largely derived from David Halperin, "Plato and Erotic Reciprocity," *Classical Antiquity* 5 (1986): 60–80.

7. The word that I have translated "desire in return" is *anteros,* a word normally used to describe women's desire for their husbands. Like boys, women are assumed not to have originary desire of their own, but once desired, they can feel reciprocating desire. Plato's innovation here is to suggest that boys feel such desire, rather than merely consenting to give pleasure to their lovers in return for personal improvement.

8. This is an often parodied and ridiculed passage. Later authors have taken great pleasure in suggesting that this is special pleading and that for all his arguments, Socrates must have enjoyed Alcibiades sexually.

CHAPTER SEVEN

1. It is not clear from the grammar whether the two lovers are both men or a man and a woman. The mention of Aphrodite in the following line argues for a heteroerotic pair.

2. Interested readers should see Christopher A. Faraone, *Ancient Greek Love Magic* (Cambridge, MA: Harvard University Press, 1999). Texts of the magical papyri (translated) are available in Hans Dieter Betz, *The Greek Magical Papyri in Translation, Including the Demotic Spells,* 2nd ed. (Chicago: University of Chicago Press, 1996).

3. See John J. Winkler, *The Constraints of Desire: The Anthropology of Sex and Gender in Ancient Greece* (New York: Routledge, 1990), 90.

4. As with everything in this poem, the context is significant. Artemis is a perpetual virgin who oversees a girl's transition to the state of being a woman, concurrent with marriage and sexual experience.

5. A good discussion can be found in Marilyn Skinner, *Sexuality in Greek and Roman Culture* (Malden, MA: Blackwell Press, 2005), 186–90.

6. Translations are my own. For the homoerotic epigrams, however, I have often referred to the elegant translations of Benjamin Acosta-Hughes in Thomas Hubbard,

ed., *Homosexuality in Greece and Rome: A Sourcebook of Basic Documents* (Berkeley: University of California Press, 2003).

7. Elegiac meter consists of couplets of contrasting lines. The first line is a six-foot dactylic line (identical to the meter of epic poetry). The second line in each pair is only five feet long. This meter was regularly used for erotic poetry in the Hellenistic period and is picked up by the Roman erotic poets discussed later.

8. The last word of the poem, which I have translated "male sluts," is of uncertain meaning. It is apparently a term of reproach and is sometimes applied to *kinaidoi.* I assume that it means something like "wanton."

9. See, most notably, Giulia Sissa, *Greek Virginity,* trans. A. Goldhammer (Cambridge, MA: Harvard University Press, 1990).

10. That is, do you have a customer right now?

11. See Kenneth Dover, "Two Women from Samos," in *The Sleep of Reason: Erotic Experience and Sexual Ethics in Ancient Greece and Rome,* ed. M. C. Nussbaum and J. Sihvola (Chicago: University of Chicago Press, 2002), 222–29.

CHAPTER EIGHT

1. A clear discussion can be found in Judith Evans Grubbs, *Women and the Law in the Roman Empire* (New York: Routledge, 2002), 83–87. A full scholarly treatment is available in Susan Treggiari, *Roman Marriage: "Iusti Coniuges" from the Time of Cicero to the Time of Ulpian* (New York: Oxford University Press, 1991), 37–80.

2. For a representative of this line of argument, see Ramsay MacMullen, "Roman Attitudes to Greek Love," *Historia* 31 (1982): 484–502.

3. A full discussion is provided by Craig Williams, "Greek Love at Rome," *Classical Quarterly* 45 (1995): 517–39.

4. Craig Williams, *Roman Homosexuality: Ideologies of Masculinity in Classical Antiquity* (New York: Oxford University Press, 1999), 64–72.

5. Ibid., 72.

6. See Jonathan Walters, "Invading the Roman Body: Manliness and Impenetrability in Roman Thought," in *Roman Sexualities,* ed. J. P. Hallett and M. Skinner (Princeton, NJ: Princeton University Press, 1997), 29–43.

7. The incident is discussed by Valerius Maximus 6.1.12 and told in detail in Plutarch *Life of Marius.* Cicero uses it as an example of justifiable homicide in *Pro Milone* 9.

8. For a full discussion, see Catherine Edwards, *The Politics of Immorality in Ancient Rome* (New York: Cambridge University Press, 1993), chapter 3; Edwards, "Unspeakable Professions: Public Performance and Prostitution in Ancient Rome," in *Roman Sexualities,* ed. J. P. Hallett and M. Skinner (Princeton, NJ: Princeton University Press, 1997), 66–98.

9. The following several paragraphs are much indebted to Williams, *Roman Homosexuality,* 172–78.

10. See, e.g., Amy Richlin, "Not before Homosexuality: The Materiality of the *Cinaedus* and the Roman Law against Love between Men," *Journal of the History of Sexuality* 3 (1993): 523–73.

11. Amy Richlin, *The Garden of Priapus: Sexuality and Aggression in Roman Humor,* rev. ed. (New York: Oxford University Press, 1992), provides a full and lively discussion in chapter 5.

12. The poem puns here on Latin *testis,* which can mean "witness" or "testicle."

13. Michel Foucault, *The History of Sexuality,* vol. 3, *The Care of the Self,* trans. R. Hurley (New York: Random House, 1986), 235.

CHAPTER NINE

1. For a brief discussion, see Craig Williams, *Roman Homosexuality: Ideologies of Masculinity in Classical Antiquity* (New York: Oxford University Press, 1999), 34–37.

2. "Fuller's juice" is urine.

3. Such arguments are the addition of later editors and are not properly part of the play itself.

4. Evidently a euphemism for sex.

5. Williams, *Roman Homosexuality,* suggests that the scene between Lysidamus and Olympio may have been inserted into the original Greek plot by Plautus, as the kind of humor that particularly appealed to the Romans. See p. 79 for an illuminating discussion.

6. A good discussion is provided by Barbara Gold, "'Vested Interests' in Plautus' *Casina:* Cross-Dressing in Roman Comedy,' Helios 25 (1998): 17–3.

CHAPTER TEN

1. See Page duBois, *Torture and Truth* (New York: Routledge, 1991), for a full-scale discussion of these procedures.

2. See, esp., Craig Williams, *Roman Homosexuality: Ideologies of Masculinity in Classical Antiquity* (New York: Oxford University Press, 1999), 138–52.

3. Francesca Santoro L'Hoir, *The Rhetoric of Gender Terms:* "*Man,*" "*Woman,*" *and the Portrayal of Character in Latin Prose* (Leiden, Netherlands: E. J. Brill, 1992), 21. In the following section (22–24), she shows that Cicero only uses *vir* of his enemies when he wants to make a rhetorical point.

4. A curious fact about Roman society is that only adult male citizens and female prostitutes wore the toga. This sentence literally says, "You made a man's clothing into a woman's." The implication is that Antony, instead of becoming a man, has become a female prostitute.

5. There is some evidence that this same Clodia is the woman whom Catullus addresses as "Lesbia" in much of his erotic poetry.

6. See Santoro L'Hoir, *Rhetoric of Gender Terms,* 22–24, for a full discussion.

7. The most famous instance is Cicero *Pro Caelio* 13.32: Cicero explains that he would refute the accusers more vehemently "if I were not impeded by my personal enmity with her husband—I meant to say her *brother*—I always make that mistake."

8. See Williams, *Roman Homosexuality,* 96–124, for a full discussion.

9. Ibid., 120. *Intestabilis* means that a man cannot call witnesses and is therefore barred from bringing legal suits in court. *Infames* carries a wider range of restrictions, including the inability to bring legal suits or to represent himself or others in court. See further discussion.

10. See especially Amy Richlin, "Not before Homosexuality: The Materiality of the *Cinaedus* and the Roman Law against Love between Men," *Journal of the History of Sexuality* 3 (1993): 569–70.

11. My discussion of *infamia* is largely dependent on Amy Richlin, "Not before Homosexuality: The Materiality of the *Cinaedus* and the Roman Law against Love between Men," *Journal of the History of Sexuality* 3 (1993): 555–61, and Williams, *Roman Homosexuality*, 193–95.

12. Most notably Richlin, "Not before Homosexuality," 555–61.

13. A.H.J. Greenidge, *Infamia: Its Place in Roman Public and Private Law* (Oxford: Clarendon Press, 1894), 117–23. On p. 121, Greenidge states that a man "who with his body has suffered womanly things" is an instance of "immediate infamia."

14. The more recent and magisterial translation of Alan Watson, trans., *The Digest of Justinian* (Philadelphia: University of Pennsylvania Press, 1985), does not translate the words *notari* and *notabiles* at 3.1.1.5 or 3.1.1.6 as meaning "noted as *infamis*," but simply as "to be blacklisted."

15. See Catherine Edwards, "Unspeakable Professions: Public Performance and Prostitution in Ancient Rome," in *Roman Sexualities*, ed. J. P. Hallett and M. Skinner (Princeton, NJ: Princeton University Press, 1997), 77.

16. Williams, *Roman Homosexuality*, 194.

17. Until the recent Supreme Court decision of *Lawrence v. Texas* (2003), sodomy (generally defined as anal sexual contact with a member of either sex), even if consensual, was illegal in 14 states in the United States.

CHAPTER ELEVEN

1. Many of these poets wrote in elegiac meter and are therefore referred to as elegiac poets. Elegiac meter presents a two-line recurring pattern: the first line consists of a six-beat line (hexameter) identical to that used in epic poems, while the second line consists of two half-lines of epic hexameter. Erotic elegy generally focuses on the speaker's frustrated relationship with some beloved.

2. It is not known with certainty whether or not Catullus placed his poems in the order that we have them. Good arguments have been made, however, for the arrangement of the first 51 poems as a deliberate book of poems. For discussion, see Marilyn Skinner, *Catullus Passer: The Arrangement of the Book of Polymetric Poems* (New York: Arno Press, 1981).

3. Ellen Oliensis, "The Erotics of *Amicitia:* Readings in Tibullus, Propertius, and Horace," in *Roman Sexualities*, ed. J. P. Hallett and M. Skinner (Princeton, NJ: Princeton University Press, 1997), 152.

4. Elsewhere in the Catullan corpus, Catullus uses phrases similar to this to address Lesbia.

5. Some texts print this as a name (e.g., "Victor"). I see no particular reason to do this, and in any case, the idea of the active partner being victorious over the fellator would be implicit in the choice of such a name.

6. A particularly good discussion of the social scrutiny assumed in Catullus's poems can be found in David Wray, *Catullus and the Poetics of Roman Manhood* (New York: Cambridge University Press, 2001).

7. That is, Mamurra has been put in charge of these provinces, recently conquered.

8. The "Romulus" addressed here is either Pompey or, more likely, Caesar, that is, a descendent of Romulus and powerful politician in Rome at the time of writing.

9. On this use of the language of business in Roman erotic poetry, see esp. Oliensis, "Erotics of *Amicitia.*"

10. The poem is inexplicably not included in Thomas Hubbard, ed., *Homosexuality in Greece and Rome: A Sourcebook of Basic Documents* (Berkeley: University of California Press, 2003).

11. The word here literally means "little eye" and is used frequently by Catullus as a term of endearment for his beloved.

12. Oliensis, "Erotics of *Amicitia*," 159, suggests that Propertius's first poem to Gallus (Propertius 1.5), in which the two poets come together over the common experience of being rejected by "Cynthia," may be modeled on this poem. She goes on to suggest that the reciprocity between men that can be found in Propertius and Horace presents "a series of interactions in which each man plays each part alternately. This intercourse may take place only on the page, but the pleasure it yields is lasting and real" (p. 169).

13. Though in poem 1.20, he writes of the love of Heracles for the boy Hylas.

14. The "thousands of troubles" may recall Catullus's thousands of kisses in poems 5 and 7.

CHAPTER TWELVE

A longer and more scholarly version of this chapter originally appeared as "Impossible Lesbians in Ovid's Metamorphoses," in *Gendered Dynamics in Latin Love Poetry*, ed. R. Ancona and E. Greene (Baltimore: Johns Hopkins University Press, 2005), 79–112. Reprinted with permission of The Johns Hopkins University Press, copyright 2005. I am grateful to the Johns Hopkins University Press, for permission to reprint that article here. In editing this essay for inclusion in the present volume, I have removed nearly all references to scholarly controversy; readers who wish a more thorough discussion of bibliography should refer to the original publication.

1. See Diane T. Pintabone, "Ovid's Iphis and Ianthe: When Girls Won't Be Girls," in *Among Women: From the Homosocial to the Homoerotic in the Ancient World*, ed. N. S. Rabinowitz and L. Auanger (Austin: University of Texas Press, 2002), 156–85; Judith Hallett, "Female Homoeroticism and the Denial of Roman Reality in Latin Literature," in *Roman Sexualities*, ed. J. P. Hallett and M. Skinner (Princeton, NJ: Princeton University Press, 1997), 255–73; John F. Makowski, "Bisexual Orpheus: Pederasty and Parody in Ovid," *Classical Journal* 92 (1996): 25–38; Shilpa Raval, "Cross-dressing and 'Gender Trouble' in the Ovidian Corpus," *Helios* 29 (2002): 149–72.

2. The Latin here contains an untranslatable ambiguity. The line could either mean "I wish I did not exist" or, with equal validity, "I wish I were not a woman."

3. Makowski, "Bisexual Orpheus," 30.

4. See, e.g., Phyllis Culham, "Decentering the Text: The Case of Ovid," *Helios* 17 (1990): 161–71. Judith Hallett, "Contextualizing the Text: The Journey to Ovid," *Helios* 17 (1990): 187–95, suggests some ways in which Ovid can be used to discern contemporary Roman attitudes. The shiftiness of the Ovidian narrator is highlighted throughout Pintabone, "Ovid's Iphis and Ianthe."

5. Susan Treggiari, *Roman Marriage: "Iusti Coniuges" from the Time of Cicero to the Time of Ulpian* (New York: Oxford University Press, 1991), 39–43, 399–400, argues that Roman men generally married around the age of 25–30, although they may have been legally able to marry as early as 14. Augustan marriage legislation may have lowered the expected age of marriage by a few years (pp. 402–3).

6. Similarly, Narcissus at Ovid *Metamorphoses* 3.466: "What I desire is with me: abundance makes me poor" (*quod cupio mecum est: inopem me copia fecit*).

7. Stephen W. Wheeler, "Changing Names: The Miracle of Iphis in Ovid *Metamorphoses* 9," *Phoenix* 51 (1997): 198.

8. Hallett, "Female Homoeroticism," 263.

9. So, e.g., Catullus tells himself to let his love go in poem 8.

10. Pintabone, "Ovid's Iphis and Ianthe," 259.

11. Wheeler, "Changing Names."

12. Antoninus Liberalis, *Metamorphoses* 17.

13. Wheeler, "Changing Names," 195–96.

14. Ibid., 200.

15. For the story, see Plutarch *Moralia* 351cff. The story about the missing penis is at 358b.

16. The most important example is Amy Richlin, "Not before Homosexuality: The Materiality of the *Cinaedus* and the Roman Law against Love between Men," *Journal of the History of Sexuality* 3 (1993): 523–73. See also Holt Parker, "The Teratogenic Grid," in *Roman Sexualities,* ed. J. P. Hallett and M. Skinner (Princeton, NJ: Princeton University Press, 1997), 60–63.

CHAPTER THIRTEEN

1. See Michel Foucault, *The History of Sexuality,* vol. 3, *The Care of the Self,* trans. R. Hurley (New York: Random House, 1986), 81–95.

2. Foucault, *Care of the Self,* 235.

3. Musonius Rufus XIIIa; see the useful discussion in Marilyn Skinner, *Sexuality in Greek and Roman Culture* (Malden, MA: Blackwell Press, 2005), 243–44.

4. This passage has been particularly well discussed by Craig Williams, *Roman Homosexuality: Ideologies of Masculinity in Classical Antiquity* (New York: Oxford University Press, 1999), 237–39, and my ideas here owe much to his treatment.

5. Ibid., 239.

6. Edward Champlin, *Nero* (London: Belknap Press, 2003), 36–52, provides a brief and illuminating discussion of the sources and their relative strengths.

7. Ibid., 36.

8. Ibid., 161, argues that Suetonius has conflated two stories and so gotten the name of Pythagoras wrong. For an alternative view, see Williams, *Roman Homosexuality,* 364 n. 19.

9. See Williams, *Roman Homosexuality,* 252.

10. Champlin, *Nero,* 150.

CHAPTER FOURTEEN

1. The identification of the historical figure with the author is generally accepted, though not entirely secure. A good, brief discussion can be found in Sarah Ruden, *Petronius' Satyricon* (Indianapolis, IN: Hackett, 2000), 129–33.

2. Encolpius compares this moment to the famous scene in the *Odyssey* in which Odysseus's old nurse recognizes him through his disguise by the scar on his thigh. It is not clear what is so distinctive about Encolpius's genitals—perhaps there is a joke here about their size?

3. Craig Williams, *Roman Homosexuality: Ideologies of Masculinity in Classical Antiquity* (New York: Oxford University Press, 1999), contains excellent discussions of many of Martial's poems.

4. Names, presumably, of known prostitutes.

5. That is, even low-class prostitutes practice their trade in cemeteries, out of plain sight.

6. Athletes traditionally performed nude but with their testicles held in place with a specialized ligature.

7. Cato the Elder lived in the late third and early second centuries BCE and was famous as a traditional moralist who criticized luxury and decadence of all sorts.

8. On this point, see Williams, *Roman Homosexuality*, 197–203; Holt Parker, "The Teratogenic Grid," in *Roman Sexualities*, ed. J. P. Hallett and M. Skinner (Princeton, NJ: Princeton University Press, 1997), 48–53.

9. The Latin here is *fututor*, a word usually reserved for men who have vaginal sex with women; see Parker, "The Teratogenic Grid."

10. It is true, however, that in the elder Seneca's *Controversiae* 1.2.23, both members of a female homoerotic pair are labeled *tribades*.

11. A legendary woman of early Rome, famous for her sexual fidelity.

12. Michel Foucault, *The History of Sexuality*, vol. 1, *An Introduction*, trans. R. Hurley (New York: Random House, 1978), 100–101.

13. See esp. Amy Richlin, "Not before Homosexuality: The Materiality of the *Cinaedus* and the Roman Law against Love between Men," *Journal of the History of Sexuality* 3 (1993): 523–73; Rabun Taylor, "Two Pathic Subcultures in Ancient Rome," *Journal of the History of Sexuality* 7 (1997): 319–71. Williams, *Roman Homosexuality*, 218–24, argues against the model of a sexual subculture for Roman society.

14. This was considered a clear sign of male effeminacy and, by extension, sexual passivity.

15. Perhaps a suggestion that he performs fellatio as well as being anally penetrated.

16. Williams, *Roman Homosexuality*, 245–52.

CHAPTER FIFTEEN

1. Excellent translations of the extant novels are available in Bryan Reardon, ed., *Collected Ancient Greek Novels* (Berkeley: University of California Press, 1989).

2. Foucault originally planned six volumes of *The History of Sexuality*; he died shortly after completing the third.

3. Michel Foucault, *The History of Sexuality*, vol. 3, *The Care of the Self*, trans. R. Hurley (New York: Random House, 1986), 228.

4. John J. Winkler, "The Invention of Romance," in *The Search for the Ancient Novel*, ed. J. Tatum (Baltimore: Johns Hopkins University Press, 1994), 33.

5. Ibid., 37.

6. Foucault, *History of Sexuality*, 3:228. This idea has required some modification; in particular, Foucault's reading of the heroine's purity misses the playfulness of the novels. See Simon Goldhill, *Foucault's Virginity: Ancient Erotic Fiction and the History of Sexuality* (Cambridge: Cambridge University Press, 1995).

7. Foucault, *History of Sexuality*, 3:230.

8. See esp. Foucault, *History of Sexuality*, 2:63–77.

9. See Foucault, *History of Sexuality*, 1:17–25, 57–61.

10. See, e.g., Paul's 1 Corinthians 6.9, Romans 1.26–27 for statements against male and female homoerotic activity. Paul clearly condemns both active and passive partners in male homoerotic relations.

11. The following discussion is heavily indebted to Eva Cantarella, *Bisexuality in the Ancient World*, trans. C. Ó. Cuilleanáin (New Haven, CT: Yale University Press, 1992), 175–91.

12. Translation is my own. Text is taken from Cantarella, *Bisexuality in the Ancient World*, 175, and is preserved in the *Theodosian Code* 9.7.3.

13. *Theodosian Code* 9.7.6. Translation is my own. Text from Cantarella, *Bisexuality in the Ancient World*, 181.

14. Cantarella, *Bisexuality in the Ancient World*, 181–82.

15. For useful discussion, see Sue-Ellen Case, "Towards a Butch-Femme Aesthetic," in *The Lesbian and Gay Studies Reader*, ed. H. Abelove, M. Barale, and D. Halperin (New York: Routledge, 1993), 294–306.

16. Dan Savage, *Savage Love: Straight Answers from America's Most Popular Sex Columnist* (New York: Plume, 1998), 189–90. Quoted and discussed in David M. Halperin, *How to Do the History of Homosexuality* (Chicago: University of Chicago Press, 2002), 133–34.

Further Readings

Abelove, Henry, Michele Barale, and David Halperin, ed. 1993. *The Lesbian and Gay Studies Reader.* New York: Routledge.

Bartsch, Shadi, and Thomas Bartscherer, ed. 2005. *Erotikon: Essays on Eros, Ancient and Modern.* Chicago: University of Chicago Press.

Bassi, Karen. 2003. "The Semantics of Manliness in Ancient Greece." In *Andreia: Studies in Manliness and Courage in Classical Antiquity,* ed. R. Rosen and I. Sluiter, 25–58. Leiden, Netherlands: E. J. Brill.

Betz, Hans Dieter. 1996. *The Greek Magical Papyri in Translation, Including the Demotic Spells.* 2nd ed. Chicago: University of Chicago Press.

Bing, Peter, and Rip Cohen. 1991. *Games of Venus: An Anthology of Greek and Roman Erotic Verse from Sappho to Ovid.* New York: Routledge.

Blundell, Sue. 1995. *Women in Ancient Greece.* Cambridge, MA: Harvard University Press.

Cantarella, Eva. 1992. *Bisexuality in the Ancient World,* trans. C. Ó. Cuilleanaín. New Haven, CT: Yale University Press.

Carnes, Jeffrey. 1998. "This Myth Which Is Not One: Construction of Discourse in Plato's Symposium." In *Rethinking Sexuality: Foucault and Classical Antiquity,* ed. D.H.J. Larmour, P. A. Miller, and C. Platter, 104–21. Princeton, NJ: Princeton University Press.

Carson, Anne. 1996 [1981]. "The Justice of Aphrodite in Sappho 1." In *Sappho: Contemporary Approaches,* ed. E. Greene, 226–32. Berkeley: University of California Press.

Case, Sue-Ellen. 1993. "Towards a Butch-Femme Aesthetic." In *The Lesbian and Gay Studies Reader,* ed. H. Abelove, M. Barale, and D. Halperin, 294–306. New York: Routledge.

Chadwick, John. 1976. *The Mycenaean World.* Cambridge: Cambridge University Press.

Champlin, Edward. 2003. *Nero.* London: Belknap Press.

Clarke, John R. 1998. *Looking at Lovemaking: Constructions of Sexuality in Roman Art.* Berkeley: University of California Press.

Cohen, Edward. 2000. *The Athenian Nation.* Princeton, NJ: Princeton University Press.

Davidson, James. 1997. *Courtesans and Fishcakes: The Consuming Passions of Classical Athens.* New York: St. Martin's Press.

———. 2001. "Dover, Foucault, and Greek Homosexuality: Penetration and the Truth of Sex." *Past and Present* 170: 3–51.

———. 2007. *The Greeks and Greek Love.* London: Weidenfeld and Nicolson.

DeJean, Joan. 1989. *Fictions of Sappho 1546–1937.* Chicago: University of Chicago Press.

DeVries, Keith. 1997. "The 'Frigid Eromenoi' and Their Wooers Revisited: A Closer Look at Greek Homosexuality in Vase Painting." In *Queer Representations: Reading Lives, Reading Cultures,* ed. M. Duberman, 14–24. New York: New York University Press.

Dover, Kenneth J. 1989 [1978]. *Greek Homosexuality.* New York: MFJ Books.

———. 2002. "Two Women from Samos." In *The Sleep of Reason: Erotic Experience and Sexual Ethics in Ancient Greece and Rome,* ed. M. C. Nussbaum and J. Sihvola, 222–29. Chicago: University of Chicago Press.

duBois, Page. 1991. *Torture and Truth.* New York: Routledge.

———. 1995. *Sappho Is Burning.* Chicago: University of Chicago Press.

Edwards, Catherine. 1993. *The Politics of Immorality in Ancient Rome.* New York: Cambridge University Press.

———. 1997. "Unspeakable Professions: Public Performance and Prostitution in Ancient Rome." In *Roman Sexualities,* ed. J. P. Hallett and M. Skinner, 66–98. Princeton, NJ: Princeton University Press.

Evans Grubbs, Judith. 2002. *Women and the Law in the Roman Empire.* New York: Routledge.

Faraone, Christopher A. 1999. *Ancient Greek Love Magic.* Cambridge, MA: Harvard University Press.

Fitzgerald, William. 2007. *Martial: The World of the Epigram.* Chicago: University of Chicago Press.

Foucault, Michel. 1978 [1976]. *The History of Sexuality.* Vol. 1, *An Introduction,* trans. R. Hurley. New York: Random House.

———. 1985 [1984]. *The History of Sexuality.* Vol. 2, *The Use of Pleasure,* trans. R. Hurley. New York: Random House.

———. 1986 [1984]. *The History of Sexuality.* Vol. 3, *The Care of the Self,* trans. R. Hurley. New York: Random House.

Fredrick, David. 1997. "Reading Broke Skin: Violence in Roman Elegy." In *Roman Sexualities,* ed. J. P. Hallett and M. Skinner, 172–96. Princeton, NJ: Princeton University Press.

Gleason, Maud. 1995. *Making Men: Sophists and Self-Presentation in Ancient Rome.* Princeton, NJ: Princeton University Press.

Gold, Barbara. 1998. " 'Vested Interests' in Plautus's Casina: Cross-Dressing in Roman Comedy." *Helios* 25: 17–30.

Goldhill, Simon. 1995. *Foucault's Virginity: Ancient Erotic Fiction and the History of Sexuality.* Cambridge: Cambridge University Press.

Greene, Ellen, ed. 1996. *Reading Sappho: Contemporary Approaches.* Berkeley: University of California Press.

———, ed. 1996. *Re-reading Sappho: Reception and Transmission.* Berkeley: University of California Press.

———. 1998. *The Erotics of Domination: Male Desire and the Mistress in Latin Love Poetry.* Baltimore: Johns Hopkins University Press.

Greenidge, A.H.J. 1894. *Infamia: Its Place in Roman Public and Private Law.* Oxford: Clarendon Press.

Hall, Edith. 1989. *Inventing the Barbarian: Greek Self-definition through Tragedy.* New York: Oxford University Press.

Hallett, Judith. 1997. "Female Homoeroticism and the Denial of Roman Reality in Latin Literature." In *Roman Sexualities,* ed. J. P. Hallett and M. Skinner, 255–73. Princeton, NJ: Princeton University Press. First published in *Yale Journal of Criticism* 3 (1989): 209–27.

Hallet, Judith P., and Marilyn Skinner, eds. 1997. *Roman Sexualities.* Princeton, NJ: Princeton University Press.

Halperin, David M. 1985. "Platonic Eros and What Men Call Love." *Ancient Philosophy* 5: 161–204.

———. 1986. "Plato and Erotic Reciprocity." *Classical Antiquity* 5: 60–80.

———. 1990. *One Hundred Years of Homosexuality and Other Essays on Greek Love.* New York: Routledge.

———. 2002. *How to Do the History of Sexuality.* Chicago: University of Chicago Press.

Halperin, David, John J. Winkler, and Froma Zeitlin, ed. 1990. *Before Sexuality: The Construction of Erotic Experience in the Ancient Greek World.* Princeton, NJ: Princeton University Press.

Hamel, Debra. 2003. *Trying Neaera: The True Story of a Courtesan's Scandalous Life in Ancient Greece.* New Haven, CT: Yale University Press.

Harris, Edward. 1988. "When Was Aeschines Born?" *Classical Philology* 88: 211–14.

Henderson, Jeffrey. 1975. *The Maculate Muse.* New Haven, CT: Yale University Press.

———. 1991. "Women and the Athenian Dramatic Festivals." *Transactions of the American Philological Association* 121: 133–47.

Hubbard, Thomas. 1998. "Popular Perceptions of Elite Homosexuality in Classical Athens." *Arion, Series 3* 6, no. 1: 48–78.

———, ed. 2003. *Homosexuality in Greece and Rome: A Sourcebook of Basic Documents.* Berkeley: University of California Press.

Janan, Micaela. 1994. *When the Lamp Is Shattered: Desire and Narrative in Catullus.* Carbondale: Southern Illinois University Press.

Joshel, Sandra. 1997. "Female Desire and the Discourse of Empire: Tacitus' Messalina." In *Roman Sexualities,* ed. J. P. Hallett and M. Skinner, 221–254. Princeton, NJ: Princeton University Press.

Kampen, Natalie, ed. 1996. *Sexuality in Ancient Art.* Cambridge: Cambridge University Press.

Keith, Alison. 1997. "Tandem Venit Amour: A Roman Woman Speaks of Love." In *Roman Sexualities,* ed. J. P. Hallett and M. Skinner, 295–310. Princeton, NJ: Princeton University Press.

Kilmer, Martin. 1993. *Greek Erotica on Red-Figure Vases.* London: Duckworth.

Kurke, Leslie. 1999. *Coins, Bodies, Games and Gold.* Princeton, NJ: Princeton University Press.

Larmour, David H. J., Paul Allen Miller, and Charles Platter, ed. 1998. *Rethinking Sexuality: Foucault and Classical Antiquity.* Princeton, NJ: Princeton University Press.

MacMullen, Ramsay. 1982. "Roman Attitudes to Greek Love." *Historia* 31: 484–502.

Makowski, John F. 1996. "Bisexual Orpheus: Pederasty and Parody in Ovid." *Classical Journal* 92: 25–38.

McCarthy, Kathleen. 2000. *Slaves, Masters, and the Art of Authority in Plautine Comedy.* Princeton, NJ: Princeton University Press.

McGinn, Thomas. 1998. *Prostitution, Sexuality, and the Law in Ancient Rome.* Oxford: Oxford University Press.

Miller, Paul Allen. 2002. *Latin Erotic Elegy: An Anthology and Reader.* New York: Routledge.

Most, Glenn. 1996. "Reflecting Sappho." In *Re-reading Sappho: Reception and Transmission,* ed. E. Greene, 11–35. Berkeley: University of California Press.

Nussbaum, Martha, and J. Sihvola, ed. 2002. *The Sleep of Reason: Erotic Experience and Sexual Ethics in Ancient Greece and Rome.* Chicago: University of Chicago Press.

Oliensis, Ellen. 1997. "The Erotics of *Amicitia:* Readings in Tibullus, Propertius, and Horace." In *Roman Sexualities,* ed. J. P. Hallett and M. Skinner, 151–71. Princeton, NJ: Princeton University Press.

Ormand, Kirk. 2005. "Impossible Lesbians in Ovid's Metamorphoses." In *Gendered Dynamics in Latin Love Poetry,* ed. R. Ancona and E. Greene, 79–112. Baltimore: Johns Hopkins University Press.

Osborne, Robin. 1998. *Archaic and Classical Greek Art.* New York: Oxford University Press.

Page, Denys. 1955. *Sappho and Alcaeus: An Introduction to the Study of Ancient Lesbian Poetry.* Oxford: Clarendon Press.

Parker, Holt. 1996. "Sappho Schoolmistress." In *Re-reading Sappho: Reception and Transmission,* ed. Ellen Greene, 146–83. Berkeley: University of California Press.

———. 1997. "The Teratogenic Grid." In *Roman Sexualities,* ed. J. P. Hallett and M. Skinner, 47–65. Princeton, NJ: Princeton University Press.

Pintabone, Diane T. 2002. "Ovid's Iphis and Ianthe: When Girls Won't Be Girls." In *Among Women: From the Homosocial to the Homoerotic in the Ancient World,* ed. N. S. Rabinowitz and L. Auanger, 156–85. Austin: University of Texas Press.

Prins, Yopie. 1999. *Victorian Sappho.* Princeton, NJ: Princeton University Press.

Rabinowitz, Nancy S., and Lisa Auanger, ed. 2002. *Among Women: From the Homosocial to the Homoerotic in the Ancient World.* Austin: University of Texas Press.

Raval, Shilpa. 2002. "Cross-dressing and 'Gender Trouble' in the Ovidian Corpus." *Helios* 29: 149–72.

Reardon, Bryan, ed. 1989. *Collected Ancient Greek Novels.* Berkeley: University of California Press.

Richlin, Amy. 1991. "Zeus and Metis: Foucault, Feminism, Classics." *Helios* 18: 160–80.

———. 1992. *The Garden of Priapus: Sexuality and Aggression in Roman Humor.* Rev. ed. New York: Oxford University Press.

———. 1993. "Not before Homosexuality: The Materiality of the *Cinaedus* and the Roman Law against Love between Men." *Journal of the History of Sexuality* 3: 523–73.

———. 1998. "Foucault's *History of Sexuality:* A Useful Theory for Women?" In *Rethinking Sexuality: Foucault and Classical Antiquity,* ed. D.H.J. Larmour, P. A. Miller, and C. Platter, 138–70. Princeton, NJ: Princeton University Press.

Ruden, Sarah. 2000. *Petronius' Satyricon.* Indianapolis, IN: Hackett.

Santoro L'Hoir, Francesca. 1992. *The Rhetoric of Gender Terms: "Man," "Woman," and the Portrayal of Character in Latin Prose.* Leiden, Netherlands: E. J. Brill.

Savage, Dan. 1998. *Savage Love: Straight Answers from America's Most Popular Sex Columnist.* New York: Plume.

Shapiro, H. Allan. 1992. "Eros in Love: Pederasty and Pornography in Greece." In *Pornography and Representation in Greece and Rome,* ed. A. Richlin, 53–72. Oxford: Oxford University Press.

Sissa, Giulia. 1990. *Greek Virginity,* trans. A. Goldhammer. Cambridge, MA: Harvard University Press.

Skinner, Marilyn. 1981. *Catullus Passer: The Arrangement of the Book of Polymetric Poems.* New York: Arno Press.

———. 1996. "Zeus and Leda: The Sexuality Wars in Contemporary Classical Scholarship." *Thamyris* 3, no. 1: 103–23.

———. 1997. "*Ego Mulier:* The Construction of Male Sexuality in Catullus." In *Roman Sexualities,* ed. J. P. Hallett and M. Skinner, 129–50. Princeton, NJ: Princeton University Press.

———. 2005. *Sexuality in Greek and Roman Culture.* Malden, MA: Blackwell Press.

Stehle, Eva. 1981. "Sappho's Private World." In *Reflections of Women in Antiquity,* ed. H. Foley, 45–61. New York: Gordon and Breach.

———. 1997. *Performance and Gender in Ancient Greece: Nondramatic Poetry in Its Setting.* Princeton, NJ: Princeton University Press.

Stewart, Andrew. 1997. *Art, Desire, and the Body in Ancient Greece.* Cambridge: Cambridge University Press.

Sullivan, John P. 2001. *Martial, the Unexpected Classic: A Literary and Historical Study.* New York: Cambridge University Press.

Taylor, Rabun. 1997. "Two Pathic Subcultures in Ancient Rome." *Journal of the History of Sexuality* 7: 319–71.

Thorp, John. 1992. "The Social Construction of Homosexuality." *Phoenix* 46: 54–61.

Treggiari, Susan. 1991. *Roman Marriage: "Iusti Coniuges" from the Time of Cicero to the Time of Ulpian.* New York: Oxford University Press.

Vertraete, Beert C., and V. Provencal, ed. 2005. *Same-Sex Desire and Love in Greco-Roman Antiquity.* Binghamton, NY: Haworth Press. Simultaneously published as a special issue of *Journal of Homosexuality* 49 (2005).

Vivante, Bella. 2007. *Daughters of Gaia: Women in the Ancient Mediterranean World.* Westport, CT: Praeger.

Waithe, Mary Ellen, ed. 1997. *Ancient Women Philosophers, 600 B.C.–500 A.D.* Dordrecht, Netherlands: Martinus Nijhoff.

Walters, Jonathan. 1997. "Invading the Roman Body: Manliness and Impenetrability in Roman Thought." In *Roman Sexualities,* ed. J. P. Hallett and M. Skinner, 29–43. Princeton, NJ: Princeton University Press.

Watson, Alan, trans. 1985. *The Digest of Justinian.* Philadelphia: University of Pennsylvania Press.

Wheeler, Stephen W. 1997. "Changing Names: The Miracle of Iphis in Ovid *Metamorphoses* 9." *Phoenix* 51: 190–202.

Williams, Craig. 1995. "Greek Love at Rome." *Classical Quarterly* 45: 517–39.

———. 1999. *Roman Homosexuality: Ideologies of Masculinity in Classical Antiquity.* New York: Oxford University Press.

Winkler, John J. 1990. *The Constraints of Desire: The Anthropology of Sex and Gender in Ancient Greece.* New York: Routledge.

———. 1994. "The Invention of Romance." In *The Search for the Ancient Novel,* ed. J. Tatum, 23–38. Baltimore: Johns Hopkins University Press.

Wray, David. 2001. *Catullus and the Poetics of Roman Manhood.* New York: Cambridge University Press.

Zeitlin, Froma. 1996. *Playing the Other: Gender and Society in Classical Greek Literature.* Chicago: University of Chicago Press.

Index

About the Author

KIRK ORMAND is Assistant Professor of Classics at Oberlin College and author of *Exchange and the Maiden: Marriage in Sophoclean Tragedy* (1999).

—